Claimed by the Sea

Claimed by the Sea

Salcombe, Langdon Bay, and other marine finds of the Bronze Age

Stuart Needham, Dave Parham, and Catherine J Frieman

With further contributions by
Martin Bates, Martin Dean, Roland Gehrels, Peter Northover,
Brendan O'Connor, Neville Oldham, Mick Palmer, and Keith Parfitt

Foreword by
Colin Burgess

Illustrations by
Tom Cousins and Stephen Crummy

CBA Research Report 173
Council for British Archaeology
2013

Published in 2013 by the Council for British Archaeology
St Mary's House, 66 Bootham, York YO30 7BZ
Copyright © 2013 Authors and Council for British Archaeology

British Library cataloguing in Publication Data
A catalogue record for this book is available from the British Library

ISBN 978-1-902771-95-3
DOI: 10.11141/RR173

Typeset by Archétype Informatique, www.archetype-it.com
Printed and bound by Henry Ling Ltd

The publisher acknowledges with gratitude a generous grant from English Heritage towards the cost of publication

**In memory of Keith Muckelroy (1951–80),
pioneering maritime archaeologist**

Contents

List of figures

List of tables

Abbreviations

ACHWS	Advisory Committee on Historic Wreck Sites (abolished in March 2011)
ADU	Archaeological Diving Unit
BGS	British Geological Survey
BSAC	British Sub-Aqua Club
CNA	Council for Nautical Archaeology
DSAC	Dover Branch, British Sub-Aqua Club
LWL	low water line
NBI	National Bronze Implements Index, British Museum
NMM	National Maritime Museum
SWMAG	South West Maritime Archaeological Group
YHA	Youth Hostel Association

Acknowledgements

With any long-running project, the debts accrued are legion. We have already acknowledged, both in the dedication and throughout this volume, the massive debt owed to the late Keith Muckelroy; our knowledge of the two key sites explored here would have been much diminished without his insight, leadership, and passionate pursuit of underwater archaeology. But equally vital to the knowledge base on which we can hang so much interpretation are the manifold contributions from the discoverers of ancient objects on the seabed and, especially, those volunteers who devoted considerable time and effort at Salcombe and Langdon Bay; we cannot hope to name all who have made a contribution over the past thirty years and more, but we nevertheless extend our appreciative thanks. Where institutions are given here, they are those of the individuals at the time of their assistance.

For the Moor Sand site we must single out Phillip Baker, the first to discover and recognise a Bronze Age artefact there. The discovery and recording of the adjacent site of Salcombe 'B' came much later, thanks to the endeavours and dedication of members of the South West Maritime Archaeology Group – David Dunkley, Andrew Elliott, Ron Howell, David Illingworth, Mike Kightley, Mick Kingston, Neville Oldham (Licensee), Mick Palmer, Jim Tyson, Mike Williams, Julie Williams, and Chris Yates. Crucial figures involved in the Langdon Bay campaign were Alan Moat (Licensee), Brian Samson, and Simon Stevens of Dover Sub-Aqua Club. As well as time, these two diving groups regularly put their own equipment at the disposal of the projects. The British Sub-Aqua Club is also to be thanked profusely for support. Volunteers came from diving clubs around the UK to give their time to help lay grid lines and search the seabed both visually and with metal detectors. Much valued help was also received from archaeological colleagues from other organisations, who gave up their holidays to assist with the project at various times. They include Barrie Andrian, Alex Hildred, and Ian Oxley, who did the painstaking hand-measured topographic survey, and Adrian Barak and Steve Liscoe, who worked hard at keeping the equipment running as well as being part of the systematic search team. More specialised help came from Martin Dean's ADUS colleague Mark Lawrence, who helped with the multibeam sonar survey, and Reson Offshore Ltd for the loan of that equipment. Earlier in the campaign an underwater metal detector had been generously loaned by Littlemore Scientific through the intermediacy of the late Professor Teddy Hall.

Despite much voluntary effort, however, the projects still needed financial, professional, and administrative support; this came primarily from the Department of Prehistoric and Romano-British Antiquities (as was) of the British Museum, and the Archaeological Research Centre (as was) at the National Maritime Museum. The early campaigns benefited from the firm support of the respective Department heads, Ian Longworth (BM) and Sean McGrail (NMM), as well as the Trustees of the two Museums, but other members of those two institutions also played significant roles. Among these, we particularly thank Ben Roberts (BM) for his support in recent years. Further financial support came from the BSAC Jubilee Trust (1981–85), while the National Trust helped facilitate operations at Moor Sand. Crucial advocates for the research campaigns were, initially, the Advisory Committee on Historic Wreck and, later, the Maritime Team at English Heritage – Ian Oxley, Jesse Ransley, and Annabel Lawrence. The Receiver of Wreck deserves full acknowledgement of its role in ensuring the retention in public care of the various assemblages over the years; this was initially uncharted territory for a site where the existence of a wreck could only be surmised rather than demonstrated. Finally, Dover Museum must be thanked doubly: firstly, for their initial role in holding together the earliest finds from Langdon Bay; secondly, under the auspices of Jon Iveson, for providing space and context in their Dover Bronze Age Boat gallery for the full display of the Langdon assemblage, a presentation that it amply warrants.

We are grateful to a number of individuals who provided specific information on relevant metalwork finds in Britain and abroad: Frank Basford (Isle of Wight Historic Environment Service), Cyrille Billard (Service Régional de l'Archéologie, Basse-Normandie), Jean Bourgeois (Gent University), Jay Butler (formerly Groningen University), Trevor Cowie (National Museums Scotland), Marie-Hélène Desjardins (Musée de Fécamp), Sophia Exelby (Receiver of Wreck), Catherine Gardiner (Poole Museum), Michel Le Goffic (Service Départmental d'Archéologie de Finistère), Adam Gwilt (National Museums Wales), Gillian Hutchinson (National Maritime Museum), Rebecca Loader (Isle of Wight Historic Environment Service), Frances Lynch (Bangor University), Jane Marley (Truro Museum), Renaud Nallier (Université de Paris Nanterre), Rebecca Peake (Institut National de Recherches Archéologiques Préventitives), Laura Pooley (Truro Museum), Andrew Richardson (Portable Antiquities Scheme, Kent), and Danielle Wootton (Portable Antiquities Scheme, Devon).

On the analytical front, we must thank Chris Salter (University of Oxford) for assistance with the chemical analyses, Brenda Rohl (University of

Oxford) for the initial batch of lead isotope results, and Matt Horstwood and Vanessa Pashley (NERC Isotope Geosciences Laboratory, Keyworth) for the subsequent batch.

Artefact drawings are largely the work of Stephen Crummy, the exceptions being noted in captions; in the cases of Figs 3.24a, 4.3 and 4.5, Stuart Needham provided primary drawings of the objects. Maps and diagrammatic illustrations are the work of individual authors in the sections by Martin Bates, Roland Gehrels and Peter Northover, and Figs 2.7 and 2.11–13 are by Martin Dean; all others were worked-up by Tom Cousins from material supplied by authors.

Collation of the present volume could not have taken place without backing from English Heritage and Bournemouth University; Elizabeth Rundle at the latter is to be thanked for assistance. We thank the Devon and Kent Historic Environment Records respectively for data relating to the Salcombe and Dover site hinterlands; in addition, Eileen Wilkes generously provided the latest information on her excavations at Mount Folly and Frances Griffith kindly commented on our synthesis of the Moor Sand hinterland sections. The British Museum supplied photographs of objects, while other photographs are taken from the site archives (lodged at the BM and NMM). Finally, we thank an anonymous referee for constructive comments on the draft.

Summary

Claimed by the Sea is centred on two remarkable Bronze Age metalwork assemblages recovered from the seabed at Langdon Bay, Dover, Kent, and Moor Sand, Salcombe, Devon. The sites have become well established in the period literature, but hitherto no full account has been published of their exploration, contexts, and contents. Their discovery marked a new chapter in the emerging field of maritime archaeology, being the first suspected wreck sites of prehistoric date in European seas outside the Mediterranean. This volume sets out in detail the history of discoveries, site environments, survey methods employed, and the evolution of thinking behind the interpretation of these two assemblages. Drawing on various strands of evidence, it also appraises afresh the circumstances of deposition – whether due to shipwreck, coastal erosion or ritual deposition at sea.

Both sites were initially found by sport divers in the mid to late 1970s, but a young pioneering diving archaeologist, Keith Muckelroy, was quick to grasp their potential importance (Chapters 1 and 2). He set up systematic surveys using dedicated amateur divers and got backing from the British Museum and the National Maritime Museum. After Muckelroy's untimely death in 1980, the campaign continued under the direction of one of the present authors (MD), continuing at Salcombe until 1982 and at Dover, sporadically, until 1989. Investigations at Salcombe were unexpectedly revived in 2004 when new Bronze Age finds were made by the South West Maritime Archaeology Group just a few hundred metres west of the earlier finds; at the time of writing, new discoveries continue to be made, but those found since the end of 2004 are not detailed in this volume.

Geomorphological studies of the coastlines at the two sites, both of which are overlooked by cliffs, consider the processes and rates of coastal erosion since the Bronze Age (Chapters 1 and 2). Also relevant to Langdon Bay is the changed configuration of the mouth of the nearby River Dour. A review of the Bronze Age archaeology of the respective hinterlands shows no phase-specific concentrations of metalwork that might have supported the hypothesis of cliff-deposited hoards having eroded into the sea. Nevertheless, intensive underwater survey failed to locate boat remains at either site and, if sunken boats were responsible for the metalwork strewn across the seabed, they must have vanished without trace in the harsh inshore environment of the Channel. Interpretation therefore hangs on the character and spatial distribution of the material assemblages that have survived the ravages of 3000 years (Chapter 3). While Langdon Bay's 360 finds are all of bronze, the 29 Salcombe artefacts reported on include other materials – gold, tin, iron, and bone. By coincidence, both sites have yielded assemblages best dated to the 13th century BC, the period of early Penard metalwork in Britain and Rosnoën in northern France, although Salcombe has also produced a later sword hilt, c 10th–9th century BC.

The range of metalwork types present is diverse, especially in the large Langdon Bay assemblage, and inter-regional comparisons are far-flung – from the British Isles to Sicily and from Brittany to Pomerania (Chapter 3). Each type is reviewed critically in the light of regional patterns of deliberate deposition and the possibility of zones of 'hidden circulation'. Although specifically Continental types are well represented, some objects are much more likely to have originated in Britain. Extensive metal analysis – using the microprobe technique, supplemented in several cases with lead isotope analysis – draws out some subtle but significant variations in the metallurgical backgrounds of the main typological groups; these variations probably reflect different zones of ultimate origin.

The two focal sites draw attention to a wider phenomenon of Bronze Age metalwork finds, of both bronze and gold, from the Channel and its approaches. Chapter 4 collates nineteen finds – of between one and six objects per site – which were either recovered from the seabed by fishermen or sport divers or appear to have been imported to land with marine-dredged ballast. They represent a miscellany of types and a wide date range (1750–625 BC). Amongst these finds, only the findspot of two gold torcs from off Sotteville-sur-Mer has received archaeological attention.

Detailed consideration of taphonomic processes indicates that the collective marine assemblage suffers from serious biases, thus making problematic any direct comparisons with contemporary metalwork deposits from land or inland waters (Chapter 5). Nevertheless, it is significant that a high proportion of the seabed finds contain objects exotic to their hinterland regions and this pattern is recognised to a lesser extent in metalwork finds made in the inter-tidal zone or on land close behind the coast. While ritual deposition remains a possibility for some finds, it is argued that the wrecking of boats will have made a major contribution to this marine assemblage. In particular, the combined evidence for Langdon Bay strongly favours the bronzes having spilled from a boat in trouble and, to use Muckelroy's phrase, thus representing 'exchange frozen in time'. The Langdon Bay objects are of varied functions and varied sizes, including small ornaments and fittings. While much of the assemblage can be interpreted as scrap-and-raw-metal, some objects may instead have been ship's equipment – the possessions of crew and passengers. Some material may have been residual from earlier exchanges, but it is considered most likely that the bulk was picked up from a limited part of coastal northern France, rather than amassed piecemeal in the course of a far-reaching itinerary.

The opportunity is taken to reappraise some of Keith Muckelroy's pioneering interpretation of Bronze Age maritime exchange in the light of subsequent research. Although elements of his 'two-tier circulation model' are critiqued, the questions he raised were insightful, challenging, and still relevant.

Résumé

Deux remarquables collections d'objets en métal récupérés en fond marin à Langdon Bay au large de Douvres dans le Kent et à Salcombe dans le Devon et datant de l'âge du Bronze forment le sujet de *Claimed by the Sea*. Ces sites sont bien connus dans la littérature spécialisée, mais jusqu'à présent aucune publication ne rendait compte de leur découverte, de leur contexte ou de leur contenu. Ces découvertes ont ouvert un nouveau chapitre dans la discipline naissante de l'archéologie maritime, les sites étant les premiers en Europe en dehors de la zone méditerranéenne datant de l'époque préhistorique. On trouvera dans ce volume un compte-rendu détaillé de leur découverte, du milieu, des méthodes de relevé employées et de l'évolution des idées menant à une interprétation de ces deux collections. L'examen de données de nature diverse permet également de réévaluer les circonstances de déposition: naufrage, érosion côtière ou dépôt rituel en mer.

Les deux sites doivent leur découverte à des amateurs de plongée sous-marine des années 1970, mais un jeune archéologue pionnier de la plongée sous-marine archéologique, Keith Muckelroy, s'est rapidement rendu compte de leur importance (chapitres 1 et 2). Il mit sur pied des campagnes de relevé systématiques, avec le concours de plongeurs amateurs et avec le soutien du British Museum et du National Maritime Museum. Après son décès précoce en 1980, les campagnes, dirigées par l'un des auteurs (MD) reprirent à Salcombe jusqu'en 1982, et à Douvres, de manière sporadique, jusqu'en 1989. Contre toute attente les recherches à Salcombe furent reprises en 2004, à la suite de nouvelles découvertes par le the South West Maritime Archaeology Group d'objets de l'âge du Bronze à une centaine de mètres du site original. De nouvelles découvertes étaient encore signalées alors que notre volume était en cours de rédaction, mais elles ne elles ne sont pas répertoriées ici à partir de la fin de 2004.

Les processus et l'importance de l'érosion côtière depuis l'âge du Bronze font l'objet d'études géomorphologiques (chapitres 1 et 2) de la zone littorale proche des deux sites—tous deux surplombés de falaises. Pour Langdon Bay, la configuration de l'embouchure de la rivière Dour est également importante. Une mise au point des vestiges de l'âge du Bronze dans les arrière-pays respectifs ne révèle aucune concentration d'objets en métal appartenant à une phase précise qui aurait pu s'expliquer par des dépôts d'objets précipités dans la mer par l'érosion des falaises. Néanmoins des recherches méticuleuses en fond de mer n'ont pas réussi à localiser des vestiges de vaisseaux ; si des embarcations étaient à l'origine des dépôts d'objets, elles ont disparu sans laisser de traces dans le milieu inhospitalier de la Manche. Notre interprétation dépend donc de la répartition et du caractère des objets ayant survécu 3000 ans de ravages (chapitre 3). Tandis que les 360 objets de Langdon Bay sont tous en bronze, les 29 de Salcombe comprennent également des objets en or, en étain, en fer et en os. Par pure coïncidence, les deux sites ont livré des collections datant du 13ème siècle avant J.-Chr., l'époque du style de Penard dans les îles britanniques et de Rosnoën en France du Nord; Salcombe a aussi livré un pommeau d'épée plus tardif, datant du 10ème ou du 9ème siècle avant J.-Chr.

Les objets sont de types divers, surtout dans la grande collection de Langdon Bay, et les pièces comparables sont à chercher fort loin, des îles britanniques à la Sicile et de la Bretagne jusqu'en Poméranie (chapitre 3). Chaque type fait l'objet d'une étude critique cherchant à déterminer les modalités de déposition intentionnelle et à identifier des zones de 'circulation invisible'. Quoique les types provenant du continent européen soient bien représentés, certains objets proviennent fort probablement des îles britanniques. Les analyses métallographiques—faisant appel à la technique des microsondes ainsi que dans certains cas les isotopes du plomb—ont révélé des variations subtiles mais significatives dans la composition des groupes typologiques principaux, reflétant probablement des zones d'origine différentes.

Les deux sites attirent l'attention sur un phénomène plus étendu exhibé par les objets en métal de l'âge du Bronze provenant de la Manche et de ses environs, qu'ils soient en bronze ou en or. On trouvera dans le chapitre 4 une mise au point sur 19 sites ayant livré entre un et six objets récupérés soit par des chalutiers, soit par des plongeurs, soit qu'ils aient été importés sous forme de ballast dragué. Il s'agit d'un mélange de types divers datant entre 1650 et 625 avant J.-C. Parmi eux, seuls les deux torques en or de Sotteville-sur-Mer on fait l'objet d'une étude archéologique.

L'examen minutieux des processus taphonomiques révèle que les collections d'objets provenant de milieux marins souffrent de problèmes de biais d'échantillonnage, ce qui rend problématique toute comparaison directe avec des collections d'objets retrouvés sur terre ou en milieu riverain ou lacustre (chapitre 5). Néanmoins, une large proportion de découvertes faites en fond marin contient des objets d'origine étrangère à leur arrière-pays ; cette tendance existe aussi, à un degré moindre, parmi les objets en métal récupérés dans les zones de marée ou dans les terres proches du littoral. Sans écarter la possibilité que certains objets aient été déposés rituellement, les naufrages d'embarcations ont dû jouer un rôle considérable. La somme des données de Langdon Bay suggère de façon convaincante que les objets en bronze proviennent d'une embarcation en difficulté, représentant selon Muckelroy 'un échange figé dans le temps'. Les objets de Langdon Bay sont de taille et de fonction variées, y compris des petits objets servant d'ornement ou d'accessoire. Quoiqu'une grande partie puisse faire partie d'un lot destiné à être fondu, certains objets pourraient représenter les possessions de l'équipage et des passagers. Une partie pourrait provenir d'échanges antérieurs mais il est probable que la majeure partie provienne d'une zone côtière limitée du nord de la France plutôt que ramassée au cours d'un long périple.

Enfin, l'occasion nous est donnée de passer en revue certains aspects du travail de pionnier de Keith Muckleroy concernant son interprétation des échanges maritimes pendant l'âge du Bronze à la lumière des études récentes. Bien que certains éléments de son 'modèle de circulation à deux niveaux' soient discutables, les questions soulevées étaient perspicaces, stimulantes et restent d'actualité.

Zusammenfassung

Zwei bemerkenswerte Sammlungen von bronzezeitlichen Gegenständen aus Metall, die vom Meeresboden in Langdon Bay an der Küste von Dover in der Grafschaft Kent und in Salcombe an der Devon Küste geborgen wurden, werden in *Claimed by the Sea* behandelt. Diese Befunde sind in der Fachliteratur recht gut bekannt, aber bis jetzt war keine veröffentlichte Bearbeitung der Umstände der Entdeckungen und des vollständigen Bestandes vorhanden. Mit diesen Befunden beginnt ein neues Kapitel in der Unterwasserarchäologie, da sie die ersten vorgeschichtlichen Fundorte außerhalb der Mittelmeerzone in Europa darstellen. Unsere Veröffentlichung berichtet ausführlich über die Fundumstände, die Umwelt, die Aufnahme der Befunde und die Entwicklung der Begriffe, die zu einer Auswertung dieser zwei Sammlungen führen. Die Ausbeutung von verschiedenen Angaben ermöglicht es auch, ob es sich um Schiffsunglücke, oder die Folgen der Küstenerosion oder rituelle Fundstätte handelt, auszuwerten.

Beide Fundstellen wurden anfänglich von Sporttauchern in den 1970er Jahren entdeckt, jedoch war es ein innovativer junger Archäologe, Keith Muckleroy, der die Bedeutung der Entdeckungen einsah (Kapitel 1 & 2). Mit Hilfe von Hobbytauchern und Unterstützung des British Museums und des National Maritime Museums organisierte er die systematische Aufnahme der Befunde. Nach seinem vorzeitigen Tod in 1980 führte einer der Autoren (MD) die Kampagne weiter: in Salcombe bis 1982 und sporadisch in Dover bis 1989. In 2004 barg der South West Maritime Archaeology Verein neue bronzezeitliche Funde in Salcombe, wenige hundert Meter westlich von der ursprünglichen Fundstelle. Eine erneute Untersuchung wurde durchgeführt, und heute noch werden neue Funde geborgen. Diejenige, die nach Ende 2004 zu Licht gekommen sind, werden hier aber nicht ausgeführt.

Geomorphologische Analysen der Küsten in den jeweiligen Zonen, beide unter Kliffen gelegen, untersuchen den Verlauf der Küstenerosion seit der Bronzezeit (Kapitel 1 & 2). Dazu sind die Veränderungen der Mündung des Flusses Dour für Langdon Bay auch wichtig. Eine Übersicht über die bronzezeitlichen Befunde in beiden Gebieten zeigt, dass es keine spezifische Konzentrationen von Metallgegenständen pro Phase gibt, die aus der Felswand erodierte ursprüngliche Hortfunde darstellen könnten. Trotzdem hat eine detaillierte Aufnahme der Daten auf dem Meeresboden in beiden Fundorten keine Schiffsspuren gefunden; wären Schiffbrüche dafür verantwortlich gewesen, sind alle Spuren in den harten Bedingungen in der Küstennähe des Ärmelkanals verschwunden. Die Deutung hängt deshalb von den Eigenschaften und der Verbreitung der Fundstücken, die nach 3000 Jahren noch überliefert sind, ab (Kapitel 3). Während alle 360 Fundstücke von Langdon Bay aus Bronze sind, bestehen die 29 Gegenstände von Salcombe auch aus anderen Rohstoffen, wie Gold, Zinn, Eisen und Bein. Zufälligerweise sind die Befunde beider Fundstellen bestens ins 13. Jahrhundert v. Chr. datierbar, was der frühen Penard Gruppe in Großbritannien und der Rosnoën Gruppe in Nordfrankreich entspricht; in Salcombe wurde aber auch ein Schwertgriff des 10.–9. Jahrhunderts v. Chr. geborgen.

Verschiedene Typen sind vorhanden, besonders in der großen Langdon Bay Sammlung, und Vergleichsmaterial muss man weit suchen—von den Britischen Inseln bis nach Sizilien, und von der Bretagne bis nach Pommern (Kapitel 3). Jeder Typ wird hier, hinsichtlich der regionalen Verbreitung von Opfergaben und eventuellen Zonen von „versteckter Verbreitung", kritisch behandelt. Obschon besonders europäische Typen gut vertreten sind, stammen einige Fundstücke viel wahrscheinlicher aus Großbritannien. Eine umfassende Untersuchung der Metalle—durch Elektromikrosondeanalyse sowie in mehreren Fällen Blei-Isotopanalyse—zeigt, dass es feine aber wichtige Unterschiede in der metallurgischen Herkunft der typologischen Hauptgruppen gibt; diese Unterschiede widerspiegeln wahrscheinlich verschiedene Ursprungsgebiete.

Für beide Fundstellen ist es beachtenswert, dass die Metallfunde, aus Gold sowie aus Bronze, einen weiteren Aspekt der Bronzezeit im Ärmelkanal und seiner Umgebung widerspiegeln. Im Kapitel 4 werden 19 Funde—von zwischen 1 und 6 Fundstücke pro Befund—untersucht; diese wurden entweder von Fischern oder von Sporttauchern vom Meeresboden geborgen, oder als gebaggerter Ballast importiert. Es handelt sich um Fundstücke von gemischten Typen und Angehörigkeit, zwischen 1750 und 625 v. Chr. datiert. Unter diesen ist nur ein Fundplatz, derjenige von Sotteville-sur-Mer wo zwei Goldhalsringe zu Licht kamen, bisher archäologisch ausgewertet worden.

Eine taphonomische Überlegung zeigt, dass Unterwassersammlungen insgesamt schwer verzerrt sind, sodass es sehr problematisch ist, sie mit gleichzeitigen Metallbefunden vom Festland oder Binnengewässer direkt zu vergleichen (Kapitel 5). Trotzdem ist es bedeutsam, dass ein hoher Anteil der Fundstücke vom Meeresboden nicht zu ihren Hinterlandgegenden gehört; dieser Trend kann man auch, in einem geringeren Maße, bei den Metallfunden im Gezeitenbereich oder auf dem Festland in der Nähe der Küsten beobachten. Obschon die Möglichkeit von einigen rituell niedergelegten Artefakten verbleibt, sind wir der Meinung, dass Schiffsunglücke einen erheblichen Beitrag zur Zusammenstellung von Sammlungen aus dem Meeresboden darstellen. Insbesondere deuten zusammengenommen die Daten von Langdon Bay auf ein Ausschütten von Bronzeobjekten, wenn ein Schiff in Not geraten ist; in den Wörtern von Keith Muckelroy stellen sie „einen Handel, in dem die Zeit stillgestanden ist" dar. Die Metallfunde von Langdon Bay haben verschiedene Zwecke, sind unterschiedlich groß und schließen Zierstücke und Beschläge ein. Obwohl man ein großer Teil der Befunde als Alt- und Rohmetalle interpretieren kann, gibt es einige Gegenstände, die eher der Ausstattung von Schiffen zu deuten sind—vielleicht das persönliche Eigentum der Besatzung oder der Passagiere. Möglicherweise ist ein Teil der Fundstücke von früheren Austauschen übrig geblieben; wir glauben doch, dass die Mehrzahl in einem beschränkten Gebiet der nordfranzösischen Küste aufgesammelt wurde, eher als Stück bei Stück während einer langen weitreichenden Reise.

Schließlich ist uns die Gelegenheit gegeben, die Pionierarbeit von Keith Muckelroy neu zu bewerten, vor allem seine Deutungen des bronzezeitlichen Seehandels angesichts der späteren Forschungen. Obschon einige Aspekte seines „zweistufigen Verbreitungsmodells" kritisch angesehen werden, bleiben die Fragen, die er gestellt hat, immer noch relevant, wichtig und fesselnd.

Riassunto

Claimed by the Sea tratta di due raccolte notevole di oggetti in metallo dal età del bronzo che sono state ritrovate sul fondo del mare a Langdon Bay a Dover nel Kent, e a Moor Sand a Salcombe nel Devon. I siti sono ben rappresentati nella letteratura del periodo, ma finora non è stato publicato nessun resoconto completo del contesto e contenuto delle scoperte, e delle circostanze della loro esplorazione. Al momento di scoperta sono stati i primi resti prehistorici trovati in un mare Europeo fuori dal mediterraneo ad essere considerati come relitti, segnando un nuovo capitolo nel campo emergente dell'archeologia marittima. Questo volume presenta in detaglio la storia delle scoperte, delle condizioni ambientali, dei metodi di indagine, e dell'evoluzione dell'interpretazione delle due raccolte. Utilizzando vari tipi di prova, richiede anche se le circonstanze di deposizione siano state conseguenze di naufragio, di erosione della costa, o di deposizione rituale nel mare.

Entrambi i siti sono stati trovati dai sommozzatori nel secondo metà del 1970, ma l'archeologo subacqueo innovativo Keith Muckelroy ha capito subito la loro importanza (capitoli 1 e 2). Ha iniziato indagini sistematiche insieme a sommozzatori amatoriali enthusiastici, ottenedo il sosetegno del British Museum e il National Maritime Museum. Dopo la morte prematura di Muckelroy nel 1980, la ricerca ha continuato sotto il controllo di uno degli autori di questo volume (MD), a Salcombe fino al 1982 e a Dover (sporadicamente) fino al 1989. A Salcombe, l'indagine è stata ripresa nel 2004 dopo che il South

West Maritime Archaeology Group aveva trovato delle nuove scoperte dall'età del bronzo a poche centinaia di metri dagli oggetto originali. Questa campagna continua a produrre nuove scoperte anche ora, ma quelle trovate dopo il 2004 non fanno parte di questo volume.

Entrambi i siti si trovano ai piedi delle scogliere, dove studi geomorfologici hanno esaminato i processi e ritmi di erosione costiera a partire dall'età del bronzo, ed in riferimento a Langton Bay anche i cambiamenti nella disposizione della foce del vicino fiume Dour (capitoli 1 e 2). Un'analisi dell'archeologia dell'età del bronzo nell'entroterra di ciascun sito non ha rivelato nessuna concentrazione di metallo specifico al momento che potrebbe avere corroborato l'ipotesi di gruzzoli caduti in mare dalle scogliere. Tuttavia, indagini intensivi sott'acqua ai due siti non hanno svelato resti di barca. Se gli oggetti in metallo provengano da nave sommerse, devono essere stati sparsiti senza lasciare traccia nell'ambiente severa vicino alla costa della Manica. L'interpretazione delle raccolte che sono soppravvissute dopo i danni di 3000 anni dipende allora dalle loro charatteristiche e ripartizione spaziale (capitolo 3). Mentre tutti i 360 oggetti di Langdon Bay sono di bronzo, tra i 29 di Salcombe ci sono anche qualche in oro, stagno, argente e osso. Per caso, i dati piu adatti per entrambe le raccolte riguardano il tredicesimo secolo, il periodo alto della lavorazione dei metalli Penard nella Gran Brettagna e nella Francia del nord. Però a Salcombe è stata trovata anche un'impugnatura più recente, dal decimo o nono secolo avanti Christo.

Nell'insieme di oggetti in metallo ci sono tanti tipi diversi, particolarmente tra la grande raccolta di Langdon Bay. I confronti interregionali si estendono per un'ampia zona, dalle isole britanniche alla Sicilia e dalla Bretagna alla Pomerania (capitolo 3). Ogni tipo di ogetto è riesaminato qui in riferimeto ai modelli regionali di deposizione intenzionale e le possibile zone di 'circolozione nascosta'. Generi dell'Europa continentale sono ben rappresentati, ma alcuni oggetti provengono probabilmente dalla Gran Bretagna. Analisi approfondita del metallo usando una microsonda elettronica (in alcuni casi insieme agli isotopi del piombo) ha dimostrato sottile ma importante variazioni della formazione metallurgica delle principali tipologie di ogetti, che probabilmente riflettono diverse zone d'origine.

I due siti richiamano l'attenzione sul fenomeno generale di oggetti in bronzo e in oro dall'età del bronzo trovati nella Manica e nelle sue vie d'accesso. Capitolo 4 riflette su diciannove scoperte (da uno a sei oggetti ciascun) ritrovate sul fondale dai pescatori o dai sommozzatori, oppure portate sulla terraferma con la massicciata dragata dal mare. Gli oggetti comprendono tipi misti ed una gamma di dati dal 1750 fino al 625 a.C. Tra queste scoperte, l'attenzione archeologica era stata dedicata precedentemente soltanto a due lunule d'oro da Sotteville-sur-Mer.

Studi tafonomici detagliati hanno trovato che il materiale dal mare mostra considerevole preju-dizio, rendendo problematici i paragoni tra reperti in metallo dell'epoca ritovati sulla terraferma o in acque interne (capitolo 5). Tuttavia, una grande parte delle scoperte dal fondale comprendono degli oggetti esotici, una cosa anche vera in misure minore per le scoperte in metallo trovate sulla battigia o sulla terra vicino alla costa. Mentre è possibile che alcuni reperti siano stati deposti rituali, si sostiene che una maggior parte della raccolta sia provenuta dai naufragi. Particolarmente i dati da Langdon Bay indicano in maniera convincente che gli oggetti siano stati caduti da una nave nei guai, o per usare la frase di Muckelroy, che rappresentino 'lo scambio congelato nel tempo'. La funzione ed i dimensioni degli oggetti da Langdon Bay sono variabile, ci sono anche degli ornamenti ed accessori piccoli. Mentre una grande parte della raccolta sembra di essere rottame e metallo grezzo, alcuni oggetti avrebbero potuto essere parte dell'apparecchiatura della barca, la proprietà dell'equipaggio ed i passageri. Alcune cose potrebbero essere rimaste da scambi precedenti, ma è probabile che la maggior parte non fosse accumulata poco a poco nel fare di un viaggio esteso, ma raccolta in una zona limitata della costa della Francia del nord.

In riferimento ad ulteriore ricerche, questo volume approfitta dell'occasione per riesaminare gli interpretazioni pionieristici di Muckelroy dello scambio marittimo dell'età del bronzo. Nonostante che guidichi criticamente certi elementi del suo modello di 'circolazione a due livelli', si sostiene che le questioni che ha sollevato siano stati penetranti, stimolanti e pertinenti.

Foreword

Dover and Salcombe

As dramatic evidence of increased traffic from France (around 1200 BC) there are now two shipwrecks, both discovered in the last two or three years, off the coast of southern England, at Dover and at Salcombe, Devon. Both have yielded French bronzes to show which way they were bound when they went down (Burgess 1980, 157).

It is something of a relief to discover that all the comprehensive researches into the nature and circumstances of the two finds in this major volume have done no great violence to what I wrote so confidently more than thirty years ago. I am relieved to see that at least I had the sense to realise the perils always attending such maritime finds by qualifying the captions of photos of the finds with quotation marks, so that both became 'wrecks'. Others in those far-off days were researching and writing in a similar vein, but I have room to mention only three names, those of scholars alas no longer with us. Two died sadly long before their time. My dear friend David Coombs, with whom I did so much work in the 1970s and 1980s, was more directly concerned than I was with the two finds. Keith Muckelroy, strangely, I never had any contact with, but he was a prime mover in the early work on the two sites, and his tragic death in a diving accident far from either site set the project back years, and must have put the publication process back considerably. The third name is that of the pioneering archaeometallurgist Ron Tylecote, whom I mention not for his archaeological work on the site but because he had a different interest in the bronzes which the authors of this volume may not have come across. Ron and his wife Elizabeth had been very kind to me when I first arrived in Newcastle University in 1963 (others were not), and we collaborated in a lot of work in the 1960s and 1970s, until he moved south in the late 1970s to an honorary chair in London. Ron came to see me after the early discoveries and was very interested in Dover in particular, because he thought it might have a bearing on research he was conducting on the seabed deposition of nuclear waste. Whether it came to anything I do not know, and certainly it is not mentioned in this work.

This brief notice is a reminder that the Bronze Age finds from the seabed near Dover and at Salcombe have been with us for nearly four decades. Material has been coming intermittently from one of the sites for much of that time, and continues to do so, forcing the writers of this volume to enforce a cut-off point of 2004 in producing this synthesis of what the two finds are all about. In the 1970s it seemed more reasonable than now to suppose that the Langdon Bay and Salcombe finds represent parts of the cargoes of boats coming from France which foundered within sight of safe haven on the southern shores of England. Even had any parts of the actual craft survived the question would still have to be asked: French boats coming from France, or English boats returning from France? Were these cargoes French or English? It has always seemed equally certain that these were products more at home in France than Britain, and thus more likely to be of French than English origin. But attention! The comprehensive inventories of the finds show that considerable parts of them were made and circulated on both sides of the Channel. In addition, a minority of them were more at home in England than France, though these can be regarded as personal equipment of the crews. But this in itself allows the possibility that the boats were English, bringing a French cargo back from France – if the material was French. The manufacture of 'British' products in France and *vice versa* is a complication we are becoming increasingly aware of: the problem of shared traditions that this volume reveals. To bring the difficulty into more recent times – and if the reader will forgive this aside by someone who has lived in France for many years – many typical and varied 'French' products have been invented and popularised by outsiders before becoming 'French'! I am particularly tickled by the case of champagne, invented by an Englishman, scientist, polymath and drinking acquaintance of Samuel Pepys, Christopher Merrett, who first realised that it was much more interesting to use stronger bottles (newly available from Newcastle upon Tyne) and keep the bubbles in than spend years, as did Dom Perignon, trying to suppress the bubbles and stop the bottles exploding to the detriment of all! Add to that the guillotine, which was effectively invented in Halifax, and had a long history of use in England before reaching France. (Perhaps less relevant in this context are baguettes and croissants, introduced to Paris by occupying Austrian troops after Napoleon). There must surely be examples which work the other way. So 'certainty' has always to be tempered with caution, in quite recent history as well as in prehistoric times. The writers of this volume feel certain enough, however, to conclude that with these two finds 'There is no compelling evidence for anything beyond a fairly straightforward one-trip collection from a location in the coastal territories of northern France or the Low Countries.'

What is clear is that regular cross-Channel traffic did not begin with the Normans, nor even with the Romans, as all the comparable bronze finds from around our shores discussed in this volume make clear. Caesar's depiction of Britain as a wild forest-covered land beyond the Ocean, peopled by woad-painted savages, was entirely for the benefit of Roman politics. It would have made much less of an impact had he admitted that the southern parts of the island had been irradiated by Mediterranean fashions and imports for decades and were well known to the maritime Gauls, and that there was a regular traffic across the Channel; and certainly not that within living memory the same king, Diviciacus, had ruled areas on both sides of the water. Cross-Channel boats had been regularly plying these waters back through the Iron Age and the Bronze Age, though in the Chalcolithic and Neolithic before that the connections had perhaps been more intermittent.

One of the most useful sections of this survey by Stuart Needham and his colleagues is a catalogue and discussion of known coastal finds on both sides of the Channel which makes clear that the traffic in metal had been going on right through the Bronze Age. The impression one sometimes had after Dover and Salcombe, that there was a peak in traffic in the Penard/Rosnoën stage, is certainly corrected by this survey, but notions that intercourse may have been lighter in some periods than others, for example in the post-Dover era, in Limehouse/St-Brieuc-des-Iffs and then Wilburton, may simply reflect differing interpretations of some of these small finds, such as Poole Harbour. In terms of its size as well as content the Langdon Bay find is unique, and for that reason alone would have deserved the exhaustive scrutiny of all the mechanisms which could explain its nature. The age in which we live demands such a treatment to establish beyond doubt why these two assemblages were found lying on the seabed, because simply to assume shipwreck is no longer sufficient. But, one by one, they are ruled out on both geological grounds and the nature of the material itself. Thus the possibility that the Bronze Age coastline was much further out, and that its retreat has left what were originally dry land collections stranded underwater is explored, but rejected – except that little certainty is possible in the sciences involved, so that one minority report has the Bronze Age coastline at Langdon Bay nearly a kilometre further out, which would turn the bronzes into an originally terrestrial deposit. There can be no such possibility at Salcombe. Another interpretation which is rejected is that these seabed assemblages represent votive deposits, but the very components of both finds

seem to rule this out. The writers conclude that the Langdon Bay assemblage 'was primarily a consignment of metal in transit … its presence at Langdon Bay is explained by an unplanned event, a ship in trouble'. Much the same is concluded for Salcombe, though here the supposed wreck may have taken place further out and the material drifted towards shore until it came to rest. Salcombe is also different because there are two periods of finds represented, Rosnoën material, like Dover, and Ewart Park bronzes of two or three centuries later.

The need to call upon all manner of arcane explanations in preference to the obvious and everyday has long since swung too far. For once the simple conclusions made about these two finds when first they came to light have survived the ensuing decades of newer archaeological theories, and the pendulum is swinging back. For example, recent work on South Welsh–Stogursey socketed axes in France (Burgess 2012) has made clear that French customers were not content with just any examples that appeared from across the water but had product preferences: they almost invariably chose examples at the larger end of the size range and avoided those with converging ribs (except in one case). But were these 'British' products brought to France by English boats or by French boats, and at what point was the selection made? There is some indication that the choice was not always made on the beach at all, but by copying the preferred forms in France itself. Whether by craftsmen from across the water or by French craftsmen would then be the next question! The same debate arises with other 'British' Late Bronze Age products in France and beyond, such as Ewart Park swords and lunate-opening spearheads.

So cross-Channel traffic in the Bronze Age presents us with many conundrums and forces us to address that problem of our business highlighted many years ago by M A Smith in addressing the 'Limitations of inference in archaeology'. No amount of scientific enquiry of the kind presented so copiously in this volume will answer beyond doubt all the problems that confront us, but we can be confident, as Needham and his colleagues conclude in their comprehensive study, that 'Of one thing we can be sure: that regular adventuring on the high seas, a major occupation of the Channel Bronze Age, must have brought its casualties. Bronze Age shipwrecks are almost certainly going to continue to be a feature of the maritime archaeological record'.

Colin Burgess, Limousin, April 2012

1   Moor Sand and Salcombe Site B, Devon

Moor Sand and Salcombe 'B' are the site names given to two groups of Bronze Age objects recovered from the seabed just off the south Devon coast. The site of Moor Sand lies between 50 and 400m off the beach of that name, and Salcombe Site B lies only a little further out to sea, to the west. The beach is set in a small, secluded bay beneath cliffs, lying roughly halfway between Prawle Point, the southernmost tip of Devon, and the Kingsbridge estuary, a large drowned estuary carrying the outflow of a relatively tiny drainage catchment (Fig 1.1). To the west of the estuary the coast follows southward as far as Bolt Head before veering west. The two sites, therefore, lie within an open bay at the mouth of the estuary between Bolt Head and Prawle Point.

Archaeological work at Moor Sand took place between 1977 and 1982, while the adjacent Site B was discovered only in 2004 and is the subject of a continuing campaign. It remains possible that the two sites resulted from the dispersal of material from a single original site. Nevertheless, the dual nomenclature is deemed valuable for historical and geographical reasons.

Moor Sand: discovery and exploration
by Dave Parham

This work has been compiled from published sources as well as from the archives of the National Maritime

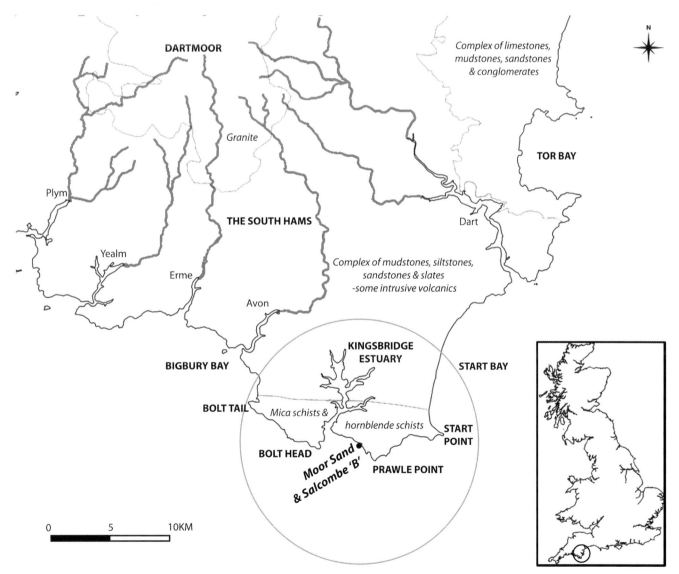

Fig 1.1   Moor Sand and its terrestrial hinterland, showing geological and topographical features (contains Ordnance Survey data. © Crown copyright and database right 2011)

Museum (which contain Keith Muckelroy's personal papers relating to the site) and the British Museum, and from material supplied by Philip Baker, the discover of the site. Figures 1.2–1.7 show the general conditions present on the site.

Environment and background

The Moor Sand/Salcombe B site, like most of the southern coasts of Devon and Cornwall, is extremely exposed to the forces of the Atlantic. It is, however, protected by land masses from northerly and easterly winds and the exposed horizon of the site is only 115°. Prawle Point, to the east, provides shelter from SE to SSE and Bolt Head, to the west, from W to WSW. Nevertheless, this restricted angle of exposure is precisely in the direction of the prevailing winds and consequent swells. To the south lies a fetch of approximately 600km to the Brittany coast, while to the south-west (the prevailing wind direction), the fetch is as much as 6500km across the Atlantic, and this can give rise to considerable swell. The wind direction records at the former Royal Air Force base at Mount Batten, in Plymouth, 30km to the north-west of the site, show that storm winds of Force 7 or above (32 mph or greater) occur, on a yearly average basis, for 1.6% of the time from the quarter to which this site is exposed. This figure rises to 3.9% for December. The

site is relatively sheltered in terms of movement of water by tidal action, but this increases to the south of the cannon site (see p 15).

The sea off Moor Sand is shallow clear water reaching depths of 4–8m inshore and 16–24m offshore in the area of the Salcombe B site. Inshore, the seabed consists of a shallow rock reef covered by a rich kelp (*Laminaria hyperborean*) forest over 1m in height.[1] The reef, which is interspersed with gullies up to 2.5m wide and crevices filled with sand and rock cobbles, has an average height of around 1m, rising to a maximum of 3m, and covers much of the sea floor. As the depth increases offshore, the kelp forest disappears and the seabed changes to rock gullies with sand infill descending to a sand and gravel seabed.

Large-scale human access to the relatively shallow waters around the coast of the UK, the equivalent of terrestrial walks in the countryside, has occurred only since the Second World War owing to the development of relatively inexpensive diving technology. The sport of amateur diving in the UK began in the 1950s, although it was not until the 1960s that it was carried out on any scale (Valentine 2003). A side effect of this activity has been the identification of relatively modern shipwrecks found by other means, such as fishing or military activity, and the occasional discovery of older, more ephemeral, shipwrecks. The point at which archaeology underwater, as opposed

Fig 1.2   Moor Sand as seen from the sea

merely to diving on shipwrecks, began is debatable. The widely accepted first true underwater excavation, as opposed to salvage, is George Bass's work at Cape Gelidonya in Turkey in 1960. In the UK, however, the situation is not so clear. One of the British pioneers of underwater archaeology, Keith Muckelroy,[2] dated the birth of the field to August 1965, when the wreck of the Dutch East Indiaman *De Liefde* in Shetland became the first major historic wreck to be positively identified in UK waters. By the mid-1970s work in the UK had expanded considerably and had made notable contributions to the understanding of various subjects, such as naval warfare in the late 16th century and European trade with the east in the 16th and 17th centuries (Muckelroy 1975, 232). However, all of the sites found by the mid-1970s were ships armed with cannon which are easily identified underwater. The oldest of these ships was the *Mary Rose*, which had been built in 1509 and lost in 1545 (Marsden 2005). No earlier maritime activity or marine vessels had been recognised.

Initial discoveries and project mobilisation

The underwater archaeology of prehistoric shipwreck sites in the UK begins with a fortuitous discovery on 4 July 1977. Two British Sub-Aqua Club (BSAC)[3] diving instructors, Philip Baker and John Hinchcliffe[4] were acting as 'Leaders' on a Youth Hostels Association 'Adventure Holiday' underwater swimming course based at the YHA in Salcombe, south Devon. The two had previously used the harbour at Salcombe for their students' first dives, but in this year they had to move the venue. The location needed suitable prevailing conditions because the students in question were complete beginners. For that reason, they chose the beach at Moor Sand.

Moor Sand is a small, deserted, sandy beach located just to the west of Gammon Head: that is, approximately 4km south-east of the entrance to Salcombe Harbour (Fig 1.1; Fig 1.2) With shallow, clear water and varied scenery, the site proved a safe and interesting venue for the students.

The team had a motor launch (*Kirby*) to allow for dives a short distance offshore. When Philip Baker took a reasonably confident and capable German student, Mrs Ursula Jurda, on the launch for her second dive, he expected another uneventful fifteen minutes underwater; but things turned out differently, as he later described:

> Ursula was on my left and she was getting perhaps 20% of my attention. On my right a large rock appeared. Behind it I glimpsed a hook – clearly metal. And I immediately thought of a lost fisherman's weight – and buckshee lead for weight belts! However the 'weight' grew longer and longer – and it tapered to a point! Putting first things

Fig 1.3 Diver in a gully at Moor Sand

first, I let go of Ursula's hand and grabbed what I imagined to be a spear head. Luckily Ursula stopped to admire my find. It lay totally exposed and free of encrustation on a gravel bottom in a gulley between large rocks, at a depth of about 6.5m. Ideas were racing though my mind. Clearly it was metal, and experience told me copper goes that distinctive green colour... but nobody ever made a spear out of copper ... but copper and ... YES ... mixed with tin it made BRONZE! With that settled we resumed our dive, looking for more goodies – and in doing so lost the exact site of my find. (Baker 2004)

On his return to *Kirby*, Baker handed his find (MS77/1; cat S15) over to John Hinchcliffe and took another student, John Clark, to search for more bronzes. Again, Baker records what happened:

... to my horror, I found myself quite alone! In near panic I retraced my steps (finnings?) and found John, sitting on the bottom – as near open mouthed as it is possible to be without actually drowning. He was holding out a much smaller, badly eroded bronze blade he had found lying on the surface gravel about 3 to 5m distant from the first find. A brief search in the vicinity revealed nothing else so in triumph we returned to *Kirby*, and after much discussion we formulated the theory that a Bronze Age sea captain had fallen overboard, taking with him his sword and dagger.

On returning to the boat, Clark handed his find (MS77/2; cat no S16) to Baker as, in his opinion, the two should remain together. Clark later recalled that he had been surprised by the sight of Baker surfacing with an object he described as looking like a rolled-up umbrella. Closer inspection revealed this find to be a sword (S15); and, excited by its recovery, Clark grabbed his equipment and jumped in with Baker, dropping straight off the boat and into a gully. Within that gully, another sword (S16) was highly visible, being almost malachite green against the white sand. Clark found the sword within 60 seconds of leaving the surface (Clark 2011).

A small number of further dives were made that day in the general area of the site, but the dive leaders' obligation to their paying pupils meant that no systematic investigation could be attempted immediately. Baker realised that he had made an important find but was concerned that news would leak out and the security of the site could be compromised. Baker and Hinchcliffe thus told the *Salcombe Gazette* of their discovery but gave a position several miles away at Soar Mill Cove. The resultant publicity caused the find to appear in the national press, *Triton* magazine (now *Diver*), and the *Underwater Book*.

Baker also contacted the relevant authorities, declaring the find to the local Receiver of Wreck,[5] who declined to record it as wreck, and Doncaster Museum (Baker's home area), which undertook conservation of the two objects and put him in touch with

Professor Keith Branigan (University of Sheffield). According to a letter written by Baker in 1977, Branigan had dated the two artefacts to the 12th century BC, identifying S15 as a rod-tanged sword of the Early Urnfield period, probably from northern France, and S16 as a sword of Unterhaching type, found mainly in southern Germany. The continental nature of the material and the maritime location of the finds suggested the real possibility of a Bronze Age wreck (Baker 2004).

Baker, a collector of naval swords, recognised the significance of the finds and, with this information in hand, he set about finding a home for them. He felt strongly that the two objects should be in a public rather than a private collection, although he felt entitled to reasonable recompense for his costs to date (Baker 1977a). He contacted a number of local and national institutions with little success. The National Maritime Museum did, however, reply to him suggesting that the British Museum or Tower Armouries might be approached, explaining that the National Maritime Museum would only really be interested if there were positive evidence that boat remains were present on site (Baker 1977b). In the mean time, ownership of the swords was in limbo; the Receiver of Wreck's refusal to accept the objects as 'wreck' meant that Baker could not establish title to them and, hence, could not pass them on to a third party. Nonetheless, he was under pressure from the Devon Archaeology Society to find a final repository for the swords. He discussed the matter with his solicitor, who suggested that he declare them to the local coroner as 'treasure trove cast into the sea'. This was not, however, a viable option as Treasure Trove, as defined at that time, was applicable only to precious metal finds with evidence that they had been hidden with the intention of later recovery. S15 was valued at £80 (Baker 1977c).

Baker and Branigan published the finds in *NATNEWS* (Muckelroy 1978l), the newsletter of the Nautical Archaeology Trust (now the Nautical Archaeology Society) and wrote a short piece for the *International Journal of Nautical Archaeology* (Baker and Branigan 1978). Baker also contacted Margaret Rule of the Mary Rose Trust, who put him in touch with Keith Muckelroy, a PhD student at Cambridge University.

Muckelroy was a 26-year-old Cambridge doctoral student working on a thesis entitled *Site Analysis and Maritime Archaeology*. Although he had only relatively recently enrolled as a research student he had already published widely, gained considerable field experience, and, from 1974, worked as a research assistant to Colin Martin at the Institute of Maritime Archaeology, St Andrews University – a post he had just left to return to Cambridge. While still an undergraduate, Muckelroy had led archaeological projects with the Cambridge University Underwater Exploration Group in mapping ancient harbour structures at Apollonia, Libya, in 1973 and Salmis in Cyprus in 1974. He had become the project archaeologist for one of the first systematic excavations of a shipwreck site, that of the VOC ship *Kennermerland*, participating in the second (1973), third (1974), and fourth (1976) seasons. He also worked under Margaret Rule on the *Mary Rose*. By 1977 he had published in *Britannia, International Journal of Nautical Archaeology, Mariner Mirror, Progress in Underwater Science*, and *World Archaeology*, in addition to writing the bulk of the text for his seminal work *Maritime Archaeology*, which was published in 1978.

The 1970s were the early days of maritime archaeology, particularly in the UK, and procedures for investigating underwater sites were still in the process of being developed as projects grew (Muckelroy 1976). As part of this development, Muckelroy had built on his Cambridge and field experience to begin to develop a methodological approach that aided the interpretation of shipwreck sites. He hypothesised that, in order to understand the original ship from which a wreck site was formed, archaeologists needed to develop a greater understanding of the processes that a ship underwent from the moment it was wrecked through to its discovery and excavation by archaeologists. He defined these processes as *wrecking; salvage; disintegration of perishables; seabed movement*; and *excavation (ibid)*.

Until this point, all UK maritime archaeological fieldwork was carried out on post-medieval wreck sites, most of which came accompanied by a wealth of historical data. Documents often dealt with the loss of the vessel and its subsequent salvage, thus providing much of the data for the first two of Muckelroy's processes. The fourth, *seabed movement*,[6] was a more difficult proposition. At the time, seabed movement on rocky shores, the environment in which most shipwreck sites had been found, was a process that had received little systematic study. Muckelroy's research into the subject indicated that the movement of archaeological objects could provide a way of studying the movement of sediment in such environments and, hence, also provide a means of collaborating with and contributing to marine science.

Muckelroy considered seabed movement to be a scrambling filter, one that mixed up what remained rather than removed it from the site. While, on the face of it these processes appeared complex, in the extreme case of the *Kennermerland*, which was wrecked in a shallow and exposed location, the finds did not appear to be as jumbled as may have been thought. In fact, the distribution of the finds on the site showed a strong correlation with the organisation of the original ship, suggesting that this process may be of only marginal significance (*ibid*).

The Moor Sand site was of immediate interest to Muckelroy. It was possibly the first wreck site found in the UK that predated AD 1500 (see discussion about 'wreck' later in this chapter). Furthermore, being dated to more than 2000 years old, it was also by definition a prehistoric site with no associated historic record. Thus, all that could be gleaned from the site would come from the remaining archaeology and the environmental conditions within which that

archaeology lay: an ideal test case for Muckelroy's methodology.

Moor Sand gave Muckelroy a free rein to start bringing his ideas into action. This site was the first at which he was in complete control of the archaeological approach to the work and the remaining site archive gives a detailed impression of both his thought processes and the practical steps that he undertook to put these thoughts into action. Consequently, the investigations of the Moor Sand site and, to a lesser extent, those of Langdon Bay (see Chapter 2), where Muckelroy was limited by the fact that Dover BSAC were 'salvors in possession', are of significant interest in the technical development of maritime archaeology.

Baker described the site to Muckelroy and indicated that he was planning to return to the site with a group of divers from the Doncaster branch of the BSAC, of which he was a member. He wished to obtain further information about the site so that it could be put forward for designation under the Protection of Wrecks Act 1973.[7] Baker was aware of his lack of experience in archaeological matters and asked if Muckelroy could either join them or suggest some relevant literature. Muckelroy agreed to accompany Baker on his return to Salcombe (Baker 1977c) over the period 15–18 October 1977 with the aims of relocating and plotting the find spots for S15 and S16 and establishing if the site was that of a wreck. There was no funding available, so each team member was expected to finance himself (Muckelroy 1977a).

Baker organised the logistics of the October search while Muckelroy advised how the work should be undertaken, even arranging to borrow a metal detector from Alan Bax of Fort Bovisand. On his first dive at Moor Sand on 15 October 1977 Muckelroy, accompanied by Derek Paling, found the water was clear enough for a close-up survey of the seabed; but the site differed from Baker's description. He had reported S15 as being found in 6m of water lying on a patch of gravel, and S16 within 3–5m of water, also lying on gravel (Muckelroy 1977b). Therefore, Muckelroy had expected a shale gravel bottom; instead, he found a more boulder-strewn seabed consisting of bedrock gullies filled with small rocks, pebbles, and broken-off bedrock, with shale bottoms (Fig 1.3). Overgrowing the seabed all around were thick kelp forests up to a metre high. Muckelroy concluded that the seabed was not gravelly, although some of the gullies did have gravel in them.

After twenty minutes of searching, the pair surfaced and were followed in the water by Baker, accompanied by Stewart Rollinson. After a further 60 minutes they located the general area of the original find spot. Following Muckelroy's directions, the divers marked the area, driving pitons into the bedrock, and set up a base line from which previously unexplored areas could be searched. The divers investigated every nook and cranny for a further 140 minutes before a third object, a very abraded weapon blade (MS77/3; cat no S17), with a patina suggestive of long-term exposure, was found by Rollinson. It was lying across a small crevice in the bedrock, well away from patches of sand or shingle. This position was in 6m of water 20–30m from the find spots of S15 and S16 and 40m away from the shore (Muckelroy and Baker 1979, 193). Again, pitons were driven into the bedrock to mark the spot, the object was photographed *in situ* and its position recorded before being lifted. With this discovery, diving ended for the day.

On the following day a further six-hour search was undertaken, but the only finds were of modern rubbish: a single brick,[8] a piece of steel mesh with a piece of rope attached (probably the base of a lobster pot), a fishing weight, and a modern ceramic sherd. Given the length of time spent searching and the area covered, Muckelroy felt that this was an unusually low concentration of modern debris for British coastal waters. On the third day, as the group sailed from Salcombe, conditions became too rough to dive so they returned and visited Moor Sand on foot. Here, they noted very little evidence of cliff erosion, except for one area of collapse along a gully above the site, which had not brought down much topsoil. They searched the beach with metal detectors, finding no archaeological material and, again, little modern debris – just a stainless steel ring pull, three or four tin cans, and the buoy that they had laid on the site two days before, which had been driven ashore by the heavy weather.

On the fourth day the weather improved enough to allow diving to resume but there was still a heavy swell with reduced visibility. Searching continued for just under two hours but, given the poor conditions and a long drive home afterwards, work was abandoned around midday with nothing further located. In the four days on site the group of seven divers had completed 27 hours 20 minutes underwater, 5.5 hours per diver (Muckelroy 1977e).

Immediately after the October programme Muckelroy considered the possible scenarios:

Deposition as a result of coastal retreat: The group had found no evidence of archaeological features above the site[9] and no evidence of archaeological features being disturbed by cliff erosion nearby. From this brief survey, Muckelroy suggested that the finds could not have resulted from coastal erosion (Muckelroy 1977c). This was backed up later by geological expertise which considered the local geology to be sufficiently resistant that there would have been few cliff falls in the intervening 3000 years (Anon 1978a). In addition, he considered that it would be extremely unusual to have a terrestrial deposit that contained only continental material (Muckelroy and Baker 1979, 205).

Deposition in a natural debris trap: The group had found relatively little modern rubbish (*ibid*, 204) on site compared to the norm for British coastal waters. From this observation, he deduced that the site was not a simple debris trap which would naturally attract debris at any time.

Deposition as a result of shipwreck: Muckelroy considered that, with four or five days of disorgan-

ised searching producing seven man-made objects, three of which were of Bronze Age date, statistically it was very likely that there was a substantial and complex deposit to be investigated (Muckelroy 1977c). He deliberately played down the possibility of a Bronze Age shipwreck; but, in writing to Margaret Rule, then of the Mary Rose Trust, he stated that it seemed to him to be the most favourable explanation by a short head and that he was prepared to reiterate this opinion in order to gain protection for the site. He signed himself a 'rather excited Keith Muckelroy' (Muckelroy 1977d).

Muckelroy felt strongly that they must now investigate the area to produce a detailed site plan and to establish the oceanographic and sedimentary patterns on site in order to give the three items a better context (*ibid*). He formulated a 'to do' list of what needed to be done, whose help was needed, and who would fund the work (Muckelroy 1977e). At this point, as a specialist maritime archaeologist with a primary research interest in the depositional processes involved in the formation of maritime archaeological sites, he recognised that he was not a specialist in the Bronze Age and needed help in this area. Furthermore, Muckelroy was keen to publish the results of the work as soon as possible, an idea that Baker supported as long as it did not conflict with Professor Branigan's interest; Baker felt that this was a 'first come, first served situation' (Baker 1977c). Muckelroy contacted Branigan asking for his help and found him to be extremely supportive. Branigan stated that, once his obligation to the *International Journal of Nautical Archaeology* (Baker and Branigan 1978) was completed, he would be happy for Muckelroy to take over archaeological interest in the project (Branigan 1977).

In an attempt to gain some understanding of the marine process in play at the site, Muckelroy sought the opinion of colleagues from other related disciplines. The Moor Sand seabed zone was thought to be a high-energy environment, thus an area of erosion (ie, an environment of net sediment loss rather than net deposition), such that it was most unlikely that a wreck could have remained buried for long periods of time and have been uncovered only recently. It was highly unlikely, he was told, that the bronzes would have lain in the position in which they were found since the Bronze Age, as water and sediment movement in such an environment would have abraded them to the point of destruction in less than the intervening 3000 years. Their condition, therefore, suggested strongly that the bronze blades had been deposited in an environment of less energy, perhaps in deeper water and/or further offshore, and had subsequently been disturbed and redeposited at Moor Sand (Anon 1978a).

Other advice given to Muckelroy regarding the movement of these blades on the seabed contradicted this interpretation. The transfer of momentum to an object on the seabed is relative to the hydrodynamic nature, or otherwise, of its shape. The more irregular the shape, the more turbulent the associated flow of water past it and the greater the transfer of momentum from the water movement, via friction, to the object. In the case of small and/or low density objects, this will allow them to move and, thus, be abraded by the subsequent tumbling movement. Bronze is a high density material which, it was argued, would almost certainly preclude any movement via transfer of momentum. Indeed, the passage of water around the blades would not only have left them unmoved, but would also gradually have eroded them to a more hydrodynamic shape, thereby reducing friction and making movement even less likely. The general hydrodynamic shape developed by the eroded objects would thus have derived from water flowing past them for a long period of time rather than movement of the objects themselves (Charles 1978).

Following this interpretation, the location of discovery would be the same as that of deposition. Moreover, as unmoving objects lying on a mobile seabed composed of materials such as sand or gravel, they would, if the sediment depth was sufficient, simply bury themselves as the lighter sediment was scoured from around and under them and redeposited on top. These processes could explain the different levels of erosion displayed by the objects: the fact that one is in near perfect condition and the others abraded is simply an accident of their precise environment (or environments) on the seabed. The well-preserved weapon had remained buried for long periods, while the others were subject to persistent sediment movement resulting from wave action (Malcolm 1977).

It was obvious that the site was exposed to full Atlantic weather and, thus, subject to heavy swells. It was protected by land masses from northerly and easterly winds and had a limited exposed horizon; however, as noted above, the horizon faced in the direction of the prevailing winds and consequent swells.

Muckelroy also learned that the seabed about 1.5 miles (2.4km) offshore and to the south-west of Moor Sand had recently been subjected to significant disturbance. A queen scallops bed extending 1 mile (1.6km) south-east of Bolt Head to 3 miles (4.8km) seaward and as far east as Prawle Point, was extensively fished for approximately eighteen months between 1973 and 1975. Heavy dredgers had been used to move innumerable large rocks, up to 350kg in weight, from the seabed. In the process, sediments shifted, exposing areas of the seabed previously covered (Worden 1978).

With regard to seabed mapping, Muckelroy made enquires of Professor Hall, head of the Research Laboratory for Art and Archaeology, who advised that the best instrument for picking up small non-ferrous objects was the 'mark 1 human eyeball' operated in a disciplined fashion. The single-beam and side-scan sonar surveying equipment (that were current in 1977) would provide depth data and some idea of seabed relief, but were unsuitable for the Moor Sand environment, as they lacked the definition necessary to distinguish shipwreck remains against the mixture of rocky reef, small gullies, and small areas of flat sand/scree that characterises the Moor Sand seabed. A magnetometer would be of little use for non-ferrous metal, but it was suggested that an underwater metal detector might help if operated in the same disciplined fashion as the human eyeball (Hall 1978a).

Muckelroy asked Cambridge University's Committee for Aerial Photography if it would take aerial photographs of the coast near Salcombe at low water. They agreed to try, as long as it could be incorporated into their own flying programme. It was suggested that low-level oblique views would provide the best images for his requirements, but they doubted whether any detail of the seabed beneath 6–10m of water would be visible (Anon 1978b). However, the work does not appear to have been conducted.

A local private museum based at Sharpitor, across the Kingsbridge estuary at Salcombe, had been broken up when the estate was purchased by the National Trust. One possibility considered by Muckelroy was that the bronzes had originally been part of this collection and found their way into the sea somehow. On making enquiries, however, he learned that no Bronze Age material had been present within the collection and that it had been disposed of in sale rooms at Torquay (Carpenter 1978).

A principal concern, highlighted by the Receiver of Wreck's refusal to accept the finds as 'wreck' under the Protection of Wrecks Act 1973, was the continuing lack of protection for the site. The Act allowed the designation of an area around a shipwreck deemed to be important by virtue of its historical, archaeological or artistic value, after which access to the designated zone had to be authorised. While the unusual nature of the objects suggested that the site might be of archaeological importance, the Act's intention was to protect shipwrecks, not other types of site. Muckelroy was very aware that, without evidence to explain how the bronze objects arrived at Moor Sand, he would have to demonstrate a reasonable presumption that the site 'is, or may prove to be, the site of a vessel lying wrecked on or in the seabed' (DCMS 1973; Muckelroy 1977c).

Prior to visiting the site Muckelroy had canvassed a number of members of the Advisory Committee on Historic Wreck[10] (ACHW) as to their opinion of the potential status of the site. They advised that the key to a successful application would be the manner in which it was made. It should contain as much information about the site as possible and be accompanied by an acceptable location plan with details of the team. It was also important that Muckelroy should explain his position within the organisation and his role as archaeological advisor (Flinder 1977). Eminent archaeologists on the committee, such as George Boon of the National Museums and Galleries of Wales, who described the find as 'dynamite', and Professor Barry Cunliffe of the Institute of Archaeology at Oxford University, were very supportive (Muckelroy 1977f).

Fig 1.4   Diver metal detecting in kelp at Moor Sand

On 19 October 1977 Baker wrote to the ACHW putting the site forward for designation as a wreck on the basis that the finds might have been from a Middle Bronze Age shipwreck which 'would be of incalculable archaeological value since nothing similar has been found and made available for archaeological investigation outside of [the] Mediterranean. At the very least, the bronzes should have their context established through survey of the site and its environment. Such a wreck would greatly extend the understanding of trade and technology of the period' (Baker 1977d). Baker's work would continue under Muckelroy's archaeological direction with conservation advice provided by Margaret Rule.

The ACHW designated the site on 8 March 1978 under Order 1978/199. This formed an important milestone for underwater archaeology as it was the first time the committee had designated an ancient site 'on spec' (Boon 1978). The Committee was particularly impressed with the application (Muckelroy 1977g) and excited by the potential of the site (Muckelroy 1977f). As a condition of the licence it was stipulated that 'in the event of any discovery of ship's structure the licensee will seek immediate specialist advice and in particular will contact Sean McGrail of the Archaeological Research Centre of the National Maritime Museum. McGrail to be contacted before survey takes place as leading UK authority on Bronze Age wrecks to advise on the kind of evidence you might expect' (Gibbons 1977).

In the hope of securing government funding for rescue archaeology, Muckelroy argued that the site was endangered by coastal erosion; but the application was unsuccessful (Pearce 1977). However, while the brief 1977 season had produced only a single additional Bronze Age find, the three bronzes found to date were sufficient to attract interest from the archaeological community. Dr Ian Longworth, then Keeper of Prehistoric and Romano-British Antiquities at the British Museum, was keen for the Museum to be involved. The later prehistoric gallery of the Museum was under renovation at that time and finds from Langdon Bay were on display (see Chapter 2) in a case on Middle Bronze Age trade. The British Museum offered to include the Moor Sand material in this exhibition (Muckelroy 1977g). Exeter Museum also expressed an interest in the ultimate display of the finds, despite the fact that Moor Sand fell outside their collecting area and, instead, within that of Plymouth Museum (Pearce 1977).

Funding and support came from multiple sources. The British Museum contributed the sum of £1500 plus specialist Bronze Age expertise in the form of staff time, the British Academy £1000 (Pearce 1978), the largest amount they had granted to an underwater project (Muckelroy 1978f), and the National Maritime Museum £500 together with access to their organic conservation facilities (McGrail 1978a). A condition of the National Maritime Museum's

Fig 1.5 Diver metal detecting in a gully at Moor Sand

involvement was that, if any boat structure earlier than the 16th century AD was discovered, they would jointly run the research project (McGrail 1978b). In addition, a metal detector was loaned by the Research Laboratory for Art and Archaeology (valued at £720) (Hall 1978b). Meanwhile, the BSAC were also keen to support the project with equipment loans, since they saw it as a model of cooperation between archaeologists, sports divers, and national museums (Muckelroy 1978h). Thus, the first archaeological season (1978) was launched.

Archaeological survey

The relatively close proximity of the finds to each other, despite their very different degrees of erosion, suggested to Muckelroy that they were being swept into the find zone from a more stable deposit located nearby. He was convinced that this deposit must originate in the marine zone as there was no evidence of eroding Bronze Age deposits on the adjacent coast. The objectives he set for the 1978 season were thus to:

• Discover what was disturbing the deposit
• Record the seabed context that the blades came from
• Establish what, if any, archaeological material remained to be found

To achieve these goals he aimed to conduct a visual search of the entire seabed within 200–300m of the original findspots as well as to undertake selective searches further away, especially in any areas found to be susceptible to erosion. His first plan was to use an underwater television sledge to search the area, but his attempts to borrow such a device from the Marine Biological Association failed owing to the perceived risk of damage to the equipment (Holme 1978). Given that the seabed was thickly covered in kelp (Fig 1.4), it is difficult to see that this exercise would have achieved much beyond crude mapping of the type of seabed. In the end, it was decided that visual survey was to be undertaken by divers who were also to search areas of deep sediment with metal detectors (Fig 1.5).

Muckelroy planned to search to the south and south-west of the original find area, as he assumed that the finds must have been swept in by the prevailing swell. To ensure that each square metre of seabed was examined, he aimed to use a corridor search pattern in which a series of adjoining, rope-defined corridors are pegged out on the seabed and then searched. To do this, he proposed laying a baseline 100m long (a length that could easily be deployed in one dive) with another (called a jackstay) laid parallel to it at a distance of 10m, a range of visibility in which divers could work safely, to create the first corridor on the seabed. The jackstay was to be laid underwater using three divers, one with

Fig 1.6   Diver surveying

a reel and the other two marking the 10m distance from the original baseline line. A shorter, second jackstay was then to be laid perpendicular to the original two, cutting across the corridor. Two divers would swim from either end of this short jackstay working towards the middle and searching a lane about one arm-span on either side of the shorter jackstay. Two pairs of divers started at each end of the corridor at the same time. With the divers turning over every boulder and disturbing every pool of sand, the search pattern would move in 2m steps from the ends of the corridor to the centre. Archaeological finds were to be left where they were, but the kelp around them would be cleared so that they could be easily relocated and inspected. Once each corridor had been searched, the baseline would be 'leapfrogged' over the jackstay (which then became the baseline) and relaid 10m further along the intended path of the search (Muckelroy and Baker 1979, 191–5). Measurements were made between corridors to ensure accuracy and seven basic datum points were established at salient locations, buoyed, and then surveyed from the shore by the Institute of Maritime Studies at Plymouth Polytechnic,[11] who were also to use an echo sounder to undertake a simple bathymetric survey (Muckelroy 1978i). Important locations (including finds) on the site were to be marked with pitons driven into the bedrock (Muckelroy and Baker 1979, 196).

The principal searching was to be done by volunteer divers drawn from branches of the BSAC.

They were not expected to be archaeologists, but they would be conducting most of the searching and seabed recording work. The archaeological recording and recovery of finds found on the seabed surface were to be undertaken by Muckelroy (Figs 1.6 and 1.7). The volunteer divers were to undertake the primary seabed search and note topography, variations in bedrock/sediment, different plant life, and anything else that seemed noteworthy; this would form the primary record of the site, to be detailed on a record sheet completed after each dive along with dive particulars. A site plan would then be drawn up at a scale of 1:100, giving a thorough picture of the seabed around the finds (*ibid*, 195). Muckelroy wanted the divers prepared for this important role, so he suggested they read a number of key texts,[12] visit local museums to handle Bronze Age metalwork to 'get their eye in', and get the feel of drawing and writing underwater by sketching objects in a swimming pool and then measuring their principal dimensions (Muckelroy and Baker 1978).

Muckelroy's plan called for surface finds to be collected, but no excavation was to be undertaken until the survey had been completed. He anticipated that this would involve working within a single gully, or gullies a few metres wide and no more than a couple of metres deep (Muckelroy 1977h). However, the site could still potentially yield the remains of a Bronze Age boat which might well be fragmentary, friable, and, hence, difficult to excavate. Therefore, excavation would require the highest level of skill and

Fig 1.7   Diver recording a find at Moor Sand

could only be undertaken by a suitably equipped and trained team in the following year (Muckelroy and Baker 1978). He considered that the initial survey would cost around £6000 with an excavation costing perhaps a further £7000, dependent upon what was found during the survey (Muckelroy 1978a).

Muckelroy was keen to introduce into archaeology the concept of ecological assessment as a means of mapping the environment of maritime archaeological sites (Muckelroy 1978h). For many years marine ecologists had been very interested in exposure scales shown by the distribution of species against physical boundaries. This work had started in the inter-tidal zone, where it had been noticed that organisms had different zoning patterns which varied depending on the physical exposure of the shore to wave action. Many years of study had refined this work to the point where it was known that this zoning was consistent around the world. As scientific diving developed, the study of seabed organisms had been taken from the inter-tidal to the submerged marine zone.

Muckelroy's early work had taken place in a range of different marine environments and had shown him that the marine environment and its impact on any archaeological deposits within it varied from site to site. He realised that the degree of preservation and gross distribution were dependent upon a number of factors, of which the overriding one was the character of the environment in which the archaeological material was deposited. Understanding the nature

of the environment would not only lead to a better understanding of the archaeology contained within it, but also allow predictions to be made about how to search for and record it. Notable among these experiences was Muckelroy's involvement with the University of Aston's second expedition to the Out Skerries in Shetland to work on the wrecks of the Dutch East Indiamen *Kennemerland* and *De Liefde*. Here, he met a marine biologist Dr Robert Earll, then a PhD student at the University of Manchester, who introduced him to the work that had been undertaken by marine ecologists (Earll 1978). Muckelroy saw a means of quantifying the nature of the environment which had great potential to assist him in his study of maritime archaeological site analysis (Muckelroy 1978h). At the time of the Moor Sand discovery this ecological work had not been used for archaeological purposes and Muckelroy was keen to involve Earll in the project to provide an invaluable adjunct to the work (*ibid*).

The 1978 diving season at Moor Sand stretched over six weeks from 11 June to 22 July. Over twenty divers stayed for periods from one to the full six weeks, with eight on site at any one time. Work took place from a self-contained shore base on the beach and the adjacent cliff top, linked by an aerial flight-way.[13] As the nearest road was 1.5km away all equipment was brought to the site by boat and kept in a site hut located at the top of the cliff overlooking the beach. Diving took place from inflatable boats, largely on SCUBA,[14] but with a small amount of work conducted using surface-supplied equipment. However, the latter was little used because of the mobile nature of the survey work. Of the 42 days available to the project, 33 days were spent diving, 5 were lost to bad weather, and the remaining 4 were taken up by mobilisation, with 341 man-hours spent underwater.

Work proceeded as planned, except that the disruption to work by poor weather was much greater than had been expected, the summer of 1978 being dominated by grey skies, intermittent drizzle, and heavy swells (Muckelroy and Baker 1980a). Muckelroy noted that, despite its obvious exposure, the site was not as heavily scoured as his initial observations had suggested. He observed that much loose material trapped within rock gullies, while often re-sorted by heavy weather, was not totally swept away. Consequently, there were many niches within the bedrock where archaeological material could be trapped for periods of time (Muckelroy and Baker 1979, 198). This observation was echoed by Bob Earll's biological assessment of the flora and fauna of the marine zone, which indicated that in fact the site was less exposed than its theoretical categorisation. Protection was afforded from northerly and easterly winds by land masses, and yet, to the south-west, the direction of the prevailing winds, there was a fetch of approximately 6500km across the Atlantic. Earll attributed the discrepancy between the theoretical and actual exposure of the site to the shallow, gently shelving nature of the seabed, which was also covered with shallow kelp reefs that acted like a series of groynes, reducing the exposure of the shore. In addition, shelter from westerly winds was afforded by Bolt Head while the gross tidal movements across the channel may also have reduced the effect of fetch and, therefore, of exposure (Earll 1979, 209).

In total, 1.5ha (3.7 acres) of seabed was searched but, despite this large effort, finds were limited to three objects. A featureless fourth blade in an advanced state of corrosion (MS78/2; cat no S23) was found by Baker 10m to the south of S15, lying beneath a boulder. Unlike all other finds from the site, corrosion products adhering to the boulder suggested that the bronze beneath it had been in this location for some time. Tests showed that, given its advanced state of corrosion, this object would not have been detected by either of the two metal detectors in the project equipment. The two further finds were both palstaves, which were found offshore and 100m or so away from the other finds. The first (MS78/1; cat no S3), recovered by Clark, was found lying within the kelp growing on the ridges between the gullies. Like the swords, being a malachite green it stood out against the exposed bedrock on which it lay. Its abraded condition immediately suggested exposure for some time. Nevertheless, Muckelroy did not believe it would necessarily have occupied the same spot for any significant period of time. The second palstave (MS78/3; cat no S4) also exhibited abrasion of its extremities, but its context was different. It was found by Chris Bennett with the use of a metal detector and had been buried under 140mm of clean, orange-brown sediment, indicating an oxygenated, unstable environment.

At the end of the season Muckelroy reflected on the implications of their discoveries and observations. The condition of the finds varied considerably from excellent to highly degraded. The excellent condition of the fine sword (S15) meant that it could not have lain for long in the exposed position in which it was found. Therefore, the object must have come from a deposit elsewhere. The varying condition of the finds suggested to Muckelroy that objects were being intermittently released from this deposit, perhaps over many centuries, and redeposited by wave and possibly tidal action to the locations in which they were found – S15 being the most recently released and the more corroded finds having been exposed for considerably longer. Lack of erosion along the adjacent coastline – particularly any events recent enough to have deposited S15 – and the fact that it would be extremely unusual for a terrestrial hoard to consist entirely of imported material suggested to Muckelroy that these objects were not originally deposited on land. Meanwhile, the dearth of modern rubbish suggested that the site was not a natural debris trap for material swept in from elsewhere along the coast; hence, Muckelroy deduced that the original deposit must be close by.

He considered many features of the artefacts themselves as well as the environment in which they were found in order to hypothesise the location of this original deposit. Corrosion on the finds indicated that they had been immersed in the marine environment for a long time. Prevailing environmental conditions would, in aggregate, move material in towards the shore. There was also a clear distinction between the zones where the two types of finds had been found. The blades (S15, S16, S17, and S3) had been found inshore, while the palstaves (S3 and S4) came from further offshore. Muckelroy realised that thin blades had a high surface area to weight ratio and may have been more responsive to water movement then the denser palstaves.

Discounting a coastal origin for the finds, Muckelroy considered that, if the objects had entered the marine environment during the Bronze Age, then it could only have been as a result of either ritual deposit or accidental loss. He thought ritual deposit was improbable as no other ritual assemblage limited purely to imported goods was known, leaving only accidental loss as a probable cause. Given the location, the most likely cause of accidental loss was shipwreck. However, he felt that the exact nature of their deposition in the archaeological record was not as important as the long-distance connections hinted at by the origins of the objects (Muckelroy and Baker 1979, 206).

One additional outcome of the 1978 season was the making of a case for an alteration to the zone of designation. The original designation protected the seabed within a 150m radius of the original finds, but, as the new finds came from outside that area, Muckelroy proposed shifting the centre of the site to 50° 12' 42" N, 03° 44' 20" W, thus including all of the seabed out to the 45-foot (13.72m) depth contour (Muckelroy 1978i). The designation order was amended on 16 February 1979 by Amendment Order 1979/56.

The 1978 season achieved its preliminary aim of establishing and recording the context of the 1977 finds, as well as locating three further finds. Although it failed in its ultimate objective of tracing the deposit from which these finds originated, their distribution did support the idea that a concentrated source might lie further out to sea, perhaps within one of the sediment-filled gullies that the ecological survey had found in 10–20m depth further offshore. These had been noted to be up to 8m wide and mostly filled with a metre or more of silts, sands, and fine shingle. This set the main objective for future survey, but seeking funding for the work proved problematic. The 1978 season had looked forward to great discoveries and, as Muckelroy noted, the funding organisations had been broad-minded and courageous to back such an uncertain proposition in a relatively unknown field (Muckelroy and Baker 1979, 189). However, the 1978 results had not been spectacular enough to justify this optimism or generate additional support (Muckelroy 1979d).

The National Maritime Museum made a grant application to the Department of Education and Science (the NMM funders) for a special fund to support underwater projects but this was rejected on the grounds of economy (McGrail 1979). Meanwhile Muckelroy's application to the British Museum (who had contributed £1500 in 1978) resulted in a much reduced grant of £100 for 1979. The museum explained that, although their purchase grant had been halved, they would like to maintain a token interest in the project (Longworth 1979b). The funding difficulties were not due just to the modest project results, but also to the state of the British economy. The winter of 1978–79 became known in Britain as the 'winter of discontent', with high rates of inflation and the country's economy in decline. The political and economic upheaval of this period led to major cuts in public expenditure. It was unfortunate for Muckelroy that he was seeking public funding for his work at a time when funding for science was being drastically cut (Muckelroy 1979g).

The substantially reduced funding base caused logistical problems and uncertainty over the scope of the work that could be undertaken. Reduced funding to cover volunteer expenses, coupled with individual people's generally diminished disposable income, resulted in fewer volunteer divers. Funding uncertainty also caused serious delays in planning the field season. As a result, it was accepted that any budget overspends would have to be made up by the sale of equipment (Muckelroy 1979e). As a consequence, the project was constrained by shortages of both divers and funds (Muckelroy 1979g).

The plan for 1979 was based on the results of the 1978 season, which had shown that finds were scattered over a large area of the seabed. Therefore, any search looking for a more coherent source deposit would need to cover a more extensive area, in particular moving further offshore from the original site. Owing to the large size of the area needing to be searched and the resource limitations, the survey could not be as intensive and comprehensive as it had been in 1978. Instead, emphasis was placed on a systematic search of areas of sand and shingle on the grounds that any substantial and well-preserved remains might be found in such deposits. Intervening areas of bare rock were to be searched visually, although not exhaustively. The area involved was to be divided up into broad east–west corridors which were generally 40m wide and 200m long and the search would, again, rely heavily on metal detectors. The divers would work in pairs, with one searching the sediment with a metal detector while the other searched the adjacent bare rock. The goal of the survey was to produce a sketch map of the seabed which would contribute to the master plan of the topography of the site started in 1978 (Muckelroy 1979h).

The 1979 season took place over June and July and involved thirteen BSAC divers with funding from the British Museum, the National Maritime Museum, and the British Academy. Blessed by good weather, the planned work was finished in the time allowed with no further finds in the 5ha (12.35 acres) of seabed searched. Muckelroy was confident that no major archaeological deposit lay in the areas searched, although he accepted that occasional isolated objects may have been overlooked. The good weather allowed the divers to move further offshore and assess an area beyond that programmed to be surveyed. Here, the depth exceeded 20m and was characterised by a seabed of rocky gullies, boulder-strewn plains, and conditions not conducive to the good archaeological preservation of organic material (*ibid*).[15]

Surplus time also allowed for a reconnaissance of the 1978 search area to be undertaken to ensure that it was still empty of bronzes and to make a comparison with 1978 conditions on site. A number of locations searched in the previous season were revisited and, in many instances, it was observed that notably less sediment was present with considerable quantities of dead kelp, perhaps reflecting the poor weather of the winter of 1978/9. The 1978 find spot of S4, at that time under 140mm of gravel, was now almost completely clear of sediment, although by the end of the season there were signs of renewed sedimentation. The sinker for the site buoy laid in the previous season had disappeared and could not be relocated. On the last full working day an eroded bronze blade (MS79/1; cat no S22) was found by Stewart Rollinson in a gully roughly in the same area as the first two finds (S15 and S16). It lay with one end covered in small stones. This area had been searched in both 1977 and 1978, when it had a very thick kelp covering, and Muckelroy thought that the blade may have been overlooked or been washed in from the unsearched shallows (*ibid*).

Muckelroy's knowledge of the seabed grew through his long-term presence on the site. Three years of failure to find a source deposit, coupled with his observations of sediment cover and movement, altered his thinking about the site. He began to move away from the theory that the bronzes were swept in from deeper water (Muckelroy 1979f) and to contemplate the possibility that the objects may have lain *in situ* for 3000 years, somehow protected until becoming exposed relatively recently owing to changes in the seabed. The site, he thought, was becoming something of an enigma (Muckelroy 1979h).

The discovery of S22 in an area already searched indicated that the site was not yet exhausted, but the very limited success of the 1979 season in producing finds discouraged Muckelroy from undertaking another full season of work until he had a better understanding of the sediment transport conditions on site (Muckelroy 1979j). He proposed that there be a regular watching brief and the monitoring of sediment movements before any resumption of archaeological work and, indeed, before any moves to de-designate the site (Muckelroy 1979h). Baker and Muckelroy thought that the extremely high winds recorded at nearby Prawle Point during the winter of 1979/80 may have washed other items out of a formerly stable deposit. To substantiate this possibility, Baker agreed to take YHA 'Adventure Holiday' divers over the site for a casual visual search which could be followed up by a working party if anything of significance was seen. However, Baker contracted an ear infection while working on the *Mary Rose* and could not undertake the YHA adventure holiday that year. As Muckelroy was due to speak in Exeter about the project in October, he and Baker planned to dive on the site in the autumn (Baker 1980). Muckelroy had left Cambridge in March 1980 to take up the post of Assistant Keeper at the National Maritime Museum as their Underwater Archaeologist (Muckelroy 1980a), but the planned October dive never came to pass. Keith Muckelroy was drowned in a diving accident while working at Oakbank Crannog in Loch Tay on 8 September 1980 (Daniel 1980, 14). With this tragic accident, further work on the site was suspended.

The 1982 season

Diving on the project did not resume until 1982, when Muckelroy's successor at the National Maritime Museum, Martin Dean, undertook a final season on the site for the Museum. Dean visited Moor Sand for two days in the summer of 1982 in the company of Phil Baker and Bill Bunting, a local dive charter skipper. His work was aimed at tying Muckelroy's surveys into the British national grid reference system by buoying Muckelroy's datums and establishing their positions by use of a theodolite. He would assess the possibility of bronzes being found in areas not yet searched as well as in areas already searched, in case these were catchments for material involved in seabed movement. Previous surveys were to be extended inshore to expand the research area (Dean 1982a). Again, poor weather prevented a thorough archaeological assessment and most of the time was spent looking for previous datums (Dean 1988). A 50m search line was laid across the area where most of the previous bronzes had been discovered and a corridor 2m wide was searched both visually and with metal detector, but no finds were made. However, during searches for Muckelroy's datum points a bronze sword hilt (MS82/1; cat no S18) was discovered lying exposed on rock some 20m from the line. Over the two days just 3.75 man-hours were spent underwater (Dean 1982c). At the time Dean thought that the bronzes were eroding from a terrestrial deposit (Dean 1988).

The site continued to be enigmatic and the appropriateness of its designation was still questionable (Dean 1982c). The National Maritime Museum continued to show commitment to the site and planned a further nine-day season involving 20–40 self-funding volunteers. However, funding for the National Maritime Museum was being squeezed and it was decided that, since there was no imminent threat to the site, it was difficult to justify the use of scarce resources. Consequently, the season was postponed. There was an intention to mobilise further work again in 1985–86; unfortunately, the Archaeological Research Centre of the National Maritime Museum closed when government funding for it was cut that year.

Since 1982 a very limited watching brief has been conducted on the site, with Dean revisiting the site in his new role as director of the Archaeological Diving Unit[16] in 1988, 1994, 1995, and 2002. Since 2000, a survey licence has been held for the site by Neville Oldham of the South West Maritime Archaeological Group, but there have been no further archaeological finds within the site's designated area. The Bronze Age seabed archaeology of the area, however, took a new turn in 2004.

Salcombe site B *by Dave Parham, Neville Oldham, and Mick Palmer*

The area off Moor Sand is a popular location for drift dives[17] and rumours had persisted for many years of a cannon site located to the seaward of Moor Sand. Over the 1992 spring bank holiday divers from the Salcombe-based dive charter boat *Panther* located and marked the site and notified Neville Oldham of the South West Maritime Archaeological Group (SWMAG), who was mapping all the cannon sites in the area. SWMAG conducted work on the site, locating finds that dated it to the mid-17th century. The 1995 discovery of gold coins and jewellery on the site led to its 1999 designation as the Salcombe Designated Wrecksite. At this point, the finds from the site were acquired by the British Museum.

Work on the site continued, but an unexpected discovery was made in May 2004 just to the east of the main 17th-century site and still within its designated area; here SWMAG recovered a number of Bronze Age objects. For the sake of clarity, the new Bronze Age concentration has been named 'Salcombe B' and the 17th-century site as 'Salcombe A'. It was felt that recent seabed movement had exposed the artefacts, putting them in danger of damage and of unauthorised removal. They were recorded and recovered and the assemblage was transferred to the British Museum because of the potential connection to the Moor Sand assemblage. A further consequence of the new discoveries was the realisation that one or two earlier found objects were of Bronze Age date. Fieldwork in 2005 included extensive survey to the east and north-east of the cannon site, towards Moor Sand, and produced additional Bronze Age material of significance (Parham and Palmer 2006). At this point, all of the material recovered from the Salcombe B site seemed to be contemporary with that recovered at Moor Sand. However, the Salcombe B material also included gold jewellery and an object identified by Stuart Needham as an *instrumento con immanicatura a cannone*, providing the first secure context in Britain for a Bronze Age object of Mediterranean origin (Needham and Giardino 2008).

Work on site continues to turn up more Bronze Age material, but the need to produce a definitive publication on the early finds led to an arbitrary cut-off date of December 2004 for inclusion in this volume. Since the cut-off date, work by SWMAG has gone on to validate some of Muckelroy's hypotheses about Moor Sand. Muckelroy's initial primary aim was to map the seabed and to understand the environmental context in which the archaeology of the site sat. His painstaking work, and that of his team, produced a map of 15,000 square metres of seabed in 1978 and of a further 50,000 square metres in 1979 which was of sufficient detail and accuracy for it to be overlain on modern electronic hydrographical surveys of the site. That this precision mapping was achieved in dense vegetation with simple surveying tools and in what are now seen as very basic diving conditions is no small achievement. Since 2005, considerable archaeological material has been found in deeper water to the west of the area that Muckelroy surveyed. This material is not a concentrated deposit of archaeological remains, but a scatter of metalwork that lies within the area in which Muckelroy suggested that a concentrated deposit might lie.

One relevant feature of the Moor Sand site is that Muckelroy started work there in 1977 as an archaeologist interested primarily in the formation of marine sites and did not consider himself to have had any particular specialist knowledge of the Bronze Age. During the time in which he was involved with this site and the one at Langdon Bay, Muckelroy's research focus changed to include cross-channel exchange (work reviewed in Chapter 5 of this volume) in the Bronze Age, and his pre-viously singular interest in the technicalities of maritime archaeology shifted to a concern with how the results of his technical investigations increased our knowledge of the past.

Sea level history and coastal geomorphology
by Roland Gehrels

The purpose of this study was to examine the history of sea level change and coastal erosion in the hope of determining whether the bronze assemblage recovered from the seabed off Moor Sand could have been an eroded terrestrial deposit. A field visit was made to study the local coastal geomorphology and evaluate possible coastal retreat. Secondary sources consulted in this study include geological, bathymetrical, topographical, and historical maps, as well as relevant scientific literature.

Relative sea level changes

Relative sea level along the south Devon coast has been rising throughout the Holocene, but reliable sea level index points are scarce. The nearest data to Moor Sand come from North Sands, Salcombe, where organic sediment at the base of lagoonal deposits was dated at 4129±59 ^{14}C yrs BP (AA-38836), placing sea level at a position of –3.1±0.3m between 2900 and 2500 BC (Massey 2004; Massey *et al* 2008). Other information comes from Slapton Ley and Hallsands (Shennan and Horton 2002), where Morey (1976; 1983) reported two radiocarbon dates with potential relevance to sea level changes (1683±40 ^{14}C yrs BP, AD 240–430, SRR317; 1813±40 ^{14}C yrs BP, AD 90–330, SRR492). However, in a re-analysis, Gehrels (2006; 2010) concluded that Morey's data are unreliable and cannot be used to constrain former sea level positions.

Given the paucity of recent geological data, the best current estimates of sea level change during the past three or four millennia are derived from geophysical model calculations. Bradley *et al* (2009) published the most recent model results for the British Isles. When applied to the south Devon coast, this model predicts a sea level position of –1.8m at 1000 BC (S L Bradley, pers comm). The model-predicted sea level at 3000 BC is –3.4m. This result agrees well with the geological evidence from North Sands and indicates that the model calculations are fairly accurate.

Coastal geomorphology

The bedrock around Moor Sand consists of greenschists and mica schists belonging to the Start Complex (British Geological Survey 2000, fig 1). These rocks are Lower Devonian in age and possibly originate from a spreading mid-ocean ridge (Holdsworth 1989; Floyd *et al* 1993). Weathering of the local bedrock has been studied by Mottershead

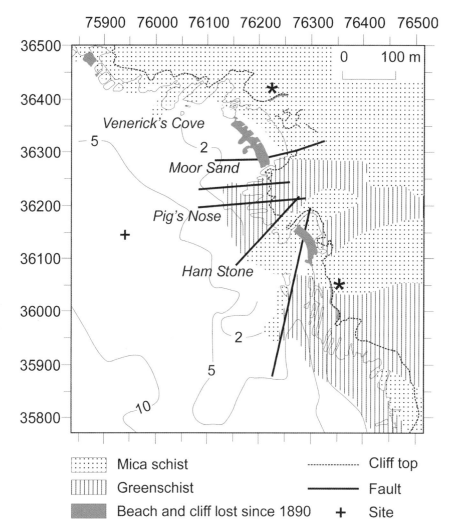

Fig 1.8   Selected geological and geomorphological features of Moor Sand and adjacent area. The coastline represented on this map coincides with the present level of Mean High Water. Beach and cliff area lost since 1890 were determined from a detailed comparison of the 1890 and 2005 Ordnance Survey maps. Sites of cliff retreat marked by an asterisk (*) are also shown in Fig 1.9. Faults and lithologies from British Geological Survey (2000). Bathymetry from UKHO 1998

(1982; 1989; 1994). In the supra-tidal zone, the schists are lowered by salt-spray weathering at a rate of 0.625mm per year (Mottershead 1989). The local bedrock forms a modern intertidal platform, but a higher platform is visible at 4–5m elevation in some locations. Similar 'raised' marine platforms have been reported by Ussher (1904) and others and are related to higher-than-present sea level positions during previous interglacials or interstadials. The 4–5m platform is the lowest of several fossil rock platforms that have been reported. Fine examples of this platform occur to the east between Prawle Point and Langerstone Point (Mottershead 1971; 1997) and to the west at Seacombe Sands. The fossil platforms are buried by an apron of head deposits, solifluction material that was formed by periglacial processes during the Devensian (Mottershead 1971). Erosion by rising sea levels during the Holocene has produced a cliff in the head deposits and has partially exposed the fossil platform. The fossil platforms would be connected to fossil sea

cliffs inland, but this connection is obscured by the drape of head.

A comparison of the modern and 1890 Ordnance Survey maps suggests that the cliff line in the Moor Sand area has remained largely stable. This observation is important as, during this period, sea level in south-west England has risen at an average rate of about 2mm per year (Woodworth and Player 2003), faster than at any time in the previous millennium (Donnelly *et al* 2004; Gehrels *et al* 2005; 2006). The low water line has moved upward since 1890 by about 0.2m, producing a narrowing of several beaches, including Moor Sand (Fig 1.8). The only substantial cliff that has noticeably retreated is the cliff in the head deposits east of the Ham Stone, but it has not changed position by more than a few metres. This cliff is marked by an asterisk in Figures 1.8 and 1.9. There are also some small erosional scarps visible in the head deposits behind Moor Sand beach (Figs 1.8 and 1.9), but these are fairly insignificant.

An important morphological feature is the extension

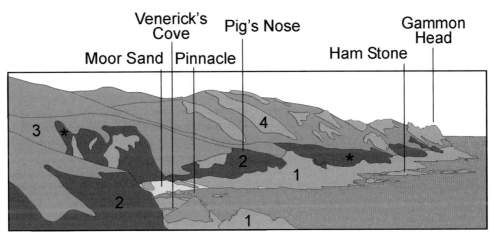

Fig 1.9 Overview of Moor Sand and adjacent coastline. 1. Intertidal rocky platform, grading into supratidal raised fossil platform at higher elevations. 2. Cliff formed in Head deposits. 3. Drape of Head deposits covered by vegetation. 4. Bedrock cliffs protruding from the Head cover, part of former interglacial cliff line

of the shoreline platform below the low water line immediately west of the eroding head cliff (Fig 1.8). The platform appears to represent a submerged extension of the Ham Stone. The Ham Stone offshore rocks are part of this former platform and can be seen in Fig 1.9. The Ham Stone consists of resistant mica schists which are separated by faults from the adjacent greenschists (Fig 1.8). It is possible that, when sea levels were several metres lower, the head cliffs occupied this platform and extended further out to sea. Indeed, further to the east at Gorah Rocks in Lannacombe Bay, the rock platform extends about 500m offshore (Mottershead 1971; 1997). It is likely that, in this locality, the rate of head cliff retreat has been much faster than at the Ham Stone.

An interesting feature just to the west of Moor Sand is an isolated 'pinnacle' of head occupying the supratidal bedrock platform (Fig 1.9). At the base of the head raised beach deposits can be observed resting on the rock platform. The pinnacle is undoubtedly a remnant of a much more extensive former head deposit which has largely been lost to coastal erosion. However, it is remarkable that the pinnacle has not changed in size since 1890. Interestingly, the pinnacle was described by Ussher (1904) during his geological mapping of the area:

At Venerick's Cove on the Prawle Coast, east of Seacombe Sands, a pinnacle of Head caps the

rock platform at a distance of 50 yards [45m] from the cliffs, between which and the pinnacle the sea has made a clean breach in the rock platform. ... To account for the isolation of the pinnacle, we must assume that it formed part of a mass of Head banked against the cliffs and overlying the old beach sand, and, that, in the denudation of the cliff and beach platform, the cliff part of the Head was washed away and the traces of the old beach preserved in the angle between the platform slope and the cliff at its termination.

The distance between the pinnacle and the cliff has not changed since the description by Ussher (1904) over a century ago.

Conclusion

The archaeological site near Moor Sand dates from roughly 1300–1200 BC. The position of sea level at this time was *c* –1.8m, so that this site would have been in 5–8m water depth at the time of its deposition. The cliffs around Moor Sand are relatively stable and coastal retreat cannot satisfactorily explain the position of the bronze artefacts. It is concluded that the materials were probably transported to their present position.

Terrestrial hinterland of Salcombe *by Stuart Needham and Dave Parham*

Assessing relevant 'hinterland' evidence can be a very different issue for maritime sites than for those on land. This is especially the case for incontrovertible shipwreck sites, since the place of wrecking may be distant from the boat's home port, the last point of landfall, and the intended destination. Hence, the boat and the particular voyage that was cut short need not have any relationship at all to the stretch of coastline on which it was wrecked. However, where there is no unequivocal evidence for a wrecked boat, the coastal hinterland may be relevant as part of a broader suite of evidence contributing to an assessment of the character of the site.

There is a second aspect of potential relevance. Even for a shipwreck, we cannot assume that the final voyage spanned a long distance. At any period networks of maritime interaction might be weighted towards short-haul coastal and cross-Channel transits rather than long-distance interaction. The nature of the ship's contents – cargo and other – may assist in the interpretation of the distance and direction travelled in the final voyage, but we should be wary of assuming that the presence of exotic types in themselves imply immediate long-distance exchange. Our preferred interpretation of the Salcombe seabed assemblage is left to Chapter 5, following consideration of all aspects of the recovered material, but the general points made here suggest that a review of the local contemporary terrestrial archaeology would be worthwhile whatever the final interpretation. Even if the local coastlands were not relevant to this particular seabed find, they might have participated in and helped support the system of maritime interaction at work in this phase of the Bronze Age. Sites discussed are shown in Fig 1.10.

The coastline around Salcombe features a series of headlands to either side of a ria, the Kingsbridge estuary; together they form a landmass jutting well into the Channel relative to flanking coastlines. The headlands, running from Bolt Tail in the west to Start Point in the east, define a strip of geology (various metamorphic rocks: hornblende-schist, amphibolite, mica-schist, quartzite, gneiss etc) different from the rest of the Devon South Hams, which is predominantly of Devonian rocks, a mix of slates, shales, and schists (Fig 1.1; Durrance and Laming 1982). This contrast could have affected both Bronze Age and later land use in significant ways. The centrally placed Kingsbridge estuary, although an impressive ria with multiple branches, drains only a very small catchment extending little more than 15km inland. Rivers to east and west have much longer reaches, their headwaters rising in southern and eastern Dartmoor: the Erme and the Avon drain into the sea in Bigbury Bay, while the Dart drains into Start Bay. These are very similar broad bays flanking the Bolt–Start headland and their rivers offer significant routes of communication inland with especial reference to resources on Dartmoor. We take both headlands and flanking bays into our main zone of consideration.

Prominent southward-jutting headlands are a particular hazard to craft being driven on prevailing south-westerly storms, or those on a course further north than intended in conditions of poor visibility. These geographical and climatic factors have had an obvious impact historically, for the local coasts are a graveyard for wrecked ships. This could well be a factor explaining the Bronze Age assemblage (or assemblages), but there are no obvious rocks seaward of the find area that would have holed a shallow-draught boat and one would have to invoke rough seas or a poorly maintained boat to account for a sinking.

Whether Moor Sand and the Salcombe B sites were the direct consequence of wreckings or not, there are good grounds for seeing this south Devon coastline as having a relatively strong level of maritime activity. This has been discussed recently for a longer chronological span by Griffith and Wilkes (2006, 70–3). They have emphasised the potential importance of seaward views of the land in the naming of distinctive land features and their associated territories in early historical times. The Bronze Age seabed assemblage is mentioned, however, as a prelude to the stronger evidence for sites involved in coastal exchange from the late Iron Age onwards.

Aside from its intermediate position in any regular pattern of long-distance cabotage, there is the probable added ingredient of tin being fed down rivers from Dartmoor to this stretch of coast (eg Griffith and Wilkes 2006, 72). The crucial importance of tin to the Bronze Age economy would have led to constant interactions between Dartmoor and the south coast (not to exclude the north coast) by way of the southerly- and easterly-flowing rivers, thus facilitating wider distribution in south-west England and beyond. The small piece of tin from Salcombe site B (S28) could be relevant here. Direct evidence for Bronze Age exploitation and distribution is scant, but a few pointers can be suggested. In their discussion of Bronze Age settlement patterns Balaam *et al* (1982, 258) suggested it was more than coincidence that 'some of the largest and agglomerated settlements in the Plym valley occur … overlooking areas that were heavily tinned in the medieval period'. Similarly, Craddock and Craddock (1997, 3–4) have noted a general association between small workings and prehistoric hut circles on Dartmoor. They also pointed out that some trench workings not far from the Grimspound Bronze Age enclosure may predate a lynchet system, potentially of Bronze Age date; the site is among headwaters of the river Dart system. Meanwhile, the Dean Moor Middle Bronze Age settlement (Fox 1957), excavation of which actually yielded cassiterite (tin ore), lies in the Avon valley. A large find of tin ingots was recovered by SWMAG from the seabed in Bigbury Bay close to the Erme estuary (Fox 1995), but unfortunately their simple plano-convex morphology is not diagnostic of any particular period of tin exploitation.

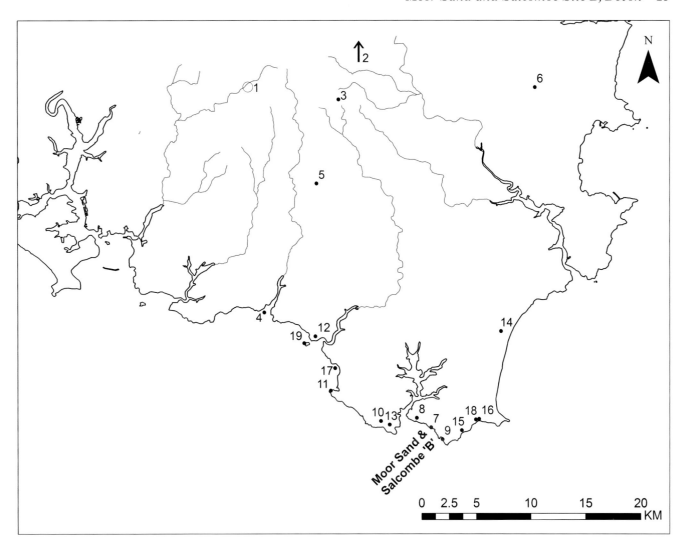

Fig 1.10   Sites in the Salcombe area discussed in the text. Key: 1. Upper Plym; 2. Grimspound; 3. Dean Moor; 4. Erme Estuary; 5. Ugborough; 6. Dainton; 7. Deckler's Cliff; 8. Rickham; 9. Elender Cove; 10. Middle Soar; 11. Bolt Tail; 12. Mount Folly; 13. Starall Bottom; 14. Slapton; 15. Chivelstone; 16. Lannacombe; 17. Thurlestone; 18. Lannacombe Beach; 19. Burgh Island

*

Dartmoor is renowned for its rich survival of prehistoric, and especially Bronze Age, archaeology. The modern agricultural landscape in the South Hams to the south and east of the moors could not be more contrasting. Traditionally this zone has yielded little evidence (eg Fordham and Mould 1982, 264, fig 24) and even casual finds of metalwork are sparse (Pearce 1983). This is undoubtedly due, in large measure, to poor survival and visibility; aerial reconnaissance has recently revealed many hitherto unknown enclosures, some undoubtedly later prehistoric in date (Griffith and Quinnell 1999b, 66, map 7.4; more have been identified since – F Griffith, pers comm). Again, until recently, there has been little excavation in the South Hams, but important new evidence comes in the form of small-plot field systems similar in character to those of Bronze Age date on Dartmoor (Yates 2007, 65–8). These discoveries are focused in zones of recent development in the Torbay hinterland, the Plymouth environs, and east of Exeter.

A site at Ugborough yielded evidence suggesting that the Dartmoor reave system continued off the moor's southern flank and into the South Hams. This all adds weight to the hypothesis that such parcelled landscapes were more widespread (though not ubiquitous) across southern Devon. Indeed, it is significant that fragments surviving as upstanding earthworks are known at Dainton in the east (Silvester 1980) and, more significantly in this context, on the Bolt–Start headland (below). Despite this growing evidence for field systems and enclosures off the Moor, it is intriguing that very few ring-ditches have been identified in the South Hams (Griffith and Quinnell 1999a, 59, map 6.5).

The immediate hinterland of Salcombe has not yielded any noteworthy concentration of Bronze Age material or sites, but there is a body of evidence that may be worth drawing attention to. Perhaps the most important evidence for later prehistoric settlement – none of it excavated or dated – comes from the remains of field systems, enclosures, and roundhouses. There is a ribbon of

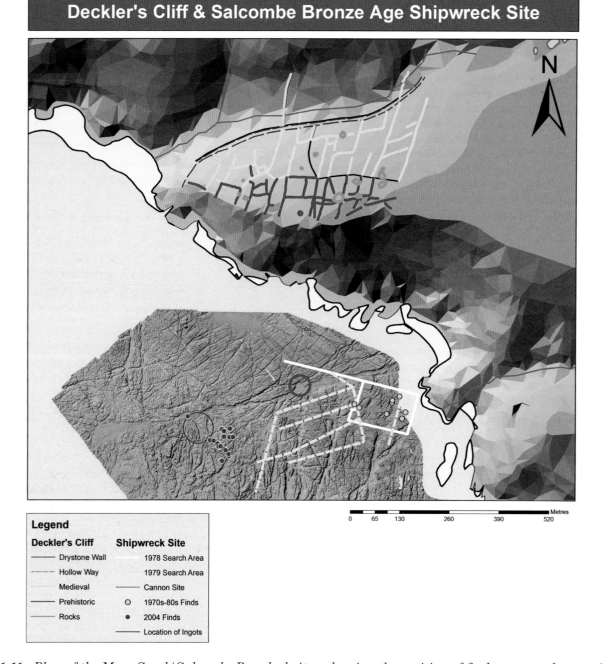

Fig 1.11   Plan of the Moor Sand / Salcombe B seabed sites, showing the position of finds recovered up until the end of 2004. The general position of the subsequent cluster of ingots is also shown, as is the plan of the probable later prehistoric field system on Deckler's Cliff, a short distance north-west of Moor Sand (after Newman 2003)

relatively rich survival running along the coastal strip between Bolt Head and Prawle Point. The main co-axial field system, comprising sub-rectangular to rhombic plots, lies on Deckler's Cliff. It is one of the best-preserved systems of small fields in the county, remaining in excellent condition, and has been recently resurveyed (Newman 2003; Fig 1.11). Blocks of similar field systems survive to the north-west, near Rickham, and to the south-east, on the cliff edge above Elender Cove, Chivelstone parish (SX73 NW162 and SX73 NE4/1), together creating an intermittent distribution of around

3km in extent. As suggested above, it seems likely that these are just marginal relics of a formerly more extensive prehistoric land-use system that has been largely erased by later agriculture, these remains lying in locations that were relatively marginal to later land-use regimes, perhaps in part because of the particular geological base.

Traces of probable prehistoric settlement, as yet undated, occur at three locations in this zone. Two clusters of circular stone-walled huts lie within the spread of field systems, one (SX73 NE69 and 69/1) comprising six or more hut circles within the

Deckler's Cliff system, the other (SX73 NE65) five hut circles within an oval enclosure situated on the coastal slope immediately above Moor Sand. The third site (SX73 NW169) lies at Middle Soar, Malborough, across the Kingsbridge estuary. It is 81m across and includes a bank 12m wide and up to 0.3m high on the north side and 0.6m high on the south. An external ditch is visible on aerial photographs. A promontory fort occupies Bolt Tail, but this is currently undated and presumed to be Iron Age (Griffith and Wilkes 2006, 83).

More positive evidence for near-contemporary occupation is beginning to appear from Eileen Wilkes' excavations at Mount Folly, overlooking the Avon estuary feeding into Bigbury Bay. Excavation targeting two or three ploughed-out enclosures has shown the principal occupation to be later Iron Age and Romano-British. However, Late Bronze Age pottery has now been recovered from pits at a lower stratigraphic horizon (Eileen Wilkes, pers comm). This horizon is due to be explored further in future seasons.

That the Bolt–Start headland was an occupied zone before the middle of the Bronze Age is clear from, for example, the presence of barrows and recorded burials of early Bronze Age date (Griffith and Quinnell 1999a, 59, map 6.5). Some of the barrows are in small groups and some occupy headlands, a siting frequently seen in coastal areas. None of the barrows has recorded burial deposits, but at Starall (Starehole) Bottom, Malborough, close to Bolt Head, it is recorded that an 'earthen pot' (therefore uncertainly of Early or Middle Bronze Age date) contained cremated remains (Devon HER: SX84 SW/11). Off the headland, at Slapton behind Start Bay, four cists were found containing cremated bones; two had Collared Urns associated (Devon HER: SX73 NW/44; Longworth 1984, 181 nos 355–6).

Given the dearth of excavation and fieldwalking, little can be ventured about domestic material of Bronze Age date. Flint assemblages have been recovered, especially from the coast at various locations (eg Fordham and Mould 1982, 262, fig 23), but little is diagnostic. Sherds of Trevisker pottery (Early to Middle Bronze Age) have been picked up at both Chivelstone, near the cliffs, and Lannacombe (ApSimon and Greenfield 1972, 373; Devon HER SX73 NE1 and SX83 NW9).

The metalwork finds are equally sparse, but much more chronologically sensitive. Two or more spearheads found at different times on Thurlestone beach (Devon HER record 58790; see also below, Table 5.4) are Late Bronze Age: one is of a distinctive Wilburton type and hence a little later than the Salcombe assemblage. The other finds are earlier: a Willerby phase decorated flat axe recorded simply as from East Portlemouth (Cambridge University Museum 22.1291); an Arreton type flanged axe from Lannacombe beach (Pearce 1983, no 438); and a stone mould fragment bearing the matrix for the blade half of a broad-bladed palstave (Middle Bronze Age) from Burgh Island, off the coast at Bigbury on

Sea (Pearce 1983, 433, no 187). A flat axe attributed to Salcombe by Pearce (1983, 453, no 289) has been discounted as it is almost certainly an Irish find (Harbison 1969, no 1206).

The permanent deposition of metalwork was probably affected by a range of factors at the time, and observed patterns will have been further modified by subsequent disturbance and recovery. Thus, metalwork distributions are far from proxies for relative levels of activity in the period. The South Hams in general are astonishingly poor in recovered finds of metalwork (Pearce 1983, 315–50). This lacuna is epitomised above all by Taunton phase metalwork (*ibid*, 150, fig 4.12), which gives the most prolific phase-specific distribution for the south-west peninsula. While the rural character of the South Hams may have reduced discovery potential relative to the built-up areas of east Devon and the Plymouth environs, this does not explain the contrast with a rural zone such as the eastern flanks of Dartmoor, which has produced far more bronze finds. Putting aside differences in modern recovery, such differences in density may reflect differences in the economic base and/or ritual customs of local groups. What *might* be more significant within southern Devon (south of Dartmoor and Torbay) is that metalwork finds, albeit modest in number, are virtually all from coastal locations. However, with the possible exception of the Thurlestone find, there is as yet no indication of a pattern of hoard deposits in this territory. This helps support the conclusions drawn elsewhere in this volume that the seabed assemblage of metalwork is not the result of a hoard (or hoards) being released into the sea by coastal erosion.

The evidence of later prehistoric occupation and land use in and around the Bolt–Start headland is not prolific and little of it can, as yet, be related closely to the phase of the Salcombe seabed material. It would therefore be unwise to conclude that there was any particular focus of settlement or exchange activity on the southernmost tip of Devon. Nevertheless, the evidence points to an occupied landscape overlooking the stretch of sea that claimed the Salcombe metalwork assemblage. The distribution of round barrows points to some occupation in the previous period and palaeoenvironmental records including dung beetles from peat exposed behind Thurlestone beach have indicated the presence of pasture and grazing animals at some point after the inception of peat growth in the Early Bronze Age (Yates 2007, 67). (In passing, we note that the report of a log-boat from the submerged forest at Thurlestone beach (Winder 1923) is unconvincing.) Such communities would have had a series of excellent vantage points overlooking the sea and could easily have tracked the passage of passing craft. The Kingsbridge estuary provided an excellent harbour within the heart of this coastal territory of headlands (even allowing for the difficult approach caused by the prevailing winds and a sub-marine bar – Griffiths and Wilkes 2006, 72, 86) and could readily have become a natural stopping point for coastal traffic. The more secluded bays, such as Moor Sand, would doubtless have been accessed by locals using cliff paths, but are less likely to have been the chosen places for regular maritime interactions.

The Bolt–Start headland may not have been a nexus for Bronze Age exchange, but it is still likely to have played a part in the chain of routine coastal interactions. Moreover, if the seabed assemblage *was* the outcome of a boat that got into trouble, it would presumably be representative of many more vessels which sought refuge and shelter along this hazardous shore. Such circumstances are bound to have brought about many unexpected meetings between Bronze Age mariners and the occupants of the Bolt–Start zone, thus adding to planned encounters.

Notes to Chapter 1

1. Kelp is a seaweed variety that consists of very large, leaf-like blades originating from elongated, stem-like structures with a holdfast – a root-like structure that anchors the kelp to the substrate. Gas-filled bladders keep the kelp blades close to the surface, forming relatively low underwater forests.

2. Keith Muckelroy was a pioneer in the 1970s of the then-fledgling discipline of maritime archaeology. He died in a diving accident in Loch Tay on 8 September 1980 at the age of 29. His work, published in his seminal 1979 publication *Maritime Archaeology*, made a major contribution to the practical and theoretical approaches to the subject and still maintains an international reputation today. An appreciation of his contribution to Bronze Age studies in trade and exchange is to be found in Chapter 5 of this volume.

3. An amateur organisation that is the governing body for sports diving in the United Kingdom. In 1977 the BSAC was the only body of any substantial size engaged in sports diving in the UK, with a membership of 25,342, about an eighth of the number of UK sports divers today (www.BSAC.com).

4. Not the archaeologist John Hinchcliffe, then of the Central Excavation Unit.

5. In 1977 the Merchant Shipping Act 1894 required that any 'wreck' found in or on the sea or washed ashore from tidal waters must be reported to the Receiver of Wreck, a local official, then often a customs officer. This Act has been superseded by the Merchant Shipping Act 1996; the duty to report is still the same, but the Receiver of Wreck is now a centralised position.

6. Now known as *sediment transport*: the movement of solid particles (sediment), typically owing to a combination of the force of gravity acting on the sediment and/or the movement of the fluid in which the sediment is suspended.

7. In 1977 this Act of Parliament was the only means of protecting cultural heritage in the UK's submerged marine zone, but it applied only to shipwrecks, not to any other form of submerged archaeological site.

8. At the time the brick seemed a strange find for a site in such an isolated location, but it may now be explained by the discovery of the wreck of the *Lord Napier*, which was lost carrying a cargo of more than 70,000 bricks. The wreck was found by SWMAG in 2007 offshore from Moor Sand.

9. This observation is not actually correct, as there is a Bronze Age co-axial field system that runs for 2km along the cliffs that overlook Moor Sand. This field system is associated with two clusters of circular stone-walled huts, one of which is situated on the coastal slope above Moor Sand.

10. The Advisory Committee on Historic Wreck Sites (abolished March 2011) consisted of a number of relevant experts who advised the appropriate Secretary of State responsible for the administration of the Protection of Wrecks Act 1973.

11. Now Plymouth University.

12. George Bass's *Archaeology underwater* (1966) and *A history of seafaring based on underwater archaeology* (1972), Philip Baker's *Techniques of archaeological excavation* (1977e), Browne's *Principles and practice in modern archaeology* (1975), John Coles' *Field archaeology in Britain* (1972), Sir Mortimer Wheeler's *Archaeology from the earth* (1954), and Colin Martin's *Full fathom five* (1975).

13. An overhead wire along which equipment was transported from the top of the cliff to the beach.

14. Self-Contained Underwater Breathing Apparatus: equipment that allows the diver to be free swimming and not tethered to the surface.

15. Ironically, it was within these gullies that, on the weekend of 15/16 May 2004, SWMAG discovered a further deposit of Bronze Age objects while working on a 17th-century site located offshore from Moor Sand. These finds consist of a collection of weapons, tools, gold jewellery, and scrap gold broadly contemporary with those found at Moor Sand. Finds recovered through to the end of 2004 are dealt with in this volume.

16. An independent archaeological diving contractor based at St Andrews University in Scotland and engaged by the UK Government from 1986 to 2002 to provide archaeological advice in relation to the Protection of Wrecks Act 1973.

17. Dives where the diver is transported by the currents, allowing him or her to cover long distances underwater usually without being aware of their exact position.

2   Langdon Bay, Dover, Kent

In early 1978 Muckelroy's involvement with Moor Sand led him to search for parallels for this site. The British Museum had recently (1977) acquired a similar, but much larger, collection of Middle Bronze Age tools and weapons that had been found in Langdon Bay, Kent, by the Dover Branch of the British Sub-Aqua Club (DSAC) in 1974 (Coombs 1976, 193; McDonald 1978, 17). Langdon Bay lies at the base of the famous White Cliffs immediately east of Dover Harbour Eastern Breakwater, on the north-western shore of the Strait of Dover (Figs 2.1 and 2.2). System-

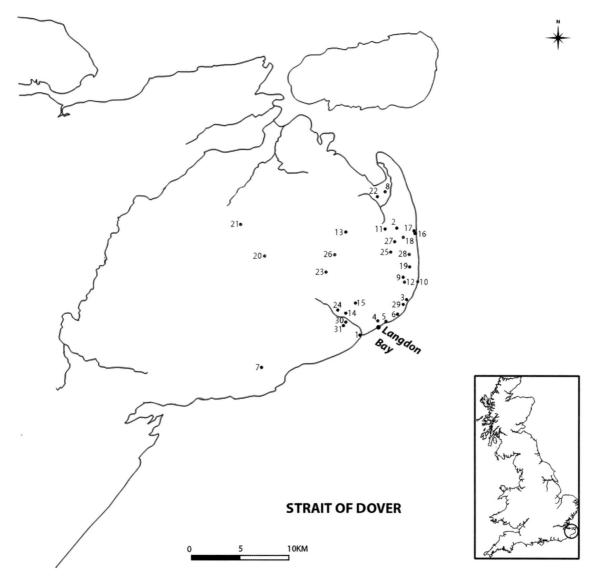

Fig 2.1 Langdon Bay and its surrounding environment, showing finds referred to in the text. Key:
1. Townwall St / Bench St, Dover; 2. Sholden Bank Primary School, Deal; 3. Salisbury Road, St Margaret's at Cliffe; 4. Swingate Aerodrome, St Margaret's at Cliffe; 5. Langdon Hole; 6. South Foreland Lighthouse; 7. Holywell Coombe, Folkestone; 8. Lydden Valley; 9. Freedown, Ringwood; 10. Hope Point, Kingsdown; 11. Sholden Bank, Deal; 12. East Valley Farm, St Margaret's at Cliffe; 13. Whitfield-Eastry bypass, Tilmanstone; 14. Dryden Road, Buckland; 15. Guston Roundabout; 16. Royal Marines S Barracks, Deal; 17. Royal Marines N Barracks, Deal; 18. Mill Hill, Deal; 19. Wood Hill, Kingsdown; 20. Wick Wood, Barham; 21. Kingston Downs, Barham; 22. Hacklinge Holes, Worth; 23. Waldershare Park, Shepherdswell with Coldred; 24. Between Old Park and Buckland, Dover; 25. Ripple Farm, Ripple; 26. Malmains Farm, Tilmanstone; 27. Church Farm, Ripple; 28. Knight's Bottom, Walmer; 29. South Foreland Estate, St Margaret's at Cliffe; 30. Buckland, Dover; 31. Union Road brickfields, Buckland, Dover

Table 2.1   History and organisation of fieldwork at Langdon Bay

Year	Lead	Main sponsors
1974	Dover Sub-Aqua Club	Dover Sub-Aqua Club
1975	Dover Sub-Aqua Club	Dover Sub-Aqua Club
1976	?	
1977	Dover Sub-Aqua Club	Dover Sub-Aqua Club
1978	Muckelroy	Dover Sub-Aqua Club
1979	Muckelroy	British Museum & National Maritime Museum
1980	Muckelroy	British Museum & National Maritime Museum
1981	Dean	British Museum & National Maritime Museum
1982	Dean	British Museum & National Maritime Museum
1983	Dean	British Museum & National Maritime Museum
1984	Dover Sub-Aqua Club	Dover Sub-Aqua Club
1985	Dean	National Maritime Museum

atic survey of the site, with limited excavation, began under Keith Muckelroy's direction in 1978 and continued on and off until 1989. After Muckelroy's death in 1980, the project was taken on by Martin Dean, his successor at the National Maritime Museum (Table 2.1).

Langdon Bay: discovery and exploration *by Dave Parham and Martin Dean*

Environment and background

The maritime environment of Langdon Bay presents more challenges to diving teams than does the Moor Sand site. The seabed consists of flat chalk dissected by eroded cracks and fissures which become more prominent towards the shore, forming gullies in some cases more than a metre deep. Most fissures are filled with mobile, loose, calcareous, sandy silt which increases towards the shore and blankets the chalk in places to a depth of 150mm. The bay would originally have been exposed to weather in a broad arc from NNE to SSW, but in more recent times some 'protection' has been afforded by the harbour breakwater a short distance to the west. However, this usually gives rise to a confused sea state caused by waves rebounding off the cliffs to the north and the breakwater to the west. Waves are also generated by shipping entering Dover Harbour or passing through the Strait[1] to the seaward. The normal sea state lifts the sediment into suspension and on most days this can been seen as a milky arc in the water whose edge is often seaward of the site, except for a period of a month or two in the summer. As a result, underwater visibility is generally poor, usually under 0.5m, only occasionally as good as 1–2m, and down to 'zero' for considerable periods after bad weather. Diving in the bay is limited to about three hours on flood tides during neap tides and one hour during spring tides (Dean 1987a).

The discoverer of the site, Simon Stevens, related these details of the initial discovery of Bronze Age materials in the *Kent Archaeology Review* (Stevens 1976, 66–7):

Fig 2.2   The area of the site from the cliffs above Langdon Bay, showing Dover Harbour in the distance

Fig 2.3   National Maritime Museum dive boat close against Dover Eastern Harbour Wall

For several years the Dover Sub-Aqua club had dived in Langdon Bay, east of Dover Harbour, mainly because of its accessibility by boat and its comparative slack water [Fig 2.3]. The bottom is very interesting being cut by chalk gullies of varying depths. The bottom is also littered with war relics ranging from odd cannonballs to World War II bombs and shells, many of which are unexploded.

On the 14th August 1974 Simon Stevens and Mike Hadlow began diving on the eastern side of the bay. We eventually swam above a small group of objects, including a spearhead and lifting only five, mainly because of the great weight, surfaced. Once back on board no one really knew what the objects were, though Mike suggested that they might be ancient tools. The following day the objects were taken to Dover Museum and shown to Mrs Coveney, the curator. Immediately recognising their importance Mrs Coveney contacted Mr Brian Philp, Director of the Kent Archaeological Rescue Unit,[2] and arranged for the objects to be examined. Mr Philp then met Mr Alan Moat, the Dover Club's Diving Officer and explained the archaeological importance of the finds and asked that a log be kept of dives and a record made of any finds [Fig 2.4].

The next task was to relocate and mark the site. On 28th August the first diving group soon found another bronze axe and marked its position. The second team dived around the marker and eventually recovered another 22 objects. The following day the site was relocated and marked with a buoy and a more detailed examination began. The finds mostly came from a narrow gully in the chalk about 79ft (24.08m) long and 2 to 10ft wide (0.61 to 3.05m) wide and 1ft (0.305m) deep. A line was placed along its axis and both ends marked with coloured buoys. These compass bearings allowed the site to be fixed and plotted on a chart. Another dive recovered 58 more bronze objects bringing the total to 86 (most finds were found in the base of the gully but a few were scattered around the banks on each side, all being found on the surface or partially buried in the sand which was 24–50mm deep) [Fig 2.5]. Sudden gales and wintry conditions brought the season's diving to an abrupt end early in September.

The 1975 diving season was very slow in starting owing to bad weather and the original marker buoys having been swept away by winter gales. The site had to be relocated and marked again, organised on a grid search pattern which took ten hours of diving. This work was hindered by bad visibility and it was not until 21st July 1975 that it was found. Two more bronze objects were found that day and finally two more on the following Sunday [see Table 2.2]. A final dive in September with the help of an underwater metal detector located another six objects.

Fig 2.4   Dover Sub-Aqua Club with finds from the site in 1974

Fig 2.5   An early find from the site: (LB37) axe lying on the chalk seabed

Table 2.2 Summary of 1974 and 1975 seasons at Langdon Bay listing minutes dived, divers and number of finds (Stevens 1976, 68)

Minutes dived

Divers	1974					1975											Total minutes dived	Total finds
	August			September		May		June							July			
	14	28	29	10	14	15	18	1	7	8	12	15	19	20	21	27		
S Stevens	50	45	125	10	5		5	20	30	40	30	30	40	40	50	60	580	46
C Osmond										40		30	40		50	40	200	0
P Mayes		40							30						60	60	190	11
K Jaynes								20	30		30			35		40	155	0
A Moat		40	30	10		5				30		30					145	20
T Stewart		45	65					25									135	13
R Player										30				35	60		125	0
M Hadlow	50				5				30			30					115	0
D Leviar		45					5		45								95	0
T Dole																60	60	0
B Atkins											30						30	0
R Mosely											30						30	0
R Shelow								25									25	0
Total minutes dived	100	215	220	20	10	5	10	90	165	140	120	120	80	110	220	260		
Finds recovered	5	23	58												2	2		

Note: the above table records the dates, diving times, and objects recovered. The cost of these 52 man dives was approximately £70.00, £40.00 for boat fees and £30.00 for compressed air. The six finds made in September 1975 are not logged here.

Fig 2.6 Median-winged axe as found at Langdon Bay

The 90 finds made prior to September 1975 were described as 23 palstaves or fragments, 26 rapier fragments, 30 median-winged axes (Fig 2.6) or fragments, 1 pin, 1 possible ferrule, 2 spearheads, 2 socketed axes, 1 socketed chisel, 1 possible knife, 2 axe blades of uncertain type, and 1 tanged axe blade. They were provisionally dated to around 1000–900 BC and thought to be from northern France (largely Brittany), with some material from areas further to the east and south-east. At the time Philp (1976) said:

> At first glance, therefore, this group appears to be essentially continental in character and origin. That it was found in the Straits of Dover suggests that the objects were in transit to Britain and had formed a cargo lost at sea. The site, only some five hundred yards from the present white cliffs, strongly suggests a wreck which, even allowing for the change in the coastline since the Bronze Age, must have been off-shore. Had any vessel been wrecked at the foot of the cliffs then the bronzes could have been collected at low water or at least subsequently buried by millions of tons of chalk rubble from the cliffs above. The evidence tends to suggest that a trader or bronze-smith was bringing a cargo of metal across the channel in a small craft when, failing to make the shelter of the wide tidal estuary of the Dour (now deeply buried under Castle Street) he was wrecked close

to the cliffs one mile further east. Of his vessel or cargo there is, apparently and logically, no trace, but his heavy bronze implements became trapped in the gully. Indeed is this the earliest evidence of a wreck in British waters so far recorded?

Immediately, therefore, the marine location of this assemblage of objects with strong continental connections suggested a possible shipwreck event, but with no evidence of a boat this hypothesis could not be confirmed. The lack of a boat was not unexpected; no such remains had been recovered from other potential Bronze Age shipwreck sites in southern France and Huelva in Spain (Coombs 1976, 194) and, moreover, the exposed conditions at Langdon would not have been conducive to the survival of organic remains over the intervening three millennia or more. However, the site is adjacent to the chalk cliffs, which are actively eroding, and it is therefore vital that we give due consideration to the possibility that the bronzes were originally deposited on the cliff top and had entered the sea as the cliffs retreated.

A copy of a primary field drawing with compass bearings which has recently come to light records the original finds as coming from a gully 80 feet (*c* 24m) long running NW–SE and lying 800 feet (*c* 244m) from the harbour wall. There are no gullies on that exact orientation, but it is possible to identify a likely candidate in the multibeam sonar image taken in 2002 (Fig 2.7, location X). This gully

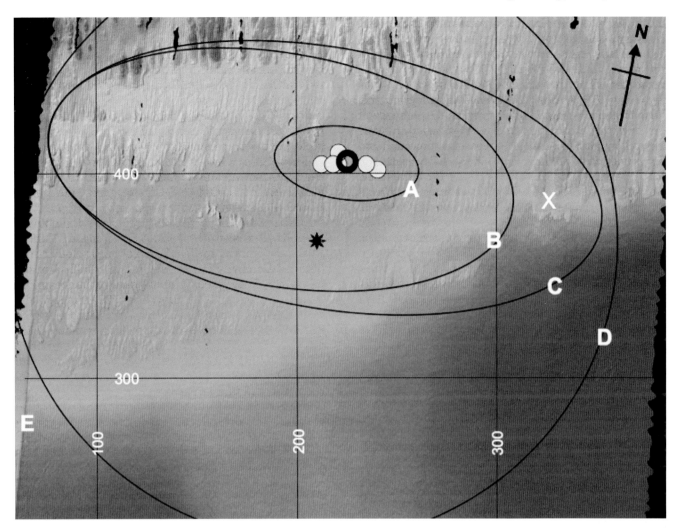

Fig 2.7 Multibeam sonar bathymetric image of the seabed with metric site grid and finds attribute distributions (see Table 2.3). O: *Mean position of all bronzes with a known find location;* O: *Six mean positions of bronzes with key attributes; A: Area containing 93% of all bronzes of known find location; B: Area containing all bronzes of known find location; C: Area probably containing all bronze find locations; D: Area designated under the Protection of Wrecks Act 1973; E: Base of the Eastern Arm of Dover Harbour; X: Probable area of pre-1978 finds;* ✳: *Centre of the designated area*

Table 2.3 Site coordinate means for bronze objects with different attributes (see Fig 2.7)

	X	Y
Heaviest 10% of bronzes	223	401
Lightest 10% of bronzes	215	406
High surface area:weight ratio (bladed weapons and fragments)	221	406
Low surface area:weight ratio (median-winged axes and fragments)	233	405
Least abraded bronzes (group a)	218	410
Most abraded bronzes (group d)	224	406
219 bronzes recovered 1978–83 (known coordinates)	221	408
c 115 bronzes recovered 1974–77 (estimated location X)	320	400
All bronzes	270	404

is 30m east of datum point H, just outside the core search area. The chart was also marked with a 'site position', probably used by Muckelroy as the centre of designation and lying about 40m SSE of the western end of his 1979 baseline; this ties in with the multibeam sonar evidence for the centre of the designated area.

When discovered, the finds were claimed by Dover

Harbour Board, which believed that it had juris-
diction over this part of the seabed. They placed
the finds on permanent loan to Dover Museum. In
fact, the objects were legally classifiable as 'wreck'
(see Chapter 1, note 5) and, in February 1976,
they were claimed by the Receiver of Wreck, which
meant that the finds should be put up for auction.
Dover Museum wished to purchase the finds, but
Dover Harbour Board declined to provide any
funds and the Receiver was left with little option
but to dispose of them via a saleroom. Since the
find was one of the most important Bronze Age discoveries of the 1970s, its highly unusual context
and composition making it internationally significant, the British Museum recognised that it would
be a valuable addition to their collections. It was
destined to be a key assemblage for understanding Bronze Age exchange and production network.
While it was initially stated that the rolled and, in
some cases, fragmentary objects would never form
a striking display (Longworth 1977a), in actuality
a selection of the material formed a key element of
a display case on Bronze Age trade and exchange
as early as 1978 (S Needham, pers comm).[3] The
British Museum persuaded the Receiver to sell
the collection directly to them without recourse to
a saleroom. Although the price of £500 was considered to be rather high in terms of open market
value, given the assemblage's condition, it was seen
as essential to keep the assemblage intact rather
than allow it to be dispersed (Longworth 1977b).
In 1977 three more bronzes were found, declared
to the Receiver of Wreck, and handed in to Dover
Museum (Muckelroy 1979a).

In April 1977 the British Museum contacted Dr
Parker of the Council for Nautical Archaeology[4]
(CNA) concerning possible archaeological investigation of the Langdon site. It was felt that it would
be difficult to find the site again without the full
cooperation of the divers who had found it; nevertheless, several council members offered to help with
the work (Cherry 1977). No archaeologist thought
it worthwhile to get in contact with the DSAC
regarding the site, probably due to the widespread
belief that there was nothing left on-site (Muckelroy
1978g). This may be how Muckelroy, a member of
the CNA, first heard of the site.

On 11 February 1978 Muckelroy contacted Mrs
Stevens, Simon's mother and the secretary of the
DSAC, expressing his interest in conditions on
the site and whether the material found had been
buried or had been lying on the surface (Muckelroy
1978b). This query resulted in an offer to explore
the site, which Muckelroy took up. He first dived
there on 20 and 21 May 1978. During this visit
he ascertained that the group had continued to
recover material, perhaps as many as 30 items,
only 3 of which had been declared to the Receiver
of Wreck. Furthermore, he spotted several dozen
more objects lying scattered around the seabed,
some of which he retrieved (Muckelroy 1978c).
Muckelroy contacted the Department of Trade with

the following report in support of the site's designation (Muckelroy 1978e):

> The site lies at 5–12m on the seabed on a fine,
> eroding, chalk surface coated with a layer of fine
> silt several mms to several cms thick. The current
> site lies about 30m away from the original site.
> Recoveries from the site include: ninety-five objects
> found in 1974–75 now in the British Museum;
> three objects from 1977 now in Dover Museum;
> eighteen objects retrieved in 1978 with at least
> two dozen seen lying around on the surface and
> signs of others being buried in an area approxi-
> mately 10m across.
>
> Arguably it is a wreck because the collection
> as a whole would be more at home in a French
> context than an English one, suggesting that
> it was accumulated in France. The number of
> objects now puts it out of the normal range of land
> hoards, the small area of seabed over which the
> deposit lies suggesting that it is not the product of
> cliff erosion. There is a concern that if word of its
> location gets out looting will occur.

In summary, his advice was that the site be designated immediately because of the 'quantity, origin
and concentration of bronzes' and the risk that
looting could occur (Muckelroy 1978c). This recommendation led to the site being designated with
'unprecedented speed', the order coming into effect
on 26 May (Gibbons 1978a) and declaring a protected
area within a circle of 75m diameter centred on
position 51:07:36N 01:20:58E (DoT 1978). The speed
of the designation process was a record for the time
(Moat 1981).

During this period, an interim survey licence was
granted to Muckelroy and Alan Moat.[5] It stipulated
that, as joint licensee, Muckelroy should provide
archaeological direction from 27 May to 10 July
1978. A condition of this licence was that a report
be presented to the Advisory Committee on Historic
Wreck Sites (ACHWS) at their next meeting on 10
July, so that a full licence application could be made
(Gibbons 1978b).

Project mobilisation and initial archaeological survey

The objectives of this first season were limited
owing to the short time available to prepare the
requirements for safeguarding the site and to gauge
the nature and degree of the problems to be tackled
in future years. A working sequence for each area
was devised by Muckelroy (Muckelroy 1978d; 1979c)
and the survey was to be left in the charge of the
DSAC (Muckelroy 1978g). A basic site plan was to
be drawn and datum points laid under Muckelroy's
direction, while the DSAC were to investigate the
surrounding area to define the limits of the site.

Systematic sonar[6] traces were to be run to define
the contours of the area and the effect of marine
life on the objects studied in order to determine

Fig 2.8 Diver laying out the search grid

the length of their exposure. Objects were to be raised only if they were likely to be lost or in order to assess the dating or identification of the 'wreck' (Gibbons 1978a). With Muckelroy's agreement, recovered artefacts were to receive immediate conservation treatment according to advice from Dover Museum or the British Museum. It was decided not to use metal detectors because of the range of other metallic items on the seabed (Muckelroy 1978e).

Although Muckelroy's intention was to excavate those areas known to contain archaeological material, he was very aware that he was working with an archaeologically inexperienced and untried team. After his initial dive at Langdon and his discussions with the ACHWS, he set down his plan of operation for the fieldwork. The site was to be gridded with frames or ropes. A 40m yellow washing line would be used as an east–west baseline across the site, and a 20m baseline was to be laid from north to south at the eastern end of the longer baseline to form an 'L' (Oram 1979). Pitons were to be hammered into the seabed with reference letters attached to create survey datum points (Fig 2.8).

From this grid, the plan was to search the 40m × 20m area in corridors 2m wide and 20m long

perpendicular to the 40m base line (M Dean, pers comm). Any features of interest were to be photographed and any silt was to be cleared away, care being taken not to disturb any objects. Divers were to note any changes in sediments, unusual stones, and so on. Numbered tags were to be nailed into the chalk alongside each find and notes made of the type of artefact given each number. Once the area was cleared up, close-up photographs were to be taken of all finds from at least two angles. Each object was to be trilaterated from four corners of the grid and from at least three nearby pitons (Fig 2.9), each trilateration plot being checked on the surface by drawing them out in the survey book, confirming that all three distances recorded actually coincided at the same spot. If any inconsistencies arose, the distances were to be remeasured. Once the plot was acceptable all objects (of whatever age) were to be recovered. Each bronze would be put into individual polythene bags on the seabed along with its tag, so that the two were not separated. Once this process was complete, the next area along would be laid out and the process repeated.

The records to be kept during excavation were as follows:

1. Diver's log. As well as usual dive details, it was to contain a note of the dive brief, the work completed, and any observations on the sediment, etc.
2. Report by that day's dive marshal containing a short report on progress.
3. Survey Book, for recording all measurements; trilaterations were then to be checked by drawing them out. All measurements, notes, and so on taken on the bottom were to be made on plastic drafting film, the sheets being kept as primary archive in case of transcription errors.
4. Finds Book, in which all bronzes recovered were to be listed, each with its own number and its distance from three pitons. Any other objects recovered would be listed in the back of the book as a group under that area's heading.

As he had done for the Moor Sand project, Muckelroy circulated a list of key texts among volunteers intending to take part here; it was a very similar list (see Chapter 1, note 10).[7]

At the same time the council of Jesus College Cambridge[8] agreed to a £90 grant from their research fund to enable Muckelroy to 'haul up Bronze Age relics from the seabed' (Sparks 1978). This phrase, perhaps better than any other, sums up the attitude of many to the then-emerging sub-discipline of maritime archaeology; Muckelroy was planning a scientific investigation of a unique site, while others saw this activity merely as hauling things up from the seabed.

Work was undertaken as planned, but was hampered by bad weather (Muckelroy 1978f). Site buoys and ground lines were badly damaged and carried away and some of the datum points

Fig 2.9　Diver recording a new find at Langdon Bay

were pulled out. In total, seventeen objects were recovered after being photographed and surveyed *in situ*; searches conducted outside the protected area located more bronzes. Pressure due to poor weather conditions meant that material had to be left on the seabed, which was a cause for concern (Moat 1978a).

When the ACHWS met in July the project was granted a full licence, although some of its members disagreed with the suggestion that the site might be that of a wreck, preferring to consider it an occupation site as the material recovered appeared to be scrap (Gibbons 1978b). One of its members, Dr David Coombs, a bronze metalwork specialist at the Department of Archaeology, Manchester University, was keen to publish something on the assemblage recovered thus far, but Muckelroy argued against this. He believed that underwater archaeology had been bedevilled by the distinctions being drawn between raised objects and the context from which they came, and he sought instead to break down this barrier and treat marine sites as one would any terrestrial site, thus establishing the context of the material before considering publication (Muckelroy 1978m).

Work that had been planned for August was cancelled after the third day owing to poor weather

and the season finished with 40–50 located bronzes still on the seabed. The DSAC continued with monitoring dives over the winter and it was observed that sediment was moving around continuously, with gullies filling and emptying, although the bronzes stayed in position (Oram 1979). The Department of Trade issued a licence for the winter period from 1 December 1978 to 31 March 1979 and was to consider a recommendation from the team that the site radius be extended from 75m to 150m (Milligan 1978). The radius was duly altered in the following year (DoT 1979). After a difficult season Muckelroy acknowledged that there was a pressing need to train divers for the next year or much time would be wasted on site repeating basics (Muckelroy 1978o).

Marine growth on bronzes consisted of the shells of marine worms of a species that could not survive if buried, suggesting that the buried bronzes must have been exposed at some time. Some of the worms were still alive when the bronzes were recovered, which was indicative of corrosion at a very slow rate, as their corrosion products would have been toxic to the worms (Aitkins 1978). Indeed, their patina was quite thin and their weight suggested that they were mostly solid metal, albeit very badly eroded (Robinson 1979).

Muckelroy was led to consider whether the

bronzes might have been exposed on the surface only as a result of the construction of Dover Harbour (Hasenson 1980). Construction of the modern harbour started in 1847 with the aim of enclosing the bay at the mouth of the Dour, thus preventing the drifting of shingle and providing a harbour of refuge for up to 20 large naval vessels. Work continued for 62 years until completion in 1909 (*ibid*, 49). The eastern breakwater of the finished harbour lies very close to the Langdon Bay site and, while no study of the changes in water movement and sediment transport caused by its construction was available to him, Muckelroy thought it likely that such a massive construction in such a dynamic environment would have caused significant changes to currents. He wondered whether the breakwaters might be causing uni-directional eddies which were very different to the conditions present prior to their construction. The new circulation pattern might then be causing the erosion of silts in Langdon Bay (Muckelroy 1978n).

The 1978 work had established that the site consisted of a central area of approximately 40m × 20m with bronzes relatively thickly spread, and a zone outside it with widely dispersed bronzes. Silt was found to reach a depth of 400mm in the deeper gullies; Muckelroy saw the potential here for stable sediments where organic material might be found (Muckelroy 1978p).

The research objectives for the 1979 season were, firstly, to recover every bronze on the seabed; this would enable the full research potential of this 'closed group' to be exploited. Secondly, Muckelroy wanted to ascertain how the bronzes came to be lying in their current exposed position. This involved determining whether the distribution of the bronzes was random or instead might hint at an arrangement of the material before it was wrecked. Alternatively, the distribution might indicate that the bronzes were in a secondary position, having been redeposited from either a sealed underwater context or a cliff-top location.

Muckelroy intended to use the techniques he had been developing for site analysis in underwater archaeology. The opinions of other relevant underwater scientists – in particular biologists, geologists, and shallow water oceanographers – would be considered as so little was known about the information content of underwater sites. Every possible clue needed to be followed in order to develop the techniques of underwater archaeology and establish a framework for the discipline (Muckelroy 1979a).

The 1978 season had shown that visibility on site was poor, and bad weather reduced this to the point of preventing active work. For 1979, Muckelroy planned to organise work at short notice to take advantage of advantageous weather forecasts, as the previous season had seen disruptions; this plan was feasible as most of the divers were self-employed. He was to be on standby at Cambridge with two to three periods of ten days' work set aside to help with the project's larger aim of completing 50

days' work between Easter and October. The seabed was to be gridded out with fixed poles to create 2m-wide corridors either side of the east–west baseline and each defined unit would then be cleared of silt and an extensive photographic record taken when conditions allowed. Muckelroy planned to use a water dredge to aid excavation and communication equipment so that he could control the work without spending too much time underwater. The main boat would remain on site for twelve hours a day with dredges on board, while a second boat would be available to ferry people to and from the shore. The bulk of the work would be undertaken with a surface-supplied 'Hookah'[9] unit to allow excavating divers to spend much greater time underwater. It was estimated that the entire cost of the project would be around £135 per day, including research and post-excavation costs (Muckelroy 1978n).

Weather conditions did not allow diving to commence until 21 April, at which time the DSAC relocated the site, laid a baseline and re-established the datum points before plotting and lifting the exposed artefacts (Muckelroy 1979i). The known archaeological area around the baseline was thoroughly searched and reconnaissance dives showed that the site continued to the west, towards the harbour wall. Pitons were established in this area and two rapiers recovered, but the area was not systematically searched.

At the end of July excavation was started along one of the corridors at the east end of the site. When a dredge was not available this process could be carried out only when a strong current was running to take away the silt, which was a severe limitation on the effectiveness of the operation. About 30 square metres were cleared of weed and sediment and a further six bronzes were found buried. An area with little silt was chosen for excavation, but it was found that in the deeper (200–400mm) gullies there was usually a layer of stiff, grey-black clay below the mobile silts. This clay sometimes contained bronzes, among them a type not previously found on the site, a broad lozenge-sectioned sword blade fragment. At least ten more days were lost to bad weather (British Museum 1979b) and the exceptional storms of August which caused the Fastnet disaster[10] led to the cessation of work on 14 August. In total, 750 square metres of seabed had been searched and 57 bronzes recovered during a total of 29 diving days; 17 divers had undertaken 192 dives, giving a total of 794.64 man-hours underwater. However, it was clear that a large area had yet to be searched and excavated, and that the project needed to continue for several years.

Muckelroy's move from Cambridge to the National Maritime Museum in early 1980 allowed him to spend more time on the project and expand his objectives. During the 1980 season he intended to extend the 1979 area greatly at the eastern end of the site and search for further deposits towards the site's western margins. He also wanted to identify the original position of the 1974–75 finds and take pH and electrode potential readings from the deposits in which artefacts had been found in order to analyse the corrosion potential of the deposit (analysis to be undertaken by freelance conservator Wendy Robinson).

He planned to use two dive teams simultaneously to improve efficiency, with one group excavating at the eastern end and the other searching to the west. As the teams would be working in areas 40m apart, it was hoped that they would not disturb each other's visibility. The eastern area had been chosen because of its heavy concentration of surface finds in 1978–79 and the presence of some gullies with sediment more than 300mm deep which could be excavated with a dredge. The western area would only be surface searched and the results added to the picture obtained from reconnaissance dives in the previous year.

The work was to be split into three concentrated periods of ten days each (in May, late June, and late July) interspersed with regular weekend diving on the site. Sufficient leeway was left so that if one or more of the earlier periods was lost to poor weather it could be reclaimed later. Before the first period, several days' work was allocated to re-establishing the site datum points, grid lines, and so on. These preliminary tasks would be carried out during weekends in April and May, while weekends between other periods would be used in preparation for the following sessions (Longworth 1980).

The start of the season was marred by bad weather, north-easterly winds bringing in silt and plankton. The site buoy had been washed away over winter and the site was not rediscovered until 6 July, during a period of unusually good visibility when Muckelroy was on site for ten days (Muckelroy 1980b). The site was found to be covered in fine sand brought in by the earlier heavy weather and it was noted that an old anchor on the site had been turned over by heavy seas. Areas that were cleared of sediment in 1979 had been refilled with similar black silt to a depth of up to 110mm. Muckelroy introduced a new marking system in which a blue tag was hammered into the seabed as near to each bronze find as possible. Excavation was undertaken and an underwater metal detector was used for the first time, proving excellent at locating smaller bronze pieces. Other divers were sent to search 15–20m to the north and south of the central area and found several artefacts in the northern sweep. In one area, twelve bronzes were located in a discrete group lying within stiff brown clay; some of them were touching the chalk bedrock, but one was noted to be overlying a modern bullet. Echo-sounding work was conducted during periods of very poor visibility. Later experience showed that many of the prehistoric bronzes were not immediately visible because of a light dusting of calcareous silt. Other bronzes were hidden deep in fissures in the chalk or at the bottom of vertical mollusc holes about 25mm in diameter and up to 200mm deep. Although a number of small bronze rivets were recovered from the bottom of some of these holes, at other times it proved impossible to recover the object indicated by a metal detector, despite ingenuity in improvised excavation tools such as teaspoons, dental probes, and thin spatulas (M Dean, pers comm).

Diving for the season ceased on 5 October (Moat and Baker 1980), by which time another 43 bronzes had been found (Needham 1981) during nineteen days of diving consisting of 109 dives and 85.21 man-hours underwater. With Muckelroy's death in September (see Chapter 1) there were problems completing the year's report (McGrail 1980; Moat 1980), which was eventually written by Alan Moat (Moat 1981).

Archaeological work after Muckelroy

In 1981 work on site resumed under the direction of Muckelroy's successor at the National Maritime Museum, Martin Dean. Archaeological work took place over two days in July, twelve in August, and one in September. Again, lines were laid parallel to and to the south of the site's baseline to form 2m-wide corridors which were then searched with metal detectors. This area covered approximately 400 square metres of seabed, all of which had previously been visually searched. Around 50% of metal detector 'contacts' were modern (fishing weights and shrapnel[11]); the rest were prehistoric bronzes, many of which were not obvious on the surface, being buried under 10–200mm of sandy silt. Forty bronzes were raised, two of which had been surveyed and numbered in 1979–80. The intensified search had changed the composition of the recovered assemblage, with an increase in the variety of items being recognised, particularly smaller, more personal items and miscellaneous pieces (Needham and Dean 1987, fig 3). Replica bronzes (distinctively marked to prevent confusion) were carefully positioned in an effort to understand seabed movements (Dean 1981). In total, 113.5 man-hours were spent underwater.

The appointment of Martin Dean as new project director offered a chance to appraise the organisation and output of the campaign. Work had been conducted with Muckelroy as archaeological director and Alan Moat as the site licensee. While Muckelroy was the only archaeologist in the team and the DSAC supplied volunteer divers the operation had not been without its problems. Experience had shown that only about 10% of divers became competent in the archaeological field techniques used on the site. When only a small group of divers was available, the useful work that could be undertaken was severely limited and considerable strain was placed on the archaeological director. As the project progressed and the experience of the team increased, the nature of the bronzes recovered changed; earlier assemblages were dominated by larger finds found on the seabed surface while later years saw the collection of smaller bronzes recovered from sediment in cracks and fissures (McGrail 1983). Working alongside the archaeological director, a few members of the DSAC had proved to be good field archaeologists, but they required the constant presence of an archaeologist on site to provide guidance.

The DSAC believed themselves to be, and were widely acknowledged as, 'salvors in possession'[12] of the site and were keen to offer their own opinions on the way things should be done; this led to disagreements as to how the project should proceed. The project had thus far failed to define the limits of the site, a particular concern for the British Museum, who wished to know how far the bronzes were dispersed or if concentrations could be established. The Museum was disappointed that, after five seasons, these objectives had not been achieved. In part, this may have been due to the scale of operation being inadequate. At Moor Sand the relative dearth of finds had led to reduced funding; in contrast, the fact that finds continued to come up at Langdon Bay acted as an inducement to continued funding. This may have led to an emphasis on object recovery, which also kept the DSAC happy. Nevertheless, there were tensions among the team regarding the extent of retrieval: some members of the team were keen to raise as much material as possible, while the priority for Muckelroy was to concentrate on correctly recording those objects already exposed. Following some discussion, Muckelroy's approach was adopted.

Another area of tension concerned the salvage award made for the bronzes. The recovered bronzes from each season ('droits') had to be disposed of by the Receiver of Wreck in the normal way. Following the precedent of the first assemblage's disposal, this was done each year by negotiation between the Receiver and the British Museum, valuation being sought from independent valuers from the antiquities market. The Museum then purchased the droit for the agreed sum and the Receiver passed on the money to the 'salvors', being the DSAC. As it had already contributed considerable sums of money towards the project's archaeological costs, the British Museum had some concerns that, in purchasing the finds from the site, it was effectively being asked to pay twice for material being recovered. Nevertheless, the mode of acquisition did not change, probably because the mainly scrap and abraded nature of the bronzes meant they would have had little appeal on the open market, keeping the valuations very modest.

The project was a joint British Museum/National Maritime Museum venture, but the British Museum supplied 80% of the project funding (£2000 annually for 1979 and 1980, although it was not able to offer a grant for the 1981 season) (Moat 1979), with the BSAC's Jubilee Trust meeting 8% of the costs (Valentine 1979), the NMM 10%, and local commercial sponsorship a further 2% (Muckelroy 1979f). As for Moor Sand, the NMM's contribution was limited because of the minimal prospects for surviving structural remains; were any to be dis-

covered, the NMM would reassess their degree of support (McGrail 1979). The NMM had made an application to the Department of Education and Science (their funders) for a special grant to support underwater projects, but it was turned down owing to the national economic situation. It was agreed by both museums that opportunities to explore sites of this nature were unlikely to present themselves often and, therefore, every effort should be made to support this project (Longworth 1979a).

The salvage awards for the bronzes were used by the DSAC for its project expenses, but the manner in which this money was spent was also a point of dispute, as some members wanted the funds to be spent on equipment, principally a larger boat, which would become the DSAC's property at the end of the project. There had been a number of objections to the valuations given to the bronzes and the British Museum was concerned that these disputes could lead to the sale of the finds by auction (British Museum 1979a). The real value of the site lay in the research potential of the finds assemblage in its entirety combined with good knowledge of its seabed context. Sale at auction risked dispersal of the finds, which would jeopardise the comprehensiveness of future research. This explains why the British Museum continued to purchase the finds and to encourage the DSAC to protect the archaeological interests of the site (Needham 1991). At the same time the British Museum also reminded the project that it could not 'look kindly on requests for funding' if a reasonable price for the recovered artefacts was not agreed.

A further complication was that some members of the DSAC wanted to keep mementoes of the finds. An attempt to solve this was the production of replicas as keepsakes, but the cost, £30 each, was six times the value of the original objects and created a feeling of injustice among some members. Despite these frictions, the DSAC were keen to show publicly how closely archaeologists and divers could liaise, a point made by Moat at the BSAC's Diving Officers' conference in November 1978 (Moat 1978b).

On a positive note, each year had brought different identifiable types to the surface, shedding new light on wider trading networks. As noted above, there had also been a noticeable change in the material as work progressed over the years and smaller fragmentary materials began to be raised alongside the complete bronzes initially recognised (Needham 1982a). The nature of the site is such that interpretation is solely dependent upon the bronzes, their distribution, and their intrinsic characteristics (Longworth 1981).

So, Dean's reappraisal of project goals and methods led to a number of changes in approach. First, a rapid survey of the seabed was needed so that the extent of further effort to be invested in the site could be determined; this ran against the desire of some to maximise the retrieval of objects. Additionally, advice was also required about underwater metal detectors, as these were the only real hope for completing a full site survey in one season (*ibid*). It was decided to aim for recovery of the largest possible sample to ensure that exceptional elements of the assemblage could be brought to light. In addition, the team should be altered to include a small group of archaeologists (four was the number suggested) to work with a larger pool of sport divers recruited from the Nautical Archaeology Society.[13] This team would deploy over a four-week field season in August and would liaise more closely with the British Museum while on site.

The British Museum was again unable to provide any funding for the project in 1982, but the National Maritime Museum continued to provide infrastructure for Martin Dean's operation despite their severely stretched finances (Baker 1982). The British Museum was unhappy with an open-ended agreement and wanted answers to a number of specific questions regarding the extent of the site and whether it was a shipwreck or the product of coastal erosion. They did, however, recognise that these questions would be difficult to answer. Given the doubtfulness by now of discovering boat remains, it was generally recognised that the distribution of the artefacts would be the key to understanding the nature of the deposition. The Department of Coastal Studies at Southampton University was contacted and suggested that, if the assemblage was a product of coastal erosion, it would be widely scattered with no visible concentration of finds (Dean 1982b). If a concentration could be seen in the find distribution, a centralised source, potentially a shipwreck, might be indicated. Therefore, the aim of the 1982 season was to attempt to determine whether the site was the result of shipwreck or of erosion. There was a fear that this aim could have led to fewer bronzes being recovered (this proved not to be the case) and thus less income deriving from the British Museum purchases, less interest from the DSAC and, consequently, the need for a greater level of costly professional help. If the season could answer the important preliminary questions, a joint British Museum/National Maritime Museum project over three to five years was being mooted. In order to achieve this end, the 1982 work needed to be well-financed (Society of Antiquaries 1982).

Work took place on the site between 2 July and 25 July. A 50m grid system was laid outward from the original baseline, extending 100m beyond the most outlying bronze yet found (Dean 1982a) and surveyed in from the shore (Anon 1982). A 1m strip along the edge of each 50m square was searched visually and with metal detectors and all finds were recovered. If nothing was detected, the sediments would be excavated down to bedrock in 1m squares every 10m along the edge of the grid with a low-powered airlift (Dean 1982a). As it turned out, the size of the assemblage recovered in 1982 (59 objects) was greater than that in all previous seasons except 1979. Nine bronzes were recovered from the search of outlying zones. The remaining 50 came from a restricted area of 60m × 30m where much of the

earlier material had been found, giving a find rate of one object per 11 square metres, compared to one per 260 square metres elsewhere (Dean 1982d). The British Museum continued to purchase the bronzes pending clarification of the objectives of the project. The 1982 season, through improved recording and lifting procedures and the increased number of finds, provided more evidence for a definite concentration of bronzes within a more widely dispersed pattern (Fig 2.10). The concentration had an apparent dual focus, while the overall extent of the scatter covered an area of at least 150m × 60m.

The National Maritime Museum wished to continue its partnership with the project and, to that end, the British Museum approved funding of £1000 for the 1983 season (Longworth 1983) with a possible further five to fourteen days being considered in 1984, depending on results (McGrail 1983a). The fieldwork timetable was provisionally arranged for 19 July to 5 August at an estimated cost of £1400. With the 1982 season results in mind, the objectives for the 1983 season were to extend the area of intensive metal detector survey outward from the known concentrations to determine the exact size of the focal area. All objects located were to be recovered. The search would then be extended to more outlying areas to determine the outer limits of the sparser distribution. Divers would also monitor the replica bronzes laid on the seabed in 1981 to assess the degree of movement caused by natural action.

Diving took place between 24 July and 6 August 1983. The main areas were searched by metal detectors in corridors 2m wide, while the outer areas were subjected to a visual search of selected corridors also 2m wide. All finds were plotted to the appropriate metre square of the grid (Dean 1983a). A metal detector search was carried out in the 50m grid laid in 1982 and outwards from the areas of greatest concentration. This search covered 4200 square metres of seabed and discovered twenty bronzes, a density of one per 210 square metres. Visual searches between the grid and the harbour wall located three further bronzes. Hence, a total of 23 bronzes was found during 233 man-hours of diving (Dean 1983b).

The second phase of the 1983 fieldwork was due to take place from 16 to 26 September (McGrail 1983b). Its aim was to determine the limits of the distribution. It was planned that the search would take in a proportion of the seabed outside the known perimeters of the site. A regular series of 10m × 20m rectangular areas was planned to the north, south, and east of the main finds distribution, each of which was divided into corridors 2m wide to facilitate systematic visual and metal-detector searching. Excavation would be undertaken only where metal detectors indicated buried metal (Dean 1984b). As soon as a Bronze Age find was made within a given box searching ceased there and instead resumed in the next 20m box outwards from the core distribution. It was predicted that, given favourable

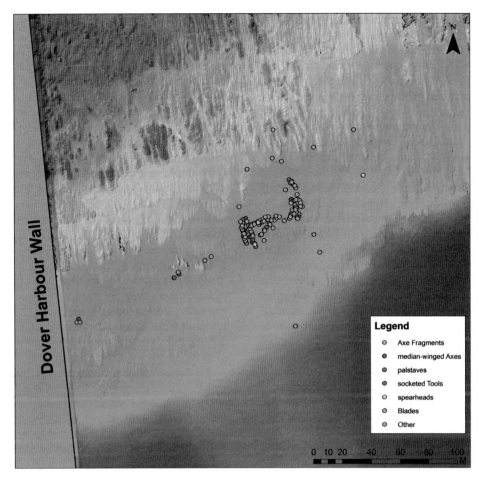

Fig 2.10 Site plan of Langdon Bay, showing search area and finds distribution

conditions, 4200 square metres of seabed could be investigated by a team of seven divers in nine days. In very good conditions as much as 5000 square metres of seabed might possibly be covered (Dean 1983b).

However, this innovative strategy could not be undertaken in 1983 and was rolled over into the 1984 season, which took place from 20 to 29 July. No bronzes were found, indicating that there was a marked fall-off in the density of finds (see search pattern in Fig 2.11) and, moreover, suggesting that the bronzes had originally been deposited in a relatively concentrated zone (Dean 1984b). Further implementation of the sampling strategy was hampered by weather conditions and deep mud which made use of the metal detector impossible and manual searches too dangerous because of the known presence of unexploded ordnance in the area.

Although work had not yet been finished on site, it was felt by the National Maritime Museum that further large-scale fieldwork was not necessary (Dean 1985). Fieldwork in 1985 was limited to the survey of datum points. The DSAC also explored the seabed between the area previously searched and the eastern breakwater using the search methods employed in 1983–84, a task they felt was within their capabilities (Dean 1985). Only three hours of diving were undertaken during July and

August owing to bad weather, with most time spent repairing damage to ground lines caused by anchors (Dean 1985). Activity was further limited by very poor underwater visibility and increased silt on site caused by the nearby land reclamation in Dover Eastern Dock (Moat 1986). Working on their own without archaeological support for the first time, the DSAC acknowledged that work on the site needed underwater instrumentation which they lacked. They felt that they could act as site caretakers on their own, but not as archaeologists (Moat 1986).

Early in 1986 Martin Dean moved to the University of St Andrews to take on a new role as director of the Archaeological Diving Unit (ADU). The Archaeological Research Centre of the National Maritime Museum closed later that year. With the ADU engaged by the government to provide archaeological advice in relation to the Protection of Wrecks Act, the ACHWS wondered if this new role would create a conflict of interest with Dean's responsibility as licensee of the Langdon Protected Wreck site. However, no conflict was identified and Dean was permitted to make site visits, although in practice he could not be present for most of the work. A further concession was to allow Dean to appoint a deputy who could agree a plan with the DSAC for the completion of basic work on site (DoTr 1986).

During 1987 the DSAC located the site, cleared it

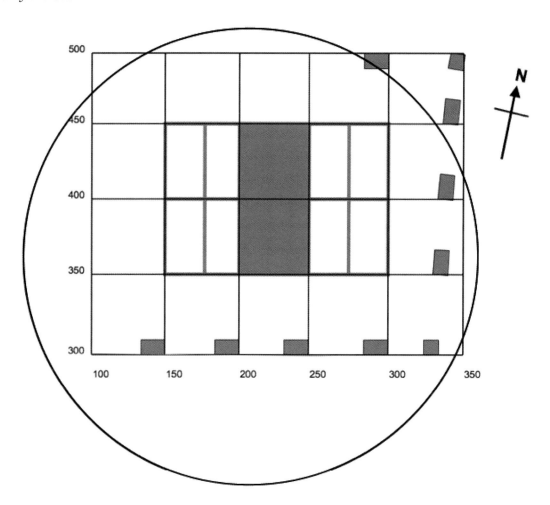

Fig 2.11   Metal-detector search pattern. These are shown as darker strips, areas and boxes within the site grid. No bronze objects were found in any of the outer boxes and the largest proportion was found between 200 and 250 East on the approximate line of 400 North (see also Fig 2.7). The misalignment of boxes along the eastern side was due to an error in setting out

of tangled rope (Moat 1987), and, in agreement with Dean, re-established as many previous datum points as possible. Although Dean was not convinced of the value of further investigatory work on the site the DSAC were keen to search up to the eastern break-water and it was felt that they had the potential to accomplish it competently (Dean 1987b). The western edge of the grid was extended towards the breakwater so that a systematic visual search of this new area could be conducted. The DSAC undertook 29 hours of diving between June and August before the weather broke and the group could do no more (Moat 1987). No bronzes were discovered, but divers noted an accumulation of new sediment covering extensive areas of the site to a maximum depth of 100mm which had resulted, as in 1986, from recla-mation in the eastern dock.

In 1988 work on the site was limited, as the licence did not arrive until June. Only 12 hours and 21 minutes were spent underwater by the DSAC owing to bad weather and poor visibility, again caused by reclamation in the eastern dock as well as by the recently started works on the Channel Tunnel.[14] These activities resulted in sediment settling on

the site and created poor visibility throughout the year (Moat 1988). Fishing had been observed taking place on the site, allegedly within the designated area, and enquiries suggested that, as investigation on the site was not active, locals assumed that it was no longer protected (Moat 1989a).

During 1989 the DSAC reported that the site was scoured, possibly by a hurricane that had struck the south coast of England on 16 October 1988; moreover, they thought that fishing activity had moved sinkers and ground lines. Some of these were relocated and five bronze items were recovered (Moat 1989b). When the ACHWS met in December 1989 Dean reported that he was uneasy with his conflicting roles as absentee co-licensee/archaeologist and the ADU Principal Field Investigator, a conclusion with which the committee concurred. Therefore, they accepted his withdrawal as co-licensee (DoE 1989), an action which resulted in the withdrawal of the DSAC exca-vation licence for the site (DoTr 1989) and effectively the close of the archaeological project.

Again, poor weather and fishing destroyed the site's survey datum points over the winter of 1989/90 and the ACHWS declined to issue excavation licences until

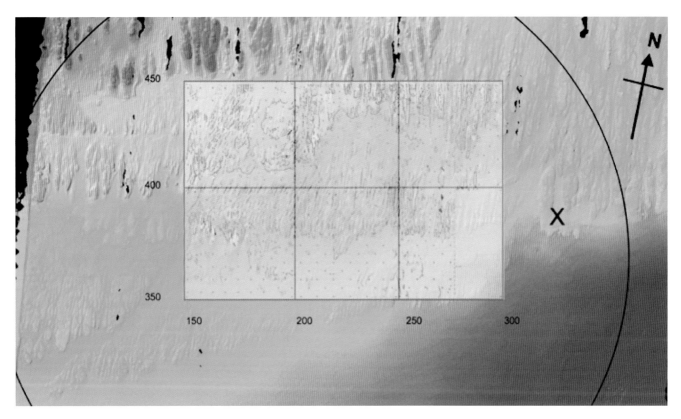

Fig 2.12 Multibeam sonar bathymetric image of the seabed overlain with a topographic survey manually drawn by diving archaeologists in 1982

these had been reliably re-established (Dean 1990a). Visits to the site continued and, in 1990, four bronzes were raised on a survey licence (Moat 1990). Lack of an archaeological advisor meant that the licence issued for 1992 was restricted to maintenance only (Roberts 1992); this new type of licence, one which did not require a formal archaeological advisor but only access to archaeological advice, was issued until Alan Moat's death in 1998. This situation allowed the DSAC to visit the site to inspect it, but not to undertake any archaeological work; all serious investigation ended with Moat's death. This certainly does not mean that no archaeological material remains on the seabed (Dean 1990b), although it would probably be buried beneath the 50–100mm of silt that accumulated on the site during the construction of the Channel Tunnel (Moat 1993).

In 2002 the ADU, in conjunction with Reson Offshore Ltd, undertook a high resolution bathymetric survey of the site and surrounding area with a Reson 8125 SeaBat multibeam sonar system (Fig 2.12).[15] This was one of the first occasions on which maritime archaeologists had unfettered access to such equipment and, although the results were extremely useful, they are not of the standard now achievable owing to recent dramatic improvements in deployment methodology and more sophisticated and accurate positioning systems. Nevertheless, images from the 2002 Langdon Bay multibeam sonar-data set show for the first time exactly how complex the seabed topography is and make the site

more comprehensible to people other than those who have first-hand experience through diving on it.

Additionally, this survey enabled the creation of a geo-referenced image of the seabed on and around the site. The diver-drawn topographic map of the seabed, incorporating the twelve datum points at the intersections of the gridlines delimiting the six 50m squares of the core search area, could then be compared with the multibeam data. This comparison showed that there was a discrepancy of 40m between the actual position of the centre of the protected area and where it had been plotted hitherto (see Fig 2.7). Although the centre is actually 40m further south, the 150m radius of the designated area still encompassed all relevant areas of the site and all known finds.

It is difficult to be certain of the precise cause of this variation, and it may not be due to a single factor. The most likely explanation is probably a mismatch of the features on the shore and chart when taking compass bearings and horizontal sextant angles. The site is close inshore, and the eastern arm of Dover harbour masks many of the easily identifiable features in the harbour and town. Identification of features was further complicated by major remodelling of the shore-side facilities in the harbour during development work in the 1980s and 1990s. The inaccuracies of the methodologies used, together with the inherent difficulty of translating the exact position of a point on the seabed to the water surface, especially when seas are not calm, all help to account for the discrep-

Fig 2.13   Detailed bathymetry of the study area, showing the incised nature of the rock-cut platform

ancy. A change in the chart datum (from OSGB36 to WGS84) on UKHO Chart Number 1698 may have also exacerbated the problem.

Coastal erosion and landscape change
by Martin Bates

The Langdon Bay 'wreck' was found (Coombs 1976; Muckelroy 1981) on a gently sloping eroded chalk rock platform at a depth of 7–13m below sea level, some 500m offshore of the adjoining cliff line cut through the chalk of the North Downs (Fig 2.13). Today the white cliffs form a historically important feature of the British landscape, the permanency and longevity of which few question. Indeed, the cliffs, and an estuary penetrating inland along the course of the modern Dour valley (Fig 2.14), appear to have been major features of the landscape by the time of Julius Caesar's expedition to Britain in 55 BC. In the 'Commentaries of Julius Caesar' he describes a place thought to be the mouth of the Dour estuary thus: 'The nature of the place was this: The sea was confined by mountains so close to it that a dart could be thrown from their summit upon the shore' (*De Bello Gallico*, Book 4, para 23).

However, today it is recognised that this landscape is an ever-changing one; and, with increasing concerns over global warming, sea-level rise, and the impact of change on the coastline, attention is turning to attempting to understand the nature of coastal change and its history in order to derive predications for rates of coastal change and retreat (Dornbusch 2005a and b). This interest may also be extrapolated to the past and, as a result of the discovery of the Dover Bronze Age boat over a decade ago (Clark 2004a), the local context and geomorphological setting of the Langdon Bay Bronze Age finds now requires clarification (Bates *et al* 2011).

Background

The creation of the English Channel and the modification of the Strait of Dover from the Middle Pleistocene onwards has been the source of debate for a number of years (Gibbard 1995; Gupta *et al* 2005), and current work in the southern North Sea as well as the Channel region may soon provide new information on the evolution of this important sea passage. However, because of the nature of the processes operating within the vicinity of the Strait, erosion predominates at the expense of deposition and little evidence exists on, or beneath, the seabed to help calibrate and contextualise these changes. Consequently, it is difficult to ascertain the local

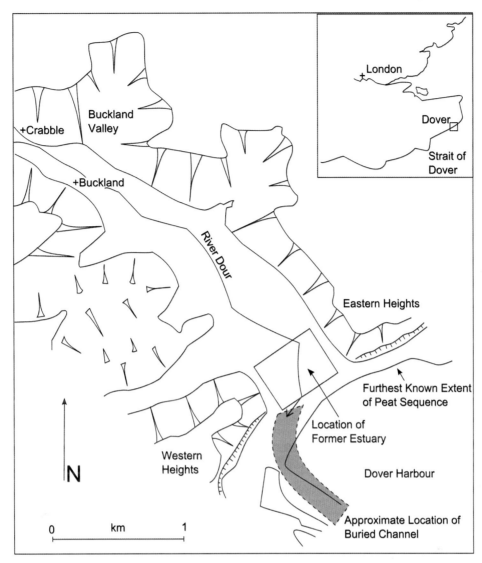

Fig 2.14 Lower Dour valley, showing position of former estuary and distribution of gravels lying within buried channel

palaeogeography of the coastal zones within the area during the later parts of the Pleistocene and much of the Holocene.

This section examines the context and geomorphological situation of the Langdon Bay metal assemblage with a view to understanding the original nature of the site as well as something of the nature of the processes likely to have been operating at the site following discard/loss. Consequently, a number of scenarios may be articulated that require examination and testing:

• The assemblage represents a cargo from a true maritime wreck resting on the seabed, lost during transport across/along the Channel margins in a situation very similar to the modern one.
• The assemblage represents a boat lost in a marine marginal situation within a topographic context different from that of the present-day open coastline.
• The assemblage represents material lost or deposited in a terrestrial context prior to erosion

and landward migration of the shore zone across the depositional site.

In order to address these three differing scenarios, two major strands of evidence may be utilised. The first comes from studies of coastal chalk cliff instability and patterns of coastal erosion in the Channel region, and the second from local geomorphological evolution and palaeoenvironmental sequences associated with the mouth of the river Dour. Evidence from these diverse sources will be articulated and discussed first so that the competing lines of evidence can be evaluated and assessed.

Bedrock geology, geomorphology, and coastal erosion

Bedrock geology

The bedrock exposed in the cliffs backing Langdon Bay consists of up to 100m of chalk exposing both

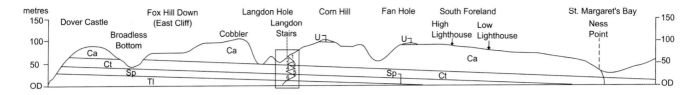

Fig 2.15   Sketch section of the cliffs between Dover and St Margaret's Bay, showing the northerly dip of the beds. Tl: Terebratulina lata *(Middle Chalk). Sp:* Sternotaxis planus. *Ct:* Micraster cortestudinarium. *Ca:* Micraster coranguinum *(from Shephard-Thorn 1988)*

Table 2.4   Chalk strata characteristics from the Landon Bay area (derived from Shephard-Thorn 1988)

Macrofossil zone	Stage	Traditional scheme	Thickness	Characteristics
Micraster coranguinum	Coniacian/Santonian		*c* 65m	Blocky white chalk with evenly spaced bands of nodular flints
Micraster cortestudinarium	Coniacian	Upper Chalk	*c* 20m	Shelly chalk with courses of flint nodules
Sternotaxis planus			15m	Hard nodular chalks, marl seams and large flint nodules at base overlain by soft white chalk. Nodular chalk at top
Terebratulina lata	Turonian	Middle Chalk	54m	Massive, soft white chalk with marl seams

Middle and Upper Chalk strata (Fig 2.15). The base of the cliff lies within the upper beds of the *Terebratulina lata* zone and the sequence upwards runs through the succeeding *Sternotaxis planus, Micraster cortestudinarium* and *Micraster coranguinum* zones (Shephard-Thorn 1988) (Table 2.4). These strata have been variously grouped into the Dover Chalk Formation, the Ramsgate Chalk Formation (Robinson 1986), and, more recently, into the New Chalk Pit, Chalk Rock, Lewes Nodular Chalk, and Seaford Chalk Member (Bristow *et al* 1997). Structurally, the chalk exposed in the cliff sections between Dover and Walmer exhibits a gentle dip in a NNE direction (Fig 2.15), thereby bringing successively more recent strata close to beach level in a northerly direction along the coast. Although no data is available to the author for the area immediately offshore from the cliffs, the nature of the strata and their dip would suggest that the seabed in Langdon Bay would be dominated by Middle Chalk of the *Terebratulina lata* zone.

Local geomorphology

Today, the local area is dominated by the Middle and Upper Chalk (Shephard-Thorn 1988) of the North Downs backing the modern beach. The North Downs form the northern limb of the Wealden anticline, with a steep scarp face to the south at Folkestone and a gentle, north-dipping dipslope extending through the study area towards Sandwich. West of Langdon Bay, the modern town and port of Dover encom-

passes the mouth of the Dour valley. The alignment of the valley (north-west–south-east) contrasts with the predominate drainage pattern in the area, in which currently dry valleys trend in a south-west–north-east direction at 90° to the strike of the modern lower and middle Dour Valley (Barham and Bates 1990). This pattern may be a relic inherited from an older drainage network of early Pleistocene or pre-Pleistocene age. For example, the strike of the modern valley may be fault guided (Shephard-Thorn 1988), with incision being initiated during the Pleistocene (the presence of a major fault in the area may influence both possible earthquake history and impact on local tectonic features dictating local subsidence rates). The nature and evolution of the valley have important implications for coastal changes in the vicinity of Langdon Bay.

Sediments infilling the Dour valley have been mapped by the British Geological Survey (BGS) and comprise alluvium, estuarine alluvium, and dry valley and nailbourne deposits in the valley bottom. Head and head brickearth along with clay-with-flints cap the adjacent downland plateaus and dry valley bases (Shephard-Thorn 1988). Within the lower Dour Valley, recent work (Barham and Bates 1990; Bates *et al* 2011) has demonstrated that the nature and patterns of sediment distribution in the area are more complex than previously documented.

Today, the cliffs at Langdon Bay rise to nearly 100m either side of a central low known as Langdon Hole (see Fig 2.1). Although no sediments survive (or are mapped) at the base of the hollow, it is probable that head deposits may once have existed

Table 2.5   Some cliff collapse events recorded for the Dover area (predominantly 19th century). Unless otherwise stated all events are recorded in a diary held in Dover Museum written by a Mr Pattenden

Date	Event type
c 1300 AD	Sea wall breached, harbour choked with pebbles (Stratham 1899)
6/4/1580	Earthquake. Cliff collapsed and outer walls of harbour came down (Stratham 1899; Batchellor 1828)
1612	Wall of the Great Pent (the Henry VIII coastal defences and harbour) breached during a storm (Stratham 1899)
1772	Several falls of the cliff caused great alarm (Stratham 1899)
14/12/1810	Seven members of family killed in cliff collapse at East Cliff. Pig buried in cliff cave after fall, dug out alive after 160 days
12/11/1844	Fall of cliff, 2 children killed
18/2/1847	40,000 tons of cliff fall from Shakespeare Cliff
21/1/1849	100,000 tons of cliff fall from Shakespeare Cliff
20/1/1853	100,000 tons of cliff fall of chalk in Limekiln Street
26/2/1853	Several thousand tons of chalk fall at Cobblers Rock, East Cliff
5/4/1859	2 men killed by fall at Snargate Street
12/5/1868	Great fall of cliff below Adrian Street
15/11/1872	Cliff collapse near castle destroys 2 houses
12/1/1877	S E Railway blocked for 2 months by fall of chalk cliff
13/3/1881	S E Railway blocked by cliff fall at Abbots Cliff

there. Little information is currently available on the origin of the hollow, but formation as a result of solifluction processes during the late Pleistocene is a possibility (Ballantyne and Harris 1994). Alternatively, the feature may be a truncated solution hollow now sectioned by the coastline. Either option would indicate probable weakness in the chalk associated with the base of the hollow.

Coastal processes

Coastal processes operating in the North Downs coastal zone are linked to meso- to macrotidal ranges. Present-day sediment dynamics are directly linked to nearshore tidal currents and are subject to a trend in longshore drift from west to east as a result of the prevailing westerly winds, which drive waves eastwards up the Channel. However, those beaches sheltered from the south-west winds may be exposed to easterly gales and local reversals of pattern can be seen, resulting in westerly drift.

Previous reports indicate that the seabed in the vicinity of the find was heavily pitted and fissured (a feature that is clear in the seabed bathymetry surrounding the site). The bathymetric map (see Fig 2.13) shows that the eroded chalk surface is progressively overlain by mobile sediment towards the southern end of the site study area. Muckelroy (1981) also noted that some gullies contained stable black-grey clays as well as the more mobile light silts. Unfortunately, the relationship of the sediments to the bronzes was not fully established.

Coastal erosion along the chalk cliff lines of Kent and Sussex is well established (eg McDakin 1900;

May 1971; May and Heeps 1985; Dornbusch 2005a) and a considerable effort is currently being made to understand the factors controlling erosion along these populated coastlines (see the 'Beaches at Risk' programme). While cliff-line erosion has been assumed to have occurred throughout the historic and prehistoric periods, little information is currently available to calibrate such processes. Erosion processes operating on a coastal cliff line are primarily influenced at a regional scale by rock type (Carter 1988), but, at smaller scales, variations in erosion rate are a function of a number of other factors (McDakin 1900; Dornbusch 2005a), including: the rock structure; water saturation; the presence/state of aquifers; precipitation; marine processes; the configuration and aspect of the coastline; the height of the cliff; the width of the shore platform; the nature of the beach; the topography of the shore platform; sea level; the presence of cliff-top superficial deposits; and human activity. Consequently, calculating retreat rates for coastal cliff erosion is notoriously difficult.

It is, however, well documented in historical literature that cliff collapse was a common feature of the Dover area (Table 2.5). The earliest attempt to calculate erosion rates was made in the late 19th century, when stakes were driven into the cliffs of the North Downs (McDakin 1900). Reported rates over a four-year period were, according to McDakin, 'unexpectedly small, only amounting to half an inch in a year'. May and Heeps (1985) suggest a mean rate for cliff-top retreat for the North Downs sector as a whole of 0.12m per year, ten times greater than McDakin's estimate. More recent calculations as part of the Beaches at Risk programme have used historical records covering the last 100 years or so

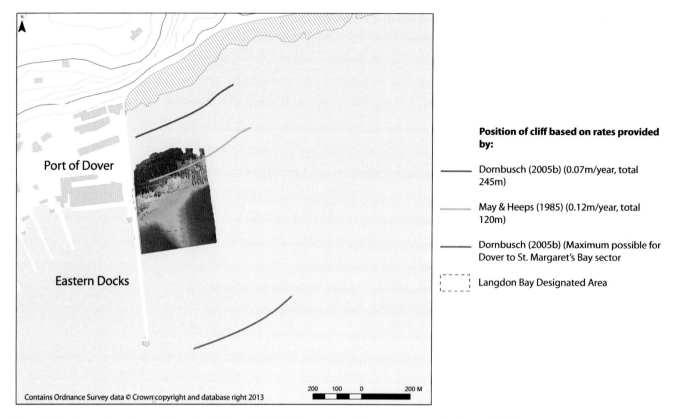

Fig 2.16   Postulated position of cliffs c 3500 BP, based on linear extrapolation of cliff retreat rates for study region

to suggest somewhat lower average rates of cliff recession of 0.07m per year for Kentish Chalk cliffs, contrasting with higher rates for the Sussex Chalk cliffs of 0.27m per year (Dornbusch 2005a). However, locally, significant portions of the Kent coast show almost no retreat at all. It should be remembered that, because these records only cover the past 100 years, any or all of these estimates may be widely inaccurate when extrapolated over longer time spans into the historic and prehistoric past. The difference in rates between Kent and Sussex may, in part, be a result of the differing aspect of the cliffs. Furthermore, Costa *et al* (2004) suggest that cliffs of Cenomanian, Turonian and Coniacian Chalk retreat less quickly than cliffs formed of Santonian and Campanian chalk. They also suggest that the latter are often subjected to frequent, but less voluminous, falls. Thus, although Kentish cliff-line retreat rates appear to be lower than those of the Sussex coastline, Kent is characterised by low frequency but high magnitude cliff-fall events (Dornbusch 2005b). Such was the collapse of January 2001, when a large piece of chalk, estimated at over 100,000 tonnes, collapsed from the cliff north of Dover.

Using the average rates of cliff-top erosion, 0.12m per year, provided by May and Heeps (1985), a total of some 390m of coastal erosion would have occurred since the deposition of the Bronze Age material (Fig 2.16). Using the alternative rates provided by Dornbusch (2005b) – 0.07m per year – projected retreat rates over 3250 years would be of the order

of 227m. However, as Dornbusch shows (2005b), the calculated rates of coastal erosion for the Langdon Stairs to St Margaret's section of the coast actually vary from less than 0.1m per year to in excess of 0.3m per year. Using these figures, retreat distances of up to 975m over a 3250-year time span might be anticipated in certain situations (Fig 2.16).

When attempting to retrodict cliff erosion rates into the prehistoric past, other factors also need to be taken into account. For example, Duperret *et al* (2004) suggest that rainfall patterns and associated ground saturation are important triggers to cliff collapse, while Mortimore *et al* (2004) suggest that further influences include storms and frost. These sorts of climatic impacts have important implications when considered in conjunction with potential phases of climate change in the past. For example, the well-known cold period of the Little Ice Age in the 17th century (Grove 2002) or the Late Bronze Age climatic deterioration noted by van Geel and Renssen (1998) are likely to have enhanced cliff erosion rates in the area. It is also noteworthy that superficial sediments present could influence the depth of weathering and consequent instability of the cliff (Mortimore *et al* 2004). Finally, patterns of marine erosion and tidal effects are also important factors (Duperret *et al* 2004; Mortimore *et al* 2004). It is interesting to note, although within a totally different system, Allen's (2002) observations of the degree of erosion on the Severn Levels over the last 1000 years, where significant variations in long-, medium-, and short-term erosion rates can be postulated. These variations are a function of an assortment of factors operating at local and regional levels and similar differences in erosion rates through time are likely for the Channel coast.

Another factor to consider as potentially influencing erosion at the coast is the influence of earthquakes, although Duperret *et al* (2004) concluded that seismic activity over recent periods is not applicable. However, significant earthquakes have been known to hit the Channel region in the past, perhaps the most famous being the Dover Strait earthquake of 1580, along with an earlier one in 1380 (perhaps associated with the fault thought to run along the length of the Dour valley discussed earlier). The former earthquake was estimated to have had a magnitude of between 5.3 and 5.9 (Harris *et al* 1996) and caused cliff collapse at Dover as well as the destruction of houses. Musson *et al* (1984) also record other earthquakes in 1776 and 1950 and have suggested that this seismic activity may be evidence for periodic earthquakes in the Channel region approximately every 200 years. Evidence of tsunamis in the Channel has also been recorded. Another factor to consider today is the impact of harbour construction at Dover and, in particular, the large building programmes resulting in the creation of the major east and west breakwaters. This construction activity is likely to have influenced longshore drift across the mouth of the Dour valley and potentially starved the Langdon Bay area of sediment from the Roman period onwards, thereby reducing the potential erosion of the cliff.

Finally, shore platform erosion also needs to be taken into account. Over time, both lowering of the coastal platform and consequent landward migration of the low water line (LWL) have occurred along the Channel coast (Dornbusch 2005b). While it is difficult to assess accurately the degree of change, an average horizontal retreat of the LWL of 68m between 1870 and the 1990s was calculated, with significant estimates for the lowering of the coastal platform. Today's platform width between low and high tide within the Langdon Bay area varies between about 50m and in excess of 100m depending on location within the bay. Similar values may also have been experienced in the past.

Summary

Coastal erosion will have taken place in the past. Erosion rates are difficult to define, but total retreat values from less than 227m to greater than 975m may be retrodicted from recent erosion rates. Changes in coastal erosion rates are likely to have occurred as a function of a variety of factors, including climatic change in the past. Accelerated erosion rates within the central portion of Langdon Bay may be expected owing to the presence of enhanced weathering zones in the bay's central region (Langdon Hole).

Humans, landscape change, and geomorphological evolution at the mouth of the Dour valley

The river Dour has been central to Dover's very existence since at least the Bronze Age (Clark 2004; Parfitt and Champion 2004; Bates *et al* 2011). By Roman times the lower part of the valley had flooded, but this did not impede the siting of a major Roman fort there (Rigold 1969; Philp 1981; Barham and Bates 1990). The estuary, however, has long since disappeared as a result of infilling with silt and shingle, and much of modern Dover is built across deep layers of natural and artificial sediment which infill the site of the ancient haven (Bates *et al* 2011).

Evidence for the earliest significant human activity at the mouth of the Dour is the presence of a Bronze Age boat of 1575–1520 cal BC, discovered during roadworks in 1992 in the Bench Street underpass excavations in the town centre (Parfitt 1993; Clark 2004). This discovery was associated with peat and tufa sequences (B in Fig 2.17) which have been traced elsewhere through the town centre and lower Dour area (Fig 2.17) and are of particular importance in the history of landscape change locally. Underlying all sequences recorded below the boat were angular flint and chalk gravels (A in Fig 2.17), a deposit first described by McDakin (1900) as a fan of gravel up to 18 feet (*c* 5.5m) thick. Geotechnical borehole records gathered by the author indicate that similar sediments can be traced from the town centre upstream to Crabble Mill and westwards to the Western Docks Train Ferry Terminal (Figs 2.17 and 2.18). The poorly sorted, sub-angular nature of the gravels, together with the discovery of mammoth teeth in Market Square and around Admiralty Pier, suggests that these gravels were laid down during cold climate conditions in the late Pleistocene. The distribution of the gravels can be used to infer the position and shape of the valley during this period (prior to 10,000 BP) of lowered sea levels (Fig 2.19).

Overlying the gravels and associated with the Bronze Age boat is a thick sequence of tufa, peats, and silts (see Fig 2.17 B and 2.20 A and B) documenting environmental change in the valley mouth in the later prehistoric period (Keeley *et al* 2004; Bates *et al* 2011). The sequence consists of interbedded tufa and compact, firm, humified peats being replaced upwards by minerogenic silts. These deposits appear to have commenced formation in a carbonate-rich flood plain or channel-margin environment that does not exist in the Dour valley today (Bates *et al* 2011) and which contains no evidence for marine or brackish water conditions (Keeley *et al* 2004). The tufa associations appear similar to those described by Pedley (1990) as forming braided fluvial systems and suggest the presence of shallow, clear-moving water bodies. The peats may have formed in areas of damp ground and contain evidence for wetland, grassland, and wooded situations. Anecdotal evidence suggests that similar

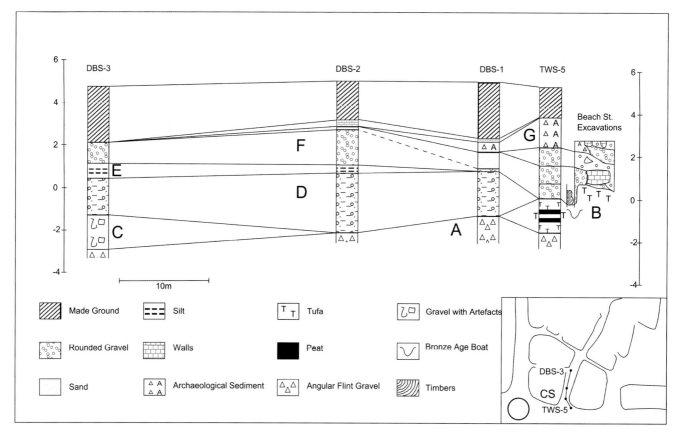

Fig 2.17 *Stratigraphic profile through town centre area, showing main units. A: Late Pleistocene gravels. B: Tufa, peat, and silt associations. C: Gravels with pottery. D: Sands and silts (brackish). E: Freshwater silts. F: Marine gravels and sands. G: Archaeological horizons (medieval). CS: Crypt site*

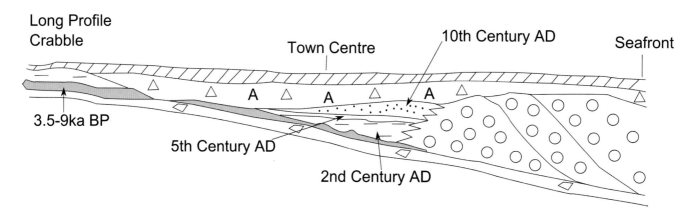

Fig 2.18 *Schematic profile through Lower Dour valley (see Fig 2.17 for key)*

sediments once occurred on the foreshore within Dover harbour, and recent borehole records along Waterloo Crescent and Marine Parade support this notion (see Fig 2.14). It is only in the deposits that consist of bedded, sometimes carbonate-rich silts that replace the peat and tufa upwards that pollen and diatoms, which suggest increasingly maritime conditions, start to appear. Age estimates on these sediment bodies indicate tufa/peat accumulation beginning in the valley by 9400 BP (Bates and Barham 1993a; Bates *et al*. 2011) and ceasing some

time after the abandonment of the boat (post 3250 BP/1500 BC).

Evidence for true marine conditions within the area is provided by the organic sands and silts found in the vicinity of the Bench Street–Market Square area (see Fig 2.17 C, D, and F). These deposits vary from poorly to well-bedded sands and silts with a variable organic content that includes plants/wood, forams, ostracods, diatoms, and pollen (Bates *et al* 2011). These sediments infill a basin-like depression that corresponds approximately to Rigold's Outer

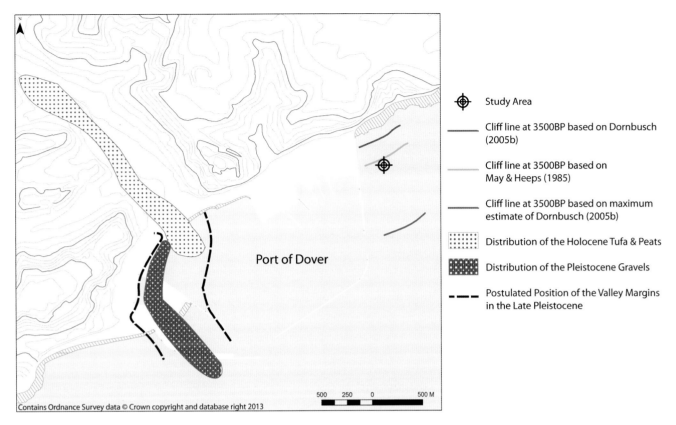

Fig 2.19   Map of the study area, showing main features relevant to the topographic history of the Lower Dour valley and Langdon Bay

Fig 2.20   A: Sequence of tufa / peat overlain by minerogenic sediments adjacent to Dover Bronze Age Boat. B: Detailed view of minerogenic sediments containing brackish water indicators

Harbour (Rigold 1969) and diatom floras indicate deposition in sub-tidal or inter-tidal situations in a brackish or saline environment (N Cameron [UCL], pers comm). Occasional pot, tile, and concrete fragments recovered from boreholes (Bates and Barham 1993b), as well as excavation records of major Roman structures (Elsted 1856; Threipland

and Steer 1951; Rahtz 1958; Rigold 1969), suggest flooding of the mouth of the Dour by the Roman period. Indeed, a major Roman harbour at the mouth of the Dour had long been assumed (Rigold 1969), but it was only excavations in the 1970s and 1980s that gave definitive proof of the existence, under the modern town, of an almost unique 2nd-century Roman naval fort (*Classis Britannica* fort) in addition to the remains of a late Roman Saxon Shore fort. Various other buildings and harbour installations (Rigold 1969; Philp 1981; 1989) have been found surrounding the harbour basin.

The geoarchaeological information allows the sequence of events associated with landscape change in the vicinity of the modern mouth of the Dour to be outlined and placed within a timeframe based on both archaeological and non-archaeological criteria (see Figs 2.18 and 2.19; Table 2.6).

The earliest sequences identified within the town centre/port area date to the late Pleistocene (post Last Glacial Maximum) and include the angular flint and chalk gravels of the valley bottom and sides described above (see Fig 2.18). The pattern of distribution of these deposits and the topography created by their deposition define the shape of the Holocene valley (ie the topographic template *sensu* Bates 1998; Bates and Whittaker 2004). This topographic template suggests that the late Pleistocene/early Holocene valley extended south-westwards along the line of Snargate Street and then south-eastwards

Table 2.6   Stratigraphic units, age ascriptions, and inferred palaeoenvironmental and geographical changes in the Lower Dour valley

Stratigraphic group	Bench Street boreholes	Crypt site	Bench Street Excavations, TWS - 5	Age ascriptions	Inferred palaeoenvironmental conditions
Made ground, anthropogenic sediments (G) and rounded flint gravels (F)	Rounded gravels and waterlogged organic silts (Norman)	Stratified cultural sediments (medieval)	Well-rounded flint gravels (medieval)	Medieval to post-medieval	Storm beach established parallel to modern coast, final infilling of valley with organic sediments in low-lying areas, colluvial deposition on valley sides and establishment of modern town geography
Sands and rounded flint gravels (F)		Well-bedded sands and rounded flint gravels (late Saxon pot)		Late Saxon	Littoral and aeolian sand infilling former Roman harbour basin
Freshwater silts (E)	Organic silts 1545±65BP 1670±65BP	Organic silts			
		Late Roman to early Saxon	Freshwater wetland growth on infilled Roman harbour, colluvial deposition continues on valley sides		
Gravel with pottery and organic sands and silts (C/D)	Interbedded sands and silts with gravel at base (with Roman pot)	Interbedded sands and silts (with Roman pot)	Roman structure	Early to late Roman	Sub-tidal to intertidal infilling of harbour basin
Bedded silts (B upper)			Bedded silts	?Iron Age	Fluvial systems rich in silt, overbank flooding with colluvial deposition on valley sides. Unstable system approach of brackish water systems, removal of barrier to marine conditions
Tufa/peat units (B lower)		Tufa and peat	Tufa and peat containing boat 4340±85BP 6315±85BP 8380±110BP	<3300 BP >9240 BP	Carbonate-rich fluvial systems with damp ground, open and closed vegetation. Stable system. Occupy valley floor in freshwater conditions, marine influence excluded
Angular flint and chalk gravels (A)	Angular flint gravels	Angular flint gravels	Angular flint gravels	>10,000 BP	Periglacial, braided channel systems, valley extended seawards via Western Docks

beneath the Western Docks (see Figs 2.14 and 2.19), implying the presence of an east bank and valley side extending across the harbour area during this period.

A shift in the nature of sedimentation followed the onset of temperate conditions in the Holocene, and tufa/peat sediments were deposited along the valley floor from Crabble Mill (Bates *et al* 2008) to the modern coast in the vicinity of the foreshore (see Fig 2.18). This alteration was followed, probably in the Late Bronze Age, by a shift towards minerogenic sedimentation and increasing evidence of brackish conditions in the valley. The relationship of these deposits to contemporary coastal geographies is of particular relevance to ascertaining the nature of the coast during the period of interest to this study. Sea-level rise during the Holocene in the Channel

region has been considered by Waller and Long (2003; 2011); however, they point out that only a limited number of sites have been investigated in the area (the closest dataset is derived from Romney Marsh). Significantly, the early Holocene is characterised by rapid sea level rise until approximately 4850 cal BC. After this time, the rate of sea-level rise slowed and is often associated with extensive peat growth. Finally, after about 1750 cal BC there was a further decline in the rate of sea-level rise, although many coastal sites in the eastern Channel were inundated by marine waters during this period. The sea level around 1300 cal BC, the period of the Langdon Bay bronze finds, is estimated by Waller and Long (2003) to be somewhere between –2 and –4m OD, just below the recorded levels for the Bronze Age boat (*c* 1500 BC), but the boat in its final resting place was certainly within reach of storm surges and floods. Consequently, the presence of the peat/tufa associations and the absence of any indication of marine influence until at least 1500 BC suggest that a substantial barrier existed to the penetration of sea waters into the valley. This hypothesis might suggest that the eastern bank of the Dour was still a major barrier until after *c* 1500 BC and that the contemporary mouth of the Dour with the sea was still a considerable distance downstream. Therefore, it is possible that significant quantities of coastal erosion have occurred since this time, trimming back the eastern valley side and exposing the valley floor to coastal flooding during the Iron Age.

Summary

A major channel of the Dour existed during the late Pleistocene, draining along the line of Snargate Street and beneath the position of the Western Docks. The aspect of the channel suggests that the eastern valley margins of the Dour valley once extended seawards, accompanying this late Pleistocene channel. Flooding of the lower valley by marine waters did not occur until sometime after *c* 1500 BC, implying a barrier to the penetration of the sea in the vicinity of the modern beach area within the harbour. Breaching of the eastern flank of the Dour valley appears to have fully occurred only during the Late Bronze Age or Iron Age.

Discussion

The evidence presented in previous sections indicates that significant local and regional changes in the topography of the channel region, and, by implication, the Langdon Bay area adjacent to the Dour valley, are likely to have occurred during, and since, prehistoric times. Therefore, the context of the bronzes recovered from the seabed requires close evaluation.

Although it will never be possible to define the precise location of the cliffs at any particular point in the past, the evidence gained from the study of recent cliff recession rates suggests that significant erosion of the chalk cliffs at Langdon Bay is likely to have occurred during the last 3500 years. Retrodicting the position of the cliff in the past (see Fig 2.19) is complex because recession rates will have varied throughout the last 3500 years as a function of (among other factors) the nature of the chalk within the cliffs themselves and changing climatic conditions (and, more recently, the impact of human constructions, such as the major harbour facilities).

Prior to sea level attaining modern datums, the degraded former cliff line established during the last interglacial would have extended beyond the modern coastline and would probably have become relatively stable after the cycle of weathering and collapse that took place during the 90,000 years of the last cold stage. Consequently, it is likely that little or no erosion of the cliff line would have occurred in the early Holocene. More significant erosion will have resumed as near-modern sea levels were attained during the Middle Holocene, at which time initial coastal erosion would have removed the unconsolidated debris accumulated from cliff degradation during the Devensian. Only following the removal of this debris would erosion of the basal rock face have resumed. Using the lowest postulated rates of cliff recession provided by Dornbusch (2005b), the distance between the site and the contemporary cliffs would be half that of today. Using the maximum possible erosion rates for the stretch of coast between Dover and St Margaret's Bay (Dornbusch 2005b), the cliff would be some 500m seawards of the site. Another factor to consider here is the water depth at the site. Regional subsidence within south-east England is now a commonly established fact (Shennan and Horton 2002), and rates of between 0.5mm and 1mm per year within the Dover Strait are possible. This observation would suggest a lowering of the wave-cut platform relative to mean sea level of between 1.75m and 3.5m in the last 3500 years (Antony Long, pers comm). This subsidence would have been exacerbated by lowering of the chalk platform through erosion at the same time. Thus, it would be expected that the water depth at the time of site formation would have been significantly less than at the present time.

The evidence from the mouth of the Dour valley (see Fig 2.19) supports the notion that the cliff line was formerly further seawards than at the present day. The distribution of the late Pleistocene gravels suggests that a substantial barrier to the direct flow of the Dour into the Channel area existed in the late Devensian. This barrier is most likely to have been a continuation of the eastern chalk valley side of the Dour valley in a south-westerly direction. That this barrier continued to be an important factor in local geography until after the Middle Bronze Age is suggested by the absence of a marine or brackish water signal in the tufa and peat sediments of the town centre. Thus, we can envisage a scenario within the early Holocene when much of the area now occupied by the port of Dover, within the modern breakwaters, was occupied by low chalk bluffs that subsequently eroded landwards. Much of this erosion would probably have occurred following the establishment of sea levels close to modern datums after *c* 6000 years ago.

Within the area of Langdon Bay itself little evidence exists to substantiate the suggestions made above owing to the predominantly erosive nature of the area. However, it is interesting to consider two aspects. Firstly, it is possible that Langdon Hole marks the headwall of a former valley that once extended seawards across the study area. If so, flooding of such a feature could have produced a small inlet in the past, perhaps an ideal location for landing a craft such as the Dover Bronze Age boat.

Secondly, the excavation records (Muckelroy 1981) note the presence of stable black-grey clays in the fissures eroded into the chalk wave-cut platform. While it is impossible to determine the precise environments of deposition of such sediments, their description resembles that of deposits usually laid down under low energy conditions of the sort normally associated with estuaries or tidal mud flats, and certainly not the open water conditions now prevalent at the site. Thus, whatever the precise nature of these sediments, they may well attest to conditions in the past that were very different to those of the present day.

In conclusion, using the geomorphological and palaeoenvironmental evidence from the local area, it may be deduced that the site area now occupies a situation very different to that at the time of site formation. If a maritime context is favoured, then the site was formed without doubt in a context considerably closer to the contemporary shoreline than at the present day, and with shallower water depths. The presence of the clays in the rock fissures might also suggest the presence of shallow and inter-tidal contexts occupying the site at some time perhaps contemporary with site formation. However, a number of very strong lines of evidence would argue that even greater local topographic changes have occurred since site formation, and that perhaps a terrestrial or estuarine context may be more appropriate to the site. The higher rates of chalk cliff erosion and the possible offshore extension of Langdon Hole might suggest, as an alternative scenario to a fully marine depositional context, that the assemblage may have been deposited within a small inlet, perhaps occupied by tidal marshes.

Terrestrial hinterland of Langdon Bay
by Stuart Needham and Keith Parfitt

As in the case of the Salcombe/Moor Sand site, consideration has been given to the terrestrial hinterland within a radius of approximately 10km from the Langdon Bay seabed find. The same caveats that were discussed in Chapter 1 apply: lack of certainty as to how the metalwork came to be deposited (our preferred conclusion is reserved for Chapter 5) and, if it is the contents of a wrecked boat, the impossibility of knowing whether that boat intended to make landfall on this part of the coast or was simply passing by.

The findspot lies close to the South Foreland, the point of Britain closest to the European mainland, from which it is separated by the Strait of Dover. It also happens to lie around the centre of a 20km stretch of coastline marked by impressive chalk cliffs – the famous White Cliffs of Dover (Fig 2.21). This striking white façade, rising in places to 150m in height, presents a full transect of the North Downs, cut through by the Channel. The geology of the chalk is outlined by Bates (above); the topography is of more concern here. At the west end of the exposure the cliffs fall quickly to give easier access to the hinterland via East Wear Bay, while to the north-east the cliffs recede more gradually, giving way to low ground at Walmer and the marshland of the Lydden Valley beyond Deal. In between, the façade is broken only twice: at Dover, where the small river Dour flows into the sea, and at St Margaret's Bay, where a local declivity in the cliffs is associated with a small beach. These are potential landing places (Parfitt 2004, 101–2). Bates (above) has conjectured that Langdon Bay itself, overlooked by the cliff-top depression of Langdon Hole, may once have been a more significant bay before coastline and cliffs receded.

Inland, our defined study zone thus encompasses a landscape almost entirely of downland, although the chalk bedrock is frequently mantled by clay-with-flints on the crests and by colluvium or solifluction deposits in the dry valleys. The prevailing surface geology, both within and beyond the radius, is indicated in simplified form in Fig 2.21. The river Dour seems, by most standards, to be a rather insignificant watercourse; nevertheless, within this landscape it serves as a thread through the heart of the zone connecting coast and inland areas. The mouth of the Dour lies 2.5km west of the Langdon Bay site today, but there is geomorphological evidence to suggest that its position has shifted a little during the Holocene, its outfall previously being further out to sea than the modern seafront (Bates above).

To the west of the study zone a short length of coastline exposes Lower Greensand (and a little Gault Clay) around Folkestone and Hythe. Beyond is today's peninsula of Dungeness, a landform that was very different in the Bronze Age. It is probable that the estuary of the river Rother fell close to Hythe and was surrounded by a complex of mudflats, saltmarsh, freshwater fen and raised bog, all trapped behind a massive shingle barrier system (Long *et al* 2007, 198 fig 6.4). While rich in certain kinds of resources and undoubtedly frequented by people, as attested by the Lydd find of flat axes (Needham 1988), this expanse would probably not have had much by way of a settled population. To the north of the study zone lies the Lydden Valley; it too has been subject to marine influences and it flanks the entrance to the Wantsum Channel, which had cut off the Isle of Thanet as the sea level rose in the earlier Holocene (Fig 2.21).

The shortness of the crossing between eastern Kent and the facing continental shores would have made this part of the Channel a favoured crossing zone for early man-powered craft (eg McGrail 1993, 200, fig 20.1), but powerful currents through the Strait of Dover would have to be combated. However, there is no reason to suppose that the bulk of cross-Channel trade would have gravitated overland to the regions immediately overlooking the Strait in order to benefit from this short crossing. Instead, we

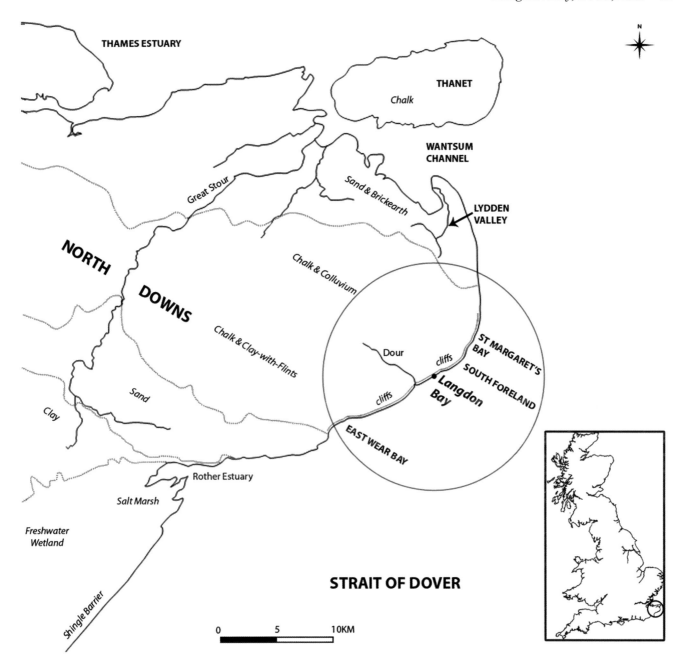

Fig 2.21   Langdon Bay and its hinterland in eastern Kent. The archaeological study zone for the terrestrial hinterland lies within the circle. Romney Marsh is as reconstructed for the Bronze Age by Long et al *2007. Base-rocks and habitats are simplified to show those prevailing in the respective zones*

have to envisage innumerable cross-Channel routes involving different combinations of near-shore coasting, crossing, and far-shore coasting. Even when the Dour valley and its environs *were* the destination in cross-Channel transits, the crossings themselves may not consistently have been across the Strait. Irrespective of varied routes, the chalk façade would have provided extremely useful marks for navigation, for both those seeking local landfall and those passing. The modern Ordnance Survey maps mark a number of names for specific locations and features along the coast between Dover and Walmer, such as Fan Point and Old Parkers Cap,

which must have been used for navigation by local mariners for generations.

Neither should we prejudge the extent to which this particular coastline was involved in cross-Channel interactions on the basis of modern preconceptions about economic trade. Such preconceptions might see economic relations being drawn preferentially towards larger or more prosperous populations, leading to the possibility that most sea-borne traffic would have bypassed 'poorer' stretches of coastline. In this context, the apparent wealth of deposited metalwork in the lower Thames valley (in many phases) and the Thames estuary (in certain phases) might encourage the view that Bronze Age mariners would have sought to round the South Foreland and head for Thanet and, via the Wantsum Channel, on to the Thames beyond. But this idea involves assumptions. The first is that maritime interactions were predicated solely on economic advantage – a dubious assumption when it comes to small-scale societies. The second is that coastal communities could have exerted some influence or control over passing boats only if they were powerful relative to others in the wider region. And the third is that the richness of deposition seen archaeologically in the lower Thames and the estuarine coastlands is directly related to the 'first port of call' of regular exchanges.

This third assumption is questionable even if the rich deposition we witness is the result of a greater regional abundance of metalwork (and this itself is by no means a given). The ability to accumulate wealth of this kind over the long term can hinge on underlying economic and political structures which cause surplus material to gravitate towards the region almost insidiously through the exchange network. There is no *a priori* reason why the region that came to monopolise surpluses should have been the first recipient of incoming material on any systematic basis. In fact, if the high level of deposition of bronzes in the river Thames – much of it weaponry – is correctly argued to be the product of ritual deposition (eg Needham and Burgess 1980), then that deposition was driven by non-economic factors rather resulting from a disproportionate share of wealth *per se*. It may be pertinent that, despite the prodigious quantities of metalwork dredged up from the Thames, items of gold are all but absent. Gold has other depositional patterns in south-east England and, as we shall see below, this pattern may have something to say about depositional behaviour in the Dover region. It is important, therefore, to assess the evidence of this region in its own right.

One key find for this discussion is, of course, the Dover boat (Clark 2004), the final resting place of which is only 2km west of the Langdon seabed assemblage (Fig 2.21). It is not an exact contemporary, having been in use in the region two to three centuries earlier, but is nevertheless unequivocal evidence for a local involvement in water-borne, probably sea-borne, pursuits during the middle stages of the Bronze Age.

Although historical circumstances have not brought about any large-scale settlement excavation in the Dover area, there is now a good-sized body of evidence for Bronze Age activity (Fig 2.1). This evidence takes the form of both smaller excavations and a growing number of field observations thanks in particular to the work of the Dover Archaeological Group over the past thirty years. Stray finds of artefacts remain important because, although lacking in context, they can often be closely dated.

The backdrop to the period of the Langdon Bay find is the landscape of barrows and burials familiar across the country at large. At least eight Beaker pots are known from the 10km zone, although only one (Sholden Bank Primary School; Grinsell 1992, 380) is definitely documented as accompanying a burial – a crouched inhumation in an oval grave. At least one other, from Salisbury Road, St Margaret's at Cliffe, is likely to have accompanied a burial, to judge from its close proximity to a subsequently discovered crouched inhumation (Stebbing 1956; Anderson 1994). One Beaker pot, found by workmen in 1917, comes from Swingate Aerodrome, less than 1km inland from Langdon Hole (Clarke 1970, 485, no 396, fig 435). None of the sites yielding Beakers had mounds surviving and not all need have been marked in this manner, but the number of ring-ditches now recognised as cropmarks suggests this was a zone of significant destruction over the course of the centuries (Parfitt 2006).

Within our study zone there is, as yet, little specific indication of occupation or activity sites contemporary with Beaker burials. Rather, there are just surface-recovered scatters of flintwork, occasionally with diagnostic barbed-and-tanged arrowheads present. Noteworthy among these is an extensive cliff-top scatter of Neolithic and Bronze Age flintwork between Langdon Hole and the South Foreland Lighthouse covering at least 45ha (100 acres). However, important Beaker occupation evidence has been identified in the last two decades just outside our radius. Immediately to the west, the Channel Tunnel preparation works revealed a settlement site with post- and stake-built structures at Holywell Coombe, Folkestone (Bennett 1988, 7–10). Meanwhile, observations over a number of years in the Lydden Valley to the north have documented the survival of a widespread buried land surface with frequent finds of Beaker pot sherds, struck flintwork, and calcined flints (Halliwell and Parfitt 1985). Exploration so far has been too limited to ascertain the nature of these assemblages, but they clearly point to significant activity on the low-lying Lydden flats flanking the entrance to the Wantsum Channel. In general, it is possible to suggest a good level of activity in this part of Kent during the main usage of Beaker pottery (c 2400–1950 BC).

At least 45 barrows and ring-ditches (combined total) are now known from within the study zone, forming part of a broader distribution focusing on the Downs of east Kent. There are records of excavation at some nine sites, these having revealed a typical variety of burial deposits and other features known from Early Bronze Age barrows. Crouched inhumations seem to be dominant locally, including some that are unaccompanied and only presumptively of this period. However, in-urned cremations are recorded, including the important burial under a barrow at Freedown, Ringwould, which had faience beads, an accessory cup, and a Biconical Urn in association (Woodruff 1874; 1880). Just two sites attest the continuation of in-urned cremation, now using

Bucket Urns, into the Middle Bronze Age: those close to the cliff top at Hope Point and at Sholden Bank (Stebbing 1936). While these will be closer in date to our seabed find, it would seem that here, and more generally in Kent, formal burial rites waned during the Middle Bronze Age.

The limited amount of fieldwork that has taken place historically in this region inevitably restricts our knowledge of Middle and Late Bronze Age settlement. Fortunately, a Middle Bronze Age residential unit has been excavated at East Valley Farm, St Margaret's at Cliffe, in downland 2km back from the cliffs running north from the South Foreland (Parfitt and Corke 2003). A classic post-built roundhouse set in a slope-cut platform retained evidence for an outer stake wall as well as the inner ring of supporting posts and a south-east-facing porch. At least two phases seem to be indicated by the mass of post and stake-holes on the platform, but the site yielded very little material refuse. This site hints at a pattern of settlement familiar elsewhere on the chalk uplands of southern England, but probably only the most easily recognised component of a settlement pattern extending onto lower ground. Other evidence in this period is vestigial (eg six Deverel-Rimbury sherds at Tilmanstone) or, as yet, poorly defined and beyond our study zone.

For the later period (and running into the Earliest Iron Age), the evidence is a little better. At Dryden Road, Buckland, in the heart of our study zone, a scatter of material was stratified in hillwash deposits and deduced to derive from occupation nearby. On the downland above, at Guston Roundabout, a scatter of shallow pits and a ditch have been excavated, most of which contained Late Bronze Age pottery as well as burnt flint and struck flintwork. One pit (F.51) yielded not only 117 sherds but also a large assemblage of charred plant material dominated by wheat: spelt and a lesser amount of emmer (unpublished report by Ruth Pelling). A sample of charcoal from this pit has been dated to 920–800 cal BC (Beta-179754).

Cut features have also been excavated at both the South and North Barracks sites of the old Royal Marines depot in Deal: at the former site a ditch complex, at the latter several pits (Kent HER records; unpublished). Dating evidence is tentative and site function impossible to assess, but the importance of these sites is that they lie fairly close to two more characteristic sites. The first is the well-known ring-work at Mill Hill Deal, which yielded a sizable assemblage of pottery and other material remains from within a circular enclosure about 50m in diameter (Stebbing 1934; Champion 1980, 233–7). Such enclosures are assumed to represent high-status residences of the Late Bronze Age. Three kilometres from Mill Hill, excavations at Wood Hill, Kingsdown, in 1984 sampled another apparently circular enclosure with a smaller diameter of about 37m. The evidence from the small quantity of pottery recovered suggests broad contemporaneity

with Mill Hill, raising the interesting question as to whether the two sites represent the pairing of ring-works that is known elsewhere, notably in Essex at Mucking (South Rings, North Ring) and Chelmsford (Springfield Lyons, Baddow) or in the Croydon area, Greater London (Carshalton, Nore Hill) (eg Needham 1992, 52).

Sites yielding various cut features, including probable field boundaries, have been excavated near Barham, north-west of our study zone, while a pit group just to the north at Hacklinge Holes, Worth, overlooking the Lydden valley, also deserves mention. The pit contained LBA/EIA pottery, animal bone, struck flints, a pyramidal loomweight, and an amber bead (Parfitt 1983). The discovery of sites of this period has been opportunistic, being primarily governed by development for towns or communications; as yet, there are too few to be confident of relative densities in different topographic zones. However, the multiple sites in and around Deal and others running northwards towards the Wantsum Channel do suggest significant occupation, with potential nodal points along the low coastlands beyond the dipslope of the Downs.

Although current evidence is focused on the lower ground the distribution of bronze metalwork of the late Bronze Age suggests that activity extended onto the uplands. Finds occur from the foot of the dipslope (Deal, Northbourne, Eastry) all the way across to the Dour valley, but evidently not further to the south-west on the highest ground, where the chalk is much mantled by clay. Most are singly found objects, but the two recorded hoards both come from within the zone of upland: at Waldershare Park (Parfitt 1997) and in the Dour valley at Buckland. Material from the latter is lost or unidentifiable in Dover Museum collections as a result of war-time disruptions, while the former was recovered during a metal-detecting rally and is distinctively of the Wilburton stage. One of three separate spearhead finds coming from within the bounds of Dover is also diagnostic of the Wilburton assemblage (Portable Antiquities Scheme SUSS-224AF6). Intriguingly, spearheads are not among the Late Bronze Age finds to the north-east, which are mainly fragments of axeheads or other tools, so there may be some differences in depositional practice in the Dour valley at this time.

Tracking backwards in time, it is apparent that Middle Bronze Age metalwork is similarly distributed, in that it avoids the high Downs south-west of the Dour. There are three important hoards, all fairly recent finds, in the Ripple to Tilmanstone zone of the lower slopes, where they are joined by some single finds. A possible related find is a pair of decorated pins, now unfortunately lost and not securely datable, which were said to have been found with traces of bone in a chalk-block-lined pit filled with rough flints at Knight's Bottom, Walmer; this feature is large enough to have been a grave for an extended inhumation (Parfitt 1994). Another decorated pin, of the so-called Picardy type with strong continental affinities, came from St Margaret's at Cliffe, overlooking the Bay (Hawkes 1942, 28–9, fig 2.4). By comparison, bronzes from the Dour valley are poor – just two single finds. The weight of bronze deposition (not to be confused with settlement or other activity) appears, therefore, to have been focused on the lower downland slopes during the Middle Bronze Age. Interestingly, only a single palstave, from Buckland, Dover (Nicholson 1980, no 16), is potentially contemporary with the seabed assemblage. One reaction might be to deduce that the pattern of exchange in the Penard phase barely touched the Dover region, but this deduction overlooks the wider pattern of deposition. In fact, setting aside the already discussed concentration of material from the Thames, there are no obvious concentrations of Penard metalwork in southern England; moreover, hoards are few and

well dispersed. So, however cross-Channel exchange was organised in this phase, it was evidently not resulting in any large-scale terrestrial deposition. Indeed, overall deposition in the Channel-facing counties, from Cornwall to Kent, seems to have declined considerably from the previous Taunton phase.

Going further back, Early Bronze Age metalwork shows a different emphasis again. There are only four or five known findspots, but these concentrate on the Dour catchment and flanking Downs. Most conspicuous is the Arreton stage hoard of three flanged axes and a tanged spearhead from Buckland, in the valley (Megaw and Hardy 1938, 283–4, fig 10, plate LVa). It is tempting to connect this mini-focus of metalwork with the Dover boat, together signalling the local importance of the Dour catchment in the Early Bronze Age.

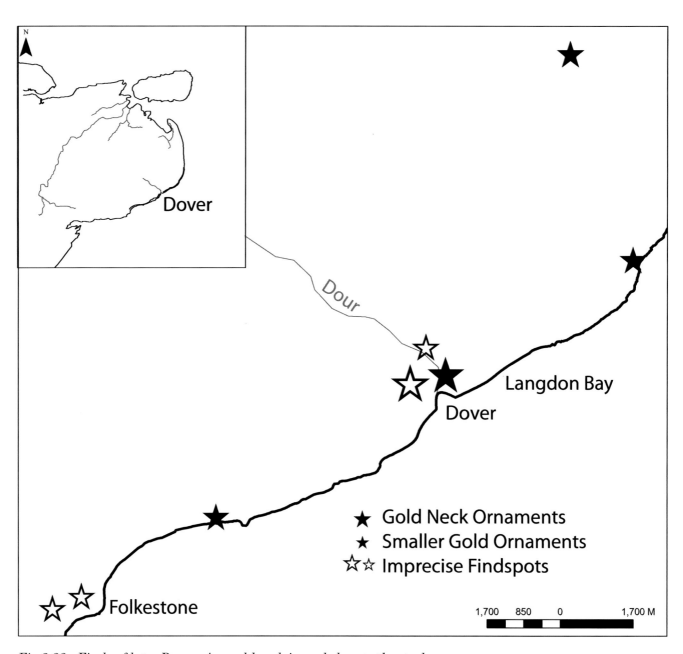

Fig 2.22 Finds of later Bronze Age goldwork in and close to the study zone

None of these bronze metalwork patterns should be read too literally as proxies for either demographic patterns or power structures, not least because, as we have seen, other contemporary evidence begins to reveal different emphases. They do, however, illustrate that the strategies and politics of deposition shifted over time and this may relate indirectly to varied aspects such as territorial boundaries, zones held in special regard, or the distribution of power within the given zone. The economics of exchange, both external and internal, may be only a small contributory factor towards patterns of permanent deposition, if a factor at all. The final category of material to be considered, goldwork, drives home the point that there is no simple or uniform explanation for deposition patterns.

Six items of Bronze Age goldwork are recorded from the study zone, and a further two are recorded as coming from just beyond, at Folkestone. They cover a date span of Penard through to Ewart stages (late Middle to Late Bronze Age), so they do not seem to represent a narrow horizon. However, what is striking is that these present a wholly different distribution from that of contemporary bronzes. With one exception (a gold-covered copper-alloy penannular ring from Ripple Farm: Parfitt 1995), these finds come from coastal locations (including the two Folkestone finds: Fig 2.22). One find, a penannular bracelet, was actually recovered from the foreshore beneath Abbot's Cliff, although it is probable that it had collapsed with eroding material from the cliff top. Two further finds were of relatively lightweight penannular rings, but the last two are more spectacular. From within the grounds of Castlemount, Dover, overlooking the Dour's mouth and no great distance from Langdon Bay, came a fine coiled and flange-twisted torc (Scott Robertson 1878; J J Taylor 1980, 82, Kt13; Eogan 1994, 128). This type of torc dates precisely to the period of the seabed assemblage. The sixth object was found in 1772, unfortunately poorly located, 'in a ploughed field near Dover' (Duncombe 1772; J J Taylor 1980, 82 Kt15). This is of the successor type to the twisted torcs, a thick bar neck-ring with tapered terminals and incised decoration. The deposition of these two weighty objects of gold at Dover, plus the more general association of goldwork with the coast, seems to indicate some specific interest in the land/sea interface. These finds do not in themselves necessarily demonstrate an engagement with maritime exchange, but they do suggest that importance was attached locally to this dramatic interface.

Notes to Chapter 2

1. Most maritime traffic between the Atlantic Ocean and the North and Baltic Seas passes through the Strait of Dover, rather than taking the longer and more dangerous route around the north of Scotland. The strait, used by over 400 commercial vessels daily, is the busiest international seaway in the world.

2. The Kent Archaeological Rescue Unit is a registered charity established in 1971 as the first county archaeology unit set up in Britain. The Unit conducts archaeological work all over the historic county of Kent and manages the Roman Painted House, Dover, and the Crofton Roman Villa, Orpington.

3. It had always been an aspiration of the Bronze Age curator to display the whole assemblage in the British Museum once more gallery space was provided for the European prehistoric collections. However, this was never to come to pass, and it was a temporary loan to Dover Museum which first gave the opportunity for full display in the context of its new Bronze Age boat gallery of 1999.

4. The Council for Nautical Archaeology (CNA) was formed in 1964, initially under the name of the The Committee for Nautical Archaeology, 'so as to ensure that the many discoveries being made by divers should not go by default through lack of contact with the appropriate learned bodies and to act as a channel of communication with the many interests that were growing up in this new field of research and exploration'. Membership included the British Museum, among others. The CNA was responsible for establishing the *International Journal of Nautical Archaeology* and was also concerned with the promotion of legislation for the protection of nautical archaeological sites, playing a key part in what became the Protection of Wrecks Act 1973. In 1984 the CNA was incorporated into the Council for British Archaeology as one of its research sub-committees (Marsden 1986).

5. At this time, Alan Moat was the Diving Officer of DSAC. In the BSAC, the diving officer of a Branch is the individual in charge of diving activities in the Branch. Moat remained the licensee for the site until his death in 1998.

6. Sonar (originally an acronym for 'sound navigation and ranging') is a technique that uses sound propagation in a range of ways (usually underwater) to navigate. In this context, sound is used to establish a depth of water beneath a boat which, if mapped, can provide a crude topographical survey of the seabed.

7. The list was divided into six sections: 'The only considerations of the fundamentals' (Bass [1966] *Archaeology underwater* and Bass [1967] *Cape Gelidonya: a Bronze Age shipwreck*); 'Why waste time on archaeology?' (Wheeler [1954] *Archaeology from the earth* and Brown [1975] *Principles and practice in modern archaeology*); 'the Bronze Age' (Renfrew [1974] *British prehistory*); 'Techniques of archaeological fieldwork' (Barker [1977] *Techniques of archaeological excavation* and Coles [1972] *Field archaeology in Britain*); 'Model final excavation reports' (Bass [1967] *Cape Gelidonya: a Bronze Age shipwreck* and Green [1977] *The loss of the Verenigde Oost-*

indische Compagnie Jacht Verguide Draeck, Western Australia 1656); and 'Archaeology in British waters' (Martin [1975] *Full fathom five* and McDonald [1978] *The treasure divers*).

8. The University of Cambridge college at which Muckelroy was reading for his PhD.

9. A system in which air is supplied to one or more divers from an air compressor on the surface via an air hose, thus eliminating the need to surface to change air tanks.

10. The Fastnet race is the supreme challenge in yacht racing in British waters. The 1979 race began on 11 August on the Isle of Wight and took the yachts westwards along the English Channel, around Lands End, across the Irish Sea, and around the Fastnet Rock off the coast of the Republic of Ireland, then back to Plymouth. On 12 August the race was hit by a storm described by some competitors as a 'great fury'. From the 303 yachts taking part, 15 yachtsmen died. The subsequent rescue operation was the biggest peace-time operation launched to that date.

11. The seabed in this area is, unsurprisingly, littered with the detritus of military activity. The cliff tops have always been a strategic position from which to observe and defend against any enemy approaching from mainland Europe. The French coast is clearly visible from the cliffs overlooking the site and, for many years, including during the Napoleonic Wars and the two World Wars, lookout posts were set up and training for invasion took place. This history of use has resulted in the seabed being liberally covered with large quantities of shrapnel from exploded ordnance, hundreds of musket balls, numerous bullets, spent mortar rounds, and projectile shells. In addition, hundreds of metres of steel cable, some of it in loose coils, had been abandoned on and around the site. It is thought that this is related to 20th-century wartime salvage activity during which crippled ships were towed into the area.

12. The term 'salvor in possession' refers to certain common law rights enjoyed by a salvor over the site of a wreck while they are actively engaged in salvage activities. It is a complicated legal concept and DSAC may not have been able to enforce it. However, at the time it was acknowledged that DSAC were 'salvors in possession' of the site.

13. The Nautical Archaeology Society is a charity whose aims are to further research in nautical archaeology, to publish the results of such research, and to advance education and training in the techniques pertaining to the study of nautical archaeology for the benefit of the public.

14. The Channel Tunnel, at 50.5km (31.4 miles), is the longest undersea tunnel in the world. It links England and northern France beneath the English Channel at the Strait of Dover. It was constructed between 1988 and 1994.

15. It is a salutary lesson to compare a diver topographic survey with the multibeam data. Perhaps the most significant difference is the objectivity of the multibeam data compared to the inevitable subjectivity of diver recording, a phenomenon observable on other sites where high resolution multibeam and diver surveys have covered the same ground. The difference in time taken to collect the multibeam data compared with the divers' topography survey is also revealing. Three divers spent twelve diving days surveying 14,000 square metres of seabed, whereas the multibeam covered 135,000 square metres in less than three hours. If the divers had covered the same area at their normal rate, it would have taken them more than 108 days of diving.

3 The metalwork assemblages: identification, connections, and metal composition

The failure to locate any structural remains and the absence of stratified deposits or other contemporary material leave the interpretation of the two seabed sites hinging very largely on their respective assemblages of metalwork. This chapter is divided into three parts. Part 1 is concerned with the description, definition and identification of the types represented at the two sites; specific parallels will be referenced insofar as is necessary for establishing an object's identity, but otherwise reference is to an established typology. Part 2 picks up from this point to explore the geographical and contextual occurrence of the type in question. The significance of individual types may be addressed here in advance of the more collective discussion of significance in Chapter 5. Part 3 sets out the results of extensive metal analyses on the objects and explores their implications in relation to broader patterns of composition across north-west Europe.

Defining the metalwork types
by Stuart Needham and Brendan O'Connor

Since Langdon Bay is by far the largest group of material, this will be classified first, followed by the Salcombe assemblage (up until the end of 2004), which has some types in common with Langdon as well as additional ones. Smaller groups and single finds from other marine sites are covered in Chapter 4, employing the same definitions where possible. Categories of objects are dealt with in the following order: tools, ornaments/fittings, vessels, weapons, metalworking debris/ingots, and unidentifiable fragments. Knives are covered alongside weapons because of the potential gradation into dirks and rapiers. The basic information on dimensions and condition for each object is presented in Appendix 1. Museum accession numbers are also given there.

Classification of condition

The classification of condition is a vital preliminary for two reasons. On the one hand, relative condition will obviously determine the degree to which an object can be classified to its original type; on the other, it may shed light on formation processes on the site and the extent to which damage was pre- or post-depositional. The condition notations in Appendix 1 are as follows.

Completeness

1. Complete
2. Small loss (eg loop, blade corner)
3. Large fragment (estimated greater than half present)
4. Approximately half
5. Small fragment (rather less than half)

Surface reduction is ignored for the purposes of this assessment (see *surface feature retention*, below). Where there is great variation in the original lengths of objects (especially swords, rapiers etc), fragments may only be attributable to a range, eg completeness 3–5.

Cutting edge profile(s)

A. Sharp
B. Rounded off
C. Very rounded (allowing for a wide variety of thicknesses at the edge)

Classification is relative to blade thickness and obtuseness.

Surface feature retention – fine morphology and decoration

a. Distinct features survive
b. Poor definition, but discernible features which are almost certainly original
c. Hint of features, but origin uncertain
d. Generally amorphous with no fine morphology
* Significant irregularities or anomalies in outline believed to be of post-depositional formation; may include surface hollows and perforations.

This categorisation provides an overview of the state of features such as edge bevels, facets, ridges, ribs, decoration, butt notches, and rivet holes. Still finer surface features, such as hammer-marks, do not survive.

Condition of breaks

1. Crisp fracture
2. Slightly rounded
3. Well rounded and smooth
L Loop only lacking

()   Uncertain breaks – applies to completeness categories 1 and 1–2 only

This categorisation might throw some light on whether apparent breaks are ancient or more recently caused under marine action, especially when compared with working edge profiles and surface feature retention.

Bending, twisting, and other features

o.   Unbent
b1. Slight bend
b2. Marked bend
b3. Doubled over
c.   Concretion attached (significant amount)
s.   Stones trapped in orifices (loops, wings)
t1. Slight twist down length, judged to be due to damage rather than initial manufacture

Langdon Bay

Median-winged axes (Nos 1–61, possibly Nos 62–63; Figs 3.1–3.6)

A substantial number of axes in the Langdon Bay assemblage may be classified to the median-winged type, which cannot be confused with any contemporary palstaves. In general, they seem to be rather standardised in form and size; there are just minor variations in the line and form of the sides and the butt notch. The relatively short blades present on some probably result from greater use, for they tend to be associated with more abrupt edge bevels which are not otherwise a characteristic of the type (but note No 36). The centre of the body, at the wings, is typically very gently waisted, while the blade tends to describe a slight bowed flare and end in a near-straight cutting edge. Two exhibit stronger waisting at the middle (Nos 22 and 38). Four examples have evidence for transverse side bevels at the wings, while seven show longitudinal side hollows. Setting aside highly eroded examples, one median-winged implement must have started as a diminutive (No 50).

There are 45 complete examples and 16 fragments with diagnostic features. At least two blade fragments (Nos 62 and 63) also seem likely to derive from this axe type. A further complete median-winged axe, in private ownership (no catalogue number), is reported to be from the Langdon assemblage. It is in similar condition.

Median-winged axes on the Continent are quite varied in detailed shape. The smooth profile of the large median-winged axes from Langdon Bay is consistent with the Swalmen variant of Kibbert's Grigny type (1984, 48, nos 76–84), as opposed to the Altrip and Nauheim variants with offset profiles (Kibbert 1984, nos 92–111). Good parallels from near parts of the Continent include an axe from the

Erondelle hoard, Somme (O'Connor 1980, fig 36B, 5) and the Seine at Paris (*ibid*, fig 37, 3). Although Langdon Bay No 50 is a slender example, its form is still consistent with a small variant of the Grigny type (Kibbert 1984, nos 87–91).

Unattributed axe blade fragments (Nos 64–67; Fig 3.6)

Four axe blade fragments are too small and/or eroded to be sure of their origins.

Palstaves (Nos 68–117; Figs 3.6–3.10)

The Langdon assemblage contains 50 certain palstaves, most of them complete in the body with just the loop damaged. As few as six have a greater part than the loop missing, No 68 being a blade edge fragment with evidence for a mid-ridge, a feature which places it as a palstave. Loops seem to have been particularly vulnerable to reduction by the erosion agencies and cannot be used to judge original completeness. However, once reduced to mere stumps, they were resistant to further erosion relative to the surrounding surfaces. Since all palstaves in fair or better condition have evidence for a former loop, unlooped palstaves would seem not to have been represented in the assemblage.

The thin flange crests were also susceptible to rapid abrasion, which may not always have acted evenly along their length. Therefore, flange shape is not very useful for classification here. On axes in fair to good condition, stop shape (in plan view) can usually be assessed with reasonable confidence, although these too can be modified by marked reduction. Among the better-preserved examples, four types of palstave may be discerned.

Type 1 (Nos 69–74; possibly Nos 75–79; Fig 3.7)

The defining attributes are a sub-rectangular hafting slot, flattish septum floor in cross section, and a flared but narrow blade. The better-preserved examples carry trident-based designs at the top of the blade; judging by well-preserved terrestrial finds, the motif may be a full trident, stem-less trident or 'ghost-trident', in which the ribs were no longer created, leaving only a pair of triangular depressions. Excluded from this type are any palstaves showing traces of only a medial ridge or rib.

The type tends to have a slight constriction at the head of the blade below the stop. Flange profiles were probably nearly triangular and butts roughly straight. Most have only hints of an edge bevel surviving, but No 71 has a steep edge bevel impinging on the tail of the decoration, presumably the result of much reworking. No 78, an uncertain member of the type, has an even stumpier blade.

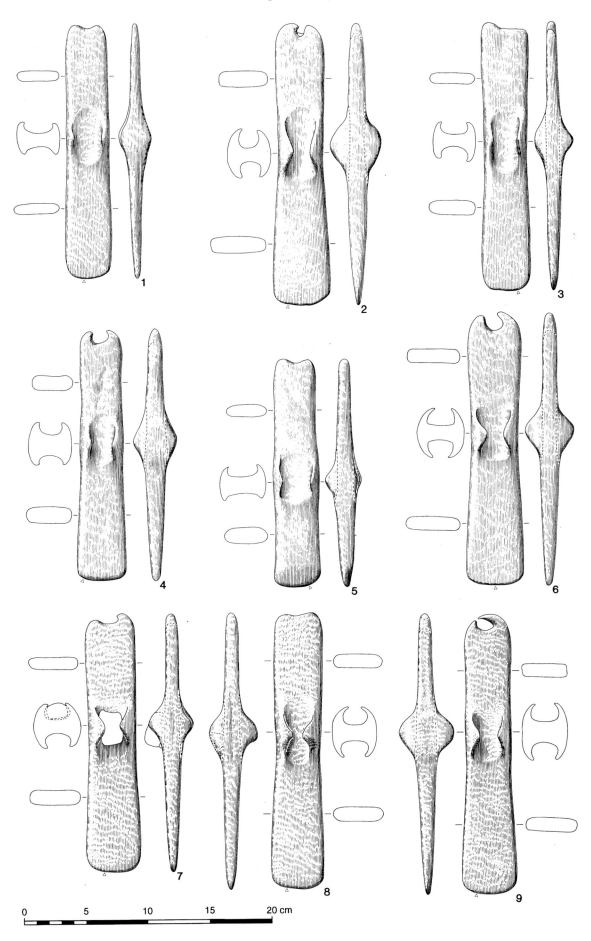

Fig 3.1 Langdon Bay: median-winged axes (Nos 1–9)

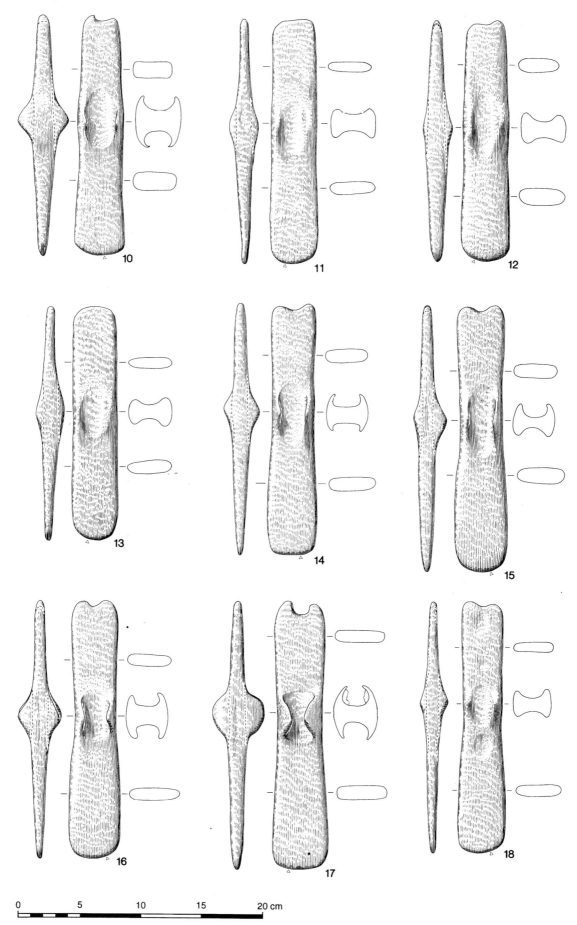

Fig 3.2 *Langdon Bay: median-winged axes (Nos 10–18)*

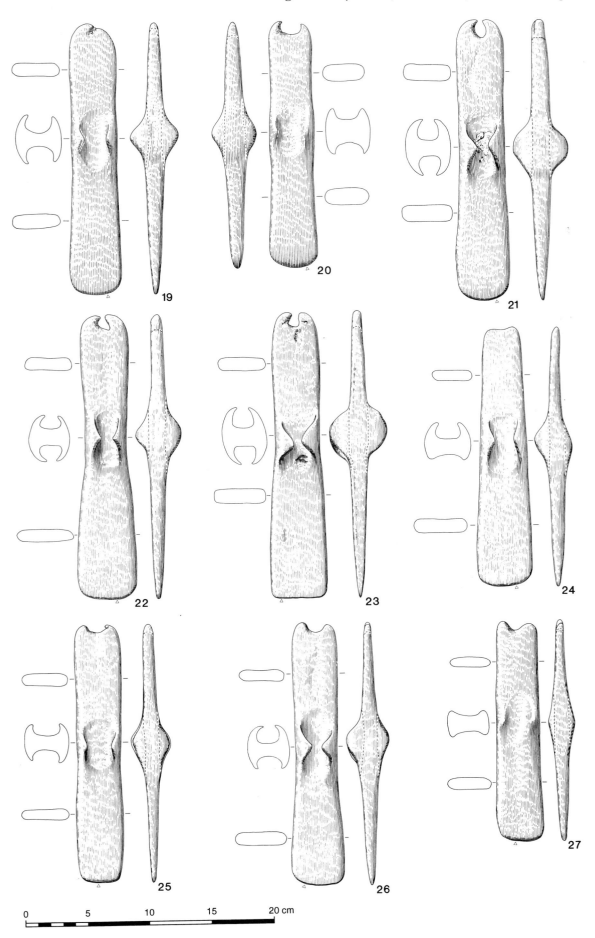

Fig 3.3   Langdon Bay: median-winged axes (Nos 19–27)

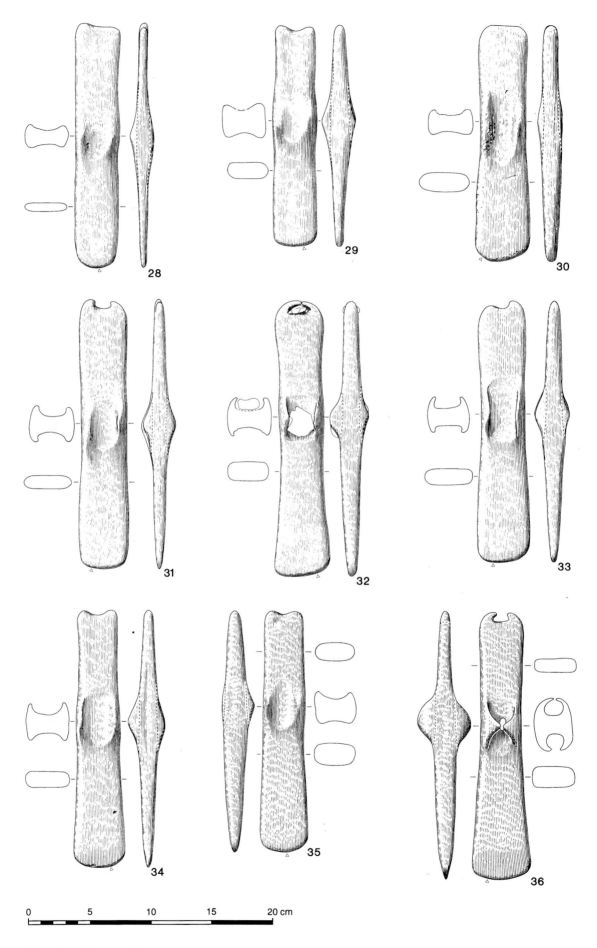

Fig 3.4   Langdon Bay: median-winged axes (Nos 28–36)

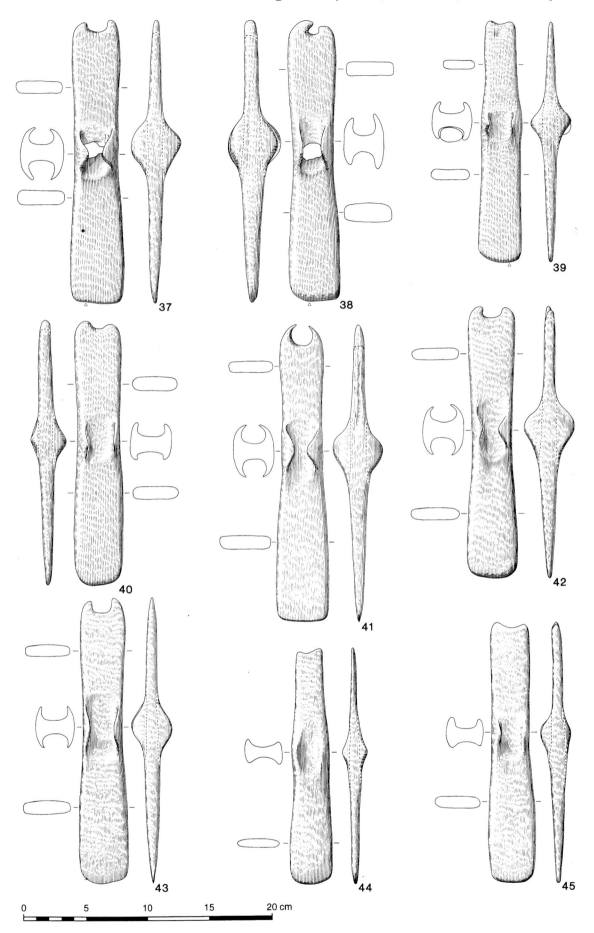

Fig 3.5 Langdon Bay: median-winged axes (Nos 37–45)

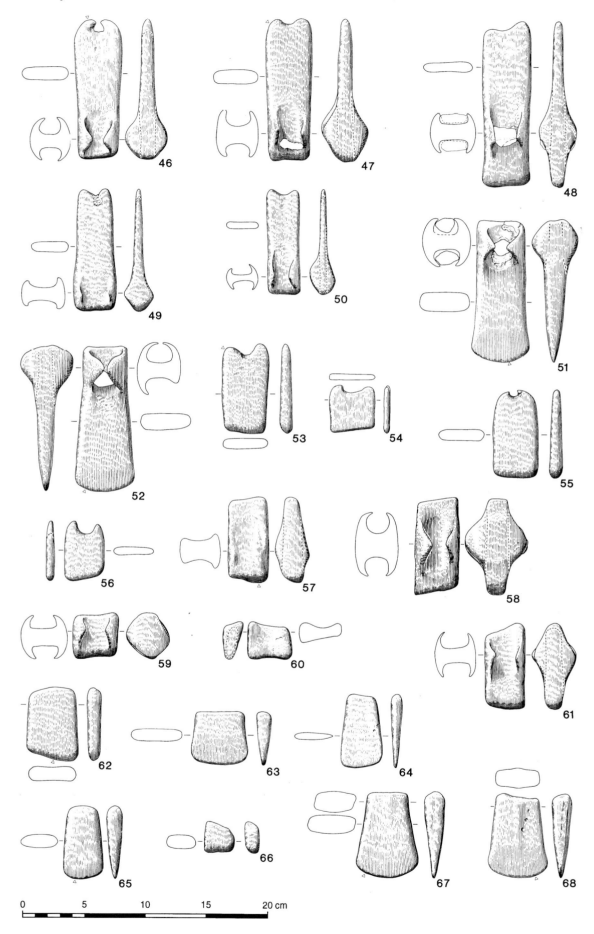

Fig 3.6   Langdon Bay: median-winged axes (Nos 46–61, ?Nos 62–63); unattributed axe fragments (Nos 64–67); palstave fragment (No 68)

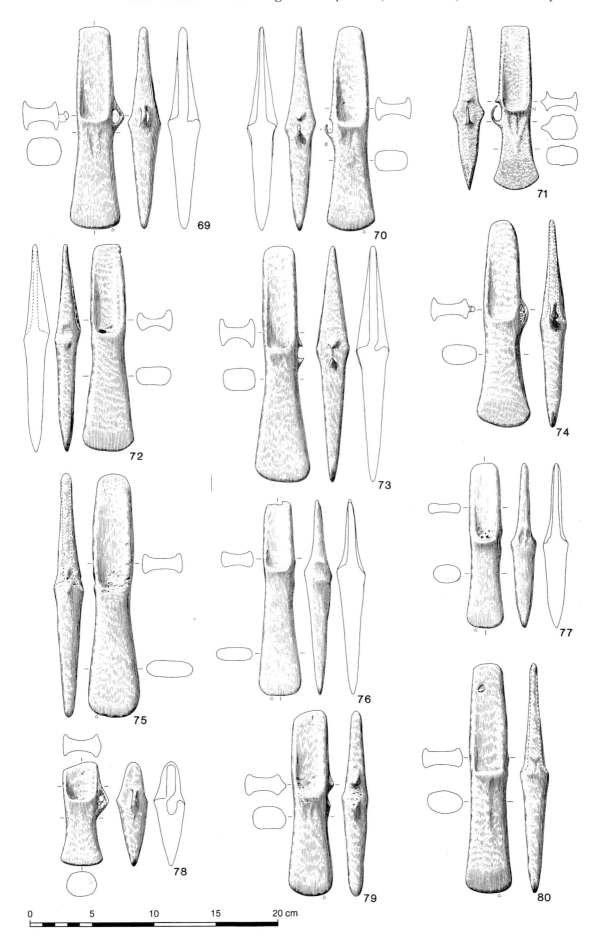

Fig 3.7 Langdon Bay: palstaves, type 1 (Nos 69–74, ?75–79); type 2 (No 80)

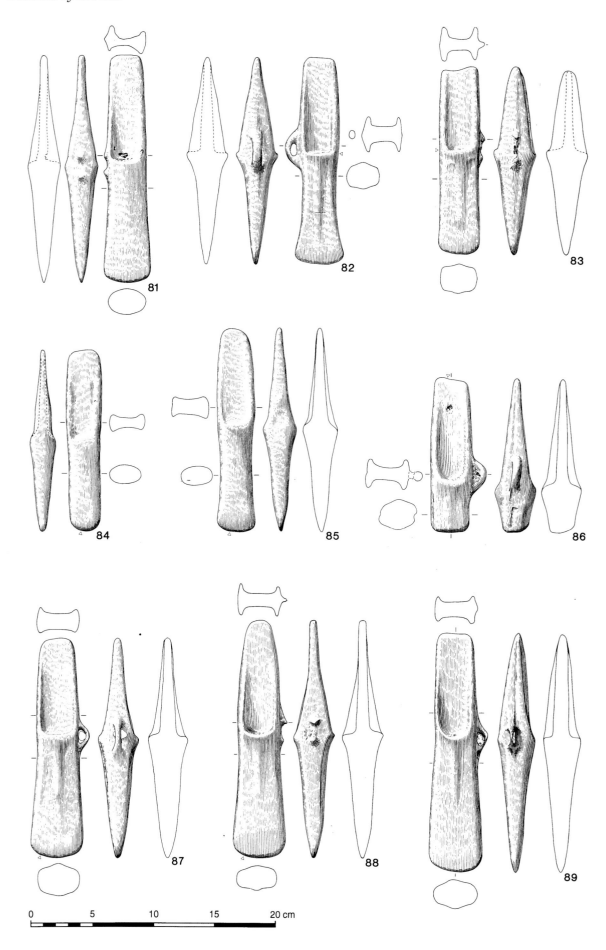

Fig 3.8   Langdon Bay: palstaves, type 2 (Nos 81–83, ?84–86); type 3 (Nos 87–89)

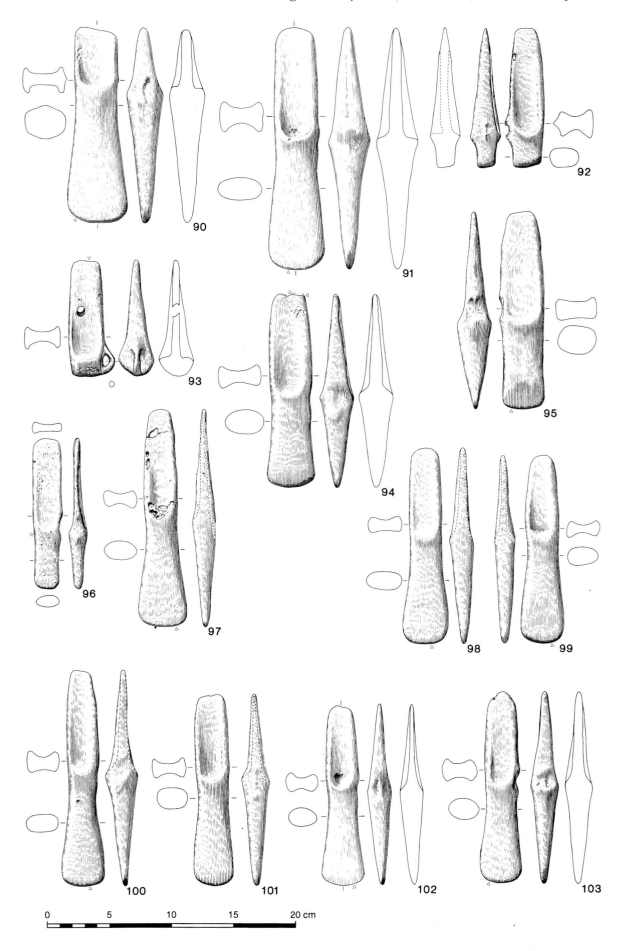

Fig 3.9 Langdon Bay: palstaves, ?type 3 (Nos 90–91); type 4 (No 92); unattributed to type (Nos 93–103)

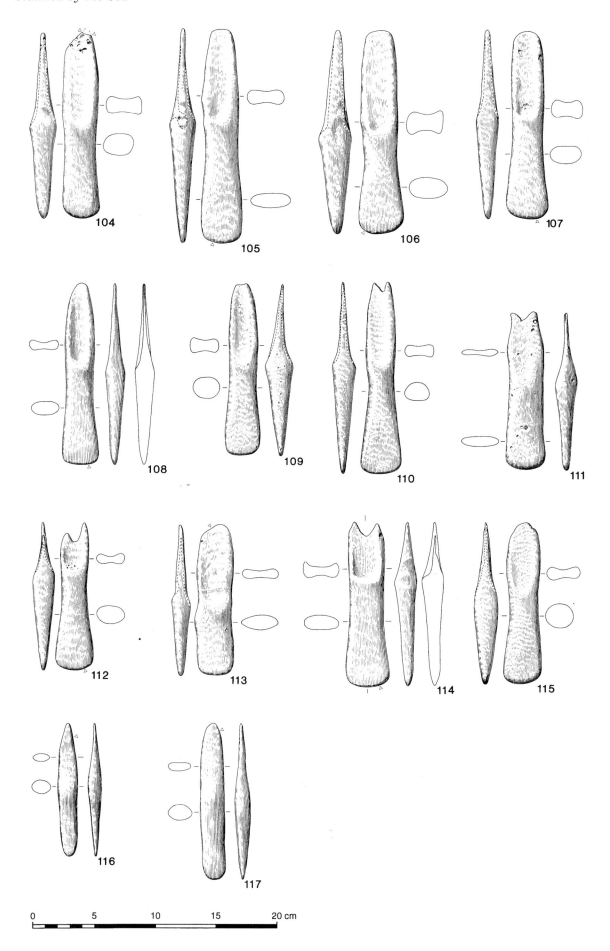

Fig 3.10   Langdon Bay: unattributed palstaves (Nos 104–117)

Type 2 (Nos 80–83; possibly Nos 84–86; Figs 3.7–3.8)

Like type 1, these have flattish septum floors and sub-rectangular hafting slots. Blades, however, are parallel or marginally flared and a single medial ridge or rib is discernible on the faces where condition is not too poor. No 82 shows that this feature can be a pronounced rib running the length of the blade, but others might have been slighter and shorter. It also shows that some at least of this class had angular stop/flange junctions and gently convex-triangular flange profiles leading to protuberant stops. Butts would seem to be essentially square. Traces of edge bevels survive on some.

This group seems to vary in mass, some being relatively lightweight while one possible example (No 86) approaches the heavier type 3. There is also a little variation in overall shape, from parallel-sided to gently sinuous bodies (especially No 82).

Type 3 (Nos 87–89; possibly 90–91; Figs 3.8–3.9)

This type is characterised above all by heavy wide blades with a distinct flare, although they still fall within the generic 'narrow-bladed' class of palstaves. Blade sides are close to straight. They carry moderately stout triangular midribs which taper out halfway down the blade, or a little beyond. Stops are gently curved or, in the case of the fairly eroded example No 89, well curved. The narrow and arched butt shape of No 88 is likely to be due to or accentuated by differential reduction. Septum floors, again, tend to be flat.

Type 4 (No 92; Fig 3.9)

One palstave in fair condition cannot be placed in types 1–3 on account of its well-curved stop in combination with a U-shaped septum cross section. Although most of the blade is missing, this clearly belongs to a slender form of palstave similar in proportion to types 1 and 2 rather than type 3. There is no certain decoration, but traces of a depression exist on one face below the stop. The under-stop profile turns out rather abruptly. Similar examples may exist among the more eroded unattributed palstaves, such as No 102.

Unattributed palstaves (Nos 93–117; Figs 3.9–3.10)

Twenty-five palstaves are too heavily rolled (or in one case too incomplete) to allow attribution to one of the above classes. Several seem to have been fairly slender varieties with gently flared bodies not unlike type 1 (eg Nos 97–103), but attribution is precluded by the loss of detail for stop and septum morphology and decoration. Two are rather broad and chunky, despite being heavily rolled (Nos 94–95), and may correspond to type 3, but if so, their blades would

appear to have been much shortened by reworking. In contrast, another is unusually slender (No 96) and may have been of palstave-chisel proportions, even though the evidence for a former loop makes it exceptional for that class of object (but see one example from the Seine at Tourville-la-Rivière, Seine-Maritime – Gabillot 2003, 350, fig 79.4).

Two objects are so excessively rolled that they have become fusiform bars (Nos 116–117). However, the different stages of reduction apparent within the Langdon palstave series allow these to be identified as extremely abraded palstaves.

Langdon type 1 palstaves have many similarities with the classic, narrow-bladed Norman type, but there are critical, if subtle, differences in style. The rectangular haft-slot and trident or stem-less trident motif are regularly found together on another form of Norman palstave of the Baux-Sainte-Croix phase, but these are virtually all broad-bladed, even the occasional examples with loops (Briard and Verron 1976a, 94, fig 3 right). The specific combination of features seen in Langdon type 1 – narrow blade, rectangular haft-slot, loop, and trident/related motif can be identified among Margaret Smith's Transitional group (Smith 1959b), as defined in Britain.

Langdon types 2 and 3 would fall within a single type in past classification schemes. Indeed, in terms of British material they too come under Transitional palstaves, which have only been sub-classified in the north, where types Shelf, Roundhay, Penrith, and Silsden contain good matches for the specific features of both Langdon types (Schmidt and Burgess 1981, nos 846–873, 883–899, 906–910, 921–926). This northern series includes variations in the blade decoration from medial ridge to midrib to stout triangular rib, thus reflecting the range at Langdon. In continental Europe the obvious region with closely comparable narrow-bladed palstaves is north-western France, especially Brittany, where they have been termed the Rosnoën type (Briard 1965, 155–7; Briard and Verron 1976a, 105–8). The type seems to continue little altered into *Bronze Final II*, where it appears in the Breton type-hoard of Saint-Brieuc-des-Iffs, Île-et-Vilaine. Again, it is clear from published examples that these palstaves vary in proportions and exact form.

The Langdon type 4 palstave, although fragmentary, can almost certainly be identified as belonging to the classic Norman narrow-bladed type because of its round-ended haft-slot, gracile proportions, and loop (Briard and Verron 1976a, 94, fig 3 left; O'Connor 1980, 47–9). This type is characteristic of the Baux-Sainte-Croix phase, broadly preceding Rosnoën/Penard, but this piece could easily be a scrap survival within the Langdon assemblage.

Socketed axes and chisels (Nos 118–29; Fig 3.11)

Twelve objects belong to this group of axe-like socketed tools. In only one example does the main body survive intact and, in ten cases, the damage is

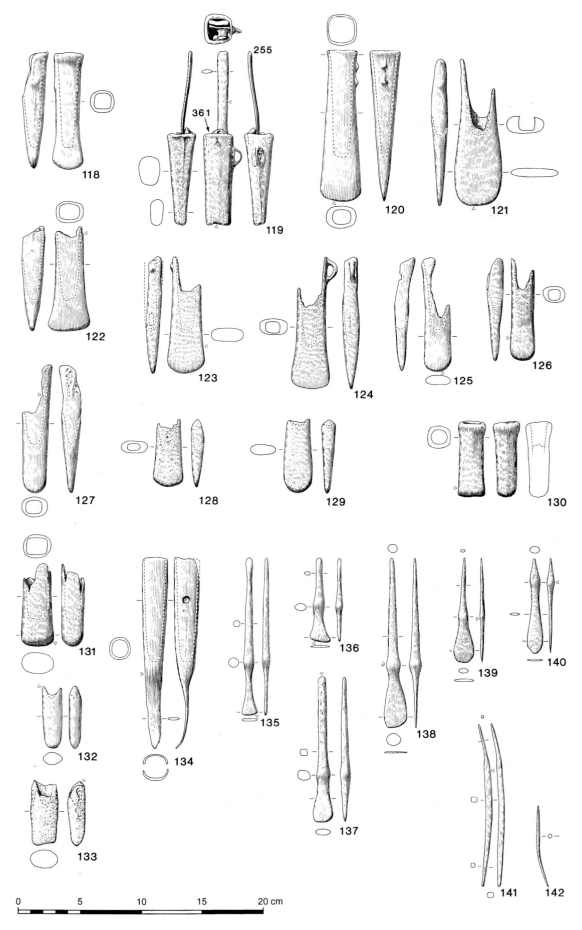

Fig 3.11 Langdon Bay: socketed axes/chisels (Nos 118–129); socketed hammers (Nos 130–133); socketed hooked knife (No 134); tanged-and-collared chisels (Nos 135–140); awls (Nos 141–142)

at the mouth end which is made more vulnerable by the thin socket walls. While the tools would obviously have been susceptible to this kind of damage during use, it must be suspected that much of the damage seen was suffered on the seabed. The one exception to this pattern of damage is No 119, where the packing of the socket with other objects would have helped the mouth to resist denting, fracture, and subsequent attrition on the sea floor.

No examples definitely lacked loops and six have positive evidence for a loop; they are placed a little below the mouth moulding, which is typical of early socketed forms (Taunton/Baux-Sainte-Croix and Penard/Rosnoën). Mouths and upper bodies are nearly square in shape, a feature that gives rise to the term 'early square-section' for this family. They are also known as the Taunton-Hademarschen type because of strong stylistic connections between the series in Britain and a group in northern Europe (Butler 1963, 75–81; Rowlands 1976, 41–3). A few of the Langdon examples retain evidence for edge bevels and associated modest expansion of the blade tips. Socket interiors consistently taper towards the lower end.

Owing to their fragmentary nature, most of the Langdon examples lack useful defining characteristics. Those in better condition are too few to suggest grouping, but three 'forms' are worthy of description to facilitate external comparisons and demonstrate some variation in detail.

Form 1

Implement 118 has a simple flared collar of moderate depth; the body is near parallel, but in fact is gently waisted low down, a feature seen on other early socketed axes. About halfway down, the faces bear signs of a transverse step or hollow. Two fragmentary axes (Nos 125 and 126) bear similar features low on their blades, producing a constriction in profile. Erosion cannot be ruled out, but this feature is known on some Taunton phase examples (see below).

Form 2

No 119 has a small beaded moulding which is unlikely to have been severely reduced by abrasion; again, the body tapers gently as far as the break. The faces bear hints of an original medial ridge, but the degree of erosion precludes certainty. If originally present, this feature and the narrow mouth moulding would suggest comparison with the axe in the Penard hoard, Glamorganshire (Savory 1980, 180, fig 32.1).

Form 3

No 120 seems to have had a small bead moulding like that on No 119, but its body is instead steadily flared from mouth to cutting edge. This makes for a generally heavier-looking implement. Fragments 121 and 123 also show clearly flared bodies, the former of which would have been heavier still prior to erosion.

Socketed hammers (Nos 130–133; Fig 3.11)

Two objects are unequivocally hammers, while two eroded fragments (Nos 132 and 133) have subtleties of form which correspond much better with hammers than with axes. The term 'hammer' refers here to any tool with a flattened working end, regardless of the surface area. The complete example (No 130) has a classic form with sub-square section and a shallow collar at the mouth with a possible triangular moulding beneath, a feature known on some parallels. It currently weighs 96g, whereas the similar mouth-damaged example (No 131) would have been a little heavier originally. Of the fragments, No 132 would be important in suggesting that more delicate hammers/punches were also represented, providing that its flattish working end is not the product of abrasion. In the latter case, it might perhaps have started as a stout socketed chisel such as seen in the Kilnhurst hoard, south Yorkshire (Smith 1958, GB 41.3).

Socketed hooked knife (No 134; Fig 3.11)

This is an unusual implement in its current form and it is not absolutely certain that the curve of the blade is original rather than due to damage. The socket is still largely intact, but the blade may have been whittled down preferentially because of its thinness. It is so fragile at one point that it has broken across subsequent to retrieval. The socket is sub-square in section rather than circular and is furnished with a pair of peg holes nearer the mouth than the blade.

Despite uncertainty about the curve of the blade, the socket form on this implement would be hard to parallel on any straight-bladed socketed knife and on balance it can be regarded as a hooked knife, an extremely rare type. It resembles the example in the Fresné-la-Mère hoard, Calvados (Evans 1881, 209 fig 247), rather than the few from Scotland which are differently proportioned and less strongly curved (*ibid*, figs 248–9).

Tanged-and-collared chisels (Nos 135–140; Fig 3.11)

The Langdon assemblage contains six examples of this small tool type. This is of considerable importance because the addition of a collar or swelling to simple tanged chisels was thought, before the Langdon discovery, to have happened a little later in the Bronze Age. Furthermore, the group is important in presenting a range of sizes and detailed forms, even allowing for differential erosion.

Overall length is very variable, to judge from the five apparently complete examples (Nos 135–139). The stop is always in the form of a biconical swelling. Tang and stop sections are rhombic on No 137, but are otherwise oval, though potentially eroded from more angular forms. The slightly expanded tang end on No 135 is likely to be original, as this is the thinnest part and thus is most susceptible to erosion.

Two blade shapes might tentatively be ventured, although the possibility must be borne in mind that some individual blades have been modified by marine action. Nos 135 and 136 show concave-sided blades, but with different proportions. The remaining four all exhibit spatulate or crinoline blades, again with variable proportions; the condition of No 138 allows at least this one to be regarded as virtually unmodified.

Awls, rods, shanks and possible anvil spikes (Nos 141–145, 147, 149; Figs 3.11–3.12)

Shanks and rods with little by way of diagnostic features are especially hard to classify when fragmentary or highly abraded. No 141 is in good condition, with a central part of square section. It tapers to two pointed ends, but the sudden narrowing towards the upper end (as illustrated) is unusual and might suggest that this part of the implement had been exposed and subject to abrasion while the remainder was protected by silt. Nevertheless, the implement can be described as an 'awl', possibly a double-ended form. The smaller piece with a round section throughout, No 142, is less certainly an awl.

No 143 may well be only a fragment of the original object and, hence, could be the tip of a pin (covered below) or the working end of an awl. The relatively constant thicknesses of Nos 144 and 145, both potentially fragments, are more in keeping with pin shanks, although the curve of the latter would also admit the possibility of it being some other form of thin-rod ornament, such as a bracelet.

A curious feature of No 144 is the flattening of one end; if original, it is not easily placed, but one possible parallel presents itself in the contemporary Bishopsland hoard, from Co Kildare. Here a thin instrument with a rectangular section has a slightly cupped flattened end with an obtuse point (Eogan 1983, 226, fig 10.16). Eogan describes it as a 'toilet article (?)' (*ibid*, 37), but another possibility is that it served as a small spoon-bit. A similar instrument comes from the Curgy hoard in Saône-et-Loire (Gaucher 1981, 202 fig 93 D1); it is 130mm long and very thin shanked with only marginal expansion for the flattened end, and is described by Gaucher as a spatula. An alternative identification for Langdon Bay No 144 is a roll-headed pin which has lost most of its head, for on this pin type the shank becomes flattened as it approaches the head. This type does

occur in contemporary contexts on the Continent, as in the Villethierry hoard, Yonne (Mordant *et al* 1976), and a small number are known from Britain (see below).

The relatively chunky tapering objects Nos 147 and 149 cannot be pins or awls. The sub-rectangular section and shape of No 147 suggest that it could be the tang end of a tanged tool, but it is far heavier than the tangs on the associated tanged-and-collared chisels (Nos 135–140) and would have to come from a different variety, perhaps a lugged stake/chisel (eg in the Lusmagh hoard, Co Offaly; Brailsford 1953, fig 12.6). In fact, the Lusmagh material offers another possibility for Langdon Bay Nos 147 and 149, as it has a three-spiked anvil whose spikes present a similar morphology. Other spiked anvils occur in contemporary hoards at Fresné-la-Mère, Calvados, and Coray, Finistère, and in the river group from the Seine at Bardouville, Seine-Maritime (Briard *et al* 1980, 62–4, fig 4).

Spurred ring-pendant (No 146; Fig 3.12)

No 146 has been termed a 'spur' simply on the basis that it tapers evenly and has a crisp D section, which rules out pins and awls. It is not absolutely clear that this has broken off a larger object, but this is likely because these very specific features can actually be matched on some continental pendants in which this spur projects from a simple ring. These occur, for example, in two east French hoards: Cannes-Écluse hoard I, Seine-et-Marne (Gaucher and Robert 1967, 191, fig 26.5–8), and Villethierry, Yonne (Mordant *et al* 1976, 191, fig 168.25–27). One of the Cannes-Écluse examples has a second ring surviving interlinked with the spurred ring and these may have dangled from longer chains of interlinked rings (arrangements of composite ornaments such as these can be seen, for example, in Eogan 2001). The complete spurs in the French hoards cited are 34mm and 40mm long respectively. This length compares well with the Langdon piece's surviving length of 41mm; widths are also similar. Moreover, two or more transverse ribs or nicks cross the spur closest to the ring and one such rib survives on the Langdon object. There is a similar spurred ring from Courchapont, Doubs (Bocquet 1969, 293), and a slightly differently styled but still tapering example in the Chailloué I hoard, Orne (Verney and Verron 1998, no 7).

Flesh-hook (No 148; Fig 3.12)

The thick-shanked and tapering object No 148 is clearly too thick to serve as a dress pin and it might conceivably be a securing pin for vehicle or vessel. The shank is sub-quadrangular in section, possibly well weathered, but the bend towards the tip appears to be original rather than a result of damage, for there is no evidence of cracking. These features and

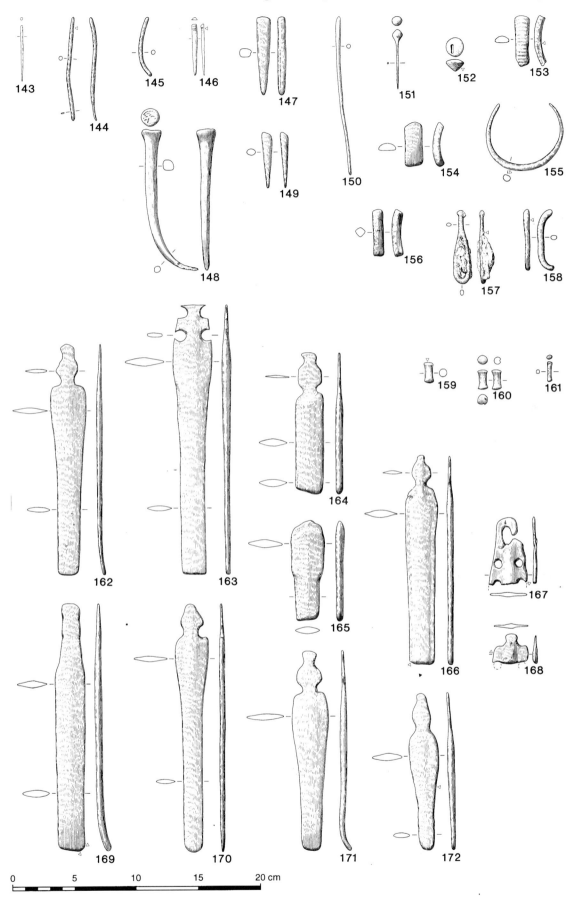

Fig 3.12 Langdon Bay: awls/rods/shanks (Nos 143–145); ring-pendant spur (No 146); ?anvil spikes (Nos 147, 149); ?flesh-hook (No 148); pins (Nos 150–152); bracelets (Nos 153–156); loop fastener/fittings (Nos 157, ?158); rivets (Nos 159–161); swords (Nos 162–169, ?170–172)

the swelling at the top end have encouraged the view that this is the prong of an early style of flesh-hook, class 2 (Needham and Bowman 2005; Bowman and Needham 2007); this identification makes the supposition that a socket has broken off the implement at the point where it met the base of the prong. If this is the case, the fracture has been well rounded by abrasion.

Pins (Nos 150–152; Fig 3.12)

None of these three pieces is likely to be intact, but all can be identified as 'dress pins' with reasonable confidence. (Note also the alternative identifications of Nos 143–145, covered above, as pins.) The only feature on the 125mm-long shank of No 150 is the gentle swelling towards one end; this might be the eroded remains of a cylindrical head, but could equally be a swelling within the shank or even an artefact of differential erosion. No 151, in contrast, has a remarkably short shank and a clear biconical head, a head form known widely on Bronze Age pins. In fact, the parallels do sometimes come with short shanks; for example, among several from the site of Saint-Pierre-en-Chastre, Oise, one is as short as 54mm (Blanchet 1984, fig 149.7), only a little longer than the surviving 48mm of Langdon Bay No 151. The conical shape of No 152 is thought to represent a slightly different head form. While the lack of any shank stump might seem to leave its identification as a pin less secure, there is in fact a scar on the flatter face which probably resulted from the join where a head was slid over the top of a separate shank. This type of union, where the head has been cast on to a pre-formed shank, is familiar among certain continental pins, notably those with comparable conical heads in the Villethierry hoard, Yonne (Mordant *et al* 1976; Armbruster and Pernot 2006).

Bracelets (Nos 153–156; Fig 3.12)

One bracelet is unbroken, but probably somewhat reduced by erosion, and a further two or three survive as fragments. As far as can be ascertained, the complete one (No 155) had simple tapering terminals and a round or an oval section. It is not certain that it was quite such a simple form prior to erosion, but there is no difficulty matching it in some phases of the Bronze Age. There are a reasonable number of similar bracelets, albeit of varied thickness and cross section, in Taunton stage hoards (Rowlands 1976, 93, type 2, pls 11–16; part of Smith's [1959b] 'ornament horizon'), but more significant for our seabed context are parallels in Penard or Rosnoën associations on the respective sides of the Channel. In Britain the hoards of Croxton, Norfolk (Needham 1990b, 255, fig 2.3), and Wallington, Northumberland (Burgess 1968b, 14, fig 10), can be cited, although their terminals tend to taper only slightly. In Brittany there are good examples in

the hoards from Plougoulm, Finistère (Briard *et al* 1980, 56, fig 2.8), and Fourdan, Morbihan (Briard *et al* 1982–3, 37–8, fig 3), while the fifteen examples in the Villethierry hoard, Yonne (Mordant *et al* 1976, 184, fig 162), cannot go unmentioned. Some of these are relatively slender and allow the possibility that Langdon Bay No 155 may not have lost much to erosion. A similar slender bracelet from Solent Water is dealt with in Chapter 4.

The sub-D sections and extant curvatures of Nos 153 and 154 are typical of many bracelet types of this phase of the Bronze Age, while the continuous transverse ribbing on the former is also an established if not especially widespread feature. It can be matched in the Chailloué I hoard, Orne (Verney and Verron 1998, no 8), and in the Plougoulm hoard, Finistère (Briard *et al* 1980, 59, fig 2, 10), where the ribbing occurs in intermittent bands with plain areas between; both hoards include other bracelets. In fact, the ribbing on No 153 is identical to type Publy, which is well known in the east of France, especially in the Jura, and occurs in the important *Bronze Final I* hoard of Cannes-Écluse 1 (Seine-et-Marne; Gaucher and Robert 1967, 192–5) as well as in the above-mentioned Chailloué I hoard.

The quadrangular-sectioned fragment, No 156, is also a strong candidate for being from a bracelet if its curvature is original. The alternative would be that it belonged to a ring-handle from a cauldron such as was present in the Salcombe assemblage (below). If it is indeed a bracelet, too little survives to know whether it is from a simple penannular bar bracelet or from a more elaborate form such as a 'Sussex loop'.

Loop fasteners/fittings (Nos 157–158; Fig 3.12)

Although much concretion is attached to the tear-shaped object No 157, it is clear that it was a cast loop leading into a tang with a knobbed terminal. Its form would best serve as a belt fitting. This is an object type which has yet to find a parallel on British soil, but the recognition of occasional examples in France begins to suggest that it was an established type there. Three of the parallels identified are almost identical: they come from a hoard at Rigny-sur-Arroux, Saône-et-Loire (Gaucher 1981, 124–5, figs 35–6A, 368), and cave assemblages at Buissières, Meyrannes, Gard (Gomez de Soto 1995, 184–5, fig 80.5), and Hasard, Tharoux, Gard (Escalon de Fonton 1970, 539, fig 48.5).

Langdon Bay No 158 would appear to represent a different type of fitting. Both ends are assumed to be breaks and, if the tighter curves adjacent are original, they suggest that it is from some kind of non-circular loop or appendage, rather than a pin or bracelet. One possibility is that it is the bow of a simple bow-brooch (see, for example, west-central European brooches published by Betzler [1974, nos 1, 7, 15, 154, 181, 185]), but this must remain tentative in the absence of critical features. Such brooches first appear at the beginning of the Urnfield culture (Reinecke Bronze D) and are thus broadly contemporary with Penard/Rosnoën.

Separate rivets (Nos 159–161; Fig 3.12)

Three loose rivets were recovered, although none survived *in situ* in any implement, undoubtedly because erosion of the rivets themselves would have quickly allowed the expanded heads to drop through their simultaneously eroding holes. All three have round sections, although No 160 is notched on one side. The two thick rivets are classic for certain types of rapier as well as for some early swords, notably the Rosnoën type. The slender example, No 161, is more likely to have secured the tang of a small tool to its handle, or even a decorative fitting to its mount.

Swords, rapiers, dirks, knives (Nos 162–348; Figs 3.12–3.18)

The assemblage contains 187 objects that may be variously described as swords, rapiers, dirks, and knives. The vast majority are fragmentary and, when lacking well-preserved hilt features, can be very difficult to attribute to broad functional classes with any confidence. Blade width is important for distinguishing between 'rapiers/dirks' and 'swords' in the Penard/Rosnoën repertoire, although it must be borne in mind that some early weapons accepted as swords, notably the Rosnoën type, are intermediate between heavy-blade swords and rapiers. Reworking of blades can obviously further complicate relationships. If we look at the Rosnoën hoard itself, crucial because of the large number of sword-like weapons it contained, most of the large weapons have blades broader than 23mm (away from tip and hilt) and these can all be regarded as 'swords', or broken blades thereof that have been reworked (Briard 1958a; Nallier and Le Goffic 2008). On the other hand, the long weapons in that hoard that are less wide have both more pronounced shoulders and two-notched hilts, features appropriate to Group IV notched-butt rapiers (Nallier and Le Goffic 2008, nos 36 and 47); the same is true of some of the shorter weapons (eg Briard 1958a, nos 10, 12, and 15).

Most of the undiagnostic blade fragments in the Langdon assemblage are narrow to medium in width, up to 21mm. The few broader blade fragments with maximum surviving widths of 21–27mm, Nos 177–183, are the most likely swords. However, some narrower examples must also be from swords, to judge from the fact that blades attached to diagnostic sword hilts can be reduced to as little as 15mm in width when heavily eroded.

Around fourteen blades seem to be close to their original lengths. Intriguingly, these split into two size categories: six are between 291mm and 462mm in length, while eight are between 78mm and 177mm. The interval between these two groups is 114mm, contrasting with average internal intervals of 14mm among the shorter implements and 34mm among the longer ones. It is difficult to know how significant this bimodality is in a broader context. Burgess and Gerloff (1981, 4–5) found 'no marked dividing line' in their analysis of the corpus of British and Irish Middle Bronze Age daggers, dirks, and rapiers, although this may be the result of conflating different phase populations together (Acton, Taunton, and Penard). Nevertheless, the two size ranges seen in the Langdon material do provide a ready distinction of convenience between swords/rapiers (>290mm) and dirks/knives (<180mm).

As already detailed, surviving blade width is not guaranteed to distinguish between swords and rapiers; instead, an identifiable hilt form must be present. Virtually all rapiers and dirks of the Penard/Rosnoën phase have just two rivet emplacements penetrating the hilt plate – either as notches or perforations just inset from the sides – whereas swords usually have four or more rivet emplacements. Occasionally they can have just three. When only two notches are present, as in the case of two sword-width blades in the Rosnoën hoard (Briard 1958, nos 3 and 11), it may be that a sword blade fragment has been rehafted. So, for Langdon, where it seems that the whole hilt is present, it is possible to attribute even eroded examples to sword or rapier/dirk/knife with a degree of confidence.

All but one of the Langdon hilts (No 167) show notches rather than holes for the rivets, but in their eroded state it is difficult to be sure what proportion started as notches. Both forms of rivet emplacement can be found on the terrestrial comparative finds. Since complete holes were usually close to the sides, the narrow strip of metal enclosing their outer sides would typically be the first part of the butt to become damaged during use (Ramsey 1993). It is also the area most susceptible to reduction by marine action. In addition to hilt No 167, we can be confident that two more examples started with holes which have subsequently been broken through by damage (Nos 163 and 175).

Swords (Nos 162–169; probably Nos 170–183; possibly Nos 210–214, 217–218, 226; Figs 3.12–3.15)

It appears that swords in the assemblage could have one of two blade sections. Blade type 1 has a lenticular section with a broad, flattish midrib and bevels to relatively narrow, hollowed cutting edges. The breadth of the midrib contrasts with the typical narrower flattened midrib of group IV rapiers/dirks. Where hilts are present (Nos 162–164 and 166) there is usually some indication of a medial ridge running through the riveted zone and onto the very top of the blade. The hilt-plate is usually at its broadest where it meets the blade, but there are no projecting shoulders here. Typically there is a distance of 20mm or more between this junction and

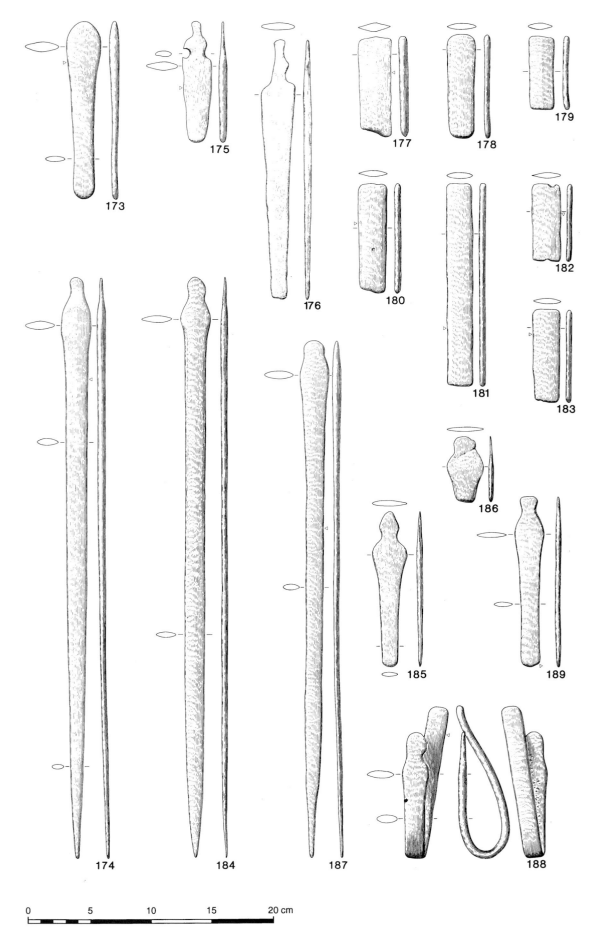

Fig 3.13   Langdon Bay: probable swords (Nos 173–183); rapiers / dirks (Nos 184–189)

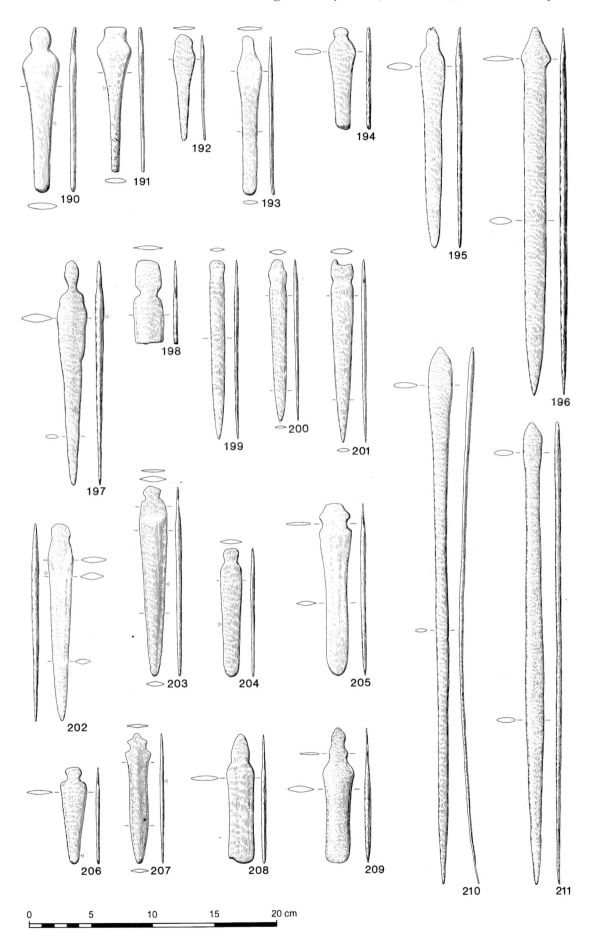

Fig 3.14 Langdon Bay: rapiers / dirks (Nos 190–196); notched-butt dirks / knives (Nos 197–207); ?reworked sword hilts (Nos 208–209); ?swords (210–211)

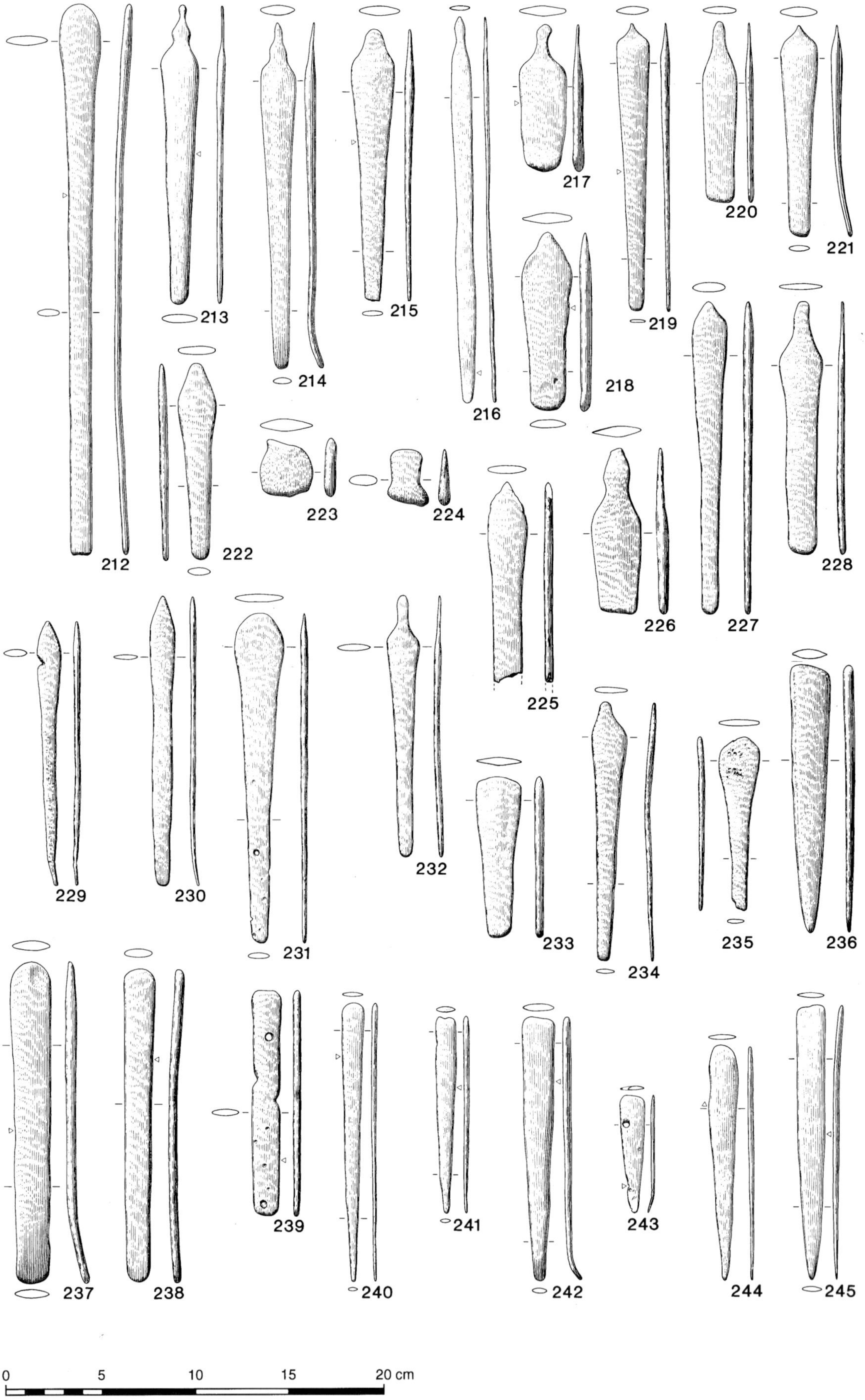

Fig 3.15   Langdon Bay: unclassified or uncertainly classified blades (Nos 212–245)

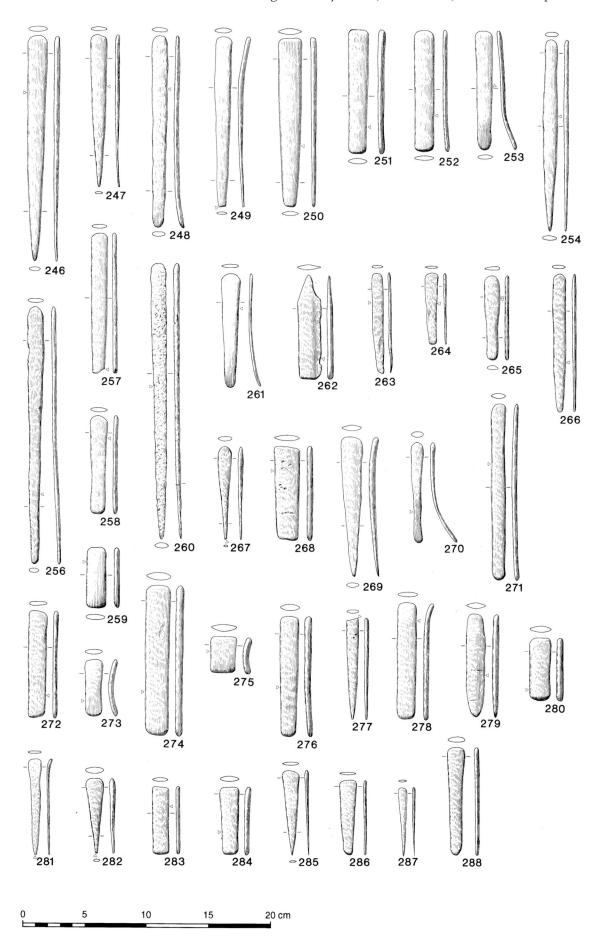

Fig 3.16   Langdon Bay: unclassified blades (Nos 246–288) [for No 255 see Fig 3.11, No 119]

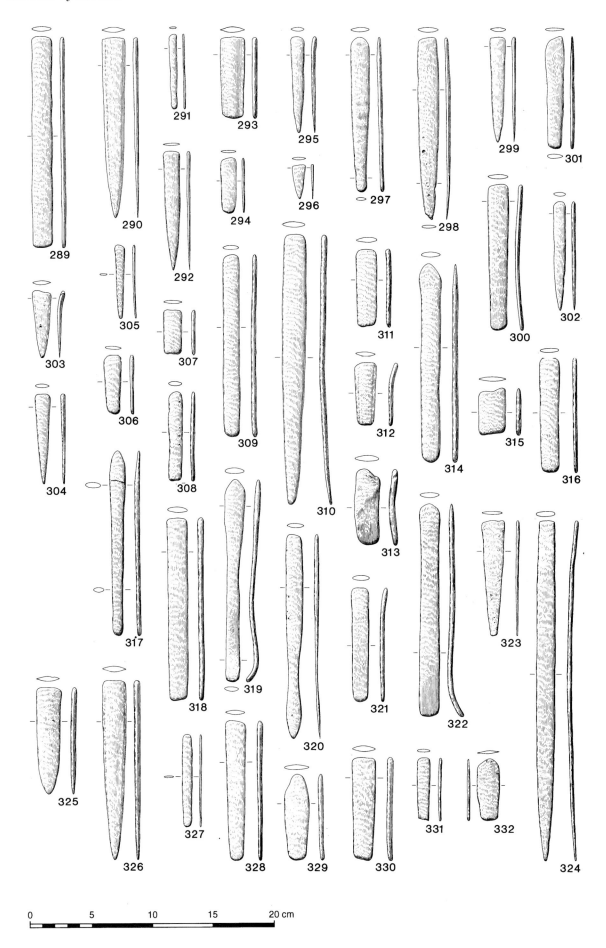

Fig 3.17   Langdon Bay: unclassified blades (Nos 289–332)

the first rivets. Reconstruction would suggest that the hilt shape was originally rectangular to slightly trapezoid. These weapons are readily identifiable as classic Rosnoën type swords (Briard 1965, 162–4; Colquhoun and Burgess 1988, nos 4–11). Rosnoën weapons, although described as 'swords', have blades of width and weight intermediate between contemporary rapiers and 'heavy swords' (Needham 1982b, 16–8 fig 4A). Five blade fragments (Nos 178 and 180–183) and two potentially reworked objects with hilts present (Nos 198 and 209) are also likely to have been from Rosnoën swords.

Langdon blade type 2 is of lozenge section, with a crisp medial ridge throughout the blade. While such a section could easily be obscured by heavy abrasion, it seems highly improbable that a neat lozenge section could be *produced* by this process. Four pieces have convincing lozenge blades, two with hilts (Nos 165 and 169), two without (Nos 177 and 179). Surviving blade widths are between 21 and 27mm. Hilt No 165 has lost its riveted zone, but retains a deep shoulder zone before the blade begins; hints of the edge bevels are present on the blade. The lozenge section seems to be present throughout the 35mm length of blade extant, so this would not be from a classic Rosnoën sword. Instead it is likely to be from a variant such as that from Highclere, Hampshire (Lawson 1984), Cannes-Écluse hoard I, Seine-et-Marne (Gaucher and Robert 1967, fig 24.2), probably Pont-à-Moussel, Meurthe-et-Moselle (Gallay 1988, 62, no 715), or the Rhine at Mainz deposit, Rheinland-Pfalz (Kubach 1973, 300, Abb. 1.1 and 1.3). It is less likely that the blade of No 165 would have been broad enough for one of the heavy sword types (Rixheim-Monza, Grigny, Ambleside-Bardouville).

No 169, on the other hand, with a blade surviving to 25mm, could well have originally measured 30mm or more wide, and is thus comparable to the various heavy swords. The hilt-plate in fact narrows from the blade into a long rectangular tang. Side notches for the rivets are vestigial and may never have been very pronounced. It seems unlikely that the hilt has suffered preferential erosion over the blade on this piece. The combination of long, contracted tang and relatively broad blade are best matched at this date on selected swords within the Grigny and Ambleside-Bardouville groups.

Another hilt fragment, No 167, is well preserved, but unfortunately has lost all of its blade. Although the square arrangement of four rivets within a trapezoidal hilt-plate is familiar on Rosnoën swords, on this piece the hilt-plate continues to taper to accommodate a fifth elongate rivet hole towards its apex. This formation is hard to parallel, but it is nevertheless not an unexpected variation in the context of early sword experimentation in the north-west of Europe and it could just as easily have furnished a heavy blade as one of Rosnoën proportions. The central rivet at the apex recalls that on Rixheim swords, though these have only three in total.

No 174, although having only one pair of rivet emplacements in evidence, seems likely to be a sword

on account of the overall depth of the hilt-plate and the lozenge section of the lower part. It is possible that the same arguments apply to the highly eroded specimens Nos 210–212, 217–218 and 226.

Two-rivet rapiers / dirks (Nos 184–196; Figs 3.13–3.14) – Stuntney and related types

Although variably eroded and of varied size, thirteen weapons are all likely to have started with similar 'bun'-shaped hilt-plates, broadest at the shoulders before tapering strongly into the blade. None of them show any indication that the notches originally started as complete holes. Blade sections are all flattened lenticular, almost certainly reflecting their original form. This group can be classified as Group IV notched-butt rapiers in terms of Burgess and Gerloff's scheme for the British and Irish material (1981, nos 654–874) or *Einfache Kerbdolche mit Absatz* by Gallay for the close French parallels (1988, nos 1051–1062). Erosion of the Langdon material precludes any attempt to place it within the more specific types defined by Burgess and Gerloff.

Miscellaneous notched-butt dirks / knives (Nos 197–207; Fig 3.14)

Although some are superficially similar to the Group IV implements discussed above, all of this miscellaneous group differ in some respect and many are in good condition, so variation cannot be attributed to the vagaries of erosion. Complete examples range in length from 78 to 177mm, so all are in the smaller range in terms of the bimodal distribution described above. Most show just two rivet notches, but two or more had four.

No 197 has a long hilt zone (45mm), recalling the swords, but only two rivet emplacements survive, while the steady taper of the blade to its tip suggests a dirk-like weapon. The distinctive cusping of both edges above the shoulders looks as if it is an original feature, even if reduced in outline a little. There are, in fact, a minority of notched rapiers/dirks that have a more elongate hilt plate than normal, especially among Burgess and Gerloff's Cutts type (1981, nos 766–807), but these are broad as well, so to make this identification one would have to invoke considerable narrowing by erosion without significant loss in length. Occasional weapons in France also show elongate hilt plates with two rivet notches and they are narrower weapons overall (eg Gallay 1988, nos 1060–1, 1068, 1071); the hilt plates of these examples are still not, however, as long as that on Langdon Bay No 197. Another possibility is that it is an eroded example of some triangular, lozenge-section daggers from the Continent which have long sub-triangular hilt-plates (eg Gallay 1988, nos 958–64 – from northern and eastern France).

Although little of the blade survives on No 198,

it is in very good condition to the point that there are traces of the edge bevels. The notches should therefore be original, rather than being broken rivet holes. Taking the notches in combination with its effectively parallel sides, the piece recalls many of the notched blades grouped together by Burgess and Gerloff as having resulted from rehafting (1981, nos 892–950). If not rehafted, however, this piece would seem to be an early lightweight sword similar to those from Methwold and Chatham Dockyard (Colquhoun and Burgess 1988, nos 14–15).

Other small blades at Langdon Bay, such as Nos 199–201 and 204, could likewise be rehafted blade tip fragments from originally longer implements; but this need not universally explain this series of notched-butt blades. Nos 202 and 203, for example, are both in reasonable condition and have thinned and gently tapering hilt-plates with side-notches; this particular form seems less likely to be the product of reworking and they are distinguished from the Group IV rapiers in lacking projecting shoulders. This feature, above all, might distinguish them as knives rather than specifically stabbing weapons. It is noteworthy that there is a fairly large series of similar notched knives/dirks from France (Gallay 1988, nos 1020–50; additional parallels are found in the Chailloué I hoard – Verney and Verron 1998, nos 19–21), some of which give good matches for individual Langdon pieces.

No 205 has a rounded end which retains a sharp edge in profile. One cannot be sure that it is not a reworked piece, but it would appear to have been a neatly shaped knife in its last use-phase. Its slightly cruciform hilt-plate might hint at a four-rivet fixing which would seem unusually stout for a knife. Nevertheless, the same could be said of No 207; and, yet, there is little doubt that this piece is in its original form which is, moreover, unique in the assemblage. It is distinguished by a small leaf-shaped blade with a lozenge section. Hints of edge bevels may be discerned. No good parallels are known from Britain or Ireland and we have to turn to continental types; even so, there are difficulties in finding exact matches. A few small to medium-sized instruments from France have leaf-shaped blades of lozenge section and four-rivet holes in a trapezoid arrangement which, after much erosion, could end up like the notched hilt-plate of No 207 (eg Gallay 1988, nos 651, 652, 661, 675, 680, 692; Billard 1993, 72, fig 14.10 – Seine at Oissel). Indeed, occasional weapons in this suite start with four notches for the rivets, though blades are usually only marginally leaf-shaped (Gallay 1988, nos 689–90, 698–701). It seems probable that Langdon Bay No 207, and perhaps 205 also, derives from this suite of knives/dirks.

Reworked sword hilts? (Nos 208–209; Fig 3.14)

The sub-squared ends of Nos 208 and 209, in both cases thinned to a sharp edge (and not, therefore, abraded breaks), suggest a particular form of cutting instrument not intended for stabbing or piercing. The squared end could have been part of the original design, but it has been noted above that No 209 at least could have begun life as a sword and, if well denuded, No 208 might have been similar in the hilt-plate.

Unclassified blades and fragments (Nos 210–348; Figs 3.14–3.18)

Of the examples grouped here, eight have already been mentioned above as possible swords; but, for the remaining 131 fragments, there is insufficient surviving morphology to suggest which variety of weapon or knife might be represented. In total, 26 retain certain or probable hilt-plates, always substantially eroded, while around 38 taper to a point. Most of the latter probably do represent the tips of the weapons, but a cautionary note relating to patterns of erosion comes from the doubled-over blade No 334, which tapers to a point at both ends, albeit more obtusely at one.

Blade fragment No 348 is uncharacteristically broad and is currently arched at one end, but in the light of its condition and lack of features it remains unidentified.

Spearheads (Nos 349–353; Fig 3.18)

Five pieces are spearheads or fragments thereof. Two essentially complete ones are 152mm and 162.5mm long, but No 350 has a greater socket-to-blade ratio than No 349. Both have peg holes through the socket. Spearhead 349 appears to have had a leaf-shaped blade, but one wing has been preferentially eroded so that it is not only narrower but also different in shape. This serves as a cautionary tale against necessarily accepting the flame shape of the blade on No 350 as original, although it can be matched in the Rosnoën phase (eg Briard 1965, 158, fig 51.1; Blanchet and Mohen 1977, 476, figs 4.25 and 4.29; Verney and Verron 1998, no 16).

Two of the fragments include the base of the blade and while one (No 352) shares a rounded midrib section with the complete examples, the other (No 351) has a more lozenge-shaped midrib section, creating a ridge along the crest. Fragment No 353 is evidently from the tip of a spearhead, but erosion has not only considerably rounded all its edges but also completely removed one face of the midrib.

Ferrules (Nos 354–355; Fig 3.18)

Two socketed ferrules of different types are represented in the assemblage. The larger fragment, No 354, tapers steadily towards a blunt tip which has an oval to sub-rectangular section. Part of the socket survives up to a break where there are also indications of crushing, perhaps as part of the scrapping

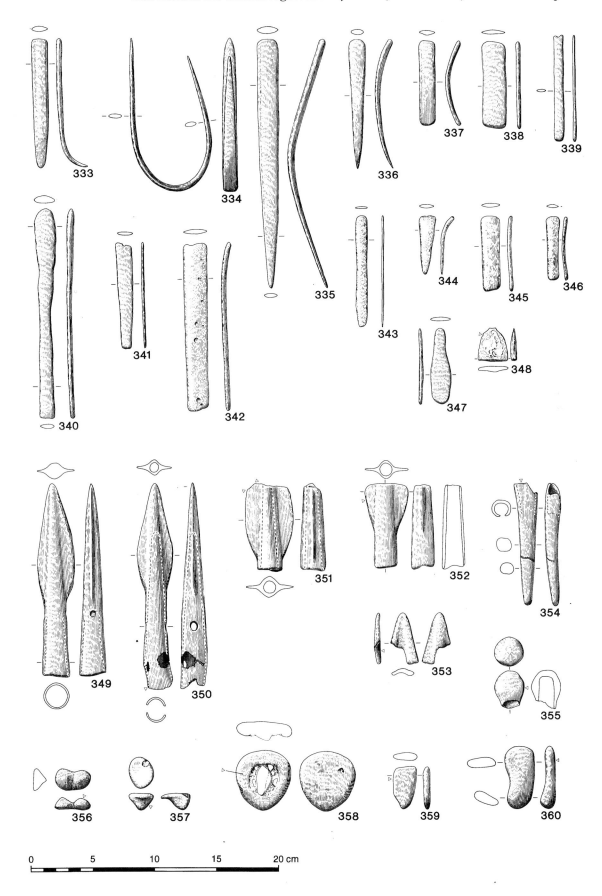

Fig 3.18 Langdon Bay: unclassified blades (Nos 333–348); spearheads (Nos 349–353); ferrules (Nos 354–355); casting jets and lumps (Nos 356–361) [for No 361 see Fig 3.11, No 119]

process; it is not possible to be sure, but the indications are that it was originally a rounded socket. The gentle curve in profile and the transverse crack are doubtless further evidence for damage. Despite the slight flattening of the faces around the middle of the fragment, the tip is blunt in profile and does not look as if it could have come to a chisel edge. Allowing for distortion and erosion, this object can instead be readily accommodated within the known series of long conical ferrules taken to be for spear butts and datable to the Penard stage (Needham 1982b, 38; additional example from Flag Fen – Coombs 2001, 261–2, no 45, fig 10.4). Lengths of British examples range from 104mm to 375mm, whereas 97mm of the Langdon example survives.

The second probable ferrule, No 355, survives as a knobbed terminal from which the very start of a circular socket emerges. Again, the original length cannot be judged, but this form of ferrule is a surprising inclusion in an assemblage of this date. Nevertheless, its metal composition is absolutely in keeping with the assemblage at large. Long examples of knobbed ferrules (over 100mm) seem to furnish Class 3 flesh-hooks in particular; but there are also shorter variants that may have furnished some other type of instrument (Needham and Bowman 2005). Generally similar knob-ended socketed fittings are known in central Europe at this time, as from the Courtavant grave, Aube, which also contains a Rixheim sword (Gaucher 1981, 160, fig 59 D1; Pare 1999, 458, fig 26.9). This generic parallel has a slightly elliptical section and need not be a spear-butt ferrule.

Casting jets, lumps, and small fragments (Nos 356–361; Fig 3.18)

The analyses of five lumps of bronze (Nos 356–360) show that they are contemporary with the rest of the assemblage. Object No 357 is a solid, sub-conical piece of bronze with a lip on one side, while No 356 has two similar cones side by side. These seem most likely to be eroded casting jets, the flatter face being the top surface with the cones leading down to a 'gate' to feed the molten bronze into the casting cavity. The larger, nearly spherical lump No 358 is unlikely to be a jet and is better interpreted simply as a spill of residual metal. Nos 359 and 360 may be fragments of implements, but are too eroded for even broad identification. Similarly, the fragments (No 361) inside the socket of axe No 119 are not sufficiently visible to be able to make any identification.

Salcombe (Moor Sand and Salcombe Site B)

Palstaves (S1–5; Fig 3.19)

Of the five palstaves from Salcombe, four (S1–4) conform well to Langdon Bay type 2, being looped palstaves with a single medial ridge or rib running the length of the blade. S1 is best preserved, even the loop being intact, although the medial ridge is more rounded on one face than the other. The flanges may be a little reduced but present a neat, triangular shape in profile leading up to a projecting stop. S2 is a blade half broken immediately above the stop. Again, the loop is present and, moreover, casting flashes survive as significant ridges down both sides; these cannot have suffered more than slight reduction. A steeply bevelled cutting edge is also clear low on the blade where it truncates the medial ridge.

The other two type 2 palstaves, both from Moor Sand, are more eroded. The size of S3 may originally have been close to that of S1, but it is heavily rolled and the blade potentially somewhat shortened and narrowed. Despite this weathering, evidence for a rib extends for 52mm below the stop; of course it may originally have been longer and stronger, but it does not seem to have been of the stout triangular form of type 3. At its haft end, which is less reduced, evidence survives for the object having been cast in a laterally misaligned bivalve mould; the two valves seem to have been displaced by around 2mm. S4 has only slight stumps representing the loop and a smoothed, curvy butt line, perhaps the result of the abrasion of a broken butt. Otherwise, its condition is fair and the long midrib is moderately strong, terminating at a now-diffuse edge bevel. Given the rounding off of all edges and corners without appreciable gross reduction, this piece would originally have been a more delicate palstave. Such palstaves are known within the Rosnoën repertoire (eg Briard 1965, 156, fig 50.4).

The fifth example, S5, is closest to Langdon type 3 in possessing a stout, triangular midrib and curved stop, but may deviate from the Langdon examples in not having a particularly heavy blade. However, there is a depression into one side at the top of the blade opposite the loop which is due to local abrasion; this part, at least, will have been a little broader than is now apparent.

Palstave-adze (S6; Fig 3.19)

Although highly eroded, the identification of this tool is certain. A slender blade terminates in a cutting edge which is set transverse to the septum, an unusual orientation. The stops consequently occur at the thickened tops of the *sides* of the blade and, indeed, there is a modest swelling towards the stops. If any flanges once existed along the haft end, which is most probable on the basis of comparable objects, these have been effectively removed except that the side edges are thickened and the septum floor between is dished. The original butt has been eaten away irregularly and the projecting corner is bent in profile.

This object type is not represented at Langdon Bay and, indeed, is rather rare anywhere. Although terminologies applied in the past have varied, such

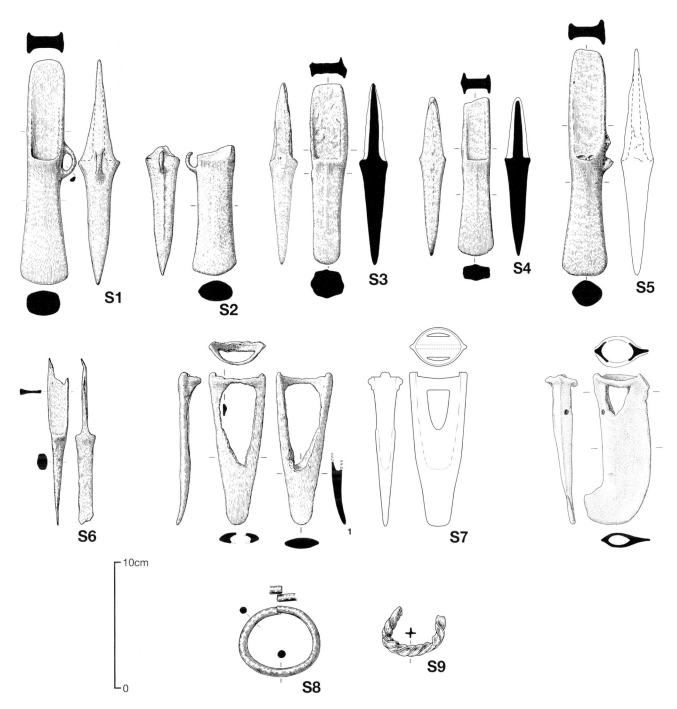

Fig 3.19   Salcombe: palstaves (S1–5); palstave-adze (S6); Sicilian tool type with reconstruction of original form (S7); parallel from Syracuse, Sicily; gold bracelet (S8); gold torc (S9)

objects are best called 'palstave-adzes' to emphasise both their relationship to and essential differences from palstave-chisels and palstaves.

Strumento con immanicatura a cannone (S7; Fig 3.19)

Although partially eroded, this is obviously a very distinctive object and one not reconcilable with bronze metalwork types in north-west Europe. In plan view, the instrument tapers from a mouth towards a rounded tip. The latter, in its current form, is rounded in profile rather than sharp. The 'blade' is solid for 44mm above the tip, expanding in profile gently. It is slightly bent in profile, presumably as a result of damage. Above the blade the object has an incomplete socket with one face almost entirely absent and the other with a gaping central perforation of sub-triangular shape. At the top of the latter a narrow strip-moulding remains to serve as one half of the mouth. Its top edge is slightly concave with some irregularities and to either side a small protuberance, or bump, projects upwards. These give the impression of being original features rather than the product of differential erosion. Along the sides of the missing face there are erratic, residual stumps and we assume that the object was originally bifacially symmetrical, allowing the reconstruction offered in Fig 3.19. The mouth is likely to have been lemon-shaped and the body, ignoring the face perforation, had a fat, lenticular cross section. The implement that survives is 121.5mm long, the socket being 77mm deep from the top. Maximum width is 45.8mm and its weight is 58.8g.

All of the features observable on this enigmatic bronze from Salcombe can, in fact, be paralleled on a class of object found only in Sicily known as *strumenti con immanicatura a cannone* (Albanese Procelli 1993, 41; Giardino 1995, 21), which falls into two broad types, both of which share the lenticular cross section, tapering socket, face perforations, and single moulding around the mouth and often also have bumps projecting from the mouth corners. Although they vary in overall size and massiveness, these implements are also united in having acutely tapering profiles. The key difference between the two types is that one has a symmetrical shield-shaped or chisel-like blade end, while in the other the blade turns abruptly sideways by angles of up to 90°, creating an L-shaped or angled implement in face view. These angled implements also terminate in rounded or squared ends.

The simplest reconstruction of the Salcombe example makes it a tapering, chisel-like form. It is conceivable that the blade end has suffered preferential erosion, causing greater reduction of its outline relative to the socket sides. The only possible evidence for this is that the lower sides are more rounded than the socket sides, which have a fairly acute profile. Of course, we cannot rule out the possibility that the blade was originally of the angled variety and had broken off above the angle prior to marine reworking. However, many examples of the angled form are asymmetric from one side of the socket to the other, whereas the Salcombe example lacks any sign of asymmetry.

Gold bracelet (S8; Fig 3.19)

Whereas no gold objects are known from Langdon Bay, two have come to light at Salcombe (up until the end of 2004). The first is a plain penannular bracelet, oval in shape, and with a round hoop section which tapers very slightly towards unexpanded terminals. This form is extremely simple, but it is entirely consistent with a Penard date (see below). Indeed, similar forms in bronze can also be found in contemporary continental hoards, as at Anzin, Nord (Blanchet 1984, 231, fig 122.1–2), or Saint-Jean-Trolimon, Finistère (Briard 1965, 159, fig 52.6). The terminals currently overlap a little which, taken together with some irregularity in the circuit, suggest that the bracelet is a little

distorted. It is impossible to know when this distortion occurred.

Gold twisted torc (S9; Fig 3.19)

A fragment of twisted four-flanged rod almost certainly belongs to a well-known Bronze Age type, the flange-twisted bar torc (eg Eogan 1994, 53–7) sometimes known as the Tara or Yeovil type. It was recovered as an outlier on the seabed some 90m north-west of the site B concentration. It is possible, perhaps, that the helically twisted flanges gave the fragment unusual hydro-dynamic properties, accounting for greater movement on the sea floor. Its metal composition is further support for the argument that it derives from the Bronze Age assemblage rather than from that of the 17th century AD from Salcombe Site A.

The extended length of this fragment is about 96mm, just a small portion of a full torc. The middle section is only gently curved and the coiled flanges are still regular in their spacing. However, this spacing breaks down towards two tighter bends, which are attributable to damage; at one of these bends the flanges are badly distorted. At both ends the fragment has been chopped through steeply and bifacially, in 'pincer' fashion. Two opposing flanges were thereby wholly crushed. This technique of chopping up Bronze Age gold bar ornaments is becoming well known (eg Needham 2007a). There is a surprising amount of surface detail extant on this piece: cut facets and associated coarse striations at the chopped ends, and considerable evidence for poorly bonded, or reopened, joins along the creases between flanges.

Cauldron handle (S10; not illustrated)

The whereabouts of this important object are unknown. It apparently went missing before being deposited at the British Museum and is currently known only from photographs taken by SWMAG and from BBC film footage in which the object is one of many laid out on a table. Its current loss is particularly unfortunate given that it is almost certainly the handle from one of the earliest sheet-bronze cauldrons, of which very few examples are known.

The clarity of the photographic images is unfortunately poor, but it can be seen that the ring-handle itself was rather badly eroded so that the thickness varies around its circuit, in places being very thin. It is basically circular, as is typical of cauldron handles. It was attached to the cauldron rim by a 'staple' or strap, the exterior of which carries three convex mouldings separated by narrow grooves; the form of the underside cannot be ascertained. The feet of the staple sit on a flat or near-flat plate of bronze which projects to either side and seems to have well-eroded edges. It is not clear whether

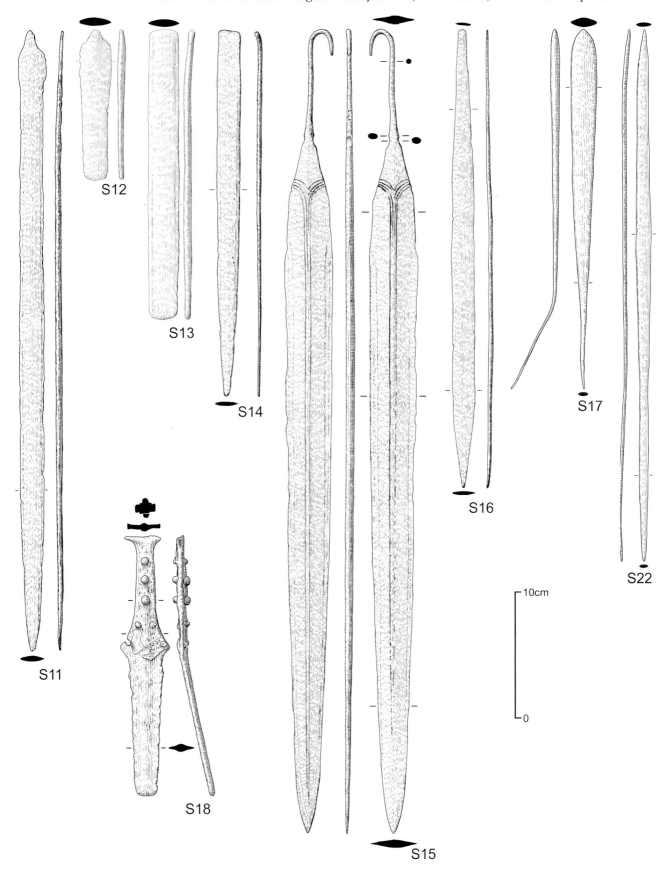

Fig 3.20   Salcombe: swords (S11–18) and sword or rapier (S22)

the staple and foot-plate were cast in one or the former cast onto the latter; this distinction would be technologically important at this early stage of the development of cauldrons. There is no image of the underside of the foot-plate. In general the triple-moulded staple form is very similar to those on Gerloff's class A0 and A1 cauldrons (Gerloff 1986; 2010, 47–80), which are dated to the Penard stage of the British sequence.

Swords (S11–18, probably S19–20; Figs 3.20–3.21)

As many as ten objects from Salcombe can be identified with reasonable certainty as having been swords, although two cannot be attributed to any type. Langdon blade type 1, with flattened lenticular section, is represented by two examples with hilt present (S11–12) and a further one or two blade fragments (S13–14); these probably represent the Rosnoën type. All have some evidence for the edge bevels and hilt fragment S12 has a vestige of a medial ridge through the shoulder zone. On both this and S11 only parts of the lower pair of rivet holes or notches survive.

Langdon blade type 2 is also represented, both by the fine complete sword S15 and two blade fragments, S16 and S17. Given the marine context, the complete sword has retained its surface detail exceptionally well. The central arris of the lozenge blade section has been accentuated by the chasing of two long grooves running most of the blade's length. They are closely set and create the impression of a narrow midrib, but actually this is not proud of the flanking blade wings. At the base of the hilt-plate the grooves splay rapidly outwards and three parallel grooves are added to create a broader Y-shaped motif. Even the edges of the sword show little damage, just slightly wavering outlines in places. Neat double bevels back the edges and feather out about 40mm below the top of the blade. The blade tapers very gradually from its widest point near the top. A triangular hilt plate continues the central thickening of the blade and leads into a fairly stout rod of round section; two slight notches constrict the plate/rod junction. The top of the rod tapers and is curled round by 180°, resulting in a length of 88mm.

S16 is relatively more eroded in its upper half, but a neat medial ridge is clear on both faces and would not be an obvious product of erosion. The second (S17) also appears to have suffered more erosion towards one end, which is whittled down to an extremely fine point that is bent in profile. Higher up, erosion has rounded off the cutting edges and possibly the central arris, but overall, a thick, nearly lozenge-shaped section survives. Erosion also accounts for the bullet-shaped end at the top, which is neither a break nor the original hilt.

A third and very distinctive blade section is also present among the Salcombe material, in S18; fortunately its hilt is extant and relatively well preserved, since this makes it clear that the sword is of a type later than the rest of the assemblage. The cross section of the blade has a distinct, rounded midrib flanked by thin tapering blade wings. The angles between midrib and wings would have been crisply defined and may even have been lightly groove-chased. The midrib tapers steadily upwards as it extends through the shoulders and onto the base of the grip. Despite rather ragged blade edges there is clear evidence for ricassos, above which are somewhat concave shoulders leading smoothly into the grip. The grip is parallel-sided for the greater part but contracts slightly before expanding rapidly to a T-shaped butt. The surfaces of the grip, like the rest of the object, are largely reduced with only limited fragments of a patinated surface upstanding. It is probable that the grip section was un-flanged, or minimally flanged, and its sides were neatly squared.

All but one of the original rivets survive, at least partially. Two are intact, with well-domed caps closing either end. In other cases the heads are damaged, allowing the construction to be seen beneath; the rivets themselves are rather slender – only 2.2–3.0mm in diameter – and the heads were deep hollow 'mushroom' caps about 4mm deep and up to 6mm in diameter. It is presumed that the rivets passed through a perforation in the centre of the caps before being clenched, but, if so, this must have been followed by extensive grinding given that no junction can be discerned on the intact heads.

The main features of S18 recall the Carp's Tongue type of sword, but the domed rivet caps seem to be exceptional and the shoulders may not have been as pronounced as is usual on the type. Given these differences, considerable thought has been given as to whether this might be an unusual type of early sword, contemporary with the rest of the assemblage (we are very grateful to Colin Burgess and Dirk Brandherm for their comments on this piece). However, virtually none of its features are those found on other early hilt-grip swords and, moreover, X-ray fluorescence analysis has indicated a leaded bronze consistent with a later date (Rohl and Needham 1998, 225, no 197). Carp's Tongue swords date to the Ewart stage of the British sequence and *Bronze Final III* in north-western France, *c* 1000–800 BC, which is around two centuries later than the bulk of the Salcombe assemblage.

Two fragments can be classified as probable swords, but of unknown type. Hilt piece S19 has the depth of shoulder zone and medial ridge characteristic of Rosnoën swords, but insufficient blade remains to be able to judge its section. Blade tip fragment S20 is likewise too eroded for confident classification (although traces of the edge bevels do survive).

Unclassified blades – sword or rapier (S21–26; Figs 3.20–3.21)

Six blades are highly eroded, normally down to extremely slender proportions. One (S21) retains part of the hilt with the remains of two rivet notches; however, there has been much reduction in the outline and it is impossible to be sure whether it orig-

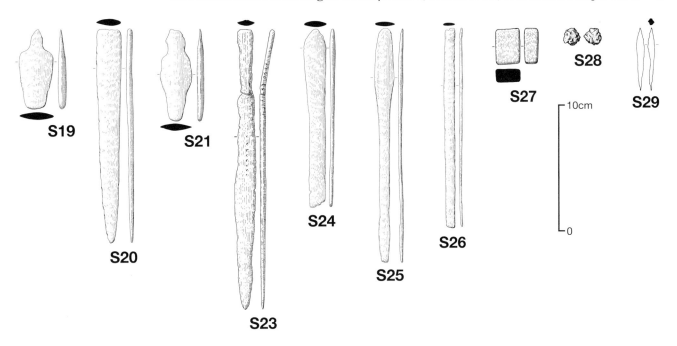

Fig 3.21   Salcombe: probable swords (S19–20); unclassified blades (S21 and 23–26); rectanguloid block / weight (S27); tin lump (S28); iron awl (S29)

inally had the subtle shoulders of an early sword or the more projecting shoulders of a Group IV notched rapier. The distance between the rivet emplacements and the start of the blade (approximately 25mm) in its current eroded state is potentially long enough for a Rosnoën sword.

The remaining five are well whittled down and somewhat amorphous; nevertheless, one (S22) survives to 421mm long. The broadening seen at the end of two pieces could be due to differential erosion rather than indicating the position of the hilt.

Rectangular block – probable weight (S27; Fig 3.21)

Among the assemblage is a very neat rectangular block. All faces are flat and smooth, save for very minor undulations, all of which are probably associated with corrosion. It is a complete object and should be contemporary with the other material given its closely similar metal composition. It is unlikely to be simply an ingot because of the neat shape. On the other hand, if it were an anvil, its small size and lack of a stake for insertion into a stabilising block would greatly limit its utility. A third and much more likely possibility is that it was a weight (44.7g). Very similar neatly shaped blocks known from western central Europe have been interpreted as weights (Pare 1999) and Coombs has suggested that some similar neat rectanguloid blocks of lead or lead alloy from Britain probably also formed part of a weight system (Coombs 2001, 291). In fact, there is a second find of a rectanguloid block from Salcombe (post-2004, so not catalogued here); it is of different proportions and has a 'design'

Fig 3.22   The second rectanguloid block from Salcombe – probable weight (not catalogued in this volume; length 48mm). © Trustees of the British Museum

of wavy mouldings on both faces (Fig 3.22). This piece is also paralleled in central European finds such as that from Richemont-Pépinville, Moselle (Pare 1999, 443, fig 17).

Tin lump (S28; Fig 3.21)

This approximately spherical pale grey lump has a nodular and partly granular surface with embedded sand grains. The surface features are probably largely the result of the corrosion of a smoother-surfaced lump. Northover's analysis (below) shows that it is almost pure tin and, therefore, of considerable importance as a potential Bronze Age find. Neither form nor composition can help to date it, but the spatial association is highly suggestive of it belonging with the Bronze Age assemblage, notwithstanding the 'Cannon' site alongside.

Iron awl in bone handle? (S29; Fig 3.21)

This object was recovered partially encased in silty concretion, but it could be seen that a metal object lay within an organic 'sheath'. The internal structure became clearer through radiography (Fig 3.23), and subsequent cleaning of the extraneous matter (Simon Dove, British Museum Conservation) revealed the organic component to be a small tubular bone. This has been identified as being from a bird, but the loss of diagnostic features and possible distortion precludes identification to species (Dale Serjeantson, pers comm).

The iron object comprises a rod tapering to both ends, and is probably an awl or similar implement. The rod is thickest about a third of the way along. The longer end tapers in somewhat irregular fashion, while the squatter end tapers evenly until close to the tip, where it thins rapidly in a nib-like fashion. It is thought likely that the shape of both ends has been altered by corrosion, as has the cross section. It is not possible to know whether the bird bone served as a container for the metal implement or was a handle that had subsequently slipped over it.

Being made of iron, this piece may be later and intrusive; however, well-stratified examples of iron implements are known from various locations in Europe from 2nd-millennium BC contexts (see further below). A small fragment of the bone handle was tested for its collagen content at the Oxford Radiocarbon Accelerator Unit, but unfortunately too little survives to allow dating.

Insular and continental affinities
by Brendan O'Connor and Stuart Needham

This section will consider the insular and continental background of the main types of metalwork represented at Langdon Bay and Salcombe. Much has already been published about the regional origins of the main types represented at these sites and some of the broader conclusions drawn in previous interims remain unchanged (Coombs 1976; Muckelroy 1980; O'Connor 1980; Needham and Dean 1987). However, some types in the assemblages have escaped attention because they are rare or difficult to identify, or were recovered from Salcombe only in more recent years. Even the main types are worthy of fresh review, for we can sometimes draw on significant additional finds or syntheses. This helps clarify further the distributions of the component types and reassess the significance of their associations in these two seabed assemblages.

One of the finds that will crop up repeatedly in our discussion is the hoard from Penavern en Rosnoën, Finistère. This hoard is eponymous for the first phase of *Bronze Final* metalwork in north-western France

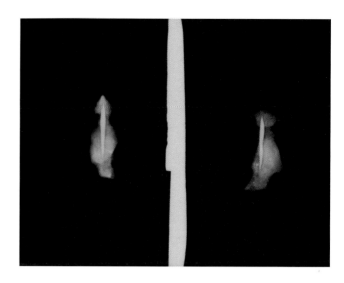

Fig 3.23   X-ray image of iron awl in bone handle (S29). The surrounding blotches are due to mineral concretions in and around the bone. © Trustees of the British Museum

and is contemporary with the Penard phase in the British chronology. Despite being exceptionally well known through Jacques Briard's publications (Briard 1958a; 1965), only more recently has it been appreciated that the hoard contained far more objects than originally reported (Le Roux and Thollard 1990, 39). Having been discovered in 1944, it came to the attention of archaeologists in 1949 with an inventory of 29 pieces. The additions, now also fully published (Nallier and Le Goffic 2008), raise the total to 88 objects.

We will discuss the implications of the various types present at Langdon Bay and Salcombe in the same order as presented above.

Median-winged axes

The large number of median-winged axes in the Langdon Bay assemblage immediately attracted attention because of the virtual absence of the type from British soil (eg Coombs 1976; Muckelroy 1980). Yet median-winged axes were numerous in much of central Europe during the middle stages of the Bronze Age and there are many variant forms. Most relevant to this assemblage are examples in the western part of the distribution, mainly west of the Rhine, and we consider all of them to fall within the Grigny type, especially variant Swalmen (see above). A thorough reappraisal of the distribution of the close continental parallels is merited.

The two eponymous examples of the Grigny type were found in the river Seine at Pas-de-Grigny, Essonne/Seine-et-Oise (Millotte *et al* 1968, 52, no 158–9; Mohen 1977, 92–3, 253 Grigny/91–23 and 24, ills 218–19); and a third fragmentary axe has come from the same place (Bastien and Yvard 1980, 247, fig 1, 2). Grigny axes are most common (165 examples) in eastern France and western Switzerland, with a smaller concentration in the Île-de-France and the Marne (Kibbert 1984, 54–5; Butler and Steegstra 1999–2000, map 3; David-Elbiali 2000, 132–4, ill 52). There is a mould from Saint-Aignan, Loir-et-Cher (Millotte *et al* 1968, no 81; Kibbert 1984, 48), which is outside the main distribution. The French distribution is complemented by about 30 examples in central western Germany, almost all west of the Rhine (Kibbert 1984, 55, Taf 84). A smaller group of Grigny axes is found on the Meuse (Butler and Steegstra 1999–2000, 129, map 4). There are ten examples from the Netherlands (Butler and Steegstra 1999–2000, nos 442–51) and seven from Belgium (Warmenbol 1989, 282). The Dutch finds of Grigny axes have been interpreted as imports from France along with Rosnoën swords and spearheads (Butler and Steegstra 1999–2000, 135).

Blanchet lists six findspots of Grigny axes in Picardy and the north of France (1984, 234, 238, nos 1–2 and 30–33, figs 121, 7, 122, 5, 125 and 128) and has published a more recent find from La Ferme Rouge, Cottenchy, Somme (Blanchet *et al* 1989, 257, fig 45). These finds include *Bronze Final I* hoards from Saint-Just-en-Chaussée, Oise (Blanchet 1984, 226–8, fig 121, 7), and Anzin, Nord (*ibid*, 228, fig 122, 5). The problematic hoard from Erondelle, Somme, includes at least one median-winged axe like those from Langdon Bay (*ibid*, 238 no 33, fig 132, 11), but also median-winged axes of different forms (*ibid*, fig 132), so the currency of the Langdon Bay axes cannot necessarily be confined to *Bronze Final I* (*ibid*, 228–30). This suggestion is confirmed by a hoard found in 1982 at Bois des Lisières, Villethierry, Yonne, which includes complete examples of Grigny axes in a transitional *Bronze Final I–IIa* context (Thévenot 1985, 210, fig 42). Such a date is also possible for the Yvoir hoard, Namur, Belgium, which contains a Grigny axe and a Rosnoën spearhead, but also an arrowhead of a type thought to be a little later (Warmenbol 1990a, 87). The earlier hoard from Malassis, Cher, which consists mainly of Bronze Moyen types alongside some of *Bronze Final I*, contains a butt fragment that has been attributed to a median-winged axe (Briard *et al* 1969, 48, figs 8, 24, and 23), although this example tapers in plan more than the butts of the Langdon Bay axes.

Outside the main concentrations, the Grigny type is more sparsely encountered in north-west France; there are some comparable examples in Normandy (Millotte *et al* 1968, nos 24, 44 bis, 87 and 146) and a few in Brittany, including that in a *Bronze Final I* hoard from Saint-Jean-Trolimon, Finistère (Millotte *et al* 1968, no 47; Briard 1965, 157, fig 50, 5–7). Further south, they are also known from the south-west of France (Coffyn 1985, 165; Gardes 1991, 185, fig 2A, 1) and there is a very outlying find in a hoard from Arroyo Molinos, Jaén, in southern Spain (Coffyn 1985, 165, 389, no 121, pl XVI). It contains two median-winged axes (Monteagudo 1977, nos 1777–8) far away from their likely origin in eastern France (Millotte *et al* 1968), significantly alongside a north-west European style of palstave and two

bar bracelets, one with incised chevron decoration (Monteagudo 1977, no 1134).

Grigny axes also occur in small numbers eastwards, in central Europe. The occurrence of a complete example and several fragments in the Rýdeč hoard, Bohemia, is significant because of the associated western swords (see below) (Kytlicová 2007, 125, n 36, Taf 89, 118). The type is also present in hoards from Lhotka and Svinárky (*ibid*, Taf 16, 62, and 172, 25) and there are two examples in a hoard of the earliest Urnfield phase from Feldkirch in the westernmost part of Austria (Mayer 1977, 144–5, nos 620–621). The datable contexts are mainly attributed to Bronze D, but Grigny axes persisted into the following phase (Kibbert 1984, 53–4; Butler and Steegstra 1999–2000, 135), echoing the situation in France and the Low Countries noted already.

The median-winged axes from Langdon Bay probably constitute 25% or more of the total number of Grigny axes recorded on the Continent. Yet despite this considerable number a few hundred metres off the coast of Dover, very few finds of any type of median-winged axe have come from British soil. A complete example said to be from Thames Ditton, Surrey, is thinner in profile than type Grigny and most other median-winged axes north of the Alps; it is in St Albans Museum (possibly part of the Captain Ball collection) but has no further history. Another complete axe was found at Sketty, Swansea, West Glamorganshire (Williams 1937), but while there is no reason to doubt the provenance it is of a type equating with Kibbert's group *Mittel- und Oberständige Lappenbeile mit Zangennacken ohne Öse*, comprising types which date to the middle stages of the Urnfield culture, later than Langdon (Kibbert 1980, nos 138–159). This is the case also for a median-winged axe provenanced to the Thames and deriving from the Thomas Bateman collection, now in the British Museum (Accession number 1995.1102.1). On the other hand, an example from Alexandra Dock, Hull, East Yorkshire (Burgess 1968b, 11, fig 7.3, 34), is likely to belong to type Grigny despite the loss of its butt; the fracture at the top of the wings has been heavily reworked by hammering. Although these examples of median-winged axes are not all contemporaneous, they are nevertheless all alien to the insular metalwork repertoire for their time. It may therefore be significant that they are all from close to the coast or a major river, though not all are from the south-east of Britain.

Palstaves

Palstaves were the predominant axe type for many centuries in north-west Europe, giving rise to an incredible diversity of styles having both regional and temporal definition. Identification of the precise types represented in the seabed assemblages therefore requires great attention to detail; quite subtle differences can affect whether a given type appears to be typical of parts of Britain or of mainland Europe.

The most regular comparisons made above for Langdon type 1 are from the British side of the channel among the Transitional type (Smith 1959b, 177, fig 7.3). These are fairly frequent in southern Britain and a few occur further north (Schmidt and Burgess 1981, nos 875–878). Surprisingly few can be identified among the published French material; these include two from the Heuqueville hoard, Seine-Maritime (Gabillot 2003, pl. 66.1–2), which otherwise contains objects appropriate to the Baux-Sainte-Croix phase (O'Connor 1980, figs 21B and 22). The same phasing applies to the Livet-sur-Autou hoard, Eure, which has one or two palstaves that are comparable, except that they have medium-broad blades (Verney 1988, 188, nos 4 and 5). There are single narrow-bladed examples in the *Bronze Final II* hoards of Luzarches (Val-d'Oise) and Erondelle (Somme) (Blanchet 1984, figs 129.2 and 132.1), the latter of which also contains a Grigny-style median-winged axe and may be transitional *Bronze Final I–II*. A stray find comes from a marsh at Manneville-la-Raoult, Eure (Verney 1988, 189, fig 6). From extant examples, it would thus appear that type 1 is more typical of the British than the continental side of the Channel.

In terms of broader comparisons, Langdon palstave types 2 and 3, which also account for all five palstaves from Salcombe, have been treated together above. Although the spotlight immediately shifts to Brittany and its Rosnoën type, in fact there is not a large number of examples there. In addition to the one in the Rosnoën hoard itself (Briard 1958a, pl IV, 9; Nallier and Le Goffic 2008, 142–5, nos 60–62, fig 12), there are further associated finds from Kergoff, Noyal-Pontivy, Morbihan (Coudrin 1905, 145, no 4, fig 3), Cornospital, Saint-Tugudual, Morbihan (Marsille 1913, 55, no 1, pl II, 1), Fourdan, Guern, Morbihan (Briard *et al* 1982–83, 37–8, fig 3), Kergoustance, Plomordien, Finistère (Briard 1965, 156, fig 50.1), and Keranfinit, Coray, Finistère (Briard *et al* 1980, 60, fig 3, 1–2). Others occur as single finds (eg Briard and Onnée 1980, 46–7, nos 1–2) or in the Saint-Brieuc-des-Iffs hoard of the subsequent phase (Briard and Onnée 1972, nos 1–6, 21–23).

Further south, in Anjou, Rosnoën palstaves occur in the second hoard from Bourgdion, Saint-Remy-la-Varenne, Maine-et-Loire (Cordier and Gruet 1975, 223, no 3, 259, fig 19, 1 and 3), in association with the blade of a leaf-shaped sword or rapier. The surviving palstave from the Becon-les-Granits hoard is also of the type (*ibid*, 170, 259, fig 19, 4) and there are isolated finds from the region as well (*ibid*, 259, figs 19, 5 and 6, 26, 5, and 6, 53, 7–10). Rosnoën palstaves, or their variants, are found in the centre-west (Gomez 1985) and south-west (Cantet 1991, 196–8; Abaz *et al* 1992) of France. There may also be occasional examples in Iberia, such as that from Fuente Urbel, Burgos, Spain (Monteagudo 1977, no 1221), but they can be difficult to distinguish from the indigenous series of single-looped palstaves there. They appear to be similarly sparse in the Paris basin, appearing in either *Bronze Final I* (Longueville) or II (Luzarches) hoards, as well as singly (Mohen 1977, 420–21 and figures on 92, 119, and 136). Nor does the type seem to be common in Picardy or the north of France (Blanchet 1984, 236, 238–9, nos 36–38). Intriguingly, however, four Rosnoën palstaves are recorded from the Netherlands (Butler and Steegstra 1997–98, 195, nos 228–231, fig 58).

Further east their occurrence is only occasional. There is an important example in the Bavarian hoard from Windsbach, Ldkr. Andsbach, Franconia (Pászthory and Mayer 1998, no 470) associated with the hilt of a Rosnoën sword and a long-socket spearhead also likely to be of western origin (Pászthory and Mayer 1998, 90–1). Müller-Karpe dated the Windsbach hoard to Bronze D (1959, 147, 176 n 7, 186, Taf. 155A); Pászthory and Mayer propose a relatively late date on the basis of the ribbed bracelet (1998, 91).

The parallels for Langdon types 2 and 3 are therefore not especially common finds in France, even in Brittany. Moreover, their associations indicate a span over *Bronze Final I–II* in terms of the established chronology, so not all will be close contemporaries of our seabed finds. Some of the British comparanda for type 2 and 3 palstaves noted above – types Shelf, Roundhay, Penrith, and Silsden – may likewise continue later than Penard proper, which could partly explain the past dispute over whether the Wallington series of hoards, in which they are frequent, belong to the Penard or Wilburton phases (Burgess 1968b; 1995; Needham 1990b; another complication is Colin Burgess' recent suggestion (pers comm) that there is a hitherto unrecognised phase falling between British Penard and Wilburton). Where catalogued, in the north of Britain, these palstave parallels are most common in northern England, thinning rapidly in Scotland (Schmidt and Burgess 1981, pl 123). There are, though, plenty of good parallels further south, including in hoards. It would seem, therefore, that considerably more parallels are known from the British side of the Channel than the continental side. More difficult to evaluate is whether there are more subtle regional or temporal variants, still less the possibility that differential deposition and/or recovery have caused the differing densities of finds on the two sides of the Channel.

The Langdon type 4 palstave has been identified as of the Norman narrow-bladed type (Briard and Verron 1976a, 94, fig 3 left). This type (discussed further in relation to the Hayling Beach/Owers Bank find – Chapter 4) is characteristic of the Baux-Sainte-Croix phase, broadly preceding Rosnoën/Penard, but this one piece could easily be a scrap survival within the Langdon assemblage.

Palstave-adze

The Salcombe palstave-adze is extremely important in providing a context for a rare type. Rowlands lists just five palstave-adzes from southern Britain, describing them as 'transverse flanged chisels' (Rowlands 1976, 44–5, 350–54). A few others occur in Scotland, where Coles describes them as 'flanged chisels', although at the same time acknowledging that the blade is set adze-fashion (Coles 1963–64, 116–17, figs 14.1–14.2, 146). In cataloguing three examples from Lincolnshire, Davey applies the term 'adze palstaves' (1973, 64). Rowlands correctly linked this adze-like form to similarly slender-bladed palstaves in which the cutting edge and septum remain in line – these are known as palstave-chisels. For consistency 'palstave-adze' is, therefore, the preferable term for the type under discussion here. The complementary palstave-chisels are also known only in limited numbers. However, these two specialised forms are readily distinguished from palstaves by their very slender bodies.

In addition to the examples listed by the above authors, others have been published from Martin Mere, Lancashire (Davey and Forster 1975, no 61); Arncliffe, West Yorkshire (Radley 1934); Lowthorpe and Burton Agnes, both in East Yorkshire (Manby 1980, figs 6.8 and 12.7); and two reputedly from Knowle Hill, Staffordshire (BM accession nos 1992 9-2 1–2; Needham 1993). A recently excavated example comes from Thorney Borrow Pit, North-amptonshire (Needham 2008). It is noteworthy that several examples come from central Britain: from Lancashire, Yorkshire, and Lincolnshire in the north, to Warwickshire and the Upper Thames Valley at Pusey, Oxfordshire (formerly Berkshire; Rowlands 1976, 350, no 1095) in the south. Indeed, Salcombe aside, it is highly significant that none is yet known from either south of the Thames or East Anglia, for these are exactly the regions that have yielded palstave-chisels (Rowlands 1976, map 12 – 'flanged chisels'; Farley 1978). This latter type has been more recently bolstered by an important new hoard find from Malmains Farm, Tilmanstone, Kent (K Parfitt, pers comm). The chisel form is also represented in northern France, from Normandy eastwards (Gabillot 2003, 350–1, pls 79–80). With such a strong mutual geographical exclusion in Britain, it seems probable that these two types were functional equivalents.

Palstave-adzes are also known in Ireland and north-west France, but again are not at all common (Evans 1881, 104–5; Briard and Verron 1976, 79). Evans described five Irish examples individually and was aware of 'several' others; a possible addi-tional one comes from the Armagh/Monaghan border (Weatherup 1982, 54, fig 22 no 115, 61). Those in the Menez-Tosta hoard (Finistère), discussed by Briard and Verron, were deposited in *Bronze Final III*, but associated is a presumably scrap-survival fragment of a Rosnoën palstave (Briard 1958b, pl I no 5), so the date of the adzes remains open.

The Salcombe example comes from the site B concentration of finds, thus providing a reasonably secure context among Penard-stage metalwork and the first association for the slender variant. Further confirmation of date comes from its impurities being entirely consistent with the main assemblage. Nevertheless, it should not be assumed that all palstave-adzes, even the slender ones, date exclu-sively to this phase, for some of the palstave-chisels undoubtedly date to earlier in the Middle Bronze Age.

Socketed axes and chisels

Socketed 'axes' dating to the Taunton and Penard stages in Britain are generally slender in propor-tion, lightweight, and narrow-edged relative to later socketed axe styles; they are collectively known as 'early square-section' forms. Their general char-acteristics would be suited to both chiselling and lighter chopping actions and it is not possible to make a clear distinction between 'axes' and 'chisels' at this stage. Early square-section socketed axes are far more frequent in southern Britain than on the opposite shores of the Channel (eg O'Connor 1980, maps 10 and 25; there are a number of additions since). Furthermore, it may be significant that the few examples known from northern France are unlooped, with the exception of an unprovenanced example in Rouen Museum (*ibid*, 98). Much further east there are similar tools from a restricted part of north-east Germany (Butler 1963, 75, 268, map V; Rowlands 1976, 41–3), but these are geographically well separated. There are also early socketed axes, a little less close in form, in southern Scandinavia (O'Connor 1980, 60–1).

Regarding specific parallel axes for the pieces found at Langdon Bay, Form 1, with its gently waisted body and traces of a transverse step or hollow about halfway down the face, has a small number of parallels mainly from a restricted region in east Dorset, west Hampshire, and the Isle of Wight (O'Connor and Woodward 2003; Needham 2005), but also in the hoard from Orsett, Essex (O'Connor 1980, fig 33.8). Langdon Bay No 119 can be compared with the axe in the Penard hoard, Glamorganshire, on the basis of a possible medial ridge and its shallow mouth moulding (Savory 1980, 180, fig 32.1). No 127 is more of a chisel form with tapering blade, much like the one found in the Manoir hoard, Logonna-Quimerc'h, Finistère (Briard *et al* 1980, 55, fig 1, 4). There is also a socketed chisel in the Kergoff hoard (Coudrin 1905, 146, no 6, fig 5), but examples also occur in Britain, including in the Kilnhurst hoard, South Yorkshire (Burgess 1968b, 18, fig 13.3).

Socketed hammers

The earliest datable contexts for socketed hammers in north-west Europe are in Taunton stage hoards and thereafter they appear in occasional contexts throughout the rest of the Bronze Age. It is not clear that there are distinctive features belonging

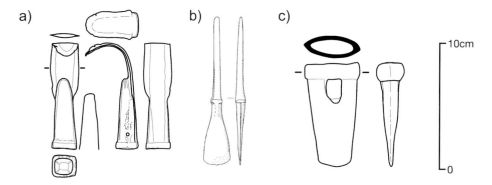

Fig 3.24   a) socketed hooked knife – Grimsby area, north Lincolnshire; b) tanged-and-collared chisel – Quidenham, Norfolk; c) Strumento *from the Modica hoard, Sicily*

to particular phases and neither do there seem to be regionally distinct styles within north-western Europe. In the Penard/Rosnoën phase, although rare in hoards, they do occur on both sides of the Channel (as well as beyond). Even in these fairly early contexts the size of the striking end and overall weight are variable.

Langdon Bay No 130, the socketed hammer with sub-square mouth and rectangular section, compares reasonably well with some examples in contemporary hoards such as Kilnhurst, South Yorkshire (Burgess 1968b, 18, fig 13.5–6), Rosnoën, Finistère (Briard 1958a, pl I, 1), Plougoulm, Finistère (Briard *et al* 1980, 56, fig 2.7, 58), and Fourdan, Morbihan (Briard *et al* 1982–83, 37–8, fig 3). The one in the Manoir hoard, Finistère, is more elaborate with slightly raised sides and a stout tapering midrib descending from the mouth (Briard *et al* 1980, 54–5, fig 1.5); this clearly imitates the stout midribs present on some palstave blades. It is possible (see above) that Langdon Bay No 130 originally had such a motif in less-prominent relief.

Socketed hooked knife

We are confident that Langdon Bay No 134 was a hooked knife of a rare type seen in the Fresné-la-Mère hoard, Calvados. The three Scottish examples of hooked knives and the one from the Thames at Mortlake are rather different and date to the Ewart stage. A previously unrecorded example, possibly from the Grimsby area of north Lincolnshire (in private possession), is also highly relevant. It is less elongate than the Langdon or Fresné-la-Mère implements, but it has a square-sectioned socket recalling the former, combined with a small flat collar such as is found on early square-section socketed axes (Fig 3.24). In profile, the blade comes off the socket end asymmetrically, a feature seen to some extent on the Langdon piece. The style of the piece from near Grimsby suggests strongly that it is a product of the Taunton or Penard traditions, and the two associated parallels from Langdon and Fresné-la-Mère may favour the latter.

Tanged-and-collared chisels

The relatively strong presence of this chisel type at Langdon Bay at a date when very few parallels can be found from terrestrial sites must be indicative of 'hidden circulation'. The metal composition is entirely consistent with the rest of the assemblage, a fact which helps establish their metallurgical and temporal connection. A rare occurrence in a context datable to this same period may be seen in the small hoard from Doncaster, South Yorkshire (Burgess 1968b, 11, fig 7.2). Burgess placed the find in his Wallington tradition, then thought to be contemporary with Wilburton, but a revised view that Wallington was largely coeval with Penard made it an acceptable contemporary of the Langdon Bay material (Needham 1990b, 265). The discussion above about Rosnoën/Langdon type 2 and 3 palstaves might allow the Doncaster find to be a little later, but the associated axe looks perfectly acceptable as of Penard phase.

There has been no fully illustrated corpus of tanged-and-collared chisels, although Burgess *et al* (1972, 217–18) have discussed the full range of variation and their possible development, while Roth has published a classification and list of those from Ireland, Britain, and France (Roth 1974). Roth focused on the shape of the blade rather than the form of the stop, which may be more critical as a temporal indicator. Many comparable chisels have other stop devices – side lugs, a ledge-stop, or a pronounced collar – rather than the seemingly more subtle swellings of those at Langdon Bay (although some reduction by erosion must be allowed for). Although there may be greater variation in blade form among the Langdon examples, we will focus discussion on the distinctive narrow or spatulate blades.

There is a small group of single terrestrial finds from Britain which seem to have similar morphology. At least five have spatulate (or crinoline) blade shapes like that of Langdon Bay No 138; they come from Mildenhall and Cavenham, both in Suffolk, Quidenham and Carleton Rode, both in Norfolk, and Tickenham, north Somerset (Roth 1974, Taf 5.1–5.2; Norfolk Museums Service Record; Norfolk Museums

Service 1977, 31, pl VI.15; Green 1973, 44, fig 6; Fig 3.24). The last was excavated from on top of a round cairn. Langdon Bay No 138 can also be compared to a tool of similar scale, though slightly different form, from Boulogne, Pas-de-Calais (Cambridge University Museum of Archaeology and Ethnography), and another rare associated find, the Saint-Brieuc-des-Iffs hoard, Île-et-Vilaine (Briard and Onnée 1972, no 87).

The chisel from Doncaster, already mentioned, has a pronounced biconical 'collar' and a long triangular blade, a form potentially seen in the eroded Langdon Bay No 140. One in the later Eaton hoard (Norfolk) is similar (Norfolk Museums Service 1977, 33–4, fig 83). We should also mention that some seemingly simple tanged chisels can have vestigial swelling at the tang/blade junction, as seen in, for example, the Burgesses' Meadow hoard (Oxford), of Taunton stage (Hawkes 1955, GB. 6 no 5).

Although datable examples are few, it appears that the narrow-bladed variants of tanged-and-collared chisels have a broad date range. As already mentioned, the metal composition of the Langdon examples confirms that they belong to the Penard assemblage, as probably should Doncaster. Saint-Brieuc-des-Iffs gives a date in *Bronze Final II*, post-Rosnoën, but perhaps now a little earlier than Wilburton in Britain, while Carleton Rode and Eaton show continuation into Ewart stage metalworking.

Strumento

A rather curious and partially eroded object from Salcombe has proved to be one of the most far travelled, almost certainly having originated in Sicily. The type seems to be a peculiarity of that island alone (Needham and Giardino 2008; and above). The full series of *strumenti con immanicatura a cannone* had a long currency through the later stages of the local Bronze Age and the early Iron Age. The absolute chronology is from around the 13th century BC to the early 8th, although the more recent examples may be old scrap in their context (Needham and Giardino 2008). One of the best published parallels for the reconstructed shape of the Salcombe example is one of three *strumenti* in the Modica hoard (Albanese Procelli 1993, 23, fig 10 B4), although this piece is only 82.5mm long and lacks any significant bumps at the mouth (Fig 3.24). The Modica hoard is currently dated to Giardino's Hoard Horizon III, around the late 11th century BC, rather late for a Penard association, but the specific type found there and at Salcombe may well have earlier origins not evident because of the poverty of associated finds in the source zone.

Awls, rods, and bars

At least one bronze awl is present at Langdon Bay (No 141, possibly Nos 142–145), but the forms of awls are not obviously phase-specific through most of the Bronze Age. The occurrence of the type is of interest, though, from the point of view of their virtual exclusion from hoards of all phases. Salcombe has also yielded an awl, but one made of iron; if contemporary with the Penard-phase assemblage, this is a very important early context for an iron object. Attention may be drawn to a broadly contemporary iron awl excavated from beneath a Middle Bronze Age trackway at Bou, Drenthe, Holland (Casparie 1984), but this is by no means an isolated case, only the nearest in a secure context. Early contexts for iron objects in Europe have been summarised on several occasions (eg Harding 1993, 155–7; Darvill 2006) and there is also indirect evidence from punched decoration on bronzes; some traditions of decoration have been shown to be executed with iron rather than bronze tools. However, this does not occur until Hallstatt A2 in central Europe (Harding 2000, 227), somewhat later than the iron awls from Bou and perhaps Salcombe.

Few scholars now doubt that iron objects were in circulation widely, if thinly, across Europe during the later Bronze Age; but accepting this fact does not help validate instances of vaguely dated contexts or ambiguous ironworking traces. Darvill's recent thorough survey (2006) of possible pre-transition ironwork from Britain highlights yet again how poor is the evidence, secure contexts tending to belong either to the Llyn Fawr/Decorated pottery horizon, which can be regarded as the earliest Iron Age (eg Cunliffe 1991; Needham 2007b), or to Ewart stage contexts which could anyway fall only marginally earlier, towards the end of the 9th century BC. These dates for ironworking should hardly occasion surprise and they still leave the Harting Copse assemblage of iron hammerscale (the context in which Darvill was writing), coming from feature fills dated to the 10th century BC (Collard *et al* 2006), in relative isolation. Sadly, the Salcombe iron find, plausible as it is in a Penard maritime context, cannot as yet contribute to our understanding of the occurrence and significance of early iron in north-west Europe.

The rod-like object with a thinned end from Langdon Bay (No 144) has not been securely identified and may be part of a pin, although a comparison can also be made with a 'toilet' implement in the contemporary Irish hoard from Bishopsland, Co Kildare. Another potentially unusual identification stems from the similarity of the tapered bars, Nos 147 and 149, to anvil spikes. Although this can only be a tentative possibility, it is entirely in keeping with the repertoire of Rosnoën metalwork known from hoards.

Flesh-hook

The suggestion that Langdon Bay No 148 is the prong of a flesh-hook of Class 2 cannot be put forward with certainty because of abrasion. However, it does give a plausible identity to an otherwise enigmatic piece. Class 2 flesh-hooks date precisely to Penard and equivalent phases elsewhere. Moreover, they have a strong international dimension, occurring in East Anglia, the centre-west of France, and Sicily (Needham and Bowman 2005).

Spurred ring

The spur fragment, Langdon Bay No 146, has been shown to belong to a spurred ring – a type found in small numbers in north-east France. The parallels cited above are exact contemporaries of the Langdon assemblage. We are not aware of any examples from Britain.

Pins

The forms of the two definite pin heads from the Langdon Bay assemblage can both be found among European Bronze Age pins. The shortness of the shank of biconical-headed No 151 has been discussed above and a French parallel found. Biconical-headed pins do occasionally occur in British Late Bronze Age contexts (eg Ivinghoe Beacon, Buckinghamshire; Britton 1968, 208, nos 14–15). The conical object No 152 has been argued above to be a pin head because it compares in both morphology and composite mode of construction with many pins in the large assemblage in the Villethierry hoard, Yonne (Mordant *et al* 1976). In total, 51 examples in the hoard have this particular head form, and the type is distributed across eastern France from the upper Rhône to upper Seine basins (Mordant *et al* 1976, 203, fig 174). The date of the hoard is more or less contemporary with the Langdon assemblage. A slightly later pin of similar two-part construction, but with a different head form, was found on the coast at Broomhill Sands, Camber, East Sussex (Bellam 1996); it too is an import from eastern France (see Table 5.4).

The Villethierry hoard is also relevant to the alternative identification of Langdon No 144 as from a roll-headed pin, as it contains many examples. The small number of the type known from Britain are mainly later when in datable contexts (Needham 1990a, 62–3), but two excavated at Dartford, Kent, were from a rich organic layer dated to the Middle Bronze Age (Needham and Rigby 2003, 63–6).

Bronze bracelets

One bronze bracelet reasonably confidently identifiable to type is the penannular example with simple tapering terminals, Langdon Bay No 155. This may be a relatively simple form, but it is not particularly abundant in associations of any phase of the northwest European Bronze Age. The occurrence of similar pieces both in Britain and the near Continent does not allow any easy assessment of the origin of the Langdon example.

The ribbed bracelet No 153 is more diagnostic in this respect. While various decorated forms do occur in the British Middle Bronze Age, type Publy is not one of them and the fragment should therefore have originated to the south of the Channel. Although their heartland appears to have been in eastern France, occasional examples were reaching the Channel coast, as at Chailloué, Orne.

Gold bracelet

Gold bracelets such as that found at Salcombe (S8) occur in a few Penard dated associations in Britain: Towednack, Cornwall; Granta Fen, Cambridgeshire; Beerhacket, Dorset; Fitzleroi Farm, Sussex; and probable fragments in a find near Cirencester, Gloucestershire (Eogan 1994, 55, fig 20, 56, fig 21; pl X; Needham 2007a). Comparable round-sectioned bracelets with no terminal expansion are also found in France, where several are relatively thick (Eluère 1982, 86–8). Some are in hoards datable to the Rosnoën phase, as at Fresné-la-Mère, Calvados, and Lanrivoaré, Finistère (Eluère 1982, 177, fig 166, 183, fig 171); there are additional unassociated finds from north-western France.

Gold twisted torc

Before the Salcombe discovery, no finds of gold bar torcs had been reported between the western tip of Cornwall and Somerset. In addition to their recurrent appearance in Britain (especially southern Britain) and Ireland, gold twisted bar torcs are present in fewer numbers over much of France (Eluère 1982, 69–75; Eogan 1994, 71, fig 32). Whether this lower frequency implies their importation across the Channel is a moot point. Certainly the intricacy and unique design of a complex and large twisted 'torc' from the Guînes hoard, Pas-de-Calais (Armbruster and Louboutin 2004), must imply regional innovation in northern France based on established expertise, even if that expertise was originally derived from Britain.

Salcombe is not the first example of a gold torc to have been recovered from the sea. There is one from The Minch off the Outer Hebrides, Scotland (Cowie 1994), and two from off the Normandy coast at Sotteville-sur-Mer (see Chapter 4; Billard *et al* 2005). When in datable associations, twisted bar gold torcs, whether formed from triangular, square or flanged bars, always occur in Penard/Rosnoën stage hoards (Northover 1989, 121–5; Needham 1990b, 263).

Loop fasteners/fittings

Of the three contexts yielding good parallels for the loop fastener, Langdon Bay No 157, the Rigny-sur-Arroux hoard contains a variety of ornaments, palstaves, a flanged axe, a knobbed sickle fragment, chisel fragment, ingots, and a pottery vessel (Gaucher 1981, 124–5, figs 35–6A, 368). The palstaves suggest a date contemporary with Taunton/Baux-Sainte-Croix or a little later. The Buissières cave contained other bronzes – a number of bracelets and a trapeze-butt, two-riveted dirk which Gomez de Soto regards as an *ensemble funéraire* (Gomez de Soto 1995, 184–5, fig 80.5; Roudil 1972, 265, no 77, fig 37). The loop fitting from Hasard is part of a well-stratified sequence and seems to come from layer 3A, datable to *Bronze Final I* (Escalon de Fonton 1970, 539, fig 48.5).

Therefore, these close parallels date to the same part of the Bronze Age as the Langdon assemblage, but it is intriguing that they are from the southern half of France, the nearest find to the Channel being south of Dijon. There is one find a little nearer to the Channel coasts that is only a little different in style, having a less pear-shaped loop; it is 50mm long, only a little shorter than the Langdon example. This piece comes from the prolific site of Fort Harrouard, Eure-et-Loir, on the western side of the Paris Basin (Mohen and Bailloud 1987, pl 8.1). Its context is unfortunately insecure, but early excavations on the site yielded material of almost every Bronze Age phase. It is worth mentioning in passing a different form of loop fitting, suggested by Kubach to be belt hooks, some examples of which have an elliptical opening (Kubach 1973, fig 3). They are contemporary and most come from a similar area encompassing the upper Rhône to upper Seine basins.

Fragment No 158 from Langdon Bay is too uncertainly identified to merit further discussion.

Cauldron

The disappearance of a cauldron ring-handle with attached staple is to be much regretted. As far as can be ascertained from extant images the typology of the piece is consonant with a Penard date, the earliest horizon for cauldron production in north-west Europe. Only a handful are known, until recently all being from Britain and Ireland (Gerloff 1986). However, an important new find of an incomplete cauldron, connected to class A0 and tentatively assigned to the Derreen variant of the Shipton-on-Cherwell type, came to light on a site with further bronzes, including a Rosnoën hoard, at Saint-Ygeaux in Brittany (Gerloff 2004, 126; 2010, 58–60, no 5A, pl 13). In addition, sheet fragments in Cannes-Écluse hoard I may also have been from a class A0 cauldron (Gerloff 2004, 102–4, no 28, pl 47), while a ring handle from Crozon, Finistère, is consistent in size and composition with class A0 (Gerloff 2004, 104–5, no 29, pl 47). This just opens up the possibility that the early types were also in production to the south of the Channel. We cannot know whether this separate handle was already scrap metal at the time of its deposition at Salcombe. There are

sheet bronze fragments from the site, but they are thought to be associated with the 17th-century AD cargo nearby (Venetia Porter, pers comm).

Swords

The swords in both the Langdon Bay and Salcombe assemblages split into two main families: Rosnoën and closely related swords characterised by relatively narrow blades with flattened midribs, and a more diverse family with broader and heavier blades which usually have a lozenge cross section. Both involve types that were developed in north-west Europe; no sword fragment positively identified to type need have been manufactured further away from the Channel than the Paris Basin.

Classic Rosnoën swords have traditionally been associated with Brittany, where they occur in several hoards, as emphasised by Jacques Briard's important publications. This need not be the specific origin of the type, however, for they occur much more widely in northern France, as we shall see. The other group is a mixture of types deriving from early western central European swords – those of types Rixheim, Monza, and Arco-Terontola. There is less consistency in feature combinations, but the types hitherto recognised are Grigny, Pépinville A, and Ambleside-Bardouville. These are important in northern France and Britain, but had less impact on western France.

The Rosnoën hoard is now known to contain 37 complete swords and 17 fragments (Nallier and Le Goffic 2008, 154); no other single find contains remotely this number. Twenty-two are complete, straight-bladed, and over 400mm long (Nallier and Le Goffic 2008, 134–42, 145–7, figs 3–4 and 6–9, 31–50; Briard 1958b, nos 25–26). Six other hoards contain at least eight fragments of Rosnoën swords: Chailloué, Orne; Condé-sur-Noireau, Calvados; Coray, Finistère; Hénon, Côtes-d'Armor; Saint-Just-en-Chaussée, Oise; and Saint-Ygeaux, Côtes-d'Armor (Nallier and Le Goffic 2008, Tab 1).

The swords in the Rosnoën hoard have a variety of hilt forms, but virtually all of the blades have proportions classic to the Rosnoën type. Just one has a rather broader blade as well as punched decoration in a cruciform design at the hilt/blade junction (Nallier and Le Goffic 2008, no 50); this was recognised to be different from the associated swords and can in fact be attributed to the Grigny type (see below). Fourteen of the swords have notches while four or five have rivet-holes, usually for four rivets but sometimes for two or six. In addition to the classic Rosnoën type, a variant with slightly angular shoulders has been identified among the new finds (Nallier and Le Goffic 2008, 145–6, nos 13–14, 37, 40–41, 46, and 48); the hilt-plate on these is correspondingly narrower than on classic examples. One of the swords in the hoard from Appleby, Lincolnshire, is of this variant (Davey and Knowles 1972, 156, no 6, fig 2).

The distribution of Rosnoën swords stretches across northern France from the Loire (Renaud Nallier kindly provided the updated list on which this discussion is based; cf Coffyn 1985, 126, map 12). The Breton finds are obviously directly across the western Channel from Salcombe. But more relevant to Langdon Bay are eleven single finds from the lower Seine area, nine from Somme, four single finds plus the Saint-Just-en-Chaussée hoard from the Oise, and two finds from the Ardennes, including what appears to be a disturbed hoard of at least three swords from Mairy (Marolles 1991). While there is no complete Rosnoën sword from Belgium, there appear to be three reworked blades from the river Scheldt in East Flanders: at Moerzeke (De Mulder 1993; Verlaeckt 1992, 74 Moerzeke-1), Schellebelle (Desittere and Weissenborn 1977, 38, no 53, fig 27; Verlaeckt 1992, 79 Schellebelle-8), and Wichelen (Warmenbol 1991, fig 20; Verlaeckt 1992, 92 Wichelen-3). In the Netherlands there is a group of three swords along the river Meuse in Dutch Limburg, a single sword from further north in Drenthe, and a fifth, unprovenanced, example (Butler 1987, 19–21, 32 n 7, figs 12–13).

Because of its relative proximity to Langdon Bay, we should mention here a straight-bladed sword from Wavrin, south-west of Lille, which has not hitherto figured in discussions of Rosnoën or Ambleside-Bardouville swords (Leman 1978, 453, fig 8; Blanchet 1984, 505, no 59). This sword has a gently tapering hilt of Rosnoën form but only two rivets, and its blade appears to have a lenticular section rather than a broad midrib.

There are two finds of Rosnoën swords from the junction of the rivers Rhine and Main. A substantially complete example in Mainz has no precise provenance, but is probably a river find from the mouth of the river Main (Schauer 1971, 81, no 270; Wegner 1976, 169 no 872, Taf. 10, 5). An incomplete sword in four fragments comes from a river concentration found in the Rhine near Wiesbaden (Schauer 1971, 81, no 272; Wegner 1976, 150, no 565a, Taf. 3,1; Taf. 75,2). This find also contains median-winged axes comparable to those found at Langdon Bay and is dated to Bronze D (Wegner 1976, 150, nos 565c, e, Taf. 3, 3 and 5; 4, 1–2; Kibbert 1984, 49, no 82, 53, Tabelle 6; Kubach 1973). In Bavaria, the Windsbach hoard contains a Rosnoën sword reworked as a knife plus a blade fragment (Schauer 1971, 82, no 273), again with median-winged axes (Pászthory and Mayer 1998, nos 670–671, 1007–1009) and is also dated to Bronze D (Pászthory and Mayer 1998, 90–1). Still further east, the hoard from Rýdeč in Bohemia, dated Bronze D-Ha A1 (Kytlicová 2007, 300–02, no 207, Taf 85B–94A), contains at least two broken hilts from Rosnoën swords (Kytlicová 2007, 175–6, 209–10, 302 nos 159–160, Taf 90; also nos 156 and 161; Novák 1975 nos 33–36) with other fragments from blades of western origin (Kytlicová 2007, 100, 105).

Rosnoën swords are rare in central and southern France. There are two finds from the river Saône,

at Tournus and La Truchère (Jeannet 1968, 88, nos 62–63, fig 6), and a fragment from Geneva (Schauer 1971, 81, no 271), plus a recent find from the Dordogne. Three finds have been mapped in south-western France (Coffyn 1985, 126, carte 12, 61–63), but Coffyn's outlying example from Palencia in Spain is apparently not a Late Bronze Age sword but instead a singular weapon of earlier date (Coffyn 1985, 386, no 25, pl II, 3, carte 12, 64; Brandherm 2007, no 828).

Compared with northern France, the Rosnoën type is actually rather rare in Britain. Classic examples with flattish midribs are known from just six sites: the Thames at Kingston, Lambeth, and Putney, from the Appleby hoard, Lincolnshire, and from Limpsfield, Surrey; the blade fragments from the Penard hoard complete the tally (Colquhoun and Burgess 1988, nos 4–5, 7–9; Needham 1987, 115, fig 5.11). Related weapons with lozenge-sectioned blades come from Methwold, Norfolk, Chatham Dockyard, Kent, and Highclere, Hampshire (Colquhoun and Burgess 1988, nos 14–15; Lawson 1984), and these might provide the best parallels for Langdon hilt fragment No 165.

We now turn to the second relevant family of swords, those with a more easterly bias – types Saint-Ouen, Grigny, and Ambleside-Bardouville. The best-preserved sword from Salcombe belongs to the class defined by Reim (1974b, 17) as Pépinville, variant A, but this is somewhat of a misnomer. Other Pépinville swords have leaf-shaped blades, whereas variant A has a broad, parallel-sided blade just like those of the classic Rixheim type and certain Monza variants of western central Europe, especially when the additional feature of longitudinal grooves are also present, as at Salcombe. Keith Muckelroy (1980, 106) recognised the inappropriateness of the 'Pépinville' nomenclature and suggested that they might better be termed Saint-Ouen swords, after one of the finest Paris Basin examples. Despite the obvious similarity of the blade to Rixheim swords, the hilting arrangement is entirely different: a hooked rod-tang projects from the top of a narrow, side-notched hilt-plate; this derives from Monza and Arco-Terontola swords, the distributions of which overlap Rixheim swords but have a more southerly emphasis.

Only six parallels are known with this particular combination of features: Champlay, Yonne (Reim 1974b, 20, fig 2.1, 25 no 10); river Seine, Essonne – ungrooved (Mohen 1977, 104, fig 229, 255); river Seine, above Villeneuve-Saint-Georges, Essonne (Mohen 1977, 104, fig 230, 254); river Seine, Île de Saint-Ouen, Seine-Saint-Denis (Mohen 1977, 104, fig 231); La Chaussée-Tirancourt, Somme – ungrooved (Blanchet 1984, 233, fig 123.1); a totally unprovenanced example – ungrooved (Colquhoun and Burgess 1988, no 2). It is worth noting that the Picquigny example listed by Reim (1974b) was apparently leaf-shaped (Gaucher 1981, 394) and would therefore be better classified as an Arco-Terontola sword. A sword from the Amiens area, Somme, lacks a rod-tang and has a broader triangular hilt-plate with side notches, but it represents a similar local derivation from the classic Rixheim type in this region (Blanchet 1984, 235, fig 124.6). Furthermore, a sword from the river Vilaine, Rennes (Île-et-Vilaine) has a damaged butt, evidently of the Rixheim format, and shows that examples of the grooved Rixheim style weapons were occasionally reaching the far west (Briard 1965, 163, fig 54.4).

The combination of long narrow hilt-plate and relatively broad blade, as on sword No 169 from Langdon Bay, are currently best matched on selected swords within the Grigny and Ambleside-Bardouville groups. Both groups are a little eclectic in terms of specific features employed, most variation lying in the precise mode of hilt attachment. Blade proportions and shape, however, are very similar, and the two groups merge into one another to some extent (Needham 1982b, 23–4). Grigny weapons typically have rather crudely fashioned tangs or bars (Reim 1974b, 29–31), but neater and broader tangs can be found, as on a sword probably from Bardouville, Seine-Maritime (Verron 1973, 396, fig 45.2). This tang is about 13mm wide, compared to 15mm for Langdon Bay No 169. Two swords previously placed in the Ambleside-Bardouville group, those from the river Trent and Essonne, have still broader 'tangs' or hilt plates (19–20mm) (Needham 1982b, 19, fig 5). In both cases, the tangs have side notches for four rivets in an arrangement very reminiscent of the hilt of No 169, and the river Trent example also has a lozenge blade section. There can be little doubt that Langdon sword No 169 belongs somewhere in the Grigny/Ambleside-Bardouville continuum and other fragments may also belong here, notably Langdon Bay Nos 167 and 174 and Salcombe No 19. Blade fragments with lozenge sections (two examples from each site: Nos 177, 179, S16, S17) should derive from one of the types within this more eastern sword family.

The later sword hilt from Salcombe (S18) has been classified above as of Carp's Tongue type despite certain unusual features. Since it must be a quite separate deposit from the Penard assemblage on the site, it will not be discussed more than briefly. Carp's Tongue swords have traditionally been seen to be a connecting type through much of Atlantic Europe (eg Coffyn 1985, 135, map 18), but their typology has only recently been analysed in detail and, in particular, distinguished from Huelva swords (Moskal 2007; Brandherm 2007; Brandherm and Burgess 2008; Brandherm and Moskal-del Hoyo 2010). They probably developed during the 10th century BC, but it has been suggested that their hoard associations belong mainly to the later 9th or even the early 8th centuries (Brandherm and Burgess 2008, 151–2).

Rapiers and dirks

These seem to occur only at Langdon Bay, where there are thirteen examples with hilts sufficiently well preserved (though often still eroded) for us to be reasonably confident of broad type. There were undoubtedly many more represented among the large number of blade fragments in that assemblage. They have been classified as Group IV notched-butt rapiers (Burgess and Gerloff 1981, nos 654–874), erosion precluding any more refined classification. This does not affect chronological considerations; when found in hoards, notched-butt rapiers/dirks of whatever variant date to the Penard/Rosnoën stage or a little later.

There are surprisingly few comparable rapiers/ dirks with bun-shaped hilt-plates from the Continent; Gallay's corpus has no more than fifteen if small knives with shoulders are excluded (among Gallay 1988, nos 1054–1073), compared with over 200 of the family recorded from Ireland and Britain (excluding some slightly heavier blades with similar hilt-plate design). They are almost all from the northern third of France, between the lower Loire and Picardy, suggesting a link with the strong British/Irish tradition in these weapons. Furthermore, the type occurs in several Rosnoën type hoards. Acknowledging the possibility of a poorer rate of recovery in France, it may nevertheless be suggested that rapiers were more rapidly replaced there by the various early sword forms. This contrasts with Britain, where some regions yield both types, sometimes in direct association, and others, such as north-east England have yielded only rapiers. We cannot exclude some limited production of these stabbing weapons on the southern side of the Channel, but it is by no means impossible from the styles involved that most or all of the French examples were insular exports.

Notched-butt knives

Notched-butt knives are again known so far only from Langdon Bay; the twelve examples thus classified are undoubtedly a minimum number, others potentially being among the smaller of the broken blade fragments. This is a fairly eclectic group in detail, but it has still been possible to find parallels for most of the better-preserved examples (above). To judge from the corpora assembled by Burgess and Gerloff (1981) and Gallay (1988), there would seem to be a broad parity in the numbers recovered on the two sides of the Channel. In part this may be explained by the suggestion that some were opportunistic reworkings of broken blades from longer weapons; nevertheless, others are very neatly fashioned and give the impression that they represent the original design.

Few of the comparisons discussed above allow us to suggest a specific source region, but No 207 and possibly 205 can be singled out as belonging to a continental type. The parallels cited above occur in eastern France and the Paris Basin with an outlier in the lower Seine region.

Spearheads

As with swords and palstaves, the Rosnoën hoard is a good starting point for comparative data for the Langdon Bay spearheads. There are now five further examples to add to the four originally published from the hoard (Nallier and Le Goffic 2008, 142, nos 55–59, fig 11). Rosnoën spearheads do not otherwise occur in many French hoards – examples are Coray and Fourdan, cited above for their palstaves – but they are common as river finds in northern France (Nallier and Le Goffic 2008, 150; Mohen 1977, 94, ills 245–267). Spearheads with long sockets and contemporary examples with flame-shaped blades have also been identified in Belgium (eg Warmenbol *et al* 1992, 92–6, nos 74–76, figs 48, 50, and 51; Verlaeckt 1992, 61 Denderwindeke-2, 75 Oudenaarde-3, 77 Schellebelle-3, fig 6, 82 Schoonaarde-8, 91 Wetteren-2, 93 Wichelen-5, 7, 9, and 10; some of these overlap with those in Warmenbol *et al* 1992) and the Netherlands (Butler 1987, 13–17). In Belgium, the Yvoir hoard from Namur contains a Rosnoën spearhead with a median-winged axe (Warmenbol 1990a).

The specific form with long socket and rivet-holes set high up represented by Langdon Bay No 350 occurs in the Rosnoën hoard (Briard 1958a, pl III, 5) and can also be matched in the Chailloué I hoard, Orne (Verney and Verron 1998, nos 16 and 17/18). However, there is also a very similar example in the Baux-Sainte-Croix hoard which we have used here as a type-hoard for the previous phase (O'Connor 1980, fig 18.11).

Ferrules

Two different types of ferrule appear to be represented at Langdon Bay. The first (No 354) is of the conical type expected for this period (eg Needham 1982b, 38). It is traditionally considered to have been developed on the Continent, but O'Connor exposed the difficulties of this derivation for the British series (1980, 102): the nearest group, in the Middle Elbe region, is too late to serve as a prototype; on the other hand, those in sufficiently early contexts are as far away as Bohemia and this either involved a big geographic leap before it came to be adopted by another cultural group, or hidden circulation making their absence in between more apparent than real. A possible alternative, indigenous derivation is raised in Chapter 5, but the main point is that, even if foreign in inspiration, the conical ferrule was adopted and then lengthened under insular production (Needham 1982b, 38).

The knobbed ferrule (No 355) is more surprising at this date for the type does not appear in terrestrial associations in the lands flanking the Channel until the succeeding Wilburton stage, but there is every reason to accept that it belongs with the assemblage given comparable metal composition. A ferrule of yet another kind has appeared in a Taunton stage association from Hayling Island, Hampshire (Lawson 1999, 101, fig 11.6, lower right); metal analysis has shown its conformity to the associated metalwork, so this is another illustration of hidden elements in the metalwork repertoire beginning to be revealed.

Rectangular block (weight)

The smooth-faced rectangular block from Salcombe has very few recognised parallels in north-west Europe. Two examples made of lead have been recorded in Ewart phase contexts in Britain, one excavated from the Runnymede settlement site on the river Thames, the other coming from a hoard at West Caister, Norfolk (Needham and Hook 1988, 261, fig 2.1; Lawson 1979b). Less closely dated, but presumably later Bronze Age, is an example from the Flag Fen Power Station site (Coombs 2001, 272, no 152, 273, fig 10.8). The Runnymede example weighs 112.3g, the West Caister one 158g.

There is a much bigger corpus of such blocks in central Europe, although they are rather variable in exact shape, size, and weight. Chris Pare (1999) argues that they functioned as weights in an early weighing system and this seems the most plausible explanation for the British finds too. The discovery of a second example at Salcombe (post-2004 and not covered in this volume; Fig 3.22) is mentioned above because its decoration gives it specific parallels among the continental corpus, thus strengthening the tie between the insular and continental series. The central European examples collated by Pare mainly occur in graves dating to Reinecke Bronze D, which is exactly the period most coeval with Penard and Rosnoën metalwork in the north-west.

Metal waste and raw metal

The few examples of metal waste and raw metal – two casting jets and a 'spill' of bronze from Langdon Bay (Nos 356–358) and a small tin lump from Salcombe (S28) – may seem to be unimportant pieces in themselves. The bronzes are confirmed to belong to the collection through analysis, whereas it is impossible to be sure for the tin lump. However, the presence of metalworking debris and raw metal makes an important point for the simple reason that these categories are virtually unknown in contemporary terrestrial hoards from neighbouring regions. In central France the Malassis and Cannes-Écluse I hoards include straight rod ingots, as does the group from the Rhein bei Mainz, but these are some distance away (Briard *et al* 1969, 60, fig 20, nos 200–205; Gaucher and Robert 1967, 198, fig 29, especially nos 1, 6, 12; Kubach 1973, figs 1.20–1.21). A group of small 'thumb-ingots' occurs on the Channel coast in the Hayling Island I hoard, Hampshire (which also yielded the ferrule mentioned above; Lawson 1999, 101, fig 11.6 left), but this belongs to the preceding phase, as does the Burgesses' Meadow hoard (Oxford), containing a straight rod ingot (Hawkes 1955, GB. 6

no 7). These minor inclusions in the seabed assemblages are therefore unusual in terms of land-based deposition practices.

Finds of unalloyed tin from the Bronze Age are extremely rare, presumably because it was in such high demand that it was almost always rapidly absorbed into the alloyed pool of metal (Needham and Hook 1988; Rohl and Northover 2001).

Metal analyses *by J P Northover*

Analysis of copper-alloy metalwork from Langdon Bay

History and introduction

The metallurgical study of the copper-alloy artefacts recovered from Langdon Bay was carried out in several stages. The first stage was in 1980–81, in connection with a study of the technical changes which took place in metallurgy in the later Bronze Age in Britain. A total of 182 objects from the assemblage was analysed and all samples were cut in order to allow metallographic examination as well as microanalysis. When it was discovered that the worn condition of the objects caused by abrasion and corrosion on the seabed had removed the worked areas of most artefacts the emphasis was placed mainly on the microanalysis of the samples. Initially, analysis was for eleven elements; at a later stage bismuth and sulphur were added to the element set and the lead levels were re-estimated. I am indebted to Prof Urve Kallavus of the Technical University, Tallinn, for this additional analysis, which was funded by a Soros Fellowship. These later analyses were made on 170 samples, the other 12 samples having been reused for lead isotope analysis by Dr B M Rohl as part of her doctoral research, later published by Rohl and Needham (1998). Subsequent to the reanalysis by Prof Kallavus, and, as part of the present publication project, a further 11 samples were reused for lead isotope analysis, making the total for this technique 23. Later still, a further 32 samples were analysed using drilled samples and an extended set of 16 elements, the sampled objects being selected to cover a number of typological gaps and to address other questions. I am indebted to Mr C J Salter of the Department of Materials, University of Oxford, for assistance with these analyses.

For each sample a minimum of three analyses were performed, and the mean values are given in Appendix 2 in weight per cent. The sampling and analysis methods are set out in Appendix 4.

Alloys

Of the 214 samples analysed, one (a rod, No 362) proved to be a relatively recent brass and consequently is not discussed further.

The remaining analysed objects were all identified as being of Bronze Age date and are almost universally cast in medium tin, unleaded bronze. A simple measure of this is given by a histogram (Fig 3.25a) and box-plot (Fig 3.25b). The distribution of tin contents is near normal with a mean of 10.3wt% and a standard deviation of ±1.8wt%. There is some slight skewing to higher tin concentrations, and a very low peak at 15wt% tin. The box-plot confirms this pattern and shows that there are very few outliers. There is one unalloyed copper, used in a broad-tanged sword (No 169); three outliers are lower tin bronzes with tin in the range 5–7%, and four are higher tin bronzes forming the minor peak in the histogram already mentioned.

The same treatment was applied to the lead content of the objects, even though almost all of them had a lead content below 1% (Fig 3.26a–b). The two diagrams show that almost all the lead contents are below 0.5%, with a mean of 0.18%. There are some outliers in the range 0.45–0.75%, but only one object has a lead content that can be presumed to have been sufficiently large to have had an observable impact on the properties of the alloy – spearhead No 350, with 1.5% lead. Rising lead contents were first identified in Late Bronze Age metalwork by Brown and Blin-Stoyle (1959), but examples of higher lead

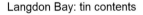

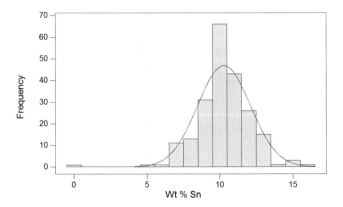

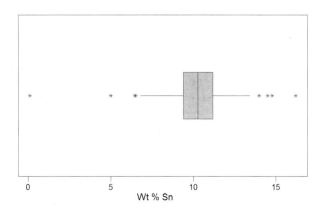

Fig 3.25 Tin content of Langdon Bay bronzes, with normal curve

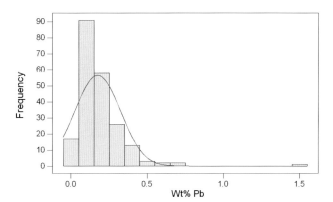

Fig 3.26   Lead content of Langdon Bay bronzes, with normal curve

were later found to occur also in the Middle Bronze Age, both in Britain and in France (Northover 1980; 1983; Briard 1984; 1985; Briard and Bigot 1989). The main period of this earlier occurrence is the Acton Park phase in Britain and the equivalent Tréboul in north-west France. However, it also occurs sporadically in later phases of the Middle Bronze Age either by chance in the charge in the smelting furnace or through recycling older metal; there is no reason to regard Langdon Bay No 350 as a deliberately created leaded bronze.

The uniformity of alloy content in the Langdon assemblage and Penard/Rosnoën metalwork more generally must reflect not only a uniformity of metallurgical style in a significant area of north-west Europe but also the effects of repeated recycling. However, within this apparently homogeneous picture it is possible that subtle variation is concealed, variation that might reflect, for example, the circulation of different alloys in different areas or the selection of different types of alloy for different products. There is, in fact, little such variation, but a simple graphical representation shows some small differences between the production technology of various different types of objects. In Figure 3.27 lead is plotted against tin for the major categories, with median-winged axes and palstaves plotted separately as they are numerically two of the largest groups. The graph does show some separation, with weapons and tools other than axes having a wider range of tin contents than either the median-winged axes or the palstaves. This observation is probably the result of these objects having been originally produced in different places and/or at different times. The median-winged axes also tend to separate from the palstaves on the basis of lead, but this separation results from the use of different metal resources, an issue discussed in the section below.

An attempt was made to make a more detailed breakdown of alloy content. Figure 3.28a–b shows the results for axes and for weapons divided by category. For the axes, all fragments were excluded and the palstaves were divided, where possible, into their three different categories. There is no clear variation among the palstaves because the total number of results is too small, but the higher lead contents of many median-winged axes are confirmed. Additionally, the socketed axes are seen to be associated with lower tin contents than the other group, suggesting a different location for their production. Among the weapons, there seem to be few differences between dirks or rapiers or swords. However, the whole picture is obscured by the number of weapon fragments which cannot be assigned to a specific type.

Previous analytical studies have shown that the medium tin, unleaded bronzes analysed here are typical of Penard/Rosnoën period bronzes, at least until the beginning of the change from pyritic to fahlerz bronzes which takes place contemporary with Ha A2 (eg Liversage and Northover 1998). In the preceding Taunton-Cemmaes period in Britain there was a very wide range of tin contents with both lower- and higher-tin alloys as well as medium tin bronzes. The lower band was probably the result of local interruptions in tin supply, while the higher band, in the range 12–16%, was the result of the import of bronze of this type from Brittany and Normandy (Northover 1983). In that part of France it appears that lower-tin bronze imported from elsewhere, most probably the Alps, was realloyed with additional tin. This process is characteristic of exactly this phase of the Middle Bronze Age and appears to have ceased relatively quickly with the establishment of new traditions. The mixing of higher-tin bronzes with locally collected or newly imported lower-tin bronzes would tend to produce the distribution of tin contents seen at Langdon Bay. The presence of some survivors from Taunton-Cemmaes metalworking that skew the overall distribution and contribute the small peak at 15% tin implies that the homogenisation process was still in progress, although possibly nearing its end. It is hard to gauge how long this process would take, but the changeover in compositions could certainly happen within a generation

Langdon Bay: alloy contents

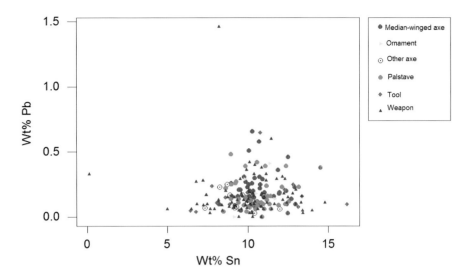

Fig 3.27   Alloy content of Langdon Bay bronzes

or so. Therefore, we may conclude from these tin contents that the majority of the assemblage dates to early in the Penard/Rosnoën period, but not its very beginning.

Impurity patterns

The impurities analysed comprise those which are indicative of the technology by which the copper ore was roasted and smelted (in this case iron and sulphur), and those which are more indicative of the mineral assemblages from which the copper ore was selected (cobalt, nickel, arsenic, antimony, silver, and bismuth). Gold and zinc are almost always at very low levels and are not detected consistently enough to be considered here.

When chalcopyrite and similar copper-iron-sulphides are smelted, it is, in theory, possible to roast, smelt, and refine the ore so that both iron and sulphur are eliminated as oxides, either to the air or to the slag. In fact, traces of both iron and sulphur often remain in the copper, their concentrations dependent both on the original smelting technology and on the extent of remelting and recycling, since both tend to be lost in this process. Thus, high values of iron and/or sulphur can be an indication that newly smelted copper has been made into bronze for the artefact, rather than existing bronze having been recycled. With the majority of values below 0.5% for sulphur and 0.15% for iron, there are no compositions in the Langdon assemblage that definitively point to unrecycled metal (Fig 3.29).

It is also instructive to look at the composition of copper ingots from the Continent in the Middle Bronze Age (there is none in Britain). Results from Switzerland (Northover 1997) show black copper from the smelter being refined at the point of use and then alloyed, leaving modest levels of iron

and sulphur in the bronze. Ingot copper from both Switzerland and France (Mohen 1977) can, before refining, have very high iron and, sometimes, also high arsenic contents – on occasion as much as 3–5%. What appears to be much more uncommon is for raw copper in circulation to have concentrations of impurities, such as arsenic, antimony, and nickel, which match the bronzes with which they are associated. The implication is that the copper in unalloyed state is not the only significant contribution to the alloyed metal in circulation at this time. Therefore, to understand the way in which metal was circulated and used, we must rely much more on the finished bronzes than on the raw copper.

Analysis of Middle and Late Bronze Age metalwork from north-west Europe (eg Northover 1980; 1983; Mohen 1977; Briard 1984; 1985; Liversage 2000; Rychner and Kläntschi 1995) shows that, in the period we are discussing, the most significant impurities were arsenic and nickel, with antimony and silver occupying a lesser place. Briard and Bigot (1989) mapped the arsenic-to-nickel ratios of all analysed palstaves in northern and western France and showed that those with Ni>As clustered immediately south of the Loire, in Normandy and in Lorraine, while those with As>Ni were from Brittany, around the Gironde, and from the Ardennes-Champagne region. At the same time, both Rychner and Kläntschi in Switzerland and Liversage in Denmark showed there could be a chronological change as well, with Ni>As being typical of a period contemporary with Taunton-Cemmaes (Period 2 in Denmark and *Bronze Moyen* in Switzerland), while the proportion of nickel declined in Nordic Period 3 and Bz D/Ha A1 in Switzerland. The present writer had reported similar changes in Britain, especially where imported bronze was concerned, results supported by the work of Rohl and Needham (1998).

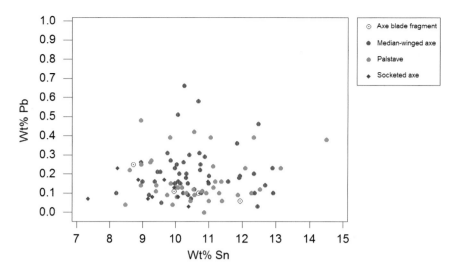

Fig 3.28a Alloy content of axes from Langdon Bay

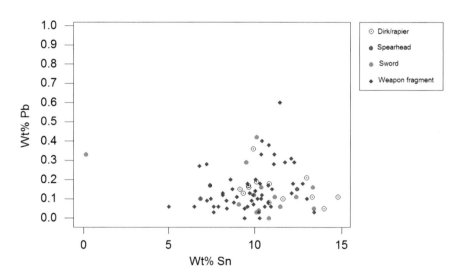

Fig 3.28b Alloy content of other weapons from Langdon Bay

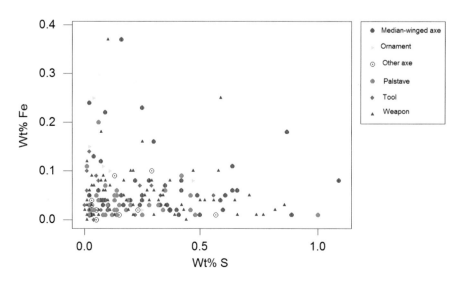

Fig 3.29   Iron and sulphur impurities of Langdon Bay bronzes

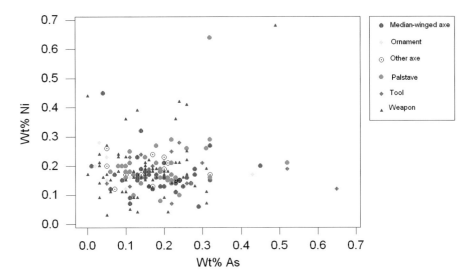

Fig 3.30   Nickel and arsenic impurities of Langdon Bay bronzes

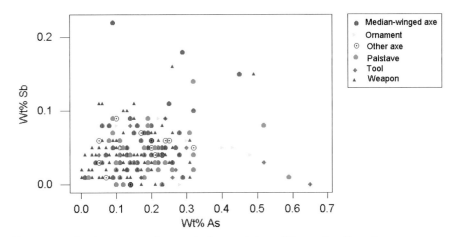

Fig 3.31   Antimony and arsenic impurities of Langdon Bay bronzes

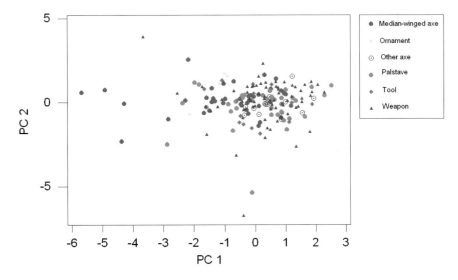

Fig 3.32   Principal components analysis of Langdon Bay bronzes

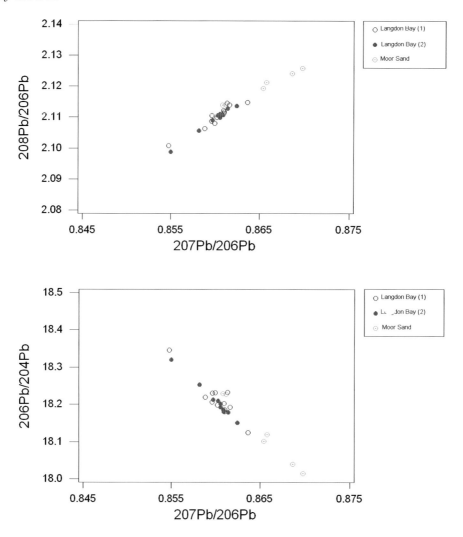

Fig 3.33 Lead isotope ratios of the Langdon Bay and Moor Sand assemblages

Accordingly, the first step in analysing the impurity patterns was to plot nickel against arsenic for the various categories (Fig 3.30). This shows that at least half the analyses have Ni>As with a bias towards palstaves and weapons for the higher nickel contents, and towards median-winged axes for the lower nickel contents. It has to be emphasised that this is only a trend and may not be statistically significant; but it does lend support to the separate character of the median-winged axes based on their lead content. Since both chronological and geographical factors must be involved, the highest nickel contents, like the highest tin contents, provides evidence of the survival of older metal in circulation and for a date early in the Penard period, but not right at its beginning.

A further significant impurity is antimony, which is present at sufficient levels to point to some use of fahlerz ores. The highest concentration of antimony in the Langdon Bay bronzes is just over 0.2%, and this indicates that the contribution of fahlerz ores to the metal supply responsible for this assemblage was not particularly great. A plot of antimony against arsenic (Fig 3.31) showed no clear trends at all. The

next stage was to undertake a principal components analysis based on a much wider range of impurities (Fe, Co, Ni, As, Sb, Ag, Pb) (Fig 3.32). The plot shows the distributions for palstaves and median-winged axes overlapping, but with the former biased towards the right and the latter to the left. For the median-winged axes, the extreme values at the left relate to high values of lead, antimony, and silver; while for the palstaves (and weapons) to the right nickel and arsenic are important. Thus, a significant proportion of the metal in the median-winged axes originated from a different source or sources and had a different history to that of a significant proportion of the palstaves and weapons.

Lead isotope analysis

In 1998 Rohl and Needham published twelve lead isotope analyses from objects in the Langdon Bay assemblage. Their conclusion was that the results, when combined with the compositional analysis, fell into their IMP-LI group 14; and that this metal spectrum in Britain 'had a substantial contribution

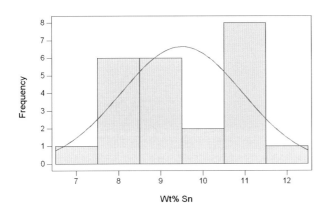

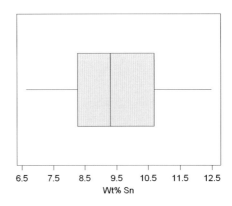

Fig 3.34 Tin content of Salcombe bronzes, with normal curve

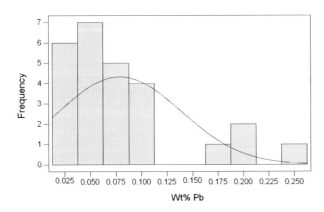

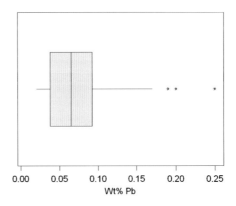

Fig 3.35 Lead content of Salcombe bronzes

from continental stocks of metal ... especially in the southern English counties' (Rohl and Needham 1998, 100). To take this study further, an additional eleven samples were analysed. The combined listing of lead isotope data is set out in Appendix 1 and the isotope ratios are plotted in Figure 3.33a–b.

The lead isotope data lend strong support to the conclusions already reached from the compositional analysis of the Langdon Bay material. There is a tight cluster at the centre of both plots where median-winged axes, palstaves, and weapons overlap. The palstave data are entirely within this cluster, while the median-winged axes trend to lower values of the Pb^{208}:Pb^{206} and higher values of the Pb^{207}:Pb^{206} and Pb^{206}:Pb^{204} ratios, while assorted blades, a rapier, a sword, and a socketed axe trend in the other direction. Clearly, the metal included in this assemblage derives from three different sources, certainly geographically separated, but almost certainly including some effects of the presence of older metal. Interestingly, the extreme

isotope ratios for the median-winged axes correlate with the raised values of antimony, silver, and lead already discussed. These isotope ratios also closely match material in the Penard hoard (Needham and Rohl 1998), but the Penard analyses do not have the antimony, silver, and lead concentrations of the Langdon Bay objects. This comparison clearly illustrates the complexity of lead isotope data where there is extensive recycling and trade, and when many ore deposits are of similar geological age and thus similar isotopic composition.

Metallography

Since the artefacts were in such an abraded state, most areas of significant thermo-mechanical treatment have been worn away. Therefore, no conclusions can be reached about the state of even the more intact objects when they were deposited – that is, whether they were unfinished, newly finished,

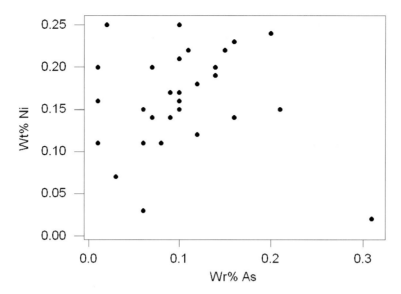

Fig 3.36   Nickel and arsenic impurities of Salcombe bronzes

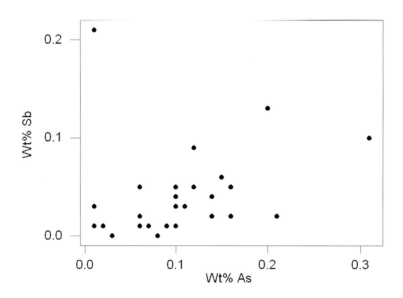

Fig 3.37   Antimony and arsenic impurities of Salcombe bronzes

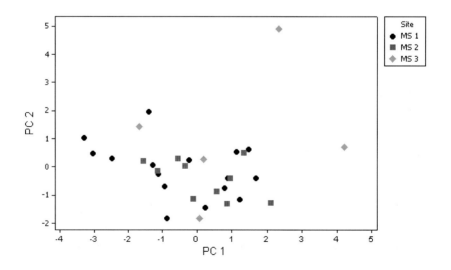

Fig 3.38   Principal components analysis of Salcombe bronzes

used or worn out. Seeing that a large quantity of material in the assemblage seems to have been destined for recycling, it is unlikely that they were unfinished or unused, and the hints of age in some of them confirm this hypothesis, but it would still have been useful to have supporting metallographic evidence. Summary metallographic data will be placed in the site archive.

Summary

The programme of analysis demonstrated that the compositions of the Langdon Bay bronze artefacts were overwhelmingly typical of the Penard/Rosnoën period on both sides of the English Channel. With two exceptions, the 213 analyses were of medium tin, unleaded bronzes with arsenic and nickel as the most significant impurities. Although the compositions showed considerable uniformity, the few combination of elemental and lead isotope analysis suggested that three streams of metal were involved, one dominated by the palstaves and overlapping with the others, one dominated by median-winged axes, and one by a variety of blades and weapons. It is proposed that these patterns relate to different source areas on the Continent, correlating with the centres of distribution of individual types, and in part also to an element of time depth (decades, not centuries), especially among the weapons and some palstaves.

Analysis of copper-alloy and tin metalwork from Moor Sand and Salcombe Site B

In total, 31 pieces of metalwork of potential Bronze Age date were analysed from the Salcombe sites. They were analysed in two groups. The first five analyses were made on those objects discovered at Moor Sand in 1978–79 (Analysis Group MS 3). These analyses were carried out at the same time and under the same conditions as the first tranche of Langdon Bay analyses. The remaining 26 analyses were made on objects discovered in 2004 (Group MS 1) and 2005 (Group MS 2)[1] using the JEOL 8800 microprobe in the Department of Materials, University of Oxford, with the much appreciated assistance of Mr C J Salter. All analyses in this group were made using drilled samples and the same conditions as the second tranche of Langdon Bay analyses, but an additional element, cadmium, was added to the set. In the event, cadmium and manganese were generally not detected. Aluminium and silicon were, however, detected on occasion and are a measure of the extent of corrosion, especially for the one tin sample.

The means of a minimum of three analyses per sample are given in Appendix 3 in weight per cent. The sampling and analysis methods are set out in Appendix 4. Also in Appendix 3 is the analysis of a Sicilian-type tool from the collections of the British Museum, which was sampled to provide a comparison for the example from Salcombe site B (S7). Besides reviewing the total collection of metalwork from both sub-sites, inter- and intra-site differences are also considered.

Alloys

The compositions recorded in Appendix 3 are all consistent with a Bronze Age date. One sample was from a piece of tin metal (S28) and one was from a high-tin bronze with 22% tin (Site ref 050918 0001). This object was a fragment of an apparent wire-drawing die which will be discussed briefly below. Excluding this object, the tin contents (Fig 3.34a) exhibit a bimodal distribution with peaks between 8wt% and 9wt% tin, and one around 10wt% tin; the box-plot (Fig 3.34b) shows no outliers. It should be remembered, though, that the population analysed here is rather small, so a few additional analyses might alter the picture considerably. A box-plot of the lead contents shows that there are no leaded bronzes, that the maximum lead value is 0.25%, and that the range of lead contents is much more limited than at Langdon Bay (Fig 3.35). Both tin and lead contents are consistent with dates in the Penard/Rosnoën period for all the medium-tin bronzes. As the number of objects in the first discovery is so small, it is not possible to make a valid comparison of alloy content between Moor Sand and Salcombe site B. All that can be said is that the alloy contents of the former group lie within the overall range.

The 22% tin recorded for the possible wire-drawing die fragment already mentioned may be enhanced by the effects of corrosion, but it was quite clear when the sample was drilled that the metal was a hard, white bronze. An alloy of around 20% would be easy to cast and would give very considerable as-cast hardness eminently suitable for a wire-drawing die. The use of such dies in the Bronze Age has been disputed, a particular objection being that no evidence can be found for their use in the form of traces on gold wires. However, it is possible that fully annealed bronze wires were both smoothed and reduced in thickness by these devices. The objects thought to be dies in the Isleham hoard (Wilburton phase, early Late Bronze Age) are convincing as such and a possible candidate for drawn wire of Penard date has also been identified (Northover 1995). The Isleham dies were, however, cast in a lower-tin, leaded bronze, and it is not clear how effectively they would have functioned, unless for drawing a softer metal.

The one piece of tin from Salcombe (S28) is very pure, apart from some aluminium and silicon from silty encrustations; removing those elements gives a purity of 99.9%. This purity is consistent with some of the tin ornaments from Flag Fen, while other pieces from that site contain small amounts of lead and copper (Rohl and Northover 2001). This find adds another example to the population of tin objects from Britain, the majority from Flag Fen, dating, perhaps, to early in the Late Bronze Age rather than to the Penard period. That tin metal did circulate in the Penard period is shown by the tin fillings of the sheet bronze handles of some shields (Needham *et al* 2012). The fact that S28 appears to be a lump rather than a finished object could place it in such a metalworking context.

Impurity patterns

The impurity content of the Salcombe bronzes is generally low, maximum values being 0.25% nickel, 0.31% arsenic (with the next highest being 0.21%), 0.21% antimony (next highest 0.13%, with only three values ≥0.10%), and 0.09% silver. A plot of nickel against arsenic (Fig 3.36) shows that the majority of samples has Ni>As, comparable to half the material from Langdon Bay. Compared with Langdon Bay, the maximum concentrations of nickel are significantly lower; and, coupled with the absence of tin contents of 12–16%, there is, perhaps, less survival of older metal. The majority of the outliers in this plot come from Moor Sand (Analysis Group MS 3), well separated on the seabed from the others, but this observation may be partially due to small differences between the two batches of analyses. Suffice it to say that four out of the five artefacts are particularly characterised by low arsenic contents. In contrast to this pattern, there is one extreme outlier with a high arsenic and very low nickel content, the intact and unworn rod-tanged sword (S15). A plot of antimony against arsenic (Fig 3.37) shows almost all antimony concentrations below 0.1%, so the influence of fahlerz compositions is almost negligible. There is more overlap in this plot between the Moor Sand and Salcombe site B objects, but the rod-tanged sword remains a distant outlier. The other outlier is one of the heavily abraded blades.

A more generalised comparison between the three analytical groups can be made with a principal components analysis (Fig 3.38). The two tranches of recent finds, from Salcombe site B, overlap very fully, but Group MS 2 has a greater spread, with the extreme values belonging to weapon blades or hilts. One of the blades from Moor Sand is relatively close to some of these, while a palstave plots in the middle of the main distribution and must be part of the same flow of metal. Again, the rod-tanged sword and one other blade remain as rather distant outliers.

Comment should also be made here on the analysis of the Sicilian-type *strumento* (S7). Its composition is entirely typical of the Salcombe assemblage, with 8.4% tin, 0.23% nickel, 0.16% arsenic, 0.08% silver, and 0.10% lead. Interestingly, the comparative example found in Sicily had 0.03% nickel, 0.27% arsenic, 0.04% silver, and 0.24% lead, and so was much less like the norm for Salcombe. One other feature of this Sicilian parallel, however, is the

cobalt content of 0.04%. An impurity pattern with Co>Ni is uncommon in the Bronze Age but can be associated with south-west England – for example, among some Crediton palstaves (Northover unpublished) – and was very important there in the Iron Age. Other locations of copper sources which can give this impurity pattern are central Italy and Cyprus. What is intriguing and surprising here is that, rather than the Salcombe *strumento*, it is the rod-tanged sword that is very close in composition to that of the Sicilian *strumento* from the British Museum collection, including having Co>Ni, both at low levels. The only difference is the rather higher arsenic content in the sword. Nonetheless, an Italian connection for the sword may be a possibility.

We may conclude from the impurity patterns that there is some overlap with the metal circulation zones from which the Langdon Bay material was drawn, but that the particular pattern associated with the median-winged axes is definitely excluded. The Salcombe assemblages drew on at least one other zone, as expressed by some of the blades, and by the rod-tanged sword. However, this sword, because of its differing state of preservation, may have a significantly different history of collection and deposition.

Lead isotope analysis

Six Penard phase objects from the first collection of finds from Moor Sand were analysed by Dr Rohl (Rohl and Needham 1998; Appendix 1). Four of the results were seen as being part of the IMP-LI group 14 to which the Langdon Bay analyses were assigned, with a consequent conclusion of a probable continental dimension to the origin of the metal. The results are plotted with the analyses of the two tranches of samples from Langdon Bay (Figs 3.33a–b). Of the six analyses, two plot with the core of the Langdon Bay distribution, confirming the overlap. These prove to be the two palstaves S3 and S4, so the grouping with the Langdon Bay data is very much to be expected. The other four analyses are the fine sword (S15) and other less-diagnostic blades (S16–17, S22) which plot in a different direction from the trend of the Langdon Bay data. This observation confirms the conclusions from the impurity patterns that one strand in the Salcombe compositions matches Langdon Bay but that there are others which do not, and that some of the implied connections may be rather distant. There is not the same difference in the impurity patterns and lead isotope ratios between the weapons and axes at Langdon Bay. Therefore, at Salcombe it would appear that the ways in which axes and tools and their fragments were collected differed significantly from the way in which the weapons and their fragments were assembled. There is no reason to doubt that the Salcombe weapons were mainly intended for recycling; but, in the western Channel and along the Atlantic coast, there were different ways of collecting them.

Summary

The Salcombe results are further evidence of how the widespread use of coppers from pyritic ore sources, a uniformity of alloying practice, and extensive recycling can produce metal of relatively homogeneous composition from a diversity of sources. In the case of Salcombe, one of the immediate sources is north-west France, even if the copper was originally smelted elsewhere. However, the material also evidently derives from one or more other regional sources yet to be clearly identified. Only extensive correlation of analyses and typology with judicious support from lead isotope analysis will unravel this complex pattern further.

Conclusions on the date of the assemblages
by Stuart Needham and Brendan O'Connor

Detailed discussion of the significance of the object compositions of these two remarkable seabed assemblages is reserved for Chapter 5. However, this is the appropriate point to draw conclusions on the dating of the two assemblages. Seabed assemblages will rarely be sealed stratigraphically, meaning there will always be a danger of the coincidental mixing of material of different periods. Ignoring the occasional modern detritus, conflation does not seem to be a significant problem at Langdon Bay. Most of the object types can be shown either to belong specifically to the Rosnoën and Penard assemblages (or their contemporaries in other regions), or, if of longer currency, to at least be present in those assemblages. The few object types that cannot, as yet, be found in contemporary hoards or other closed finds might at first raise concerns of intrusion. However, in all cases the metal composition of the items in question shows them to be integral components of the main assemblage. This instead forces us to consider the extent to which the non-deposition of types in regular circulation can lead to hidden elements of the repertoire – a point made with specific reference to the Langdon Bay find in an early interim account (Needham and Dean 1987).

Until the close of the 2004 season at Salcombe (our cut-off for this volume), much the same could be said of its assemblage. Just one object was identifiable as belonging to a quite discrete phase: the Carp's Tongue sword, S18. However, later discoveries are altering the picture, as there is certainly another sword of Ewart date in the same general area of the seabed and it remains to be assessed whether the large group of ingots also belongs to that phase (Dave Parham and SWMAG, pers comm). This does not, however, alter the integrity of the Penard phase group discussed in this report, as the majority of objects have been identified to specific types and the

more eroded pieces have been shown to have comparable compositions.

Both the absolute dating of Penard/Rosnoën metalwork and its chronological correlation to central European sequences are extremely complicated matters and this is not the place to do more than summarise recent views. Divergent opinions are in part due to different methodological approaches. Sabine Gerloff has provided the most recent detailed consideration of correlations between north-west and central Europe (2007) using traditional methods of cross-associations as her basis, with radiocarbon evidence introduced as a supplement. In contrast, the 'DoB' programme for southern Britain (Needham *et al* 1997) used high-quality radiocarbon determinations empirically in order to try to free the regional chronology from the assumptions traditionally made about inter-regional synchronisations and/or directions of influence. Both approaches can have their limitations. Samples datable by radiocarbon can be biased towards certain bronze types, for example, those that tend to occur with organic haft remnants in waterlogged environments, or those that were regularly placed in graves in those regions where metalwork was acceptable for funerary use. In the case of haft remnants, there is also the question of the growth-age of the wood sampled. While the specialist involved in the DoB programme assessed most samples to be young wood, Lanting and van der Plicht (2001/2; also Brindley 2007, 380) have taken the view that more mature wood would be chosen for hafts and shafts, and have consequently slightly down-dated the British metalwork assemblages relative to Needham *et al* 1997.

The perennial problem of making alignments on the basis of cross-associations is that there are generally very few critical associations relating to well-separated regions. This makes it difficult to evaluate, firstly, whether some isolated long-distance displacements might be long-circulated objects and, secondly, how well synchronised the beginnings and ends of period assemblages in one region are with those in another. Thus, the evidence might clearly point to two assemblages overlapping, but not be of good enough resolution to indicate the degree and direction of overlap. These problems have been long understood by many specialists attempting correlations, but, ultimately, only the construction of robust regional chronologies for each relevant region can resolve these conundrums.

Gerloff (2007, 126, table 13.2, 145–9) equates *Bronze Final I* and earlier Penard (Penard 1), relevant to Langdon Bay and Salcombe, with Reinecke Bronze D and Hallstatt A1 (though we would not accept her identification of the majority of the Langdon Bay winged axes as Bronze C2 types). There is good evidence for widespread contacts at this time, when various types of prestige metalwork were introduced into Britain. She gives a chronology of 1300–1150 BC, while stressing the paucity of relevant absolute dates. Nevertheless, in their wide-ranging survey of radiocarbon chronology Lanting and van der Plicht (2001/2, 134) came to the range of 1325–1125 BC for Bronze D plus Hallstatt A1.

There are virtually no absolute dates relating directly to the bronze types present at Langdon Bay and Salcombe on either side of the Channel; indeed, dates for broadly contemporary material of any kind are scarce. Recent evidence for west-central Europe is provided by absolute dates for cremations with pottery from Elgg-Breiti, Canton Zürich, Switzerland, which suggest a 13th-century BC date for Bronze D (Mäder and Sormaz 2000; Mäder 2002, 147–75; Lanting and van der Plicht 2001/2, 131; Gerloff 2007, 124–5; Harding *et al* 2007, 83–4; Przybyła 2009, 59–62, fig 4). Radiocarbon dates for *Bronze Final I* contexts in France have only just begun to appear (Gouge and Peake 2005, 352, fig 14; Peake and Delattre 2005, 16–17).

The small group of radiocarbon dates for British Penard metalwork is helpful, even though they bear only indirectly on the particular bronze types from Langdon Bay and Salcombe. These were used to argue for a *core* date range for Penard of 1275–1140 BC (Needham *et al* 1997) or 1250–1125 BC (Lanting and van der Plicht 2001/2, 142–3; summarised in English by Brindley 2007, 375 and 380). While these limits provide useful 'watershed' dates between one metalworking tradition and the next, it should be recognised that they do not necessarily constrain the beginnings and ends of the respective traditions. There is always the possibility of overlap with preceding and succeeding traditions and it is eminently possible that some Penard and Rosnoën styles began earlier, around the beginning of the 13th century BC. Similarly, one cannot rule out a late facies of Penard (Penard 2), characterised above all by early flange-hilted swords (Types Hemigkofen, Erbenheim, Clewer, Limehouse etc) continuing through to the late 12th century, as argued by Gerloff (2007, 146) in order to explain the Hallstatt A2 knife in the Ffynhonnau hoard. Placing the two seabed assemblages more closely within this two-century span hinges primarily on the sword types present, as no other types have been recognised to show significant typological development over the course of the tradition. Although one object at Langdon, the Norman palstave (Langdon type 4) is typical of the preceding phase, this is a single object in a very large assemblage and cannot be taken to indicate a specifically transitional date.

The swords at both sites suggest a date in the earlier rather than the later part of Penard. The Saint-Ouen (formerly Pépinville A variant) sword from Salcombe is seen to be one of the very early types accounting for the spread of the heavy bladed sword to north-west Europe (Needham 1982b). Meanwhile, Langdon Bay has fragments which are most likely to belong to other early derivatives of continental Rixheim and Monza swords – notably the Grigny and Ambleside/Bardouville series and perhaps other 'hybrids' with Rosnoën weapons. Rosnoën swords are regarded as an early north-west French response, though need not be exclusively early. However, on both sides of the Channel the subsequent introduction of flange-hilted swords with leaf-shaped blades from Hallstatt A1 of central Europe is believed to have stimulated a range of new regional types (mentioned above) perhaps from as early as the turn of the 13th/12th centuries (Gerloff 2007, 126, table 13.2, 148). These forms are not apparent in either seabed assemblage. Thus, overall, we would suggest that both of these assemblages are best dated to the 13th century BC or a little later on the basis of typology, associations, and relevant absolute dating (see Table 5.3 for their position in the longer trajectory of metalwork traditions). This conclusion finds further support from Peter Northover's deductions from the temporal dynamics of changing metal compositions.

Note to Chapter 3

1   These objects are not catalogued or discussed in this volume, but it seemed useful to publish the analytical results alongside the others obtained.

4 Other marine finds of Bronze Age metalwork from Britain and the near Continent

by Stuart Needham

It was clear from an early stage in the campaign of exploration on the two key seabed sites that it might be instructive to consider other marine finds of Bronze Age metalwork. To this end, both previously published examples and new finds that have come to our attention have been logged over many years (the cut-off date was the end of 2004, just as for the growing Salcombe assemblage). Deciding on what precise contexts might be most relevant for comparison is not, however, straightforward, for the obvious reasons that the coastline may have shifted since the Bronze Age with consequent reworking of artefacts from terrestrial to marine contexts or vice versa. Even without reworking, the submergence of low-lying ground through sea level rise might take original terrestrial deposits into the marine domain (as, for example, at Minnis Bay on the north Kent coast; see also the Whitstable finds below). Moreover, the intertidal zone presents a 'grey area', neither land nor sea; and a final difficulty comes in deciding when sea becomes river – are estuarine finds relevant?

Only occasionally can one be reasonably confident that coastal or off-shore finds originated in their respective contexts; therefore, we have had to take a pragmatic approach to the inclusion of material in the following catalogue. Finds covered are either: (i) unambiguously *recovered* from the seabed below low-tide, but with no assumption that they were necessarily deposited in the sea; or (ii) recovered from

Fig 4.1 Locations of seabed finds from the Channel and its approaches. Numbers correlate with the catalogue entries in this Chapter

a coastal location where there is some evidence that they had been brought onto the coast with material from the seabed. In restricting the dataset in this way we would hope to get close to an assemblage of metalwork that was genuinely deposited (by whatever means) at sea. There are a good number of further finds located in the intertidal zone; some of these will be mentioned in the discussion (Chapter 5).

The catalogued finds are from the English Channel and its approaches as far as Pembrokeshire in the west and East Anglia/Holland in the east (Fig 4.1). The finds are dealt with in geographical order from west to east along the British coastline, then from west to east along the continental shore. The exact list of finds differs significantly from that recently published by Alice Samson (2006, table 1): she included two that were not found off-shore (Thurlestone beach, Devon, and Alexandra Dock, Hull) and another for which there appears to be no evidence for a marine context (Whitstable sword). Furthermore, Samson treated Seaford and Salcombe each as two sites, whereas we have combined them; so her tally of eighteen sites comes down to thirteen, which have corresponding entries below. We can add a further eight certain or probable sea finds from the Channel and its approaches. In addition, attention is drawn in Chapter 5 to two finds from Scottish waters.

1. Off Llanrhian, Dyfed (Pembrokeshire)

Rapier: cf Drumcoltran and Talaton hoard examples (Fig 4.2)
National Museum Wales, 88.121H
Sources: Unpublished; inf Martin Dean; author's study (National Bronze Implements Index [NBI]).
Circumstances: Found by Bill Randall about 1985 in *c*10m of water between the headlands of Penclegyr and Ynsdeullyn (inf Martin Dean). Randall gave a 'best guess' grid reference of about SM 828337; this is in the region of a kilometre from shore.
Dimensions: Length (extended) 530mm; width at hilt-plate 13.9mm; thickness 6.0mm; weight 99.0g.
Description: (Notes by the author 1986) Although the whole implement is present, the blade is snapped in two at a slight bend (*c* 40°); this break appears to be recent. Approximately half of the surface is eroded but stable and dark brown-green to yellow-green with pitting. The rest of the surface has flaked thinly to a very pale bluish-green powdery surface with some brighter green patches. There are some small irregularities in outline. The blade edges are quite sharp, but this is probably due to erosion whittling since the butt edges are also sharp. To judge from the amorphous, spatula-like hilt end, this piece would seem to have experienced much erosion, fully removing the original rivet emplacements if any were present. A small proportion of rapiers do not actually have any well-defined emplacements, but their hilt plates are always much wider than that remaining on the Llanrhian weapon. If the hilt has

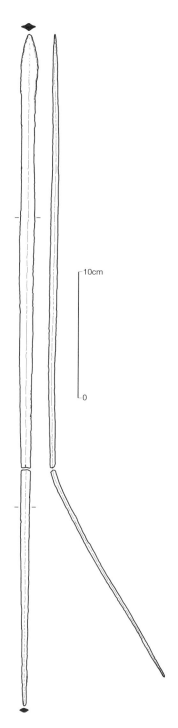

Fig 4.2 Rapier found off Llanrhian, Dyfed (Pembrokeshire)

indeed been well whittled down, then the blade must also have suffered, although its stoutness may have slowed the rate of attrition significantly. The upper blade, in particular, has a pronounced, rounded midridge with concave, flanking blade faces.
Identification: The three predominant cross-sectional forms of rapiers and dirks – broad lozengic, triplearris or flattened midrib (Burgess and Gerloff 1981, groups II, III, and IV respectively) – are unlikely, if substantially reduced by erosion, to have resulted in the narrow yet still thick blade with lozenge tendency seen in this find. It is reasonable to conclude that it

could only have come from a relatively narrow and strongly lozengic-sectioned blade which had seen only modest sectional loss. The consistent hollowing of the blade wings could suggest that concavity was significant in the original profile.

Blades comparable to that deduced are rare, but occur in two important hoards, those from Talaton, Devon, and Drumcoltran, Kirkcudbrightshire (Burgess and Gerloff 1981, nos 410, 425–426, 451). Significantly, perhaps, two of these examples would have been very long; no 410 is actually incomplete at 400mm, while no 425 from Drumcoltran is 627mm. There are a good number of other rapiers of this order of length – over 500mm – and, among them, those from Lissane, Co Derry, and 'Ireland' are note-worthy in having extremely slender blades (Burgess and Gerloff 1981, nos 387–388). These examples are of triple-midrib section (Group III), but of an unusual variant which is extremely thick in the centre with the flanking arrises close to the edges. If whittled down, this section too might result in the profile seen at Llanrhian. Other potentially relevant blades occur in the Beddgelert hoard, Caernarvon-shire (Gwynedd): one very similar to the Lissane variant, and one of lozenge section (Burgess and Gerloff 1981, nos 437, 285).

This list of blades having both similar proportions and appropriate cross sections may not be totally exhaustive, but it would seem highly significant that they all occur in the lands flanking the Irish Sea.

Date: Taunton assemblage, *c* 1400–1250 BC.

Assessment: The grid reference supplied by the finder seems too far offshore to correspond with the stated depth, but it is presumed that this is the approximate area of discovery.

2. Off Sennen Cove, Cornwall

Sword or rapier: Possibly an Irish variant of a Gund-lingen type sword (Fig 4.3)
Truro, Royal Cornwall Museum, 1992.29
Sources: Unpublished; inf Martin Dean.
Circumstances: Found by a sport diver, Mr Terry Crocker, in May 1990. Acquired by Royal Cornwall Museum via the Receiver of Wreck.
Dimensions: Length 473mm; width at shoulders 28.8mm; width at blade waist 14.0mm; maximum width of blade 17.5mm; maximum thickness 6.6mm.
Description: The weapon has a varied, dull-green, textured surface with small corrosion deposits and much mini-pocking; many of the tiny pocks have become deep voids and there are frequent grains of probable sand embedded in others. The very tip of the blade is lacking and the last 15mm extant is a separate fragment reattached to the main piece. The long profile is virtually straight.

In its current state, the weapon has a rather rhombic 'hilt-plate', around 60mm long and between 5.5 and 6.6mm thick, surmounted by a small, tapering tang. A long and slender blade tapers initially from the

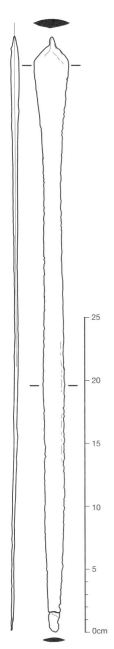

Fig 4.3 Sword or rapier found off Sennen Cove, Cornwall

hilt-plate, but then begins to expand very gradually to the middle before again contracting. The blade is thin with an essentially flat cross section tapering to semi-sharp edges on both sides. The hilt-plate is thicker, but still basically of lenticular section, the edges being more obtuse but still pointed.

The cutting edges carry almost continuous small notching due to loss from corrosion and limited abrasion; however, the retention of an acute profile indicates that it has not been heavily rolled. Moreover, given the overall symmetry still seen in the object, it seems unlikely that the original outline has been reduced by a great amount. The only part of the weapon with indications of differential abrasion is the butt, where one face has a slight, near-central ridge which is smooth and slightly wavy; it is still possible, however, that this is a relic of an original central feature. The small tang-like feature has a rather asymmetric section, suggesting that it has been whittled down more than the rest of the implement; if this is the case, it is possible that it was originally longer and/or broader. It is conceivable that either side of the 'tang' has a remnant of a rivet notch, but, if so, the rivet emplacements were set rather close together, even allowing for drift due to erosion.

Identification: The outline, in its current form, is not easily recognised as an established type of long-blade weapon. Nevertheless, the blade presents a sinuous outline with no sign of differential loss along its length; the swelling is slight by comparison with the vast majority of leaf-bladed swords. The latter are also generally considerably broader, and it seems unlikely that massive erosion of such a sword would result in this regular shape with thin blade edges. The narrowness of the blade might suggest instead a rapier, but its sinuous shape presents difficulties. Rapier/dirk-type weapons only occasionally have slightly leaf-shaped blades (Cutts type – Burgess and Gerloff 1981, nos 766–807), and these are rarely as long as the surviving Sennen object. Moreover, the Cutts type does not show the long steady tapering from the shoulders downwards; in common with all rapier types, it has, instead, a more rapid contraction which is lacking on the Sennen Cove object. The thickened rhombic 'hilt-plate' might compare with the hilt-plates of certain early 'swords' within the Rosnoën spectrum – see, for example, Nos 162–166 and 170–176 in the Langdon Bay assemblage. These examples have suffered varied erosion of the rivet emplacements, and it is possible that further erosion would result in just a tang-like stump. Rosnoën type weapons rarely have blades which are more than marginally leaf-shaped, but it would be unwise to wholly rule out such an identification.

A more likely reconstruction can be found in a limited series of Gündlingen-type swords from Ireland. Unlike virtually all other true swords of the later Bronze Age, these pieces tend to have gracile leaf-shaped blades with a simple flat blade section, contrasting with British equivalents. Those illustrated by Eogan (1965, especially nos 501, 505, 514, 515, 531) have blade widths ranging down to 21mm, or, in one case, 18mm. Allowing for erosion, the 17.5mm of the Sennen Cove blade could well have fallen within this range. If the piece is interpreted in this way its hilt and shoulders would have seen more dramatic reduction, but two details seem to support the interpretation. Firstly, the well-splayed shoulders are similar to those seen on Gündlingen swords, albeit that Sennen Cove has had the lines of rivet holes stripped off. Secondly, the tang is consistent with a thicker tongue of metal which projects from the shoulders into the base of the sword's grip.

Date: possibly Llyn Fawr assemblage, *c* 800–625 BC.

Assessment: The evidence for embedded sand in the object's surface is consistent with a sandy bay environment, as seen at Sennen Cove. Unfortunately, it is not known how far offshore the find was made. The blade does not seem to have been exposed to excessive erosion, but if the preferred interpretation is correct the shoulders have been more substantially reduced.

3. Off Moor Sand, Salcombe, Devon

See Chapter 1.

4. Off Chesil Beach, Dorset

Socketed axe: Armorican type (Fig 4.4)
Private ownership, Mr M May (1979)
Sources: R Taylor 1980.
Circumstances: Discovered 150m off Chesil Beach (*c* SY 6675) by Mr M May while diving in 1979. It lay in 12m of water.
Dimensions: Length 122mm; width at mouth 27mm; breadth at mouth 37mm; width of cutting edge 33mm; weight 250g.
Description: This is a long, plain socketed axe with a single pronounced mouth-moulding and side loop immediately beneath. The sub-rectangular socket has its long axis perpendicular to the blade. Its body flares steadily towards the blade's edge, which had evidently not been prepared for use after casting. Taylor suspected some wear of body angles, but there was neither extensive reduction of form nor extensive corrosion. A piece of grit was trapped within the loop's aperture and grey concretion adhered to parts of the surface.
Date: Premier Age du Fer (equivalent of Llyn Fawr assemblage), 800–625 BC.
Assessment: Although incontrovertibly found in open water, the scale of long-shore drift along the Chesil stretch of coast gives plenty of opportunity for this object to have been eroded at some stage from land. It is correctly identified by Taylor as being of the Armorican type (R Taylor 1980; Briard

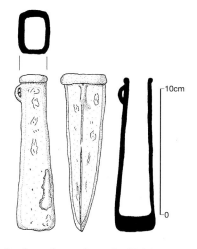

Fig 4.4 Socketed axe found off Chesil Beach, Dorset (drawing: Taylor 1980)

and Verron 1976b, 47–60), a good number of which have been found on land in the southern counties of Britain (O'Connor 1980, 235–6, 586). Indeed, a second example was found 'under the pebble beach at Portland' some 6km down-current of this find and could conceivably derive from the same original deposit, whether on land or at sea (R Taylor 1980, 136). The condition of the Chesil Beach find argues against it having been exposed on the seabed for long, so it must have been buried for much of its history in stable terrestrial or marine sediments.

5. Poole Harbour entrance, Dorset

Winged axe: End-winged type (Fig 4.5)
Poole Museums Service, OR 1985 A
Ferrule: Tubular (or cylindrical) type (Fig 4.5)
Poole Museums Service, OR 1985 A
Sources: Samson 2006, table 1 no 13 – described as 'winged palstave'; inf Dave Parham; author's study.
Circumstances: Two interlocked bronzes found by Philip Butterworth while diving in the narrow entrance to Poole Harbour. Samson states that 'possible pins/needles' were also found (2006, table 1 no 13), but it is not known on what evidence.

Winged axe

Dimensions: Length 138.5mm; width at cutting edge 36.2mm; width at butt 23.5mm; breadth at flanges 37.5mm; minimum breadth of loop 5.6mm; weight (with ferrule) 323g.
Description: The surface bears a light sheen, possibly due to lacquering, but is otherwise characterised by four surface textures. Parts of the faces and sides appear to be dark green nearly intact patina remnants which are much broken by mini-pocked or undulating dull green areas. Inside the 'sockets' created by the wings are some pale green dusty patches; and, finally, all body angles and extremities, including the strong bends along the wings, exhibit smooth, even, green-brown surfaces. The latter, seen in contrast to the partially corroded

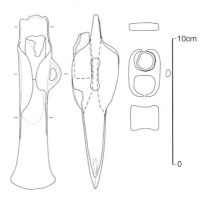

Fig 4.5 Winged axe and ferrule fragment (interlocked) found in the entrance to Poole Harbour, Dorset

surface elsewhere, are probably the result of physical abrasion.

The cutting edge is essentially intact, but lightly blunted by the abrasion noted above; thus, the tips are somewhat rounded. Small notches into one wing may have been small 'imperfections' arising from production, but the much larger indent on another wing (face view in Fig 4.5) is more likely to be due to a fracture occurring either in manufacture or in later use – the surrounding broken edges are all well abraded. The two notches into the butt probably derive from the original shape after the casting jet had been removed and the butt trimmed up. There are slight blade-tip hollows, showing that the cutting edge had been expanded by post-cast forging.

The blade/septum junction is defined by weak U- or V-shaped bevels, as is normal for the type, but this axe actually retains evidence for two bevels 7.5mm apart in the centre. The loop has a sub-D cross section.
Identification: End-winged axes are a familiar type in the Ewart stage hoards of south-east Britain in particular and more scattered examples occur in the south-west peninsula (Burgess 1968a, fig 14; O'Connor 1980, 159–60). Highly comparable axes are also found in northern French hoards, with a concentration in Armorica. In general, they have often been considered to be a key type within the 'Carp's Tongue complex'. Equivalent axes in the Urnfield zone of central Europe are stylistically distinct.

Ferrule

Dimensions: Length 37mm; maximum width 16.5mm; wall thickness *c* 0.5–1.7mm.
Description: A tubular object is rammed into the socket on one face of the winged axe and is further secured by corrosion deposits. The surface is partly a green patina, but much has flaked to a mid-green surface. There are also patches of the dusty pale green seen on the axe. The walls are not of constant thickness and thin towards a rounded top edge. The section of the tube may originally have been circular, but this is distorted by damage. The upper, exposed end is very irregular owing to breakage and a resulting corner is bent; the concealed end is more or less straight, but corrosion makes it impossible to assess whether this is an original end. Two perforations through the wall are irregular and encircled by corroded metal – hence, neither was necessarily originally a peg hole.
Identification: The diameter of the tube is consistent with the tubular ferrules well known in Late Bronze Age contexts and interpreted as spear-butt fittings. Those in Wilburton assemblage hoards are very long, but even the shorter ones of the Ewart stage are significantly longer than this presumably fragmentary example (Burgess *et al* 1972, 216; Needham 1990a, 58). While one cannot rule out this being a fragment of a long Wilburton ferrule, its inextricable asso-

ciation with the end-winged axe strongly favours a Ewart-stage type.

Date: Ewart/Plainseau assemblage; *c* 1000–775 BC.

Assessment: The variations in surface condition are consistent with the object (axe plus ferrule) having suffered from post-depositional corrosion, but at the same or different times having also been subjected to physical attrition (eg rolling) of extremities and angles. There are no signs of heavy battering, however, and the attrition appears to have been a relatively gentle process. This observation is curious in the context of Poole Harbour's entrance, which is notorious for its strong tidal surge through the gap, and perhaps implies that the axe and ferrule had been buried in seabed silt for long parts of their depositional history.

Although finds of end-winged axes are less numerous in Britain than on the opposite side of the Channel, the number is greater than is obviously accounted for by direct imports; it is more likely that they were part of a shared tradition initially stemming from the near Continent.

6. Off Southbourne ('Hengistbury Head'), Hampshire

Shaft-hole axe: Sicilian type (Fig 4.6)
British Museum, 1937, 1109.1
Sources: Brailsford 1953, 28, fig 8.2; Cunliffe 1978, 26 fig 9.2, 29–3; author's study.

Circumstances: The circumstances are best quoted direct from the original correspondence from Mr H C Audin of Bournemouth. His initial letter of 18 September 1937 stated:

> Recently while beach-fishing at Hengistbury Head I discovered an axe-head attached to a cluster of sea-weed and other matter entangled with it. I am enclosing a drawing of the implement. The head weighs nearly a pound and is a kind of bronze or brass. It is crusted with a green mould and has a stoney deposit adhering to it. I should be pleased if you could enlighten me regarding it.

Christopher Hawkes responded from the Museum and sought to clarify the provenance: 'If you could state the distance and direction of the spot from some recognizable land-mark ...'. On 19 October 1937 Audin wrote again:

> I fished it up at a point called Southbourne 1¼ miles from Hengistbury Head, due south, and as the compass shows to the west side of the Head. I believe at one time there was an old pier [Southbourne Pier] washed away practically in the very spot where I hooked it up.

Hawkes queried the ambiguity in this statement, to which he received (2 January 1938) the affirmative that it was:

> ...fished up due south of a point on the shore at Southbourne 1¼ miles from the POINT or the

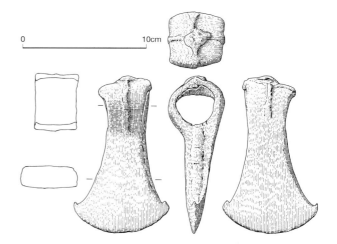

Fig 4.6   Shaft-hole axe found off Southbourne ('Hengistbury Head'), Hampshire

REAL top of the HEAD. Yes, I should say it was to the EAST end of Southbourne Overcliff Drive.

A sketch map accompanied this letter and showed in addition that the find-spot was 100 yards east of where a 'new prom' terminated.

Dimensions: Length 125mm; width at cutting edge 79.1mm; minimum width 30.0mm; width at butt 44.8mm; breadth at butt 45.6mm; diameter of perforation 30.5–33.8mm; breadth at blade top 24.8mm; weight 596.1g.

Description: The axe has a slightly shiny, dark greeny-brown surface which is partly smooth with mini-undulations. Smaller areas are slightly textured; on one face there are patches up to 8mm across over which a very thin patina has flaked to reveal a matt dull-brown surface. Rubbing at the butt projection, the blade tips, and around the rims of the shaft-hole has created a smoothish, dull, coppery-brown surface. Beige soil or silt deposits survive inside the socket and locally alongside casting flashes; inside the socket they include a whitish inclusion (>1 millimetre) which is possibly calcareous and not obviously shell. It is mainly in good, unrolled condition with limited scratches and dents. Apart from occasional nicks or dents, the edge retains a good outline, but it is rather blunt.

The axe is narrowest where the blade meets the shaft-hole, and the curves from butt to the two blade tips are not symmetrical. The blade expands in a sweeping curve and then more strongly at the tips; there are no associated blade tip hollows. The socket is also not symmetrical in relation to the blade profile, and there is no indication that this is due to damage; the socket is sub-triangular rather than circular. One blade face carries a diffuse edge-bevel, the other is entirely smooth in profile.

Manufacture of the axe was rather crude. The casting flashes and a thick feeder at the butt were only partly fettled, the residual stumps then having been roughly hammered down, causing significant lipping. The rims around the shaft hole are roughly flattened by hammering, leading to internal lips more or less all round; in places they have cracked. The medial rib encircling the socket is not neatly cast, and it too has suffered some hammering.

Identification: Single-bladed shaft-hole axes are mainly a feature of Italy and Sicily, with scattered examples further afield (Coffyn 1985, 157, map 25), but this classification embraces a range of types in detail. The Southbourne example is best matched in Sicily, although most from that island have more slender blades, seen face on. The rib encircling the socket characterises one of the variants among central Mediterranean parallels (Albanese Procelli 1993, 37, fig 6), occurring, for example, on two butt fragments in the Lipari hoard, one of which also shows the sub-triangular shaft hole (Giardino 1995, fig 7A no 2). Others, as in the Badia Malvagna hoard, can have decidedly oval shaft holes, but the two ribbed examples here have splayed blades more like that of Southbourne (Giardino 2004, 349, fig 1D nos 1 and 3). Other ribbed-butt axes have been found in hoards from Cannatello 1 and Erbe Bianche (Giardino 2004, 349, fig 1C, 351, fig 2A).

Date: Sicilian Hoard Horizon I, *c* 13th century BC (Needham and Giardino 2008).

Assessment: The correspondence is convincing on the point that Audin did indeed find the axe at Southbourne. The only remaining uncertainty would then be whether it had been deposited there in more recent times, especially since a pier once stood near the site. Although the surface exhibits only minimal mechanical damage from contact with other hard objects (such as pebbles), the weight of this object could well have led to it remaining stationary on a seabed until it had become engulfed in protective silt. However, closeness to the shore on a coastline with strong long-shore drift makes an original terrestrial context equally feasible.

7. Solent Water, Hampshire

Bracelet: Penannular with tapering terminals (Fig 4.7)

Private ownership (1978)

Sources: Unpublished; British Museum archives; author's study (NBI).

Circumstances: Brought up from the waters of the Solent 'impaled on an oyster fisherman's anchor fluke' (inf John Lavender, Christchurch Museum). The same fisherman had dredged up three 'Thames picks' and a tranchet adze from other locations in the Solent.

Dimensions: Diameter 71mm × 66mm; maximum thickness of hoop 4.5mm.

Description: On much of its inner face a dark-green patina is well preserved. The outer face and terminals are dull ruddy-brown with intermittent green and seem rather eroded. The terminals are currently out of alignment by a few millimetres in both planes. The section is approximately round at

Fig 4.7   Bracelet found in Solent Water, Hampshire

the thickest point and becomes elliptical as the hoop tapers to either terminal.

Identification: Despite erosion, the even tapering towards the terminals strongly suggests that it never had any terminal expansion. It is, therefore, an extremely simple type of penannular bracelet which is not closely datable (and might even be an ethnographic loss). Comparable simple bracelets are known in the British Middle Bronze Age and have been discussed above in relation to Langdon Bay No 155 (Chapter 3); this is a possible identification.

Date: possibly Taunton/Baux-Sainte-Croix to Penard/Rosnoën assemblages, *c* 1400–1125 BC.

Assessment: There is much shallow water in the Solent which is known to have become drowned during the later Holocene (Allen and Gardiner 2000). Without any precise location it is impossible to assess whether this piece is more likely to have been deposited at sea or on land which has became submerged since the Bronze Age.

8. Off Bembridge, Isle of Wight

Rapier: Wandsworth type (Fig 4.8)

Isle of Wight Heritage Service, IOW2005–176

Sources: Unpublished; inf Sophia Exelby and Frank Basford; author's study.

Circumstances: Recovered from the seabed during fishing operations and reported to the Receiver of Wreck in 2005 (inf Sophia Exelby, Receiver of Wreck).

Dimensions: Length 393mm; width at shoulders 62mm; maximum thickness 6.0mm; maximum thickness at butt 1.0 millimetre; weight 195.5g; *rivet*: length 16mm; minimum shank diameter 5.9mm × 6.7mm; maximum head diameters 7.9mm and 8.5mm.

Description: Several matt blackish patches, mainly smooth, are probable remnants of the rapier's original surface; some parts are also textured. The rest is flaked to a lower surface comprising mottled varied dull greens, predominantly light chalky green. There are limited orange-stained patches, possibly incorporating fine sediment, and a small patch of an off-white calcareous deposit on the hilt-plate. Recent scraping of the blade's central arris has exposed a 30mm-long stretch of brighter metal close to the tip. The hole of the missing rivet is unbroken and the weapon is unbent throughout its length.

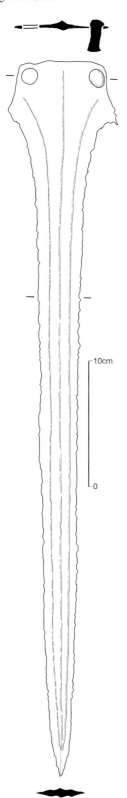

Fig 4.8   Rapier found off Bembridge, Isle of Wight

expanded domed head at one end and a less-convex head at the other. The butt is very thin but thickens a little at the centre, where the midrib terminates. The hilt-plate sides are slightly thicker and flattish.

Identification: Despite some edge damage, little of the original outline has been lost and the hilt-plate is unequivocally trapezoidal with acute, down-turned shoulders. Trapezoidal butts combined with the distinctive triple-arris blade characterise Type Wandsworth in Burgess and Gerloff's classification (1981, nos 342–386). Examples with downturned shoulders are not common in the series (eg nos 360, 363, 364), but this is probably just one extreme of the shape variation of the hilt-plates. Triple-arris rapiers of comparable forms to British/Irish Type Wandsworth are extremely rare in northern France (Gallay 1988, nos 807B, ?807C, 848, 858, 896, 896A), most of these being fragments from the Chéry hoard.

Date: Taunton assemblage, *c* 1400–1250 BC.

Assessment: The character of the surface is in keeping with a marine depositional environment. Damage is primarily due to chemical attack rather than physical attrition; indeed, the lack of evidence for rolling, hard impacts or 'sand-blasting' suggests that this item has probably been largely sedentary in its seabed location.

9. Possibly the seas around the Isle of Wight

Socketed axe: Sompting type (Fig 4.9)

Private ownership (1981)

Sources: Dean 1984c, 78; Isle of Wight Historic Environment Service records no 1400.

Circumstances: Found by a workman mixed in with marine ballast that was being shovelled into a concrete mixer at Chilton, Isle of Wight. On this basis, the piece was suspected to be from an unknown site on the seabed (Isle of Wight Historic Environment Service). The finder reported the object to the Carisbrooke Castle Museum in 1981.

Dimensions: Length 126mm; width at cutting edge 51mm; width at mouth 35.5mm; breadth at mouth 38mm; weight 475g.

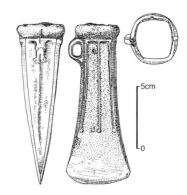

Fig 4.9   Socketed axe possibly found in the seas around the Isle of Wight (drawing: Isle of Wight Historic Environment Service)

The hilt-plate is trapezoidal with slightly concave sides leading to acute, downturned shoulders, to judge from the more intact one. In fact, both shoulders and much of the blade edges are damaged by ragged notching. The blade section is triple-arris throughout its length. One of two rivets survives in the hilt-plate; it has a thick circular shank with an

Description: (Based on drawing of 1981) The axe has a sub-rectangular mouth with a slightly longer axis perpendicular to blade edge as well as a bulbous upper mouth-moulding; immediately below this is a fine horizontal rib, from which issue three more long, fine ribs, each ending in a pellet. A prominent loop springs from the underside of the upper moulding. The body of the axe flares steadily towards the cutting edge. There are indications of scratches/striations on the lower blade, but it remains unknown whether they are ancient.

Identification: Virtually all of the classic features of Sompting socketed axes are present (Schmidt and Burgess 1981, 241, nos 1575–1603): a mouth perpendicular to the cutting edge, pronounced mouth-moulding, and the steady flare of the body; the decoration is also one of the frequent designs seen in the class.

Date: Llyn Fawr assemblage, *c* 800–625 BC.

Assessment: Having been found in a secondary context, little certainty can be attached to this being a marine find. It is not known whether there were any adhering encrustations indicative of such an environment.

10. Hayling Beach, Hampshire, or Owers Bank, off the Sussex coast

Six palstaves: Norman (4), Breton (1) and Broad-bladed (1) types (Fig 4.10)
Sources: Lawson 1999, 95; author's study (NBI) British Museum, 1988, 0602.1–6.
Circumstances: The six bronzes were found by Brian Kilshaw and Daniel Clahane on the beach on Hayling Island close to Eastoke Point. They were recovered on more than one occasion over a period of up to five days in November 1985, all coming from the same area of the beach between one pair of groynes and between the tidal limits. The finds were made just after the importation to the site of large quantities of gravel dredged offshore, the purpose of which was beach reinforcement. Kilshaw and Clahane worked as a gang on this project. They believed that the axes had come in with the gravel, which was being imported between April and December 1985 from an underwater extraction site at Owers Bank, 13km out from Littlehampton, Sussex, with a contract run by South Coast Shipping. The gravel was won by the use of suction pumps working over the surface and then loaded into bottom-opening barges; these were floated over the beach at high tide and the ballast let out. At low tide, the gravel was redistributed by the workmen.

Two palstaves found on one occasion were 'within a couple of steps of one another'. Later, three were found in a linear formation along the shoreline at low tide perhaps 10–15m apart. Kilshaw thought these pieces had washed out of the dumped gravel spread across the beach above. He also remarked on 'black timbers' appearing all along the water line after dumping; specimens shown to the author

were two small wood pebbles and a larger piece of roundwood with no sign of working.

Palstave 1 (Fig 4.10a)

Dimensions: Length 149.5mm; width at cutting edge 39.5mm; breadth at stop 27mm; weight 312.6g.
Description: The surface is mainly a dull green-brown with areas of powdery pale green; crests, angles, and the stumps of a broken loop are partially rubbed to golden-coloured metal; the butt, flange crests, and cutting edge are chipped and generally 'worn'.

Flanges and stop form a U-shaped slot, more curved on one face than the other. The septum base is slightly concave in section; inner flange faces become vertical. Despite damage, the flanges seem to be ogival in profile. The blade is narrow with a gentle, steady flare and no sign of cutting edge expansion. There is a triangular shield motif on both faces beneath the stop – one survives as three slight, converging ribs, the other as two triangular depressions, the ribs perhaps having fully eroded away.

Identification: This is a classic Norman-style narrow-bladed palstave, a type which is also found in a number of locations along the south coast of England (Briard and Verron 1976, 91–5; Verney 1988; O'Connor 1980, 47–9, 781, map 5; Needham 1980).

Palstave 2 (Fig 4.10b)

Dimensions: Length 150mm; width at cutting edge 35mm; breadth at stop 26mm; weight 246g.
Description: Most of the surface is yellow-green to bluey-green, but patches are dull brown and gold-flecked. An iron-stained patch on the non-loop side may be a fragment of the original surface. Some parts are severely reduced by corrosion and abrasion – the loop is reduced to stumps and the flanges on that side are heavily reduced. There is also a deep cavity at the centre of the septum end, penetrating into the stop. The blade edge is very blunt and the butt is lacking a corner.

Flanges and stop create a U-shaped slot. The septum base is slightly concave in section and the inner faces of the flanges are steep. Although the blade faces are eroded, one retains a vestigial triangular shield or trident motif – there is a hint of a ridge beneath the three convergent ribs.

Identification: Despite heavy erosion, this piece is clearly of Norman type (as Palstave 1).

Palstave 3 (Fig 4.10c)

Dimensions: Length 142mm; width at cutting edge 34.5mm; breadth at stop 26.5mm; weight 299g.
Description: The surface is largely a dull, dark brown with areas, especially crests, rubbed to a gold colour. There are mixed pale-green/brighter green/

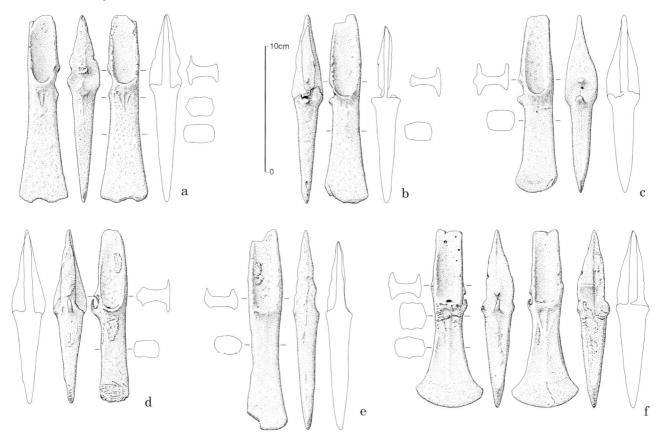

Fig 4.10   Six palstaves found on Hayling Beach, Hampshire, possibly from the sea at Owers Bank off the Sussex coast (drawings: Phil Dean)

purple surfaces in the hafting slots, while limited patches of ferrous brown on faces and sides are probably original surface remnants. There is also some reduction of the cutting edge, flange crests on one face, and loop stumps which, although projecting, are well rounded.

The flanges define a U-shaped slot with slightly bowed sides. In profile, the flanges have a strong ogival shape. The septum base is almost flat in cross section with a sudden turn to steep inner flange faces. A cavity penetrates the end of one septum. The blade is nearly parallel until it expands modestly close to the cutting edge – this transition is associated with a fairly steep edge bevel, as seen in profile. Both blade faces retain vestigial evidence for a trident motif, the stem of which is evident only as a marginally hexagonal section to the blade.

Identification: Norman type (as Palstave 1).

Palstave 4 (Fig 4.10d)

Dimensions: Length 138mm; width at cutting edge 24.5mm; breadth at stop 27.5mm; weight 236.3g.
Description: The surface is mostly a pale bluey-green; some parts are light greeny-brown. There are also patches of dull dark green, especially in the hafting slots, which are probably remnants of the original surface. One septum is encrusted with barnacles and a small patch of fine, mesh-like cal-

careous concretion. The cutting edge is very thick and ragged owing to considerable outline loss. The gullies running across the edge bevel may be due to preferential etching of particular metallographic structures in a well-worked zone. The loop is well thinned by erosion, which has resulted in a small gap. The butt is rather rounded and the flanges on the loop side are heavily reduced.

The hafting slot is U-shaped and, in profile, the more complete flanges are ogival. The septum base is gently concave in cross section, but there is a sharp turn to vertical inner flange faces. The blade, in its eroded form, has very modest expansion. No real surface detail survives, but there is a possible ghost of a trident or V-motif beneath the stop.

Identification: Despite severe erosion, there are sufficient distinctive shape characteristics to indicate the Norman type (as Palstave 1).

Palstave 5 (Fig 4.10e)

Dimensions: Length 159.5mm; width at cutting edge 33.5mm; breadth at stop 22mm; weight 267.9g.
Description: Much of one face and side retains a dark greeny-brown and slightly shiny 'patina'; sandy deposits adhere in spots. The rest of the surface has deteriorated to purply-brown and powdery pale-green with localised gold-flecking. The cutting edge is very blunt with one large corner broken off; there

is a similar missing corner at the butt. The flanges have irregular outlines in profile from chipping and/or abrasion – one is reduced to a stumpy ridge.

The axe has a nearly rectangular slot whose sides are lightly bowed. The best-preserved flange is triangular in profile, but originally it may have been bowed. The septum base is approximately flat in cross section with sharp angles to the steep inner flange faces. The blade is distinctly waisted, contracting 5mm from the stop; and, despite significant rounding of the body angles, it retains the evidence for a medial ridge down half or more of either face. The blade and flange sides tend to be angled in cross section. There is not the slightest hint of stumps from a former loop.

Identification: Slot and septum form, lack of loop, waisted blade, and medial ridge are all paralleled on most narrow-bladed palstaves of Breton type (Briard 1965, 110–18; Briard and Verron 1976, 101–4).

Palstave 6 (Fig 4.10f)

Dimensions: Length 142mm; width at cutting edge 54.5mm; breadth at stop 27mm; weight 321.9g.

Description: There are small remnants of original shiny surface/patina which is fir-green to brown; elsewhere it is reduced to powdery light green, in places yellow-green, and still further to the dull, dark-brown underlying body. In parts of the cutting edge, some golden metal has been exposed by rubbing. The cutting edge is, in fact, nearly intact and backed by a neat, if no longer crisply defined, edge bevel. The butt and two flanges seem little reduced. On one face, however, the flanges are reduced by about half. This face and the non-loop side have extensive pitting and fissuring of the zone around the stop, possibly due to differential etching of inhomogeneous cast metal here, which presumably also accounts for the longer fissure crossing the decorative motif. Both septum ends have cavities. About a third of the loop is missing and the rest is thin and bent inwards.

The slot is rectangular. Flanges are ogival in profile and contract a little just before the protruding stop. The septum base is almost flat in cross section with sharp angles to steep inner flange faces. Beneath the stop, the sides contract marginally before steadily expanding to form a broad or medium–broad blade; a distinct out-swing towards the blade tips is associated with forging of the well-formed edge bevel. Both faces retain a strong trident rib motif, the stem extending virtually to the edge bevel. The blade faces to either side of the stem are hollowed, thereby emphasising the body angles. The non-loop side has a neat bar-moulding running across just half of the flange, up to a step representing the valve junction of the mould; this feature is not obviously functional or stylistic and was probably a fortuitous impression made during the manufacture of one valve of a presumed clay mould.

Identification: Unlike the associated axes, this one has a relatively broad blade (excluding the outturned blade tips). Broad-bladed palstaves occur on both sides of the Channel and even the specific style features of palstave 6 do not prevail on one side or the other. The trident motif is quite frequent on Norman broad-bladed palstaves, essentially contemporary with the narrow-bladed form dealt with above for nos 1–4 (Verney 1988). However, these continental versions are predominantly unlooped. Briard and Verron (1976, 92) believed that the looped version was added to the Norman palstave repertoire late in the period in question.

In Britain a number of broad-bladed palstaves illustrated by Rowlands have both trident decoration and a loop (eg 1976, pl 28 nos 810, 551, 561, pl 30 nos 394, 754, 811, 595) and there are other examples with medium–broad blades (Rowlands 1976, pl 32 nos 957, 697) which seem to grade into narrow-bladed versions. Whether there is a continuous spectrum here requires future research and I have not distinguished in this section between straight-pronged tridents and those with curved outer prongs. Important hoard finds for the broad-bladed version are those from Hunstanton, Norfolk (Lawson 1979a, fig 2.2a), Taunton Workhouse, Somerset (Smith 1959a, GB43 no 29), Little London, Sussex, Peartree Green, Hampshire, and Eglesham Meadow, Dorset (Rowlands 1976, nos 151, 66.7, 32.1), all belonging to the Taunton assemblage, whereas narrow-bladed versions occur in Penard associations.

The precise distribution of this palstave style in Britain is difficult to determine because Rowlands classifies them into different classes. However, they are essentially a southern British type, including Wales and the Marches (Savory 1980, figs 22 and 23), as seen, for example, in the Cemmaes hoard, Powys (Montgomeryshire) (Savory 1980, fig 31 no 263), and that from Deansfield, Gwynedd (Caernarvonshire) (Smith 1959b, 166, fig 5.2). Relatively few examples have been found north of the Humber, where Schmidt and Burgess have classified them as type Carleton (1981, 139–40). Those authors make the important point that the type has close parallels which differ only in lacking the loop. Looped and unlooped variants seem to be contemporary, and it is hard to evaluate the significance of presence or absence.

Date: Taunton/Baux-Sainte-Croix assemblage; *c* 1400–1250 BC.

Assessment: Although the degree of erosion seen on the six palstaves is variable, none is so heavily rolled that it can no longer be identified to specific type. Therefore, they cannot have been exposed among beach shingle for any length of time. If they were originally land finds it must be concluded that they had eroded out into the beach only relatively late in their depositional history. On the other hand, the marine concretion on no 4 suggests, instead, a marine environment, as does the general surface condition of all of the axes. It seems more probable that the bronzes originated on the seabed at Owers Bank than that they were *in situ* terrestrial deposits at Hayling Beach. Given the vicissitudes of the intervening transport from seabed to beach, and the chances of being spotted by the groundsmen, it would seem highly likely that these six objects were part of a larger group at the original seabed site.

11. Off Seaford, East Sussex

Two palstaves, copper ingot fragment, and 'needle-like object'
Palstave 1: Broad-bladed type (Fig 4.11a)
National Maritime Museum, AOA 0596
Palstave 2: Broad-bladed type (Fig 4.11b)
Whereabouts unknown
Possible ingot fragment: (Fig 4.11c)
National Maritime Museum, AOA 0775
'Needle-like object': (not illustrated)
Whereabouts unknown
Sources: Dean 1984c, 78; author's study.
Circumstances: These finds were reported during 1982–83 and 1991, having probably been found on different occasions in the same general area of seabed close to the shore. The spatial relationship of the finds is not known, although they are thought all to be from within a kilometre of each other. Palstave 1 is described in the National Maritime Museum's records as having been 'found on the seabed by a sport diver beneath the cliffs at Seaford …'. The diver is identified as Alan Loader of Bromley BSAC branch, who made the find in or before August 1982. The position of the find is given as latitude 49° 46' 10s, longitude 0° 5' 15s E. The lump was found in October of the same year by Bromley BSAC branch close to the findspot of the palstave. A 'needle', said to be of bronze and *c* 200mm long, is reported to have been found in the same area as the other Seaford bronzes; it was reported to Martin Dean in April 1983 by Russel Brammah of Xenopus Sub-Aqua Club, apparently having been found by a colleague who was 'working out of the country'.

Palstave 2 has a more specific findspot, having been found by a diver (unnamed) not far offshore, lying on the seabed close to the sewage outlet (TV 488981) in about 6–7m of water. It was studied (by the author) while on loan to Museum of London, 1991, from the finder's girlfriend.

Palstave 1

Dimensions: Length 146mm; width at cutting edge 34mm; breadth at stop 17.3mm.
Description: The piece has a crinkly surface all over due to many small depressions. It is very dark green, except where it has been rubbed and/or flaked along crests and edges to a mid-green. None of the surface can be original given evident extensive reduction in outline. Both sides at the stop are very gently swollen, but one also features a series of small cavities which might conceivably have derived from the as-cast metal structure around the foot of a loop. An even slighter bump lower on this side can be felt rather than seen; the original presence of a loop is, therefore, not certain. The curved cross section of the septum base may reflect the original profile. There are diffuse but definite indications of a double tri-angular depression below the stop on each face; the blade faces immediately beneath are smooth, with no sign of a long central rib. The central swelling of the lower blade is almost certainly an artefact of differential erosion, which has also caused consider-able loss of surface and outline here. The notching of the butt is ragged and, as a feature not normal to the type, can be regarded as damage.
Identification: Allowing for some loss of outline, the blade would have been broad enough to define this as a broad-bladed palstave. It was decorated with a 'ghost trident' motif in which two (sub-) triangular depressions were separated by a vertical 'rib'; the heavy erosion does not allow us to identify whether there was originally a longer-stemmed rib, but both motif variants (with or without long rib) are familiar on broad-bladed palstaves. The axe may have had a loop, but this would not significantly alter its dating.

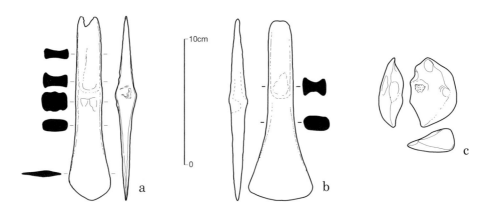

Fig 4.11 Bronze metalwork found off Seaford, East Sussex; a) palstave 1; b) palstave 2; c) possible ingot fragment

Comparable palstaves for either of the motif possibilities can be found in northern France, particularly in the Norman series (Briard and Verron 1976, 91–5; O'Connor 1980, among figs 17–25). Both decoration variants are also found in southern Britain; Rowlands illustrates a number of examples which are either broad- or narrow-bladed (Rowlands 1976, pl 1 no 16, pl 4 nos 48.1, 51.1, 80.2, pl 5 no 158.1, pl 6 nos 66.9–10, 12, 73.5–6, pl 7 no 31.1, pl 10 no 82.14, pl 11 no 34.2, pl 28 no 831, pl 30 no 663; also O'Connor 1980, among figs 1–16). No detailed cross-Channel inter-comparison has been undertaken to evaluate the extent of exchange or shared traditions involved among these very similar palstave repertoires.

Palstave 2

Dimensions: Length 143mm; width at cutting edge 52mm; breadth at stop 16mm.

Description: The edges and corners have generally been well rounded by erosion. The end of one septum retains what appears to be a patch of original patinated surface around 20mm long. The flanges are much reduced, but the concave septum cross section is probably original. No decorative design survives on the blade faces; one is flat up to the stop, but on the other face the top of the blade and the stop have been largely removed by a deep pit. This area is likely to have been preferentially scoured because of a weaker metal structure or as-cast vacuoles here; the feature recalls the 'swallow holes' that often developed in the end of the hafting slots of palstaves during casting.

Identification: Despite erosion, the blade is clearly broad, while there is no sign of a loop. Undecorated broad-bladed palstaves are actually rather rare in Britain, but they are occasionally found in Taunton stage hoards, as at Gosport, Newport/Fairleigh, Leavington, Birchington, and near Canterbury (O'Connor 1980, fig 4.7, fig 9A.8, fig 9B.2, fig 11.12–3, fig 12B.6). Rowlands illustrates occasional further examples. In France there are a few undecorated palstaves among the Tréboul group of Armorica (Briard 1965, 84; Briard and Verron 1976, 88), but these tend to be more massive than the Seaford example. The type appears to be equally rare in the later Baux-Sainte-Croix assemblage of northern France (O'Connor 1980, fig 21B.4, fig 22.5). O'Connor also illustrates one from Schoonaarde, Belgium (O'Connor 1980, fig 27.5).

Ingot fragment

Dimensions: Maximum dimension 55.5mm; width 38.5mm; thickness 18.5mm.

Description: A highly 'polished' dull coppery surface has just limited areas of brighter green. Abrasion has produced a scalloped effect along the thinnest edge. Some scallop bases and limited areas elsewhere have rich fir-green smooth surfaces which are a very thin layer overlying that mainly exposed. Two

deeper depressions contain more craggy deposits, probably a mix of corrosion products and concretion. These depressions are the only possible indication of the vesicular structure normally encountered in standard Bronze Age plano-convex ingots. Ignoring the scallops, one face could have started essentially flat and would thus be the upper one of such an ingot. If this interpretation is correct, the fractured edges have been considerably abraded to become totally rounded.

Identification: The form of this lump is consistent with it being a highly abraded edge fragment from a plano-convex ingot. In Britain associated finds of such ingots are almost exclusively from hoards of the Ewart assemblage (*c* 1000–800 BC), possibly late within that phase. If this ingot was originally associated with the palstaves, and therefore of earlier date, it is possible that it is a rare example of the deposition of material that was normally kept in circulation until converted into artefacts. Rare ingot finds from pre-Ewart phases of the Bronze Age can be of different forms: for example, small 'thumb-ingots' were found with a Taunton stage hoard from Hayling Island, Hampshire (Lawson 1999, 101–2, fig 11.6), but the basic plano-convex form is likely to have been an initial product of smelting at the copper sources at any stage.

Needle-like object

Dimensions: Said to be 200mm long.
Description: Said to be of bronze.
Identification: It is conceivable that this was a highly eroded weapon blade.

Date: Taunton/Baux-Sainte-Croix assemblage, 1400–1250 BC (palstaves); the ingot and needle-like object should not be ruled out as having been contemporary.

Assessment: Too little is known to assess the nature of the association. The two palstaves are of similar date. Coastal erosion is well known in modern times along this part of the coast with its chalk cliffs. The hillfort on Seaford Head (500m east of the findspot of palstave 2) and another further east at Belle Tout seem to have been significantly truncated by cliff collapse, but quantifying the loss depends on assumptions about their original full plan. Both palstaves, especially 1, seem to have been rolled on the seabed for some while, but this still could have been for a shorter duration than the time elapsed since initial deposition in the middle Bronze Age.

12. Off Hastings, East Sussex

Flanged axe: Derryniggin/Balbirnie type (Fig 4.12)
Rouen Museum
Sources: Needham 1983, 380 Sx13; author's study.
Circumstances: A printed label accompanying the

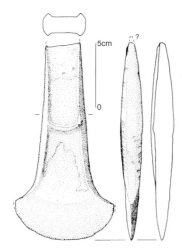

Fig 4.12 Flanged axe found off Hastings, East Sussex (drawing: Needham 1983)

find states: 'en mer, en face d'Hastings'. It was presumably pulled up by a French trawler or dredger.
Dimensions: Length 156mm; width at cutting edge 81mm; breadth at flanges 18mm; thickness at stop 15.5mm.
Description: A reed-green patina partially survives on all faces; the rest of the surface is flaked, slightly undulating, and of varied dull to bright green colours. The cutting edge is a little irregular. Modern interference is evident at the blade tips and across the butt, which has been truncated. There is a distinct bump-stop (1mm high), which is gently curved in plan. The body is medium–broad and expands gradually from butt to low on the blade, where it expands more markedly to the flared cutting edge. The edge bevel is emphasised to form a slight ridge and there are traces of a furrow concentric with it, but there is otherwise no sign of face decoration. The septum is flat in cross section with obtuse angles to the sloped inner flange faces. The sides have a longitudinal triple facet, and there are traces of superimposed cable decoration.
Identification: In general terms, this axe corresponds with those of Arreton type in southern England and northern France. However, certain features, especially the bump-stop, are exceptional in the Arreton series and are more frequent among the related Irish and north British axes of Derryniggin and Balbirnie types respectively (Harbison 1969; Schmidt and Burgess 1981).
The following flanged axes from Britain are the most similar, but their bump-stops are sometimes only marginally raised while blade tips can be more expanded, even swept back: Brambridge, Hampshire (unpublished); the Totland hoard, Isle of Wight (Sherwin 1942, no 10; Needham 1979, 273, fig 6.1A); Lambeth, Greater London (Megaw and Hardy 1938, 301, no 93); the Poslingford hoard, Suffolk (Megaw and Hardy 1938, 276, fig 4a); Burwell Fen, Cambridgeshire (Fox 1923, 54, pl VI.6); Attenborough and Clifton, both Nottinghamshire (Needham 1979,

268, figs 3.2 and 3.4, 272); Brough-under-Stainmore, Cumbria; Whittington Fell, Northumberland; 'Yorkshire Moors'; and Duggleby, North Yorkshire (Schmidt and Burgess 1981, nos 406, 407, 407A, 514). Other southern flanged axes such as those from Staunton, Gloucestershire (Evans 1881, 73), and Grunty Fen, Cambridgeshire (Megaw and Hardy 1938, 299, no 18), are narrower-bodied with higher flanges, but have the bump-stops, rather spatulate lower blades and the ridge- or furrow-defined edge bevels seen on many of this group. Additional north British axes may conform, but bump-stops are not always clearly distinguished from stop-bevels in published drawings.
There are a good many axes among the Irish Derryniggin series which match that from Hastings in having a medium–broad body, fairly low cast flanges, and well-splayed lower blades. Some of these undoubtedly have low bump-stops as well, such as that from the Bandon hoard, Co Cork (Harbison 1969, no 29), but, again, published drawings rarely allow clear differentiation between this feature and a simple bevel. There would appear to have been a complex pattern of feature exchange between the major series of flanged axes at this time. However, on balance, it seems most likely that the Hastings piece was of a style rooted within the Irish Derryniggin tradition, even if a minority were actually produced in Britain.
Date: Arreton/Derryniggin assemblage, c 1750/1700–1500 BC.
Assessment: Although some morphological detail is retained, the axe's surface condition is not incompatible with a marine burial context. However, it does not appear to have been exposed to erosion agencies for any length of time. This axe almost certainly originates in Ireland or Britain, rather than from the Continent; nevertheless, it may still be substantially displaced from its place of production, since close parallels from south-east England are scarce.

13. Off Sandgate, near Folkestone, Kent

Rapier? Unknown type
Whereabouts unknown
Sources: Dean 1984c, 78; inf Martin Dean.
Circumstances: In October 1982 Martin Dean (then of the National Maritime Museum) was told of a 'Bronze Age sword' found off Sandgate by a diver who 'wants to keep it for himself and not let archaeologists see it'. The finder has evidently succeeded – nothing more is known of the find. The informant was Alan Moat, a key diver involved in the discovery and survey of the Langdon Bay site; indeed, the finder of this piece had also dived at Langdon.
Dimensions: not known.
Description: Dean saw only a poor-quality photograph of the object, but thought it looked similar in form and condition to the Langdon Bay rapiers.
Identification: not known.
Date: not known.
Assessment: Provenance should be treated as uncon-

firmed and it is conceivable that this was actually a find from Langdon Bay illicitly withheld.

14. East Wear Bay, off Folkestone, Kent

Sword: Limehouse type (Fig 4.13)
Private ownership, Mr H Brice (1952)
Sources: Cowen 1952; Colquhoun and Burgess 1988, no 120.
Circumstances: Dredged from the sea in the net of a Folkestone fishing smack in April or May 1951 about 40 yards from the shore. The finder was Mr H Brice and the first to recognise its archaeological significance was Mr G F Finn. It remained in private ownership.
Dimensions: length 625mm; width at shoulders 64mm.
Description: (Based on Cowen 1952) The sword was 'in sound condition but a little water-rolled'. The hilt has a 'fish-tail' finial and the gently swollen grip is perforated with a single slot. The shoulders are widely splayed with convex outline above and strongly concave ricassos below; each accommodates two rivet holes. Cowen detected a 'moulding' descending in a curve from each of the outer rivets for two inches; on the strength of parallel swords, this feature may have been the metal left upstanding between a pair of grooves rather than a moulding as such. The blade, as illustrated, retains a gentle, leaf-shaped form broadest close to the tip, but the extent of edge loss cannot be ascertained from the drawing alone.
Identification: This weapon is clearly an early form of British flange-hilted sword belonging to a pre-Wilburton tradition. Colquhoun and Burgess place it in their type Taplow (1988, no 120), but its widely splayed and convex shoulders are better matched among type Limehouse (Colquhoun and Burgess 1988, nos 95–106). Although not diagnostic in itself, the fixing arrangement of slot plus two rivet holes per shoulder is also well matched in that group, as is the grooved blade decoration. Reclassification does not affect the suggested chronology of the piece and, in reality, types Limehouse and Taplow may in fact be variants within a basic format. These swords actually have close parallels in Atlantic France, where they are more numerous (Colquhoun and Burgess 1988, 34); several, for example, come from the Seine in the Paris Basin, some with the groove decoration and some with rivet slots in the hilt grip (Mohen 1977, figs 438–51). These often grooved swords are doubtless the antecedents of the Saint Nazaire type discussed below for the Sandettié Bank sword (No 19).
Date: later Penard/Saint-Brieuc-des-Iffs assemblage, 1200–1100 BC.
Assessment: The water-rolling noted by Cowen implies that the object had been in the sea for a while. However, it could not have been exposed for much of its post-depositional history given the typological detail that survived.

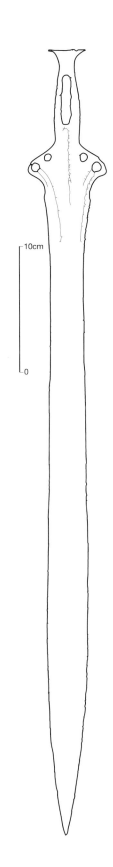

Fig 4.13 Sword found in East Wear Bay, off Folkestone, Kent (drawing: Cowen 1952)

15. Off Langdon Bay, Dover, Kent

See Chapter 2.

16. Off Whitstable, Kent

4 socketed axes
Socketed axe 1: south-eastern type, plain (Fig 4.14a)
Maidstone Museum, 38.1916
Socketed axe 2: south-eastern type, plain (Fig 4.14b)
Maidstone Museum, 182.1916
Socketed axe 3: ?south-eastern type, plain (Fig 4.14c)
Whereabouts unknown
Socketed axe 4: southern English ribbed type (class B) (Fig 4.14d)
Maidstone Museum, 85.1953
Sources: NBI; Grove 1954; Samson 2006, 373, table 1 no 5.
Circumstances: According to an early record in the NBI: 'In a letter dated 24.vi.16. Mr Wells says "I have in my collection 3 bronze socketed axes which were found at Whitstable. They were brought up by oyster dredgers nearly a mile from shore. I understand that the oyster dredgers know the exact spot where they are found and look out for specimens".' One (No 1) and possibly another (No 2) of the axes were purchased by Maidstone Museum from W C Wells in 1917; No 3 was said to have been given to the museum by Wells and later returned to him. Axe No 4 was purchased by Maidstone Museum much later, in 1953; it had come from the Fenton collection (Grove 1954) and was recorded as being 'from the sea at Whitstable'.

Socketed axe 1

Dimensions: Length 95mm; width at cutting edge 40mm; width at mouth 36mm; breadth at mouth 38mm; weight 191.3g.

Description: (Based on the NBI record) The surface is rusty-brown coloured; a little light-coloured sediment adheres, especially inside the socket. A mouth-moulding is shown, but not a second which, if present, may be slight. The body is nearly parallel and gently waisted, leading to modestly expanded blade tips. The socket mouth is oval, the slightly longer axis being perpendicular to the blade edge.
Identification: The main features are of the south-eastern type of socketed axe (class A in Needham 1990a).

Socketed axe 2

Dimensions: Length 97mm; width at cutting edge 43mm; width at mouth 37mm; breadth at mouth 35mm; weight 184.3g.
Description: (Based on NBI entry) The surface is rusty brown coloured and rather rough. A double mouth-moulding is in evidence, the lower moulding being slighter. The body is nearly parallel with a gentle expansion towards the blade tips. The socket mouth is sub-rectangular with the long axis in line with the cutting edge.
Identification: Typical south-eastern socketed axe (class A).

Socketed axe 3

Dimensions: Length 96mm; width at cutting edge 37mm; width at mouth 32mm; breadth at mouth 35mm.
Description: (Based on NBI entry) The surface is rusty-brown coloured. The drawing does not show mouth-mouldings, but the axe is unlikely to have lacked any. The loop is still intact, so the extent of abrasion would not have been great and the mouldings may have been slight. Irregularities in the outline of mouth and cutting edge suggest minor damage. The body expands very gently to the cutting edge and the socket mouth is slightly oval.
Identification: Probably of the south-eastern type.

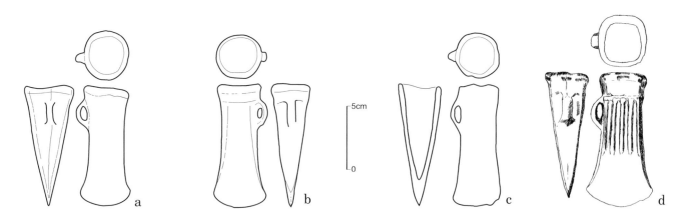

Fig 4.14 Bronze metalwork found off Whitstable, Kent: a) socketed axe 1; b) socketed axe 2; c) socketed axe 3; d) socketed axe 4 (drawings after National Bronze Implements Index)

Socketed axe 4

Dimensions: Length 106mm; width at cutting edge
c 54mm; width at mouth *c* 40mm; breadth at mouth
?41mm; weight *c* 305g.
Description: (Based on NBI entry) The axe has
an uneven brown surface and is chipped (unclear
where). There are remains of marine bryozoa inside
the socket. It has a strong upper mouth-moulding
around an almost square socket. There is a slight
lower moulding well below the upper one from
which issue five vertical ribs, the outer two of which
emphasise the body angles. The body expands
gently towards the blade tips, which appear to be
undamaged.
Identification: Classic southern English ribbed axe
(class B in Needham 1990a).

Date: Ewart assemblage, *c* 1000–775 BC.
Assessment: The implication of Wells' original communication is that bronzes were pulled up from the
seabed at a given location sufficiently frequently
to attract the notice of the oystermen and it is
possible that more than four examples were found.
Three further entries in the NBI record three more
socketed axes from Whitstable in the ownership of
Captain J H Ball early in the twentieth century. Two
appear to be class A socketed axes and the third is
a class B axe on which five ribs terminate in pellets.
While not recorded as having come from the sea, one
of these axes is described as having gravel in the
socket and they could easily be further seabed finds
from the same area.

The depth of water one mile (1.6km) from shore
would still be only a few metres as the location falls
within the extensive area of 'Kentish flats'. There has
been submergence of low-lying coastal land along
the north Kent coast even since the Late Bronze
Age (Champion 1980), and it is possible that these
axes came from a relative high point in the topography which, in the Late Bronze Age, was exposed
at low tide at least. On nautical charts there is, in
fact, a thin spur of very shallow water running for
almost exactly one mile northwards from Whitstable; this feature is known as 'Whitstable Street', but
is thought to be a bank formed under marine conditions rather than a former terrestrial feature (inf
Dave Parham).

17. Off Southend, Essex

Rapier: Group II (Fig 4.15a)
British Museum, 1942, 0410.1
Flanged axe: Stop-ridge axe (Fig 4.15b)
British Museum, 1942, 0410.2
Sources: Rowlands 1976, 281, no 203, 403, no 1701,
pl 42; Burgess and Gerloff 1981, no 71; author's
study.
Circumstances: These two bronze objects were
purchased in 1942 by the Christy Trustees for the
British Museum from F Rehberger Esq, The Old

Rectory, Winkleigh, Devon. An adhesive label on
the rapier states 'Off Southend 1935', a similar
one on the palstave 'Off Southend 1932'; these
were probably applied by the former owner. The
1942 acquisition also included two flints from West
Mersea 1939, presumably the location of that name
further north along the Essex coast.

Rapier

Dimensions: Length 469.5mm; width at butt
63.7mm; maximum thickness (at the middle of the
blade) 6.6mm; weight 330.7g; *rivets*: lengths 20.6mm,
21.0mm; head diameters 8.3–8.8mm; minimum
diameter 6.9mm × 7.5mm.
Description: The surface coloration is varied with
one face generally duller than the other. It is largely
lightish green/dull greeny-gold with some darker
patches; very limited areas (mainly at the edges) are
rubbed down to brighter, golden metal.

The butt is thin and slightly irregular; in plan it
describes a broad, gentle curve. The base of the hilt-
plate is defined by a strong omega-shaped hilt-line,
comprising a sudden step down from the plate to the
top of the blade. This feature, although more pronounced on one face, is present on both, resulting
in the hilt-plate being almost a millimetre thicker
than the adjacent blade. The definition of the step
is rather diffuse towards one shoulder, probably
because of erosion; the surface condition does not
change across this step, but, even so, it may have
been caused by differential erosion during the period
before the organic hilt decayed. Of four original
rivets, the middle two remain *in situ*; these are thick
with minimally expanded, gently domed heads.

The blade contracts below the hilt-plate, but then
becomes more gently tapering for the greater part of
its length. The cross section is concave-lozenge, the
arris being slightly rounded, perhaps by erosion. A
pair of grooves runs from each of the outer two rivet
holes, eventually converging low on the blade. These
are relatively consistently preserved and it therefore
seems surprising that there are much more vestigial
traces of two further grooves immediately outside
the obvious pairs. These grooves are best preserved
over a length of only 30mm, with just hints of them
elsewhere. Similarly, there are only slight hints of
edge bevels, and it would appear that a very thin
surface layer has been stripped off the whole object.
It can only be surmised that the inner two grooves of
initially quadruple groove bands were more deeply
chased. The cutting edges are sharp from the surface
reduction but retain an even outline.
Identification: The rapier belongs in Burgess and
Gerloff's Group II on account of the lozenge-shaped
blade section, but they were unable to place it in a
specific type, just a small sub-group having shallow
butts and four rivet holes (Burgess and Gerloff
1981, no 71). They compared the butt/rivet arrangement to certain Tumulus rapiers in central Europe
(*ibid*, 43), but the similarity is quite general and the

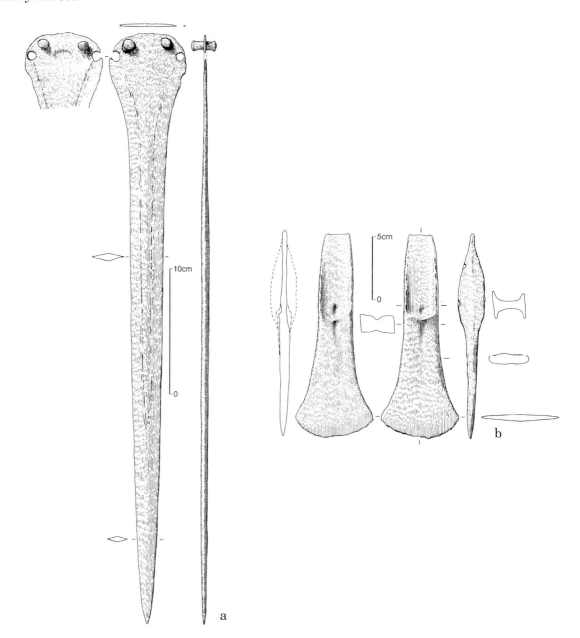

Fig 4.15   Bronze metalwork found off Southend, Essex: a) rapier; b) flanged axe

stronger connections are with the Tréboul/Saint-Brandan and related rapiers of north-west France (Briard 1965, 86–94) and Belgium (Warmenbol 1992, 83, fig 42 a and b), plus a few similar weapons in Britain and Ireland. The French examples usually have six rivets (the outer two set in side notches) and bands of four or five grooves. They also have rounded midribs, which differentiates them from the Southend weapon. However, one rapier from the Saint-Brandan hoard itself has a very similar shape and four-rivet arrangement (Gallay 1988, no 566). There are a number of grooved-blade dirks and rapiers from Britain and Ireland which clearly relate to the Saint-Brandan development across the Channel, but none closely match the combination of features at Southend. Overall, therefore, this blade can be interpreted as a near-unique variant on the Saint-Brandan grooved dirk/rapier model.

This makes it difficult to suggest its specific region of production.

Flanged axe

Dimensions: Length 162mm; width at cutting edge 64mm; width at shoulders 29.2mm; width at stop 27.5mm; width at butt 18.2mm; breadth of flanges 22.3mm, 22.1mm; maximum height of flanges 9.0mm; height of stop above septum *c* 2.5mm; depth of hollows from blade surface 4.0mm, 1.5mm; maximum thickness of septum *c* 6mm; weight 257.4g.

Description: The surface is mainly a matt, darkish brown with green areas, especially in the hafting slots. It is generally rather battered, being covered in dents and depressions of varied character, some probably the result of corrosion or differential etching. One butt corner is slightly bent. The cutting edge is somewhat irregular and no defined edge bevel survives. The flanges are fairly thin, again with irregular crests. Ghosts of the casting flashes are present running down the flange sides.

The flanges are leaf-shaped, a little asymmetric, and largely restricted to the haft-end. There are good internal angles where they meet the gently convex cross section of the septum. The haft end is close to parallel in plan and the blade expands significantly only towards the cutting edge. Erosion leaves it uncertain, but there could be the hint of vestigial shoulders at the base of the flanges, a feature often present on short-flanged axes. The blade is thicker than the septum, but, unlike on true palstaves, the stop is not fully level with the flanges; instead it dips significantly towards the centre line, where there is a linear furrow stretching from the end of the septum well into the upper blade. Consideration was given to whether these might be preferential erosion features caused by a differing metal structure along the medial axis. However, this scenario cannot be the cause since, even though the stop becomes low in the middle, it is still present running across the furrow, rather than being broken by it.

Both the sharpness of the cutting edge and the thinness of the flanges are likely to have resulted from surface reduction which might also account for the rounded blade sides. However, the overall symmetry of the object may suggest that loss has not been great. It is concluded that the longitudinal furrows are original features of the axe.

Identification: This axe would appear to relate to the 'stop-ridge' or 'bar-stop' series which primarily occur in southern Britain, northern France, and the Low Countries (Butler 1963, 45). French examples have been termed type Plaisir (Blanchet and Mordant 1987). However, the majority of these, throughout their distribution, retain full-length flanges extending along much of the blade's sides. The axe from off Southend also differs in the medial furrow traversing the stop position. This is an extremely unusual feature, potentially deriving from the flow and shrinkage of the metal during casting.

Although no exact parallels are forthcoming some important comparisons may be made, firstly, with three Welsh implements. Of these, the most similar in overall proportions is an axe from Abertillery, Monmouthshire (Savory 1980, no 130). The leaf-shaped flanges cease a little below the stop and are only a little broader than those on the Southend axe. The stop is much more pronounced, but there is a slight medial hollow straddling it. There is also the slightest intimation of shoulders at the flange bases. The two other pieces to be discussed are curious lightweight flanged implements, too light for axes and yet with broad blades. The one from Holyhead Mountain, Anglesey, has a narrower body and is waisted below the blade, where there is an oval hollow beneath the low stop (*ibid*, no 128). Although in plan view its proportions are different, its profile

is close to that of the Southend axe. The flanged 'axe' from the Moelfre Uchaf hoard, Denbighshire (*ibid*, no 261:1), is comparable in both profile and plan, but it lacks any stop feature between its septum and thin blade. There is a related narrow-bodied flanged implement from the Voorhout hoard, Zuid-Holland (Butler 1995/6, 223 fig 145), but this is an extremely slight implement. The Plaisir type flanged axe from the river Maas at Maastricht should also be mentioned on account of having a pronounced depression immediately beneath its stop (Butler 1995/6, 228, fig 36b no 157).

It is possible to see the Southend axe and the Welsh pieces discussed as representing an experimental 'type' or group leading to a more regular palstave type with a shield-shaped hollow beneath the stop set within a thicker blade (eg Savory 1980, nos 132–42); this type probably ran in parallel with the classic Acton palstaves, which instead bear a shield-shaped rib beneath the stop.

Date: Acton/Tréboul assemblage; *c* 1525–1375 BC.
Assessment: It is unfortunate that more is not known of the circumstances of discovery and whether Rehberger was the finder. According to the attached labels thought to have been applied prior to acquisition by the museum, these two objects were recovered from the sea three years apart. If this information is correct, it is noteworthy that two objects of the same phase should have been brought up on separate occasions from 'Off Southend' and it seems unlikely that they were totally unrelated deposits. It is possible that the original findspot was rescoured simply because a fisherman repeatedly returned to a favoured patch of the sea. The alternative is that one of the dates was incorrectly inscribed. Either way, the implication of these two bronzes is that they might have been part of a larger find.

18. Off Sotteville-sur-Mer, Seine-Maritime

Gold torc 1: flange-twisted type (Fig 4.16a)
Gold torc 2: flange-twisted type (Fig 4.16b)
Musée des Terre-Neuvas, Fécamp, D.30.1–2
Sources: Billard *et al* 2005; Marcigny *et al* 2005a, 108 no 108.
Circumstances: These torcs were brought up in the net of professional fishermen Claude and Denis Dufour on separate occasions almost two years apart, but at the same location (established each time by positioning equipment). They were declared to the department of *Affaires Maritimes* in 1994. The findspot was about 3 nautical miles (5.5km) from the coast around Sotteville-sur-Mer, where the seabed is some 30m deep. Subsequent archaeological surveys were conducted in 1994 and 1995; during the latter season 7200 square metres of seabed (120m × 60m) were systematically scanned with the aid of metal detectors in corridors 5m wide. No further Bronze Age finds were made. This area is thought to have safely encompassed the relatively precise recorded

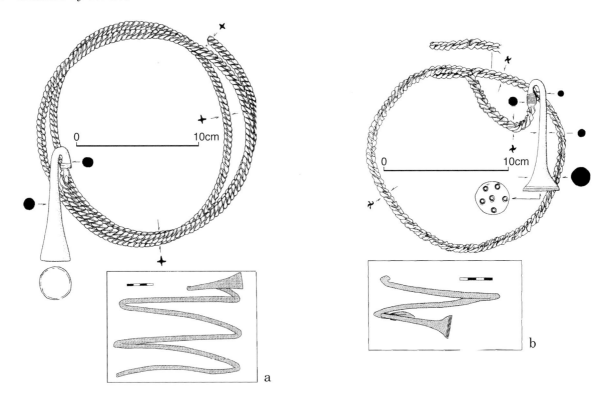

Fig 4.16   Gold torcs found off Sotteville-sur-Mer, Seine-Maritime: a) torc 1; b) torc 2 (drawings: Billard et al 2005)

location of the finds. The seabed is sand of variable thickness, up to 1m, overlying a rock platform which outcrops in places (Billard *et al* 2005).

At the time of discovery the torcs were covered in thick calcareous concretion, but this had been cleaned off by the finders prior to reporting.

Torc 1

Dimensions: Length uncoiled *c* 1.33m; maximum diameter of coils 183mm; maximum diameter at terminal 27mm; diameter of twisted bar *c* 5.5–8.5mm; weight >600g.

Description: (Based on Billard *et al* 2005) This torc is incomplete, but still retains over two and a half coils of very evenly twisted bar of cruciform cross section. The coils wind helically with good spaces between them so that the overall depth of the helix is about 135mm. At the intact end a tightly doubled-back trumpet terminal has been soldered or brazed onto the bar. After the tight U-bend, the round-section terminal expands fairly steadily with slightly concave sides. It is plain apart from two fine encircling grooves, one incomplete, close to the junction with the bar.

Identification: The cross section is that of a crisp four-armed star, or cruciform, making it specifically flange-twisted within the broader 'bar'-torc series (Eogan 1994, 53–7). The terminal, although a large example, is typical of the type. Eogan's distribution map (Eogan 1994, fig 32) shows major

concentrations of gold bar-torcs in southern Britain and eastern Ireland. However, there are also a number of finds spread across north-western France and beyond (see also Billard *et al* 2005, 299, fig 4) and it seems eminently likely, especially given the extremely elaborate example from the Guînes hoard, Pas-de-Calais (Armbruster and Louboutin 2004), that the type was being produced on the continental mainland. This is probably an example of a shared tradition of metalworking embracing regions separated by the Channel.

Torc 2

Dimensions: Length uncoiled *c* 0.70m; maximum diameter of coils 159mm; maximum diameter at terminal 27mm; diameter of twisted bar *c* 6.8–8.2mm; weight 222g.

Description: (Based on Billard *et al* 2005) This is an incomplete torc with approximately one and a third coils of twisted bar. The bar has a cruciform section, but, unlike Torc 1, the four arms frequently curl as they radiate outwards. The twisting is also much less regular and there seem to be many crimps at intervals along the flange crests. It is not clear to what extent this is a less accomplished flange-twisted bar or whether it has just suffered more damage. Again, the intact terminal is of doubled-back trumpet form, but expansion is slight for much of the length and only increases dramatically close to its flat-faced end. The latter is decorated with six small inscribed circles, one roughly central and the others distributed around the edges; their spacing is not very regular. The sides of the terminal alongside this face carry three fine encircling grooves, while a set of eleven encircles the opposite end, where it meets the bar. Deformation of the flanges at this junction suggests that the twisted bar has been inserted into a socket in the terminal. Very different metal compositions for bar and terminal confirm that they started as separate components.

Identification: This torc is also of the flange-twisted type, but the more ornately decorated terminal is a rare feature. Eogan (1967, 129) listed only two bar-torcs with decorated terminals, and only a couple of further examples have been found since his corpus (eg Mohen 1977, 98; Armbruster and Louboutin 2004).

Date: Penard/Rosnoën assemblage, *c* 1275–1125 BC.

Assessment: Coastal retreat of the Norman coast has been only modest since the Bronze Age, in the order of hundreds of metres, not kilometres (Billard *et al* 2005, 296). Despite archaeological underwater prospection, there is unfortunately no further evidence to shed light on the context of deposition and those authors review a wide range of possible explanations for this deep-water find. They were, however, able to argue that it was unlikely to be due to loss during the sinking of a modern ship on which these were carried as antiquities. They favoured instead loss as a result of shipwreck in the Bronze Age, but also drew attention to the practices of watery deposition well known for rivers and other terrestrial wet zones. Intriguingly, there is another find of a flange-twisted torc from The Minch, between Skye and Lewis in the Scottish island archipelago (Cowie 1994), and two fragments have now been retrieved from Salcombe site B (only one of which is catalogued in this volume).

19. Sandettié Bank, the Channel/North Sea

Sword: Saint Nazaire or related type (Fig 4.17)
Private ownership?
Sources: Verlaeckt 1996.
Circumstances: Recovered in December 1994 by a fishing boat trawling the middle of the North Sea approach to the Channel at Sandettié Bank, some 32.5km north of Calais and 36km east of the coast near Sandwich. Mr R Barbaix took it to Ostend for recording. The find is stated to have come up from international waters at about latitude 51°16' and longitude 1°55' E, placing it on the north-west flank of the long SW–NE-aligned Sandettié Bank. The point of the sword was distorted and broken off by the net winding gear, but the missing part of the hilt was not present at the time of discovery (Verlaeckt 1996).

Dimensions: Length 693mm (including tip); maximum width of grip 17mm; width at shoulders 38mm; maximum width of blade 40mm; maximum

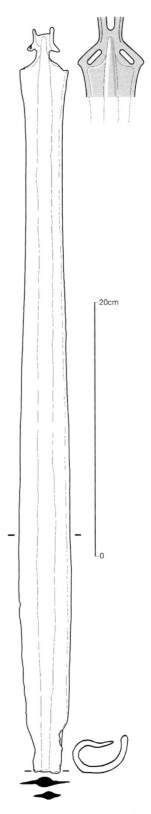

Fig 4.17 Sword found on Sandettié Bank in the Channel / North Sea (drawing: Verlaeckt 1996), with suggested reconstruction of original shoulder form

thickness of grip 8mm; maximum thickness of blade 7mm; weight 594g.

Description: (Based on Verlaeckt 1996) The sword has a golden- to red-brown patina with green corrosion pitting. The extant base of the hilt grip has side flanges; the large notch at the break is probably either the result of heavy attrition around the lowest rivet hole or the base of a rivet slot. The very tops of the shoulders have survived and are strongly out-turned from the grip (approximately 50° from the long axis), but most of the shoulders have broken or eroded away. The rivet holes or slots in the shoulders would have made that zone particularly susceptible to erosion. Even allowing for this increased erosion, the evident alignment of the shoulder perforations (see reconstruction in Fig 4.17) suggests that the shoulders could not have curved downwards by more than a small amount. There is no certain sign of indented ricassos, but, being blunt, these would have resisted abrasion much more than the very thin sharpened edges immediately below; hence, with time, it is possible that the latter would be reduced sufficiently to come into line with the former. The blade is leaf-shaped with the broadest part much nearer the tip than the shoulders, as is classic for flange-hilted swords. There are traces of decoration in the form of a quadruple groove on either side of a slight 'midrib'. It is not clear whether this is a true midrib or instead simply a thickened mid-blade delineated by the grooving.

Identification: Identification of a sword severely eroded around the diagnostic shoulder zone is bound to pose problems. This is clearly a flange-hilted sword within the generic Atlantic tradition of the Late Bronze Age. Verlaeckt suggested it belonged to *Bronze Final IIb–IIIb* in the French system, or Hallstatt A2–B2/3 in terms of central European chronologies (1996, 52). Furthermore, he drew a comparison with north-west French Saint Nazaire swords, which are characterised by multiple groove bands, as seen on the Sandettié Bank example. Many swords of Saint Nazaire type have less-splayed shoulders than would seem to have been the case here (Briard 1965, figs 63–64), but closely related swords from further south may be more comparable, including from the Saint-Denis-de-Pile hoard, Gironde (eg Coffyn 1985, fig 11.5, pl IX, 13 and 18, pl XII, 3 and 4). Sadly, the condition of the Sandettié Bank sword is not good enough to be sure of precise typological comparisons. Multiple grooving appears on a few earlier flange-hilted swords of late Penard date, some of which have widely splayed shoulders, notably among type Mortlake (Colquhoun and Burgess 1988, nos 127–134), with close parallels in northern France (Mohen 1977, fig 444). However, the Sandettié Bank sword is unlikely to have belonged to this very broad-bladed and broad-shouldered form.

Interestingly, there is a Belgian find of a triple-grooved sword from Harelbeke, West Flanders. Warmenbol (1990b, 41, fig 11) classified it as Carp's Tongue, but it is more similar to the Saint-Nazaire type.

Date: Saint-Brieuc-des-Iffs assemblage, *c* 1150–1000 BC.

Assessment: This find, discovered at such a considerable distance from any coastline, must have been deposited at sea. The extent of erosion evident around the shoulders is consonant with it having suffered from corrosive attack and/or physical abrasion for some time.

20. Off Westkapelle, Zeeland, Holland

Palstave: Rosnoën type (Fig 4.18)
Private ownership
Sources: Samson 2006, 373, table 1 no 2 – described as 'axe (stop-ridge)'; inf Jay Butler and Hannie Steegstra.
Circumstances: Dredged from the North Sea in April 1998 about 500m west of Westkapelle, the extreme western tip of Walcheren, Zeeland (inf David Fontijn and Jay Butler).
Dimensions: Length 194mm; width at cutting edge 49mm; breadth at stop 32mm; weight 616g.
Description: (Based on information supplied by J Butler) This is an unusually massive, narrow-bladed palstave. It has a green patina with black patches and some golden-coloured metal showing through. The flanges and stop together form a long, slightly swollen U-shaped slot. The septum base is flat in the middle, but the flange inner faces are rather sloped. A short tapering rib descends from beneath the stop. The blade is modestly flared with no additional expansion towards the blade tips, one of which may be a little damaged. Its faces are convex in cross section.
Identification: It is very similar to the palstaves defined in this volume as Langdon type 3, among which Nos 88 and 89 at least are of similar size (190mm). Palstave S5 from Moor Sand is also similar in most respects, but has a stouter midrib. These are a variant within the Rosnoën palstave spectrum.
Date: Penard/Rosnoën to Saint-Brieuc-des-Iffs assemblages, *c* 1275–1000 BC.

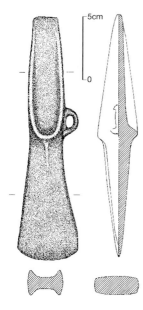

Fig 4.18 Palstave found off Westkappelle, Zeeland, Holland (drawing supplied by Jay Butler)

Assessment: Changes to the Dutch coastline have been complex during the later Holocene. A dune/peat coastal formation established by the late third millennium BC passed through the western tip of what was later to become Zeeland, and this barrier system shielded extensive intertidal flats behind it (Van Gijssel and van der Valk 2006). While the findspot of this palstave may have been open sea in the Middle Bronze Age and the object deposited directly in the water, it is also entirely feasible that the object arrived there as a result of subsequent erosion of the coastal barrier system locally. The lack of significant feature reduction on the object favours either a long-stable underwater burial environment, or redeposition into the sea in more recent times.

21. Possibly the seas around Vlieland and Terschelling, Friesland

Palstave: Broad-bladed, Flevoland type (early midribbed palstave) (Fig 4.19)
Private ownership; on loan to 't Behouden Huys Museum, Terschelling
Sources: Samson 2006, 373, table 1 no 1 – described as 'axe (stop-ridge)'; Butler forthcoming; inf Jay Butler and Hannie Steegstra.
Circumstances: Found in February 2000 among crushed shells on a shell-path and presumed to have been dredged up by a suction dredger from either the inshore Waddenzee or the North Sea between or north of the islands of Vlieland and Terschelling (inf Jay Butler).
Dimensions: Length 133mm; width at cutting edge 57mm; breadth at stop 18mm.
Description: (Based on information supplied by J Butler) The axe has a light-brown patina with areas of golden-coloured metal showing as well as some green, damaged areas (possible corrosion spots). The flanges and stop together create a long U-shaped slot. The septum base is fairly evenly curved in cross section. Neither flanges nor stop are very high and it seems unlikely that this slightness was due to substantial reduction from rolling, since the ribs on the blade are still prominent features, much as would be expected of the type. The upper blade is slightly waisted, but then it expands strongly with straight sides. In addition to the strong ribs along its sides ('side-flanged'), the blade carries a central rib from stop to edge bevel. The edge bevel is steeply chamfered for the full width of the cutting edge.
Identification: This is a broad-bladed and unlooped form of palstave. Butler (pers comm) draws attention to three very similar axes, possibly from a hoard from an unknown provenance in Flevoland (the reclaimed polders on the south-east side of Ijsselmeer; Butler and Steegstra 1997/8, 191–2, fig 56 nos 222–224). These three share the low flanges and stop of the present example. The form is related to southern British 'early midribbed palstaves' (Butler and Steegstra 1997/8, 191–2; Schmidt and Burgess

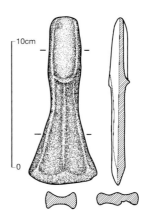

Fig 4.19 Palstave possibly found in the seas around Vlieland and Terschelling, Friesland (drawing supplied by Jay Butler)

1981, 125–8), but the low flanges are unusual. A less-extreme version may come from the Acton Park hoard, Denbighshire (Savory 1980, no 262.6), but Margaret Ehrenberg (1982) has shown that there is some doubt about the association of that particular palstave.
Date: Acton/Tréboul assemblage, *c* 1525–1375 BC.
Assessment: Even assuming that this was a dredged find, there are many imponderables as to its origin. Firstly, it is not known whether it came from the seas to the south or north of the West Friesian islands and, as in the case of the Off-Westkapelle find above, coastal landform changes have been considerable since the Bronze Age. At the beginning of the Bronze Age the islands of Vlieland and Terchelling were probably engulfed in a wider area of dune and peat formation spreading a little further seaward, but more particularly extending for 50km landward before meeting, at different points, intertidal flats and higher land (Van Gijssel and van der Valk 2006). Therefore, it is quite likely that the depositional environment of the axe was not so much open water as an extensive complex of barrier system and tidal flats.

Summation

At first sight, this list of marine finds of Bronze Age metalwork from the coastlands of southern Britain, northern France, and the Low Countries is fairly impressive. Moreover, the finds discussed may be only the reported and/or identifiable 'tip of the iceberg'. However, perusal of the details of discovery given above will quickly highlight the degree of uncertainty surrounding the original contexts of deposition of many of the finds. In part, this situation is a function of the unstable state of coastal environments when seen against timescales of millennia; but it is also in part due to the suspicion with which archaeologists and archaeological bodies have traditionally been regarded by those most likely to make significant marine discoveries. Careful evaluation of the condition of the objects can help confirm that there has been marine influence, but without precise locations, follow-up underwater investigations, and knowledgeable consideration of local coastline changes the prospects for a good understanding of these scarce and important prehistoric deposits and their contexts are small.

A fuller evaluation of the collective significance of the catalogued finds is reserved for Chapter 5, but it is worth noting in summary here that the objects are varied in type and date, spanning much of the Bronze Age, and that they come from widespread locations within the Channel and its approaches (see Fig 4.1). Another point that will receive attention below concerns the fairly high proportion of these finds that certainly or potentially lay beyond their core areas of distribution. This observation obviously assumes interest in light of the foreign components present at both Salcombe and Langdon Bay.

5 Bronze Age metalwork from the sea – taphonomy and significance *by Stuart Needham, with Martin Dean, Catherine J Frieman, Brendan O'Connor, and Dave Parham*

Opinion on the two main assemblages covered here has traditionally leaned towards their marking the sites of wrecked or foundering ships of the Bronze Age, or at least representing cargoes (Coombs 1976; Baker and Branigan 1978; Muckelroy 1980c; 1981; Needham and Dean 1987). Some consideration has always been given to the possibility that they might instead have resulted from coastal erosion (Muckelroy and Baker 1979; Muckelroy 1980c, 100), however, and this hypothesis can now be addressed more fully with the detailed geomorphological reports presented in this volume. Coastal submergence since the Bronze Age is another potential cause for the recovery of land-deposited bronzes from the sea, but, as there has been little relative rise in sea level since the period in question, in practice this explanation is only relevant to restricted zones, such as the north Kent shelf (see, for example, the Whitstable find – Chapter 4). Another possible scenario of deposition is introduced in the case of the Salcombe site because of the proximity of the new Bronze Age concentration (site B) to the 17th-century AD 'Cannon' site. Might the Bronze Age material have merely been a part of the 17th-century cargo? This idea is not just a theoretical possibility; the cargo of *The Colossus* which went down off St Mary's in the Scillies in 1798 included a collection of Greek antiquities being brought back for Sir William Hamilton (Morris 1972). In discussing the torcs found off Sotteville-sur-Mer, Cyrille Billard and his co-authors covered these possible explanations and also raised another: the deliberate deposition of metalwork in the open sea as an extension of the recurrent practice of watery deposition elsewhere in north-western Europe. However, on balance, this was not the interpretation preferred for the Sotteville find (Billard *et al* 2005, 296–8). Even Keith Muckelroy had given some thought to the possibility of ritual deposition for the Moor Sand site, but he thought it improbable that a ritual offering would be limited to imported French objects (Muckelroy and Baker 1979, 205).

Nevertheless, ritual deposition has been taken up with vigour in a recent article by Alice Samson (2006). Samson argues that, by treating all seabed finds as debris from shipwrecks, they are categorised as 'profane' deposits, while she seeks instead to 'explore the possibility of another realm of Bronze Age practice' (Samson 2006, 376, 379). It is documented in various ancient cultures that the sea can be used as a specialised deposition zone (Lindendauf 2003), but to get beyond the theoretical possibility to a reasoned argument it is essential to undertake careful analysis of seabed finds individually and collectively. Samson's comparative and taphonomic analyses are poor in a number of respects and she fails to come up with convincing criteria for establishing a pattern of deposition that might be diagnostic of deliberate deposition in the sea, as opposed to accidental losses in the same environment. Either process could give rise to an aggregate seabed assemblage with distinctive elements relative to terrestrial assemblages. In fact, interpretation of patterns is extremely hamstrung by the smallness of the dataset (even our enlarged dataset relative to Samson's) and by the dearth of good contextual evidence for the seabed assemblages such that we have no 'control' sites. What, for example, should we expect of a genuine shipwreck in north-west European waters? We venture some very general predictions below. Samson (2006, 379) makes the tacit assumption that we can look to well-established wrecks such as that at Uluburun, off the southern Turkish coast (Yalçin *et al* 2005); but it is surely a mistake to assume that a ship's contents in such an entirely different social environment would necessarily bear any close resemblance to contemporary examples from north European waters.

Other negative forms of evidence introduced by Samson in arguing against shipwrecks are the lack of any actual boat remains, pottery or ballast on the three archaeologically investigated sites (Langdon, Salcombe, Sotteville). This betrays a startling under-appreciation of the harshness of the underwater environment in the Channel; one only has to look at the extreme whittling down of some recovered bronzes – a relatively durable material – to appreciate the point. Indeed, it is not improbable that some bronzes have been reduced to the point of disintegration. Nevertheless, relatively durable material such as bronze does have the opportunity over a fairly extended period to find its way into stable, non-erosive contexts, such as silt-filled gullies, and still be recognisable for what it is. This would not be the case for prehistoric pottery, which would have had to have benefited from that protection almost immediately if it was not to have been washed away and/or disintegrated in the high-energy shallow water environments of Langdon and Salcombe, with their strong tidal surges. If occasional ceramic finds did get into stable sediment or gullies, they could remain buried and undetected without extensive

Fig 5.1   Large block of stone with a cupped depression, potentially a lamp or mortar, found at Salcombe in 2005. Length 240mm. © Trustees of the British Museum

excavation and sieving. It must be remembered that most of the underwater work at the key sites has involved only surface survey, and only the very limited excavation of sediment pockets when metal detectors have indicated the potential presence of buried bronzes.

The taphonomic issues relating to the survival of a boat are different. Firstly, it is a large artefact compared to its contents. If a boat had sunk to the seabed at Salcombe or Langdon Bay, either entire or as large segments, it is most likely that it would have come to rest on an exposed surface rather than in any protective crevice. Without any rapid covering of sediment, storms and currents would soon break it up and disperse it. Smaller fragments could of course have found their way into gullies, but even these would have been subject to continued attrition unless quickly buried in sediment. It is crucial to recognise that the environments of these sites are not those of the *Mary Rose* or Uluburun.

Samson's points may be more valid in relation to other kinds of durable material that might be on board a prehistoric boat, notably lithic material. Stone would resist erosion better than most materials and its weight could prevent any undue dispersal. The absence of identifiable worked or non-local lithic material at Langdon Bay does suggest that there was no lithic ballast, but early sail-less boats with a low freeboard may not have had any

need for ballast. If additional weight was a benefit, we should not forget the bronze material itself, especially since we cannot know how much larger the original metal assemblage was than the 65kg recovered. The rocky nature of the Salcombe coast and seabed introduces difficulties for the recognition of intrusive stone. However, the discovery on the site in 2005 of a large block of stone with a cupped depression, potentially a lamp or mortar (Fig 5.1), may be an early indication of a novel component to the Salcombe assemblage.

Although we question the *basis* on which Samson made her case for ritual deposition at sea, that does not mean we do not accept it as a possible explanation for some material deposited in the maritime environment. Some aspects of such deposition are raised hypothetically in this chapter.

Finally, before proceeding further with analysis, we do need to accept that, whatever the full range of modes of deposition at sea in the Bronze Age, it is inconceivable that foundering boats were not a component. The finds catalogued here span a millennium or more, and it can be speculatively ventured that many hundreds of boats and their cargoes would have sunk over this period, a proportion doubtless in circumstances and locations susceptible to later discovery. Indeed, it is well understood that, although some boats will have been overset in open water, wrecks tend to be distributed close to the coast, often concentrating around ports and other landing areas. The surf zone is exceptionally dangerous, with waters that are more confused than those further offshore, increasing the risk of boats being swamped in heavy weather or poor conditions. Additionally, in coastal areas vessels in difficulty are in danger of hitting either the shore or rocks just offshore. Shallower draught craft will have inevitably been closer to the shore before they made contact with the seabed or submerged rocks. A small Bronze Age boat of the size capable of transporting the Langdon Bay assemblage may have come to grief in the very shallowest and highest-energy water: that is, the surf zone.

In summary, a Bronze Age shipwreck site in the Channel might only yield remains of the boat under exceptionally benign seabed conditions. This leaves three other potential components: related maritime equipment (anchors, navigation instruments, etc); domestic assemblage belonging to the crew; and cargo. Since there is no evidence in northwest Europe of any specialised maritime objects for the Bronze Age, we are left with the latter two categories.

Mode of recovery and recovery biases

The distribution of the known seabed sites is intriguing (see Fig 4.1). The study area has been selected to embrace finds from the Channel and its approaches from west and east, but actually known finds do seem to peter out beyond this zone. Along the east coast of Britain only one is known to the authors north of Southend, Essex: a socketed spearhead recorded as having been dredged from near St Margaret Hope in the Firth of Forth in 1916 (Cowie and Hall 2001, 7, no 8; T Cowie, pers comm). The site is just off Rosyth, where the tidal estuary is still 3km wide. The Hull median-winged axe listed by Samson (2006) was found during construction of the Alexandra Docks alongside the Humber estuary and is not strictly a marine find, although we do introduce it into a broader discussion of land/sea interface finds below. On the west coast, the only find known to us north of Llanrhian, Dyfed, is right up in the Outer Hebrides: a gold twisted torc from the waters immediately west of the Shiant Isles which are towards the mainland from the Isle of Lewis (find known as 'The Minch' – Cowie 1994). Finds do not appear to have been reported from southern Scandinavia – although this could be due to the region's history of isostatic recovery – nor from the western coasts of France. Of course, there might well be taphonomic reasons for some apparent lacunae. Even within the study area there is an apparent concentration along the south English coast from Dorset to the Thames estuary. There are, however, several beach finds from the south-west peninsula (Chapter 1) and Wales, as well as elsewhere, that would amplify the western distribution if some had washed up from eroding seabed contexts (see also below). To gain a better apprecia-

Table 5.1   Summary of mode of recovery of the seabed finds

	Site	Mode of recovery
1	Llanrhian	Diver
2	Sennen Cove	Diver
3	Salcombe	Diver
4	Chesil Beach	Diver
5	Poole Harbour	Diver
6	Southbourne	Beach-fishing
7	Solent Water	Sea-fishing (on anchor)
8	Bembridge	Sea-fishing (net)
9	Isle of Wight?	Dredged?
10	Hayling/Owers Bank	Dredged?
11	Seaford	Diver
12	Hastings	Sea-fishing?
13	Sandgate	Diver
14	Folkestone	Sea-fishing (net)
15	Langdon Bay	Diver
16	Whitstable	Sea-fishing (net?)
17	Southend	Sea-fishing?
18	Sotteville-sur-Mer	Sea-fishing (net)
19	Sandettié Bank	Sea-fishing (net)
20	Westkapelle	Dredged
21	Vlieland/Terschelling	Dredged?

tion of the significance of the seabed distribution we also need to consider the mode of recovery.

Most of the finds have been made by sport divers or fishermen (in roughly equal numbers); a minority have come from material dredged from the seabed (Table 5.1). There is geographical bias, with diver finds in the majority to the west of the Isle of Wight, while to the east most were recovered by fishermen. It is not obvious why fished-up finds should be so relatively restricted given that material clearly exists further afield and, one assumes, fishing activity has been fairly evenly distributed along these coastal waters, both inshore and offshore. One possible factor could be the nature of the seabed. Flat-bottomed or sediment-laden beds are presumably much more likely to deliver large objects into dragged nets than those with craggy topographies. Deep fissures in particular could prevent objects being caught in nets. This contrasting potential might favour discoveries through fishing around the lowland zone of Britain, with its generally softer, erodible rocks yielding flatter seabed platforms.

It is clear that the later 20th-century growth in sport diving is responsible for a significant increase in seabed discoveries and, moreover, in the extension of the distribution to more westerly waters. The amount of diving activity along the various coastlines will be an important factor in the pattern of recovery established, particularly as one can imagine that there has been a bias towards diving on the more interesting, rocky coasts of western Britain rather than in the siltier environments to the east.

Analysis must proceed on the basis that our seabed dataset may be an unusually fuzzy representation of the real seabed assemblage. Recovery bias is, of course, one important factor to be considered; but we must also be aware that a proportion of the finds will not have started their depositional life in the sea, while others that did may subsequently have been redeposited on land or eroded to the point of disintegration.

The most probable recovery biases include the retrieval, firstly, of metal at the expense of other materials (although note probable differential survival, as discussed above); secondly, of objects with form as opposed to those made amorphous by erosion; and, thirdly, of objects large enough to be brought up in nets and noticed onboard ship. Underwater survey can at least partly address these imbalances. At Langdon Bay many small and amorphous pieces were recovered only as a result of persistent searches over several years (Needham and Dean 1987). The analyses presented in that paper clearly showed how both the size distribution and the type range of the bronzes changed over the course of a multi-season campaign. The new work at Salcombe is also turning up small and unusual objects – for example, the tin lump (S28) and the iron awl in bone handle (S29) – the latter of which also highlights the possibility of occasional organic survival. A further encouraging outcome of the concerted underwater survey campaign on that site is the recent recovery of a cupped block of stone (Fig 5.1), mentioned above; although not proven, this object seems likely to have belonged with the Bronze Age assemblage.

Few of the other finds catalogued here have offered the opportunity for underwater prospection because they were old finds, the find-spot was too imprecise, or they were already clearly redeposited at the time of discovery. Survey work at Sotteville-sur-Mer was uninformative as to the original context of the two gold torcs (Billard *et al* 2005).

Object condition and implications for representation

Naturally, one of the most significant questions is how much material might there be, or might there have once been, in the seas surrounding north-western Europe? The modest corpus of data gathered here actually has the potential to give some important insights into this question. The more thoroughly examined sites demonstrate that material of the same age recovered from the same limited stretch of seabed can be in highly variable condition, ranging from near-pristine to amorphous and virtually unrecognisable. Highly eroded objects have, in fact, been reported only on the sites where finds that were more recognisable had already been recovered. The most heavily rolled blades and axes from Langdon Bay would scarcely attract much attention if found singly; they are barely recognisable to the specialist, let alone the lay-person, and it is not unreasonable to suppose that many such pieces have been overlooked by sport divers, fishermen or those working with marine-recovered ballast.

That a high proportion of the *recognised* seabed finds comprises objects that have not suffered particularly heavy erosion, either by chemical corrosion or mechanical attrition, suggests that most of these finds have not been exposed to destructive agencies for very long – certainly only a minor part of their full age. In some cases this could well be due to their having been reworked into the sea from coastal deposits only relatively late in their buried life. However, this scenario is unlikely to explain all known examples, for we know that relatively well-preserved objects were lying in protected seabed contexts, namely silt-filled gullies, at Salcombe and Langdon Bay. If the Hayling Beach axes did indeed come in with ballast from Owers Bank, these too must have lain relatively undisturbed for long periods well out to sea. The same conclusion might also be drawn for the Sandettié Bank sword, although it may have lain in deeper waters than the coastal finds and thus not been subjected to such strongly erosive conditions. Similarly, any long-standing sediment abrasion could be expected to have worn even the gold of the Sotteville torcs more than is evident. It is hard to escape the conclusion that the identifiable objects that make up the recognised seabed assemblage are but the tip of the iceberg in terms of what once existed in that domain.

The generally good condition of objects recovered from the seabed extends to their degree of completeness. Setting aside the two sites that have been subjected to intensive, long-term survey work, virtually all objects from the other nineteen sites are either essentially complete or large fragments – usually well over half of the original object. The only exception is the ferrule from Poole Harbour, which may be a smaller fragment, but this was recovered lodged within a larger object. Rather than reading this evidence as a true reflection of the material on the seabed, it is far more likely that it derives from the casual mode of recovery and the failure of lay-people to notice or report small or fragmentary items. Yet the clear evidence of underwater survey at Langdon and Salcombe is that small and fragmentary objects are present on some seabed sites; indeed, they may predominate over more complete and/or larger objects. This is another reason, additional to the related problem of form loss from erosion (which also makes things smaller), for believing that the material recovered so far is a tiny fraction of that present on the seabed and, moreover, not a faithful representation in terms of condition and range of object sizes.

Table 5.2 Summary of the phasing and contents of the seabed assemblages of metalwork

Site		Assemblage	No objects	Categories	Production zones (best estimates)
1	Llanrhian	Taunton	1	W	Near-regions or Ireland
2	Sennen Cove	Llyn Fawr?	1	W	? Ireland
3	Salcombe (to end 2004)	Penard/Rosnoën	28	W, A, T, O, M	Mixed – cross-Channel regions; Seine basin; one, central Mediterranean
		Ewart/Plainseau	1	W	Cross-Channel regions
4	Chesil Beach	*Premier Âge du Fer* (= Llyn Fawr)	1	A	Cross-Channel regions
5	Poole Harbour	Ewart/ Plainseau	2	A, M	Near-regions or cross-Channel regions
6	Southbourne	Sicilian Hoard Horizon I (≈ Penard)	1	A	Central Mediterranean
7	Solent Water	Taunton/Baux-Sainte-Croix to Penard/Rosnoën?	1	O	? Near-regions or cross-Channel regions
8	Bembridge	Taunton	1	W	Near-regions
9	Off the Isle of Wight	Llyn Fawr	1	A	Near-regions or further afield in Britain
10	Hayling/Owers Bank	Taunton/Baux-Sainte-Croix	6	A	Cross-channel regions; one possibly near-regions
11	Seaford	Taunton/Baux-Sainte-Croix	4	A, W? M	Near-regions or cross-Channel regions
12	Hastings	Arreton/Derryniggin	1	A	Central to northern Britain or Ireland
13	Sandgate	?	1	W?	?
14	Folkestone	Penard (late)/St-Brieuc-des-Iffs	1	W	Near-regions or cross-Channel
15	Langdon Bay	Penard/Rosnoën	361	A, T, W, O, M	Mixed – cross-Channel regions; further south in eastern France; near-regions
16	Whitstable	Ewart	4	A	Near-regions or cross-Channel regions
17	Southend	Acton/Tréboul	2	A, W	Mixed – Western Britain; ? local, cross-Channel inspired
18	Sotteville-sur-Mer	Penard/Rosnoën	2	O	Near-regions or cross-Channel
19	Sandettié Bank	St-Brieuc-des-Iffs	1	W	Along Channel (western France)
20	Westkapelle	Penard/Rosnoën to St-Brieuc-des-Iffs	1	A	Along or cross-Channel
21	Vlieland/Terschelling	Acton/Tréboul	1	A	? Local, cross-Channel inspired

Note: A = axes; M = metalworking debris and miscellaneous; O = ornaments; T = tools other than axes; W = weapons

Object categories and representation

The range of metalwork from the sea is as varied as that from the land (Table 5.2). This range of variation is seen not only within the large assemblages, where there is natural scope for the incremental addition of new types and categories, but also in the small groups and single objects taken all together. The large finds both include all five major categories defined: axes (A), tools of other types (T), ornaments (O), weapons (W), and miscellaneous objects (M), including fittings and metalworking debris. The nineteen smaller finds, which have between one and six objects per site, need to be taken in aggregate, but the pattern thus

established will not be directly comparable to that for the large assemblages because they conflate seven different phases of the Bronze Age rather than representing just one. Among the smaller site assemblages, axes are the dominant category, occurring on eleven of the nineteen sites. Contrary to Samson's attempts to find significance in the frequency of axe finds (2006, 382), the category is far too ubiquitous in both circulation and the deposited record to draw any useful conclusions from the sea/land comparison. Weapons – all swords and rapiers – are a little less frequent, occurring on up to eight sites. Ornaments occur on only two of the smaller sites, but that might be because most ornament types, such as bracelets, rings, costume fittings, and pins, are small and relatively light-weight and can be rendered rather nondescript after only limited erosion. Miscellaneous material may be poorly represented for similar reasons, and it is noteworthy that in one case (Poole Harbour) the 'miscellaneous' object was inextricably locked together with an axe, while in the other (Seaford) it was probably spotted only because a palstave had already been recognised on the site. Other tools are not represented, perhaps because most are smaller than axes or are hollow-cast and therefore prone to greater erosion, thus escaping notice.

Overall, then, there is little evidence for any selectivity in the categories deposited at sea relative to those found on land. It is true that, among the 'single' finds, weapons (5 + 1?) are as frequent as axes (6), but this observation hardly seems a compelling argument for interpreting the maritime assemblage *en masse* as the product of any deliberate deposition strategy, particularly since it is possible that longer weapons would get caught in nets or catch the eye more readily than axes. Samson's claim that 'the temporal and compositional patterning described … suggests another scenario: that of deliberate deposition in the sea' (2006, 380) cannot be substantiated on the basis of aggregate composition, unless the argument is actually that, because most land finds are now being considered in terms of deliberate ritual deposition, the similarity of the seabed assemblage points to the same depositional background. This comparative deduction would be too simplistic.

Taking all finds together, there is also a wide range of more specific types: a flanged axe, winged axes, palstaves, socketed axes, a shaft-hole axe, chisels, hammers, knives, awls, a possible flesh-hook, ferrules, loop attachments, raw metal, neckrings, bracelets, pins, swords, rapier/dirks, and spear-heads. The last type is surprising in that, despite its frequency on land and in rivers, it occurs on only one seabed site in the study area – Langdon Bay – and in very modest numbers (5 of 360 bronzes; but also note the Firth of Forth example mentioned above). It is evident from the Langdon examples (see below) that the hollow-cast and thin-bladed form of a spearhead may be prone to more rapid erosion than solid cast types; even if erosion has removed only one face or side (eg No 353), it can make interpretation of original form difficult. If this is a valid argument, it could mean that socketed axes were also more readily reduced to unrecognisable forms than earlier axe types, palstaves, and so on, which has implications for the chronological distribution (below).

The nature of the multiple-object sites

Eight of the sites have yielded more than one object and these multiple finds allow some assessment of those sites' coherence in temporal terms. One site, Poole Harbour, is discounted for this purpose as the two objects are locked together and thus constitute a single discovery. In all other cases, individual objects were recovered on two or more occasions which were sometimes spread over years rather than just within one season. Despite the spread of recovery times, in almost every case the material brought up from a given site appears to belong essentially to a single-period assemblage. At Langdon nothing in the vast haul seems anachronistic except a modern copper-alloy rod and other dismissed modern detritus. The Hayling Beach palstaves are all coeval despite being of three different types; so too are the socketed axes from Whitstable, apparently brought up by the fishermen over time. Sotteville-sur-Mer and Southend yielded just two objects, in both cases apparently discovered two or three years apart; yet both comprise contemporaneous pairs of objects. We cannot be so sure about the Seaford bronzes because only the two palstaves are really diagnostic; a third object is missing and the fourth, the piece of raw metal, would be an extremely unusual inclusion in a terrestrial hoard of the period. However, this assemblage may reflect on the selective nature of deposition on land, rather than on chronology.

Salcombe is beginning to look like an exception in this respect. Until recently (ie the 30 objects catalogued in Appendix 1), virtually all the prehistoric objects were of Penard/Rosnoën date; the one clear exception was a Carp's Tongue sword, while the iron awl must remain uncertainly dated for the present. Finds since 2004, however, include more that are best dated to the Ewart stage, so the site seems to have received bronze metalwork on at least two occasions in the Bronze Age. There is no evidence as yet for long-term continuous deposition rather than two temporally separated episodes. Salcombe aside, therefore, these multi-object groups are temporally restricted to within a particular metalworking stage. In this respect, they are temporally coherent groups akin to hoards, but other features suggest that they cannot all be regarded as equivalent to hoards.

Nor, evidently, do the multi-object sites represent extensions out into the sea of the long-term practices of deposition seen in the rivers. Assemblages from particular reaches of rivers can occasionally be temporally confined (see also discussion of river-mouth groups below), sometimes to the point that a group of river-found metalwork has been referred to as a 'hoard' – as in the case of the Broadness (Burgess *et al* 1972, 238–9) or Taplow Creek groups (Ehrenberg 1977, nos 113–119; Colquhoun and Burgess 1988, nos 167 and 186). More usually, however, reaches that have yielded metalwork represent more than one phase and at times quite diverse assemblages (eg Needham and Burgess 1980, 452 fig 7). There is no indication yet of this more normal riverine pattern in the offshore zone.

Given the serendipity of recovery and the infrequency of archaeological follow-up, the multiple-object sites give the strong impression

Table 5.3   Chronological distribution of the seabed finds

Date (BC)	Metalwork assemblages	No finds	Multiple finds
1750/1700–1500	Arreton/Muids/Derryniggin	1	0
1525–1375	Acton (2)/Tréboul	2	1
1400–1250	Taunton/Baux-Sainte-Croix	4 (+1?)	2
1275–1125	Penard/Rosnoën	6 (+2?)	3
1150–975*	St-Brieuc-des-Iffs	1	0
	Wilburton		
1000–775	Ewart (including Blackmoor)/Plainseau	3	2
800–625	Llyn Fawr/*Premier Âge du Fer* (Hallstatt C)	2	0
	Total	19 (+2)	8

* A recent suggestion by Colin Burgess (in prep) is that this actually conflates two metalwork phases, St-Brieuc-des-Iffs being earlier than Wilburton. St-Brieuc-des-Iffs may in fact largely equate with *later* Penard material in Britain (sometimes referred to as Penard 2), so there may be more than usual overlap in the attributions given in this volume for the Penard to Wilburton span.

Note: The proposed date ranges deliberately overlap to express both the degree of imprecision and the likelihood that there were genuine periods of transition.

that many may originally have been larger assemblages, perhaps much larger. This may not be the case for Sotteville, where subsequent survey work yielded only recent objects. The two torcs on that site could, of course, be the only surviving remains of an upset boat, but the total lack of other contemporary finds in this expanse of open water away from reefs certainly admits the possibility of a deliberate deposit (*pace* Billard *et al* 2005, 296–8).

The circumstances of the Hayling Beach group suggest another picture, for there were a number of potential filters in the recovery process restricting the number of finds recovered: firstly, there is the possibility that objects were dispersed on the seabed such that not all were dredged up; secondly, there could have been differential erosion, as seen at the main sites, resulting in unrecognisable pieces; and, thirdly, there is no guarantee that, once dumped on the beach, all ancient artefacts would have been obvious to the workmen. It would be very hard, in this instance, to conclude that the six palstaves recovered were the full complement.

It may be conjectured, then, that the number of objects known from any individual seabed site is potentially considerably fewer than the original number deposited. Even setting aside all the survival and recovery biases set out above, this factor alone has serious implications for attempts to make statistical comparisons between seabed assemblages and those from dry land. A second difficulty in making sea to land comparisons is that, on land, where initial observation was good we can often be confident of the 'closed' nature of a group of objects. The vicissitudes of the marine environment make it intrinsically difficult to have the same confidence for sea finds. Only if an enclosing vessel were to be found might a 'closed group' be claimed with certainty, but evidence for associated ship remains has eluded us thus far.

Chronological distribution

It is clear that metalwork spanning a long part of the Bronze Age, from at least 1750/1700 BC through to 625 BC, was finding its way onto the seabed one way or another (Table 5.3). In general, multiple finds seem to be in proportion to the total number of finds through this time span. Given the still small number of finds and the many taphonomic issues discussed, their distribution through time should not be taken to represent true relative levels of activity. For example, there is an apparent peak during the Taunton/Baux-Sainte-Croix to Penard/Rosnoën phases which includes the two major assemblages and the next largest (Hayling/Owers Bank); but socketed axes, like socketed spearheads, may be more susceptible to serious damage than palstaves and Late Bronze Age finds could thus be under-represented relative to those of the Middle Bronze Age.

If, however, the peak noted is a genuine reflection of relative maritime activity (of whatever kind), it is intriguing that it does not coincide exactly with the chronological distribution of metalwork on land to either side of the Channel. Although there was large-scale terrestrial deposition in the Taunton/Baux-Sainte-Croix phase on both sides, the quantity of metalwork permanently deposited in the succeeding Penard/Rosnoën phase decreased considerably, particularly in Britain. The seabed record is also at variance with the terrestrial one when we come to consider the later phases. Land deposition was at an all-time high during the Ewart/Plainseau phase, even greater than in that of Taunton/Baux-Sainte-Croix; this pattern is not reflected in the seabed distribution and only future surveys and discoveries may indicate whether this difference is just down to the hypothesised under-recovery of Late Bronze Age socketed implement types. Nevertheless, it may be that the composite pattern seen in the seabed finds is the product of a balance of circumstances that was *not* the same as that governing land deposition.

Origins, foreign-ness, and the problem of 'hidden circulation'

Great interest has naturally been taken in the presence of 'foreign' objects in the two key assemblages. The existence of these exotic objects was recognised early on by Coombs (1976), Muckelroy (1980; 1981) and O'Connor (1980) and has been reinforced by subsequent finds and analyses (Needham and Dean 1987; Needham and Giardino 2008; Chapter 3 above). It is significant, then, that the other seabed finds described here (Chapter 4) augment this pattern in having a good proportion of objects potentially foreign to their immediate hinterlands.

The question of assessing foreign-ness needs to be approached with the regional scale of Bronze Age polities in mind. For example, an object from northern Britain found in the south may have been just as alien, if not more so, than one from immediately across the Channel. There is also the question of the perception of the source by the receiving communities; looking at the Low Countries evidence for imports of western bronzes, David Fontijn (2009) has wondered to what extent those of insular origin would be differentiated from those of north French origin. With the growth of more regular traffic across and along the north-west European seaways, a phenomenon that has been dubbed elsewhere the 'Channel Bronze Age' (Needham *et al* 2006; Needham 2009), perceptions of foreign-ness may well have shifted. The processes behind the Channel Bronze Age led to a degree of cultural convergence in the lands flanking the Channel (see also Gabillot 2003; Marcigny *et al* 2005) manifested in both artefact forms and aspects of settlement and landscape organisation. Some metalwork types, such as the gold twisted bar-torcs, seem to be sufficiently frequent on both sides of the Channel to suggest they were being manufactured in both regions rather than being the products of one shore that were exported across the water. For such types, we need to think in terms of shared traditions. However, the pattern is not uniform for all regions, nor for all types; some types remained essentially characteristic of one region, albeit with seeming distributional outliers (eg the Breton palstave), and others seem not to have been acceptable for use on one shore of the Channel or the other (eg the median-winged axes; looped socketed axes/chisels). The result is a complex pattern that renders difficult the drawing of neat culture-zone or shared-tradition boundaries.

The enduring problem we face is in having to interpret production and circulation densities from the modern, recovered distributions, for it is well accepted that processes of differential recovery have an influence, sometimes profound, on regional densities of finds. An even more intractable problem is that of 'hidden circulation', cases where a type of object did actually circulate within a region as an accepted part of the systemic repertoire, but for some reason was not deliberately deposited in the ground or watery environments. Growing evidence points to this form of bias in many metalwork distributions;

at Langdon Bay it is exemplified above all by the tanged-and-collared chisels, for which very few terrestrial finds can be shown to be contemporary.

So, in reading a distribution (strictly, a 'map of recovery') with, say, a finds zone of high density, areas in which finds are less densely spread, and, beyond, just occasional 'outliers', it is easy to deduce a 'core zone of production' with distribution outwards. However, such interpretations usually overlook potential differentials in both deposition and modern recovery and mould finds often show that production was taking place in zones that have yielded few finds of the type in question. Sometimes like-with-like comparisons, for example one type of sword with other contemporary swords, can help in deciding whether low-scale presence is due to importation rather than local production which happens to be under-represented in the archaeological record. Yet even this approach is not infallible, as we cannot assume that complex social interactions would always result in any regional production being focused on a single style of sword. Assessment of the foreign-ness, or otherwise, of the seabed finds is, therefore, not always straightforward, but nevertheless has to be attempted (see Table 5.2).

Several finds are unequivocally of types that were shared between cross-sea regions, such as those from Llanrhian, Poole Harbour, Bembridge, Seaford, Folkestone, Whitstable, and Sotteville-sur-Mer, as well as some of the types at Langdon. While it may seem most economical to regard such examples as coming from their respective closer shores, this need not have consistently been the case. A few finds would, on current interpretations, be seen unequivocally as objects that have crossed the Channel: Salcombe (most of the assemblage), Chesil Beach, Hayling/Owers Bank, Langdon (much of the assemblage), Vlieland/Terschelling, and perhaps the Southend rapier. Others have evidently been transported *along* one or another of the north-western seaways – Hastings, Southend, Sandettié Bank, and Westkapelle. We should not make too much of the distinction between along-coast and coast-to-coast passage of goods. More crucial in terms of contemporary perception would have been, firstly, the degree to which the displaced material was patently of a foreign type in the reception zone and, secondly, the association of any past history (biography) that reinforced its foreign-ness. In addition, there are, of course, the two examples of long-distance displacement of objects which came all the way from the central Mediterranean and were found at Southbourne and Salcombe.

A conservative estimate suggests that as many as 10 of the 21 finds catalogued include objects significantly displaced from their probable zone of manufacture. This proportion is very noteworthy (almost 50% of sites), in that it contrasts starkly with the normal incidence of foreign material from terrestrial locations. On this basis alone it is obvious that the pattern of offshore deposition does not simply reflect that seen in the respective hinterlands. The balance of components is very different. It is also of note that, despite the small size of our dataset, the identified foreign objects come from a variety of regions: northern Britain/Ireland, Armorica, northern France/Belgium, the Seine Basin, and the central Mediterranean.

This difference observed in the proportion of foreign objects adds to the perception that the collective seabed assemblage is not simply an echo of that found on land (including inland waters). This particular distinguishing feature is, of course, even more strongly reflected in the two large seabed finds. Detailed consideration of the geographical catchment of those two assemblages is discussed in a later section.

Between land and sea: deposition across the interface

Thus far, discussion has been strictly confined to the material known or believed to have been recovered from the seabed; this stricture was necessary in order to get the best possible characterisation of the marine assemblage. However, for the purposes of interpreting the significance of the coastline in terms of metalwork deposition in the Bronze Age, it may be an advantage to relax the criterion to allow consideration of finds made on the intertidal zone and a short distance inland.

The growth in the Middle to Late Bronze Age of large-scale seaborne movement of material, especially metal, must have focused ever more attention on coasts, estuaries, and rivers as interface zones for socially important transactions. Indeed, the location of many Arreton hoards may suggest that such a focus was already developing towards the end of the British Early Bronze Age (Needham *et al* 2006, 78, fig 38). Seen from a coarse-grained, cartographic perspective, the coast can appear to be a simple, linear meeting point of two very different domains – the land and the sea. Yet, even setting aside diverse human reactions to such a dramatic ecotone, more careful thought suggests it could be viewed as a more complex series of topographic and perceptual zones. Since topographic zonation was evidently of great importance in the deposition of Bronze Age metalwork (eg Fontijn 2002; Yates and Bradley 2010), it is worth considering hypothetically what micro-topographic zones might have been distinguished within the 'coast' by prehistoric communities. Figure 5.2 is a schematic attempt to show the components that can make up this interface.

The strong likelihood that some material will have been reworked from one zone to another by subsequent processes has already been stressed. However, this reworking may not materially alter the distinctive, foreign-rich character of the maritime bronze assemblage. Although we have not quantified them in proportional terms (it would be a major project in its own right), there are a number of other bronzes from coastal locations that conform to the criteria of foreign-ness adopted here. As examples, one can cite

the median-winged axes from Alexandra Dock, Hull, and Sketty, Glamorganshire; a biconical-headed pin of Rhine-Swiss-eastern French type from Camber Sands, East Sussex; a Hunze-Ems socketed axe among the bronzes from the marsh platform site just behind the coast at Shinewater, East Sussex, and another from the Minnis Bay hoard, Kent; a plate-extended flanged axe probably of Danish origin from Reculver, Kent; and a continental barbed and tanged arrowhead from the Penard hoard, Gower, Glamorganshire (Table 5.4). Many of the British finds of Norman palstaves also come from sites close to the coast.

Table 5.4 is far from an exhaustive record of foreign-looking bronzes from the coastal strip. Indeed, they form only a small minority of the many other finds which are consistent with being relatively local products. Further inland, the proportion of foreign objects declines. There are, of course, examples of clear foreigners well inland, such as the Bohemian palstave from Horridge Common in the heart of Dartmoor (Fox and Britton 1969) or the Breton and Norman palstaves from the Wantage hoard, Berkshire (O'Connor 1980, 319, no 1), and, in particular, the large hoard of mainly imported palstaves from Marnhull in Dorset, some 37km as the crow flies from the south coast. The Marnhull assemblage could perhaps have been imported through Christchurch Harbour and up the river Stour (Lawson and Farwell 1991; O'Connor 2009). These are just illustrative examples; it would be a massive and partly subjective exercise to quantify 'imports' in relation to inland regions, not least because of the difficulty of clearly defining one region's output from that of neighbouring regions. Nevertheless, there is little doubt that only a tiny proportion of objects could be identified specifically as foreign to their region of deposition using similar criteria to those adopted here for the marine finds.

Therefore, there would appear to be something of a gradation with regard to the distribution of the most obviously alien bronze types. One plausible explanation would be that coastal communities initially commandeered goods carried by sea and then usually recast them into local types before redistribution to groups further inland. If the explanation lies primarily in such economics of exchange and production, rather than ritual concerns (see below), it nevertheless needs to be recognised that cross-Channel and long-shore exchange may have been organised differently at different stages of the Bronze Age, giving rise to different deposition patterns. Coastal communities would always have had the greatest potential for controlling sea-to-land interactions, but this control would not necessarily have been exercised, depending on the socio-political relations of the time. The case of Early Bronze Age amber is instructive; there is certainly a case to be made for the exercise of some control by south coast communities (Beck and Shennan 1991, 77–85; Needham *et al* 2006, 75–6), but the mere fact that a goodly amount of amber

Table 5.4 Examples of bronze metalwork found on or close behind shores in Britain

Site	Context & circumstances	Object, collection	Date	Origin	Reference
Anglesey, Menai Bridge SS 555 716	Overlooking Menai Strait, c 200m north of coast; found 7ft deep, covered by two stones while quarrying, 1874/5	Hoard: 8 Arreton type flanged axes *National Museum of Wales: 44.172/1 British Museum: 1881,1224.1 Bangor Museum*	Arreton		Britton 1963, 318–19; Lynch 1991, 218–21
Cornwall, Camel Estuary, Doom Bar Sands SW 9168 7743(?)	Large expanse of estuarine foreshore; metal-detector find 1999	Side-looped spearhead *Unknown?*	MBA		*Royal Institute of Cornwall County Museum & Art Gallery Newsletter no 27*
Cornwall, Breage, Praa Sands c SW 58 28	Sea-front behind beach; digging foundations for bungalow, pre-1932	Arreton type flanged axe *Helston Museum: 1079*	Arreton		Thomas 1963, fig 22
Devon, Chivelstone, Lannacombe Beach SX 801 371	Beach close to Lannacombe stream; below high water mark, lodged in rocks; found c 1973 by Mr I Mercer; a submerged forest is preserved lower on the beach	Arreton flanged axe *Private*	Arreton		Pearce 1973
Devon, Thurlestone (or South Milton), Leas Foot Beach SX 674 421	Beach, exposed after winter storms; found March 1998; there is a submerged forest near this site	Peg-hole spearhead *Plymouth Museum*	LBA		Devon SMR record no 58790; Samson 2006, no 9
Devon, Thurlestone (or South Milton), Leas Foot Beach SX 67 42	Beach, found 2008; reports of further metal-detector finds of LBA metalwork in same area, 2 spearheads and axe fragment – possibly dispersed hoard	Peg-hole spearhead, offset blade bases *Private*	Wilburton		PAS scheme DEV-2B4697; Danielle Wootton, pers comm
Devon, Berrynarbor, Smallmouth Cove SS 55 48	Beach; found June 1981 by metal-detectorist; tip of ash shaft in situ	Spearhead *British Museum: 1982,0702.1*	Penard –Ewart		Pearce 1983, 556 fig 20
Dorset, Portland, presumably the E end of Chesil Beach c SY 67 74	Beach; 'under the pebble beach at Portland … waterworn and corroded by the action of the sea according to Evans	Armorican socketed axe *Ashmolean Museum (Evans collection)*	Llyn Fawr equivalent	Continent (NW France)	Evans 1881, 115; R Taylor 1980
Dorset, Weymouth Backwater SY 676 788	Lowest reach of River Wey; dredged 1900	Sword, Ewart type with Gündlingen features *Dorset County Museum: 1939.35.1 (loan to Weymouth Museum)*	Ewart/ Llyn Fawr		Pearce 1983, 487 no 475; Colquhoun and Burgess 1988, 86 no 440
Dorset, Weymouth Backwater SY 677 792	Lowest reach of River Wey, 50ft N of Wesham Bridge; dredged 1936, apparently with skull and ulna	Wilburton type sword *Dorset County Museum: 1937.10.1*	Wilburton		Pearce 1983, 487 no 476; Colquhoun and Burgess 1988, 49 no 217
Dorset, Weymouth Backwater SY 677 792	Lowest reach of River Wey; dredged about 1921	Wilburton type sword *Weymouth Museum: 1921.2.1*	Wilburton		Colquhoun and Burgess 1988, 49 no 218
Glamorgan (West), Gower, Oystermouth SS 6172 8832	Apparently close to high-tide mark on very broad foreshore; found sticking out of mud on beach, 1979	Ballintober type sword *National Museum Wales: 79.77H*	Penard		Green 1985; Colquhoun & Burgess 1988, no 775
Glamorgan (West), Margam, Margam Sands SS 769 852	Foreshore; found in clay exposed by erosion of overlying peat, 1972–73	Arreton type flanged axe *National Museum Wales: 74.34H.I*	Arreton	South-east England	Savory 1980, 102 no 122
Glamorgan (West), Pennard (Penard), Langrove; c SS 56 88	Exact location unknown but probably about a kilometre behind coast; 1827, while quarrying	Hoard: 2 Ballintober swords, Rosnoën sword, spearhead, socketed axe, arrowhead *National Museum Wales: 15.227.1–6*	Penard	Arrowhead: Continent	Savory 1980, 117 no 266, 180 fig 32; Colquhoun & Burgess 1988, nos 3, 31, & 32
Glamorgan (West), Swansea, Crymlyn Burrows, Elba Tinplate Works c SS 70 93	Within a few hundred metres of current coast; found 16ft deep during digging for foundations, 1926; palstave reported to be near right knee of an extended skeleton	Acton type palstave *Swansea Royal Institution*	Acton		Williams 1937; Burgess 1976, 84 fig 1a, 85 no 2

Table 5.4 (*cont.*) **Examples of bronze metalwork found on or close behind shores in Britain**

Site	Context & circumstances	Object, collection	Date	Origin	Reference
Glamorgan (West), Swansea, Sketty SS 623 924	A short distance inland from coast; 1898, while enlarging pond near Sketty Green entrance to Sketty Hall	Median-winged axe, *Swansea Museum*	(Penard–Wilburton equivalent)	Continent	Williams 1937
Gwynedd, between Tal-y-bont and Barmouth SH 5 2	Shore; thought likely to have been eroded from adjacent peat	Basal-looped spearhead, slender leaf blade; with remains of wood shaft *Private?*	MBA		Frances Lynch, pers comm
Isle of Wight, Totland, Highdown (Tennyson Down) SZ 3216 8536	Cliff top (approx 200m back from present cliff)	Hoard: tanged spearhead, Arreton socketed spearhead	Arreton		Northover 2001, 434, 443
Isle of Wight, Totland, Colwell Bay SZ 329 884	Beach? 'waterworn and abraded' according to Rowlands	Palstave & palstave fragment *Carisbrooke Castle Museum*	Taunton		Rowlands 1976, 309 no 570; Northover 2001, 443
Kent, Capel-le-Ferne, Abbot's Cliff TR 268 384	Foreshore, 1991; thought to have come down with cliff collapse	Gold penannular bracelet *Dover Museum: 1991.5*	Ewart		Unpublished
Kent, Birchington, Minnis Bay c TR 284 697	Foreshore; possibly associated with submerged land surface and pits, exposed after gale, 1938; hoard found in low gravel bank above scoop in chalk bedrock	Hoard of many pieces *British Museum: 1961,1006,1ff*	Ewart	Continent (at least one piece)	Worsfold 1943; O'Connor 1980, 384–6
Kent, Birchington, Minnis Bay c TR 27 69	Beach; single find	Pegged spearhead with flame-shaped blade; remains of wood shaft *Private*	Ewart		Needham *et al* 1997, 65, 96 fig 22.1
Kent, Herne Bay, Reculver c TR 22 69	Exact location unknown, but hamlet and Roman shore fort right up against coast; found 1884?	Flanged axe, Danish type *Ashmolean Museum: 1927.2380*	(approx. Arreton equivalent)	Continent	Needham 1979, 279 fig 9.3, 280
Kent, Isle of Grain TQ 8 7	Foreshore, no exact location; found at low tide line, 2003, by W Green	Dirk/knife – 2 rivet holes; triple arris blade; possibly reworked rapier tip *Private*	MBA(?)		NBI
Kent, Lydd, Whitehall Farm TR 0466 2194	Gravel deposits forming former coastal barrier system; objects picked off conveyor belt carrying extracted gravel by K Atkinson, 1985	5 decorated low-flanged axes *British Museum: 1986,1101.1; 1986,1102.1; 1986,1103.1; 1986,1103.2; 1987,1002.1*	Willerby		Needham 1988
Kent, Margate, c TR 35 71	Beach near a chalk outcrop; metal-detector find 2005	Socketed gouge; with remains of wood handle *Private*	LBA		Andrew Richardson, pers comm; PAS KENT-ACD9F3
Norfolk, Mundesley c TG 31 36	Beach; said to be associated with cliff collapse, 1879	Arreton type flanged axe *Spalding Museum: 87*	Arreton		*Norfolk Archaeology* **9** (1884), 361
Northumberland, Berwick-upon-Tweed c NU 00 53	In arable field a short distance behind coast; found 2005 by J Minns while metal-detecting	Large hoard, many objects fragmentary: 6 gold lock rings, 4 bronze bracelets, 6 rings, 3 pins, 2 bugle-shaped fittings, 6 socketed axes, 3 gouges, knife, 2 razors, spearhead, chape, ingot, pottery sherds; wood remnant in one axe dated 2771 ± 26 BP (OxA-15102) *Newcastle-upon-Tyne, Great North Museum*	Ewart		Needham *et al* 2007
Pembrokeshire, Freshwater West, c SR 882 999	Beach; metal-detector find at lowest tide	Group of 28 objects: 2 sword blade frags (1 Ewart, 1 Carps Tongue), 3 socketed axe frags (1 ribbed, 1 plain, 1 indeterminate), 23 ingots frags	Ewart		Adam Gwilt, pers comm; Dyfed Archaeological Trust HER (PRN14393)

Table 5.4 (*cont.*)   **Examples of bronze metalwork found on or close behind shores in Britain**

Site	Context & circumstances	Object, collection	Date	Origin	Reference
Suffolk, Reydon ('Covehithe'), Easton Cliffs c TM 515 790 & 513 790	Cliff & beach: 1, on beach at foot of cliffs 35–50ft high, believed to be in slumped soil; found about 1980 by P Burbridge 2, in ploughed field immediately above, c 200m from cliff	2 flat axes: 1) class 3E flat axe; 2) class 3B (Killaha type) flat axe *Private*	Brithdir	2) Ireland/ northern Britain	Martin *et al* 1981, 74; NBI
Sussex (West), East Wittering, Bracklesham Bay c SZ 80 96	Presumed beach find; found before 1849 'in the bed containing so many shells of the *Venericaidia planicosta*'	Littleport type dirk *Alnwick Castle Museum: 1880.242*			Dixon 1849; Burgess & Gerloff 1981, 30 no 172 A flanged axe subsequently said to have been associated is probably a fake
Sussex (East), Eastbourne, Beachy Head c TV 585 952	Cliff & beach, 1806; axe first found exposed in cliff face, 10ft down; other objects then discovered in collapsed debris below	Carp's Tongue sword frag, end-winged axe, 4 gold bracelets *British Museum: Payne Knight collection*	Ewart		*Archaeologia* **16** (1806), 363; Smith 1958, GB.40
Sussex (East), Birling, Birling Gap c TV 550 961	Beach; 1991 or shortly before	Transitional type palstave *Private*	Penard (–early Wilburton)		NBI; unpublished
Sussex (East), Camber, Broomhill Sands TQ 992 178	Beach; found 1991–92 by Mr Murfet low on foreshore after storms had carved troughs; pin pointing downwards in or below sand covering shingle	Disc-headed pin, with decorated head and collar beneath (previously classified mistakenly as a *Spindelkopfnadel*) *Hastings Museum: 993.90*	(approx. Wilburton equivalent)	Continent (eastern France or near)	Bellam 1996; Brendan O'Connor, pers comm
Sussex (East), Eastbourne, Shinewater Marsh TQ 6155 0295	Platform occupation in peaty embayment immediately behind coast	Variety of bronzes including Hunze-Ems socketed axe *British Museum: 1997,1002.2*	Ewart	Axe: Continent	Greatorex 2003
Sussex (East), Fairlight, Cliff End TQ 888 128	Foreshore, among stones c 50ft below high-water mark; found c 1971 by Mr O'Dowd	Peg-hole spearhead *Hastings Museum: 971–4*	M-LBA		Baines 1973 There is a submerged forest in this part of the beach, prostrate trunks are still visible; it is likely that this and the next two finds were deposited just behind the contemporary coast before marine incursion
Sussex (East), Fairlight, Cliff End TQ 888 128	Foreshore, resting in clay amongst rocks at low tide; found 1937 by Mr F J Britt-Compton	Dirk/rapier fragments (3 blade frags) *Hastings Museum: 937–72*	MBA?		Baines 1973; Rowlands 1976, 420 no 1921; Needham 1988, 81
Sussex (East), Fairlight, Cliff End c TZ 887 126	Foreshore, close to low-water mark, wedged between rocks on shore of mixed sand and rock outcrops; found 1981, by J E Thwaites; this was evidently found close to earlier finds	Dirk; broad flattened midrib, 2 rivet emplacements; possibly reworked blade tip of Group IV rapier or Rosnoën sword *Private*	MBA		NBI
Yorkshire (East), Barmston Cliff c TA 172 593		Roundhay type palstave *Bridlington Museum: A134*	Penard (–early Wilburton)		Schmidt & Burgess 1981, 150 no 897
Yorkshire (East), Barmston Cliff c TA 172 593		Silsden type palstave *Private?*	Penard (–early Wilburton)		NBI; unpublished
Yorkshire (East), Hull, Alexandra Docks TA 12 29	Close to estuary shore; ?found during construction of docks	Median-winged axe *Hull and East Riding Museum*	(Penard equivalent)	Continent	Burgess 1968b, 11 fig 7.3, 34
Yorkshire (East), North Ferriby SE 991 252	High on foreshore, about 75m NE of Ferriby boat F1; found by E V Wright 1939–40	Tanged knife, probably reworked blade tip of rapier or dirk *Greenwich, National Maritime Museum*	MBA?		Wright 1990, 17, 164 fig 7.25

Topographic complexity at the coastal interface

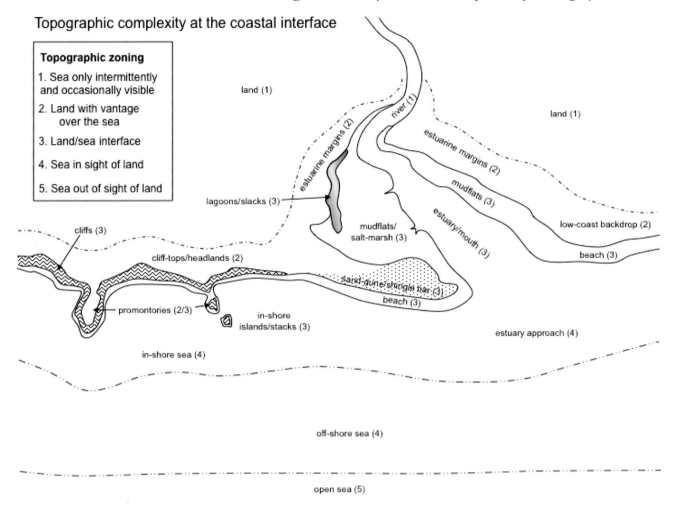

Topographic zoning

1. Sea only intermittently and occasionally visible
2. Land with vantage over the sea
3. Land/sea interface
4. Sea in sight of land
5. Sea out of sight of land

Fig 5.2   Schematic map of the components of the land / sea interface in the Bronze Age

reached central Wessex (even allowing for over-representation there) suggests there were preferential arrangements favouring that destination. Political or, more probably in this case, spiritual dimensions could account for this bias, which, intriguingly, is not evident at all among contemporary bronze metalwork (Willerby and Arreton assemblages).

An alternative possibility is that some deposition around the coastal interface and, in particular, the preferential deposition of foreign objects, stemmed from some kind of ritual behaviour. Although we suggest that the high proportion of foreign types present in the seabed assemblage is significant in terms of the original systemic assemblage, it is not necessarily helpful in relation to the question of deliberate deposition or accidental loss. In the case of intentional deposition, the types deposited might well reflect different social perspectives and depend on who was making the deposit; an obvious contrast would be between people from the proximate shore and travellers from afar. Likewise, different choices for deposition might reflect the occasion that was being marked – as examples, celebrating a successful transaction, a safe home-coming or a safe arrival. However, what this foreign-ness characteristic tells us clearly is that *either* a different assemblage was circulating on the seaways and in the interface zones

compared with that circulating inland, *or* quite different rules governed deposition at sea and coast from those inland. In practice, of course, it could well be that both of these explanations are correct and that one reinforced the other in determining the coastal interface assemblage.

Regardless of the exact interpretation put on a given phase system, the more nuanced categorisation of the land/sea interface suggested in Figure 5.2 could allow some finds deposited near the coast to be viewed in a new way. Traditionally, we regard such finds as part of a 'terrestrial' distribution, perhaps related to areas of intense occupation, even when acknowledging the potential contribution of newly imported material from across the sea. However, it is possible to suggest greater ambiguity in contemporary conceptualisation of their locations of placement. They might be seen as constituting as much a part of the maritime interaction zone as of their hinterland territories, representing an interface zone which had special social regulations for the conduct of essential maritime interactions. This suggestion has been made before for coastal promontories (Cunliffe 2001, 9–10), but deserves wider consideration. For example, in the Isle of Thanet all but one hoard of Middle and Late Bronze Age date lie close to the former coast (Moody 2008, 103, fig 54); this distribution pattern is most unlikely to represent the distribution of settlement as such and is more likely to relate in some way to the islanders' relationship to the sea and sea-borne traffic. Another special-case topographic scenario is seen at Lydd, Kent, where a growing barrier system of shingle was evolving during the later Holocene, trapping a complex wet zone behind (Long *et al* 2007). This place was chosen for the deposition of five Early Bronze Age decorated axeheads, an act which, I have argued elsewhere, could have had a propitiatory function (Needham 2009, 25). The location of the Voorhout hoard, Holland, is also relevant here (Fontijn 2009). One might also question the significance of the striking concentration of Taunton phase hoards spread along the coastal strip from the Solent to West Sussex, including several notably large hoards (Lawson 1999, 100, fig 11.5; to which can also be added his Hayling Island 1; Rowlands 1976, map 26). Is this pattern something more than a settlement-related distribution?

More subtle ways of categorising elements of the land/sea interface by early communities would certainly further complicate our attempts to compare marine and terrestrial assemblages. On this matter, it *may* also be appropriate to think of the find locations of the few median-winged axes in Britain already mentioned above as being extensions of the maritime domain or, at least, as having been deposited at the boundary between two domains. In Chapter 1 it was noted that, although Bronze Age metalwork is thinly spread in south Devon, it has mainly been found close to the coast. Similarly, the recognition in Chapter 2 that later Bronze Age goldwork is distributed along the White Cliffs coastline incorporating Langdon Bay is also relevant here. If it is indeed appropriate to think in terms of some metalwork deposition having taken place close to the coast as part of ritual concerns with maritime engagement, it is equally apparent that this was not a universal reaction, since there are many coastal regions for which no such focus on the coast itself can be discerned. Independent consideration must be given to each region and each phase, rather than seeking or assuming universal patterns of behaviour.

Langdon Bay and Salcombe: material in transit?

Our analysis so far suggests a number of interesting points. While the single and small groups of objects from the seabed give us valuable evidence for a wider phenomenon, we need to be circumspect in their interpretation, whether taken as individual sites or as a group. Without systematic and long-term survey, their small size and extant type compositions cannot be relied upon as faithful representations of the originally deposited assemblages. This caveat applies no matter which

explanation for deposition is being entertained. To suggest that a number of these finds might originally have been larger and more diverse does not rule out the possibility that some others *were* genuinely very restricted deposits – this seems to have been the case for the pair of torcs from Sotteville-sur-Mer.

Although it would be a mistake to attempt to argue the mode of deposition for most of the seabed sites, we are duty bound to form an opinion on the two key sites of Langdon Bay and Salcombe. As already noted, the central debate has been between accidental loss and votive deposition, but this division simplifies the potential scenarios and five hypothetical possibilities can in fact be put forward:

- Land deposits (probably hoards) redeposited through coastal erosion
- Votive deposition at sea as a single act – hoard mode
- Votive deposition at sea as many successive acts – accumulative ritual deposit
- Foundering ship, off-loaded cargo
- Shipwreck site

The key distinction between option 1 (original land deposition) and the others (original sea deposition) has often been considered in the context of these finds. The condition of the metalwork finds does not help with this question; nor do the assessments of changes to the coastline since the Middle Bronze Age. Neither of the detailed reports on coastal geomorphology (Bates and Gehrels above) can be absolutely specific on the amount of coastal loss through erosion since the Penard/Rosnoën phase, approximately 3300–3125 years ago. Modelling coastal change is crucial for understanding the contemporary site environment, but even accurate information on the contemporary position of the coast would not rule out the possibility of subsequent movement of objects on the seabed by tidal currents. The condition, shape, and precise contexts of the bronzes at Langdon Bay and Salcombe may help evaluate these possibilities.

Langdon Bay

Topographic reconstruction

The range of estimated rates of coastal retreat leaves it unclear whether the Langdon Bay site would have been land or sea in the later 2nd millennium BC. The preferred figure, an average of 0.12m per year (Bates, Chapter 2), places the chalk cliff immediately north of the site of recovery, such that the bronzes, if largely unmoved, would have been very close into shore. However, this estimate is based simply on the erosion rate of the chalk rock in this stretch of the coast and Bates introduces another potentially important factor. Up until the later 2nd millennium BC the Dour valley immediately to the west was accumulating a series of peats and tufaceous silts which were unaffected by marine tidal surges.

He suggests that the eastern bank of the river's mouth may have continued southwards and thus projected seawards of the more recent coastline. An alternative might be the accumulation of a shingle barrier across the mouth as sea levels rose during the later Holocene, as seen in many other south coast locations. Without knowing the extent of such a deposit, of either kind, it is hard to extrapolate what effect its existence and then later removal would have had on rates of cliff retreat just to the east.

Much regarding topographic change remains uncertain, so we have no firm basis for establishing the original context of the Langdon bronzes and we need to turn back to the material itself for clues as to its depositional background. Firstly, this large haul of bronzes seems all to be contemporary, within a single metalworking stage. Secondly, it is an absolutely unprecedented assemblage, the like of which cannot be found on either side of the Channel (Fig 5.3). Its singularity lies in both its size (65kg plus, undoubtedly, more not recovered) and the particular range of types. The issue of type range can be further broken down as: i) an unusually wide range of types associated together, although this might be a function simply of assemblage size; ii) types that are extremely rare on the British side of the Channel (as discussed above) and yet may be abundant on this single coastal site (notably median-winged axes); iii) types that are rare anywhere in terrestrial contexts at this date, even to the point of seeming anachronistic (notably tanged-and-collared chisels). Anachronism has been ruled out, however, by the metal compositions.

Fragmentation patterns and assemblage function

Another important aspect of the assemblage is the inclusion of a large proportion of fragmentary objects (Muckelroy 1980c, 101). This level of fragmentation is unusual in contemporary hoards from Britain, but those south of the Channel have variable and sometimes high percentages of fragmentary pieces (Nallier and Le Goffic 2008, 155, tab 1). It appears, furthermore, that there are very different patterns for the major types present at Langdon; the retrieval of much small material through systematic survey gives good grounds for assuming that inter-type comparisons in this respect will broadly reflect the original assemblage. Table 5.5 summarises the balance of complete to fragmentary examples for each major type; it also serves as a useful summary of the overall type composition.

Fragmentary objects are clearly in the majority, but the high total is mainly made up of the various blade weapons. In fact, there is actually a strong representation of complete objects, especially among the axes, but also proportionally among the tanged chisels and small blades (ie knives and dirks). In contrast, the great majority of socketed tools, weapons, and fittings are fragmentary, and it was argued above that the thin socket walls were much more susceptible to physical attrition and, ultimately, breakage in the seabed environment. It is probable that many more, perhaps most, of these implements were originally complete. On the other hand, one cannot dismiss the broken solid-bladed axes as the result of post-depositional damage. Since these fractures run transversely through thick blades or medium–thick butt ends the breakage would not have come about through rolling or even underwater impacts with moving gravel. It would seem that the many complete axes (palstave and median-winged types) were accompanied by smaller numbers of broken examples.

The categories of small objects – awls/rods/shanks, ornaments/fittings, miscellaneous/lumps – are all very difficult to evaluate in terms of their completeness profile. They either started out relatively amorphous (lumps) or are intrinsically more fragile than the larger tools and weapons; in either case, just limited abrasion can result in uncertainty over their original form and completeness. However, it is probable that some were complete, particularly among the ornamental category.

Taking the blade weapons all together, at most 15% seem to have been complete. This proportion reduces to 11% if one excludes the small knife category. The possibility that some of the thin blades were broken by marine agencies cannot be excluded, but that is less likely for thicker examples; indeed, the chopped-up look of much of this material is suggestive of ancient scrapping. This suggestion is reinforced by the two long fragments which are doubled back (Nos 188 and 334), and several more that have tight bends in profile close to breaks. These features can only be realistically attributed to human actions. With eight exceptions – these mainly being complete swords or rapiers – all of the weapon blades have lengths of less than 220mm, regardless of whether they were complete or not. This consistency could be the result of a pattern of scrapping, especially of the longer weapons and less consistently of those already less than 200mm in length (hence explaining the high proportion of small knives that remained complete). Of course, some of the breakage could have occurred during use rather than specifically at the hands of metalworkers.

A possible reconstruction of the original character of the Langdon assemblage is ventured in Table 5.6. This reconstruction not only takes account of the above discussion on the balance between complete and fragmentary examples but also includes a prediction regarding whether the given type may still be under-represented in the recovered assemblage. The fact that a good quantity of scrapped objects appears to be present in the assemblage could lead to the assumption that the whole assemblage constitutes scrap (Muckelroy 1980c, 101). Certainly the median-winged axes, although predominantly complete and functional, would probably be regarded

Fig 5.3   The whole Langdon Bay assemblage. © Trustees of the British Museum

Table 5.5 Summary of type representation and completeness in the Langdon Bay assemblage

Type	Complete (or near)	Fragmentary	Possible example	Total
Palstaves	44	6	0	50
Median-winged axes	45	16	2	63
Axe-blade fragments	0	4	0	4
Tanged-and-collared chisels	5	1	0	6
Socketed tools/implements	3	15	0	18
Spearheads & ferrules	2	5	0	7
Notched-butt knives	10	1	0	11
Rapiers/dirks	5	8	0	13
Swords (& possible swords)	3	27	0	30
Swords reworked as knives	2	0	0	2
Unidentified blades	?9	122	0	131
Ornaments & fittings	3	3	4	10
Awls/rods/shanks	?2	?5	–	7
Rivets	3	0	0	3
Miscellaneous/lumps	?3	?3	–	6
Totals	125 + ?14	208 + ?8	6	361

Table 5.6 A possible reconstruction of the original character of the Langdon assemblage

Type	Complete examples	Scrapped material
Palstaves	Many; various stages of use	Very few
Median-winged axes	Many; few used, but in various stages of use?	Minority
Tanged-and-collared chisels	Small number	Very few/none
Socketed axes/chisels	Moderate number	Few/none
Socketed hammers/punches	Small number	Very few/none
Socketed hooked knife	One at least	
Awls	Small number	
Socketed flesh-hook	One (?)	
Ornaments/fittings	Small number	Uncertain
Miscellaneous pieces/lumps	Small number	
Swords	Small number	Great majority
Rapiers	Small number	Great majority
Knives	Moderate number	Minority?

as raw metal on the British side of the Channel, as Muckelroy realised. However, the palstaves do not obviously conform to this pattern. Very few scrapped examples were recovered and all the complete and functional palstaves that could be identified are of types that would be perfectly at home in southern Britain, even if they had actually been produced on the Continent. If they came ashore as functional and stylistically acceptable objects, they may well have been put into use rather than immediately melted down. The same might apply if their intended destination was actually the southern shores of the Channel.

Despite these cogent arguments for much of the assemblage having comprised, from the perspective of a recipient group in southern England, of raw metal rather than imported objects, it would be a mistake to rule out other components being present. A range of small tools are represented – chisels, knives, hammers, awls, and lightweight axes – such as are only infrequently seen in terrestrial hoards of this phase; many of these were probably complete, functional objects. Could these be the essential equipment of the ship's company for carpentry repairs, leatherworking, cloth working, food preparation, and even metalworking? To take this idea further, it would not be unreasonable to see some of the complete weapons as ship's arms; this scenario could explain the smallness of the complement of spearheads (even allowing for under-representation) and the handful of intact swords and rapiers – perhaps one for each seaman on board? The ornaments, too, might conceivably have been those in service among the crew and any passengers.

Comparative land assemblages

It has already been emphasised that there is little on land that can be compared to the Langdon Bay assemblage. One 'terrestrial' find that is similar in some respects to Langdon Bay and, moreover, includes Penard phase metalwork, is the accumulation at the Fengate Power Station site, near Peterborough (Pryor 2001). This assemblage is fairly large and diverse in the types represented, but differs significantly not only in spanning the whole of the later Bronze Age but also in having later elements of Iron Age and Roman date. Unlike the Langdon assemblage, Flag Fen is patently an accumulation over a long period of time in a long-venerated location. In this respect, it bears comparison instead with the typical river assemblages touched upon above.

Terrestrial hoards of Penard date from the British side of the Channel are all small in size, never more than several objects. The pattern is a little different for the contemporary Rosnoën material in northern France and Brittany, where half the recorded hoards have ten or more objects and two are large: Chailloué with 53 pieces and Rosnoën itself with 88 (Nallier and Le Goffic 2008, 155 tab 1). Nevertheless, seven of the nine largest hoards (comprising more than twelve objects) are dominated by swords, sometimes accompanied by significant numbers of rapiers/dirks. Axes are present in small numbers except at Fourdan, where palstaves are the most frequent type (12 examples), followed by spearheads (8). At Saint-Jean-Trolimon, however, spearheads are most common (5). Small numbers of tools (excluding axes) and ornaments are recurrent among the larger hoards. There are, therefore, elements of similarity between Rosnoën hoards and the Langdon Bay assemblage, notably the inclusion of most of the broad categories of metalwork available. However, the high frequency of axes and broken blade fragments of weapons set the seabed find apart, especially when it is remembered that over half of the many axes are of the median-winged type, which are present in the land finds only occasionally and in very small numbers. Even if we hypothetically conjectured that exceptionally large terrestrial hoards might once have existed, normal land deposition rules are unlikely to have led to the composition of the Langdon assemblage, so we would have to infer a unique hoard arising from an exceptional circumstance.

There are, then, no really comparable deposits of metalwork from the Penard/Rosnoën phase in the coastlands flanking the Channel. Neither are there obviously similar assemblage compositions from other phases (bearing in mind that inter-comparison becomes more difficult as specific object types change). It is this uniqueness of character that, above all else, argues for a kind of context with which we are unfamiliar in the archaeological record. To state this fact does not in itself prove that the assemblage *was* deposited in the sea, but it does allow us to suggest a specific relationship to the *maritime domain* regardless of whether it was initially deposited at sea or on the edge of the land. In the broad sense of making a connection to a particular part of the systemic sphere, the precise context of deposition may not matter too much. However, the question of land or sea still irks in terms of the specific historical scenario and it might also have a major impact on our future expectations of Bronze Age maritime sites.

If the Langdon Bay assemblage were the product of a single *deliberate* act of deposition, rather than a maritime accident, it would be, as we have seen, a truly exceptional deposit in terms of both its size and composition. This clear differentiation might conceivably signal a new kind of deliberate deposit that has hitherto remained hidden from archaeological view; unless further comparable finds come to light, it is impossible to evaluate this hypothesis. If its size militates against a single deliberate deposit on the grounds of there being no precedent, could it have been the product of repeated deposition over a fairly limited period of time? Such a scenario of repeated ritual deposition has been raised by Marisa Ruiz-Gálvez for the Ría Huelva find in Spain (see further below) and the Langdon Bay assemblage could thus, theoretically, represent a kind of boundary deposit placed by mariners regularly crossing the sea to and from this location. This scenario could explain, for example, the presence of many foreign objects. Such an interpretation would have some quite intriguing ramifications. It would imply, firstly, that there was a specific and repeated pattern of maritime contact, for which one terminus was Dover; secondly, that this regular travel resulted in many similar acts of deposition on, for example, an annual basis; thirdly, that, although this deposition was an enduring pattern, it was, nevertheless, limited to a span of time falling within one metalworking phase of about a century and a half; and, fourthly, that the depositors were able to locate the appropriate place of deposition with reasonable accuracy over time – in fact, repeated relocation would not have been too difficult close in to a distinctively configured coastal topography with cliffs and an adjacent river mouth.

Comparative river mouth assemblages

The question of topographic position leads us to consider other concentrations of metalwork in similar locations. Depending on the state of the coastal barrier system at Dover around the 13th century BC, the Langdon assemblage would have lain close to, or even at, the mouth of the river Dour (discussion above, this Chapter). Discoveries from estuaries may actually be under-represented relative to those dredged from further upstream; tidal scour can readily maintain navigable channels, hence there is less need for artificial dredging. Moreover, the broadening of the waterway gives the potential for deposits to occur away from the navigable channels that might be dredged from time to time. As a consequence, discoveries have rarely come from the mouths of the rivers (insofar as the mouth can be closely defined). Some concentrations have much the same character as seen more generally for riverine assemblages. For example, a 20km reach of the river Tay (Perthshire) spanning the transition from river to estuary has yielded a modest but important cluster of riverine finds of metalwork along with other prehistoric objects (Cowie and Hall 2001, 8–11, fig 3; Cowie and Hall 2010). The Bronze Age metalwork ranges in date from Acton to Llyn Fawr and, as we saw for Fengate, there is no suggestion here of any mass deposition over a short period. Similarly, many later Bronze Age bronzes, especially weaponry, have been recovered from the lowest reaches of the river Loire, between Nantes and the mouth (Briard 1965; Coffyn 1985).

Perhaps of more relevance to the present discussion are groups that have a much more constrained chronology. One such is a large deposit of Ewart stage bronzes dredged up from the tight bend of the tidal Thames at Broadness (Burgess *et al* 1972; Needham and Burgess 1980, 451 fig 6). Although a mixture of types is represented, it is spearheads that dominate that assemblage, a point which led Burgess *et al* (1972) to link it to their Broadward complex. Other Broadward 'hoards' are terrestrial, but there is a frequent association with wetlands (Burgess *et al* 1972).

A concentration of some 50 bronzes from the river Seine at Vatteville-la-Rue, some 20km from its mouth, seems to be primarily of material belonging to the Rosnoën phase (Verron 1973; O'Connor 1980, 360; Billard *et al* 2005, 297). Verron has suggested that it might represent the cargo of a wrecked ship, but the idea of a phase-specific set of deposits may again be raised. It is of further, perhaps incidental, interest that this particular deposit is broadly contemporary with Langdon and Salcombe.

Much further away from the Channel is the famous 'Ría Huelva hoard' from south-west Spain (Anon 1927; Ruiz-Gálvez 1995; Brandherm 2007; Burgess and O'Connor 2008). The material was dredged up in 1923 from the lowest reach of the river Odiel about 5km above the modern confluence with the river Tinto, which, itself, is only about 5km from the Atlantic coast. However, palaeogeographic reconstruction suggests that this confluence zone was a much more open expanse of water in the 2nd millennium BC, being some 10km in breadth, into

which the Huelva peninsula jutted (Ruiz-Gálvez 1995, 17–18, figs 2 and 3). According to this reconstruction, the metalwork was deposited or lost with a shipwreck in the western channel (the Odiel) level with the end of the peninsula.

The Huelva assemblage is best dated on typology and three radiocarbon dates to the 10th century BC, contemporary with the Blackmoor (early Ewart) stage in Britain. It has very strong components of swords, spearheads, and spear ferrules, with good numbers also of daggers, buttons, elbow fibulae, and arrowheads. There are smaller numbers of other diverse types, including helmets and ornamental gear, but no obvious tools. It is therefore a specialised assemblage of types and extensive metal analysis has shown that all the material could have been produced from metal that was in circulation in the immediate region (Rovira in Ruiz-Gálvez 1995). Even the distinctive lunate-opening spearhead (Ruiz-Gálvez 1995, 245, pl 15.22), a type more familiar in Britain, Ireland, and the north-west of Europe, could not be distinguished on the basis of its metal composition.

Past researchers have wondered whether this 'hoard' might be the cargo of a sunken boat. This scenario would certainly be one way of explaining its temporal homogeneity, but Marisa Ruiz-Gálvez has suggested another explanation, having considered wider patterns in the specific siting of metalwork deposits in Iberia. She believes that the assemblage is best interpreted as votive in intent, but nevertheless still reflecting changing economic interests in which certain points in the landscape were now seen to be strategic points of exit/entry (Ruiz-Gálvez 1995, 21, 157). For her, strong symbolic importance went hand-in-hand with the recognised geographical significance of the nodal position of this site within the new economic rationale of the Late Bronze Age. Such deposits had both a sacred and profane character at the same time.

The comparison with Langdon Bay is, in some ways, seductive. Both have compositionally and typologically coherent assemblages and seem to be from rather limited patches of the seabed or estuary. Further, both may have been deposited close to the mouth of a river, albeit not in exactly the same topographic relationship. A point of clear differentiation, however, lies in the origin of the material. Whereas all of Huelva's could be local, it is possible that none or little of the Langdon assemblage was made or circulated in the adjacent territory (east Kent); certainly, a large proportion came from external metalworking spheres. Another difference lies in the more restricted type range at Huelva. So it may be a mistake to draw too close an analogy and, if there is a case for votive deposition, the two situations may be linked only in terms of generic principles relating to the ritual use of metalwork.

None of the above cited examples, all of which are widely spread across western Europe, provides a particularly close parallel for the combination of topographic siting and object composition seen at Langdon Bay. Despite the potential problem of under-representation of river mouth finds, at present there is no sense of a pattern within which the Langdon Bay site falls. The large phase-specific assemblages deposited in watery environments are then equivocal in their interpretation. It is possible to see them theoretically as the product of repeated acts within a phase-specific system of interaction, but the overall character of the Langdon Bay assemblage favours another conclusion.

In summary, the important overall characteristics of the assemblage are:

• relatively tight distribution on the sea floor (allowing for marine redistribution)
• very large size
• a good proportion of foreign types, most of which would have been regarded as raw metal by adjacent communities in southern England
• much fragmentary material, evidently already scrapped at the time of deposition

Combined, these features clearly suggest that this assemblage was primarily a consignment of metal in transit and that its presence at Langdon Bay is explained by an unplanned event, a ship in trouble. It is also possible to identify a minor component of objects – selected complete weapons, tools, and fittings – which plausibly represent the gear of the ship's company, rather than cargo.

Salcombe and Moor Sand

Ongoing work on the Salcombe site requires this discussion to be briefer than for the Langdon assemblage. The first small group of material recovered at Salcombe, in 1977–82, came from an area of about 140m east–west and 60m north–south just to the south-west (140m) of Moor Sand. The eight objects were relatively scattered (see Fig 1.11) and although seven could be contemporary with one another, the eighth – a Carp's Tongue sword – is definitely of a later phase. Even though the anachronistic object was found later, in 1982, during Martin Dean's continuation of the campaign, Keith Muckelroy believed there was some chronological spread among the others. This belief was partly based on identifying both palstaves as of Breton type, a type mainly of pre-Rosnoën date, whereas we now classify both as Rosnoën palstaves. In addition, it was due to an erroneous indication that one weapon blade contained 5.9% lead, which suggested a post-Rosnoën date; subsequent analysis shows no such high lead content.

The wide dispersal of finds led Muckelroy to consider the possibility that the bronzes had been gathered in this area by prevailing currents: that it was somehow a tidal trap for mobile material initially deposited elsewhere. After due consideration, however, he decided against this conclusion because of the lack of modern detritus (Muckelroy

1980, 104). One argument against displacement over any great distance is the fact that two of the weapons are in good condition and the two palstaves were not excessively rolled. Nevertheless, that does not rule out a shorter distance of displacement, with the bronzes being 'swept piece by piece into this area over a long period of time, the fine sword being the latest arrival' (*ibid*), and he was encouraged in this model by the fact that the thicker objects (the palstaves) were further out to sea than the sword/ rapier blades (Muckelroy and Baker 1979, 205). It is noteworthy that the 1982 sword was found lying exposed on rock in an area which had previously been systematically searched by Muckelroy's team; Dean believes it likely that it had recently emerged from soil profiles under erosion.

Despite attempts by Muckelroy and then Dean to locate material up to 200m further out to sea, nothing was found. It was only the later discovery by SWMAG of another scatter of contemporary objects some 400m further west (Salcombe site B – 22 objects catalogued here and a number more since 2004) that provided a potential source area for the theory of short-range dispersal. Most of the diagnostic types among these subsequent finds are, again, of Penard/Rosnoën age and, when analysed, they are consistent in their metal composition (a few are included in Northover's analyses in Chapter 3). Hence, it is possible to contemplate that a single event or limited phase of deposition might have deposited material at or near site B, and that some objects were later dispersed shorewards. Moreover, the post-2004 finds may also be providing a better context for the Carp's Tongue sword, as there is at least one further Ewart stage sword as well as a large consignment of ingots of copper and tin[1] which would, if found in terrestrial contexts, be expected to be contemporary.

The close proximity of site B to the 17th-century AD Cannon site (site A) is intriguing but almost certainly irrelevant except insofar as it may indicate a time-honoured wrecking ground for vessels attempting to find harbour in Kingsbridge estuary, or alternatively trying to clear Prawle Point, during south-westerly driven storms. Only one or two Bronze Age objects have come from the main concentration of 17th-century material and, conversely, very little of the latter came from within the Bronze Age find zone. The fact that contemporary bronzes occur well to the east at Moor Sand, away from the Cannon site, makes it clear that very special pleading has to be made to entertain the idea that the Bronze Age objects were in transit on the 17th-century AD ship. Therefore, we can proceed on the basis that, in all probability, a significant assemblage of metalwork was lost or deposited on sea or land at Salcombe in the Bronze Age, around the 13th century BC. Further metalwork was lost or deposited later, in the 10th–9th centuries BC.

Gehrels' report (Chapter 1) shows that elements of the coast around Moor Sand are vulnerable to erosion, particularly the Head deposits, but this is much less the case for the underlying solid geology of schists. One coastal feature, the Pinnacle, 300m west of Moor Sand, seems to have been unchanged over the past century despite being ringed by the sea. Coastal retreat seems extremely unlikely to have been so rapid that the coastline was as far out as site B in the late 2nd millennium BC. The small possibility that the Bronze Age artefacts were originally deposited on land would, therefore, depend on invoking a fair degree of seaward migration once they had been eroded out of their putative terrestrial context. This explanation seems rather unlikely given that a concentration of material, the greatest concentration yet known on the site, has emerged in one particular gully in site B as much as 450m from the closest part of the modern shore. That gully includes material that is in good condition and has evidently not suffered much rolling. It is hoped that further evidence relating to potential dispersal will emerge as fieldwork and analysis of new finds proceeds.

Our conclusion here must be strongly in favour of an original marine context of deposition for the Salcombe Bronze Age material. Two metalworking phases are currently represented and these are separated by some two centuries, or perhaps longer. Just as argued for Langdon, the Salcombe material seems to be of phase-specific deposits (albeit of two phases), rather than representing the continuum of deposition typical for riverine assemblages. Again, we need to allow for the various alternative explanations outlined above. If either of the modes of votive deposition – two single large deposition events separated by a long passage of time, or successions of smaller deposits confined to two specific phases well separated in time – were responsible, it would surely imply that there was something very special about this particular patch of the seabed which did not apply to most comparable inshore patches. Could the site mark a regular end point of sea voyages in both the two phases in question?

Although Moor Sand itself could conceivably have been a traditional beaching point, it is surrounded by cliffs and faces directly into the prevailing south-westerlies; this position would seem to be a strange choice of venue for regular harbourage and maritime exchange activities when the shelter of the large Kingsbridge estuary could be accessed just 3km to the west (albeit with the hazard of an underwater reef across the entrance). A prediction on the basis of 'strategic interest' in maritime interaction would suggest, therefore, that the Salcombe site B/Moor Sand assemblage was 'off-mark'. If it were to be argued that Moor Sand or the adjacent headland of the Pig's Nose had, in the eyes of Bronze Age depositors, some other special qualities not related to exchange and associated interactions, it is difficult to guess what those might have been.

If there is a lack of persuasive evidence for ritual deposition of the Salcombe metalwork, do the options of shipwreck or foundering ship make any

more sense? We still have to account for a minimum of two separate Bronze Age losses fortuitously close together, but we need to remember also that the large assemblage of 17th-century AD material (the Cannon site) is almost certainly the debris resulting from a wreck.

The rocky south-west peninsular coasts are a notorious graveyard for boats caught up in bad weather. Shipwreck sites in the seas around Salcombe (as elsewhere) are not documented in historical records until the mid-18th century. However, the area is something of a magnet for sailing ship wrecks and no fewer than fourteen have been located within a few kilometres; many others are known to have been lost in the general area but have yet to be located (McDonald 1994). An analysis of their losses provides clues as to the potential causes of shipwrecks in the area. The *De Boot* (1738), *Dragon* (1757), *Lintor Ken* (1765), HMS *Crocodile* (1784), *Gossamer* (1864), *Glad Tidings* (1882), *Meirion* (1879), *Volere* (1881), and *Halloween* (1887) all sank in shallow water after running aground owing to navigational error. *Lalla Rookh* (1873) and *Herogin Cecilie* (1936) are also in shallow water, but differ from the others in that they originally struck elsewhere and, whilst sinking, were then carried on by their momentum, the tide, and the wind until they eventually ran ashore elsewhere. Three wrecks are in deeper water: the unidentified 17th-century AD Salcombe Cannon site already mentioned, whose cause of loss is unknown; HMS *Ramillies* (1760), which became embayed (unable to sail past a headland), tried to anchor in a near hurricane and then was driven ashore against the cliffs and sank in deep water; and the recently located wreck of the *Lord Napier* (1912), which sank after springing a leak.

Bronze Age site B, whilst relatively close to the shore, is actually in fairly deep water away from any kind of obvious hazard that could have led to the loss of a shallow-draught boat. This detail would suggest that, if this is a shipwreck site, the vessel must have struck elsewhere; or, alternatively, it sustained damage in a conflict, or just proved to be unseaworthy in rough seas. To the west of the site lies the headland of the Bolt (see Fig 1.1), the second most southerly point of mainland Britain and, as a result, a notorious false marker in later periods for ships who thought they were safely in mid-Channel. To the east are a number of reefs which are relatively shallow, although probably too deep for a Bronze Age ship to strike. One plausible scenario, then, is that the site B vessel struck one of the reefs around the Bolt and was then propelled in a damaged, sinking state by prevailing south-westerly winds towards Gammon Head. Seeing nothing but cliffs ahead, her pilot would have sought out the safest place on which to wreck – the beach at Moor Sands. Such a scenario can be no more than conjecture and still leaves questions about whether the boat would have spilled all its contents at one spot or several.

The catchment of the assemblages and the conduct of maritime interactions during the later Bronze Age

Keith Muckelroy's two-tier circulation model for Bronze Age metalwork

During his tragically foreshortened career Keith Muckelroy had a significant impact on the development of maritime archaeology. Moreover, the novelty of suddenly having two important Bronze Age seabed sites in British waters, both of which he was able to subject to systematic archaeological survey, gave him a particular impetus to comprehend their implications for both deposition and trade in the Bronze Age. His rigorous analysis of site formation processes provided an excellent foundation for interpretation; there is much that he wrote that we still adhere to today. He was open to varied potential scenarios for the accumulation and deposition of the two assemblages. The evidence was weighed up carefully before drawing conclusions, and he felt that these could be drawn more firmly for Langdon Bay than for Moor Sand because of the latter site's relatively small and dispersed assemblage with very variable condition; at one point he hypothesised that material on that site had been swept in from a 'coherent central deposit' (Muckelroy and Baker 1979, 206) further out to sea. This last prediction was shown to be vindicated by the discovery 25 years later of site B.

Muckelroy's contribution, however, was not simply the application of good methodology and post-recovery analysis. He also set about researching in depth the metalwork finds themselves with a view to understanding the origins of different types, the way in which the respective assemblages had come about, implications for the organisation of bronze metalworking on land, and implications for metal distribution systems across land and sea. Only with this detailed background could he draw well-grounded conclusions on the significance and roles of the maritime sites. In the process, he achieved perhaps the most sophisticated view of the circulation of Bronze Age metalwork hitherto. Given such early promise, it is salutary to wonder where his research might subsequently have led.

The analytical foundations were laid down in the interim accounts of archaeological survey at Moor Sand (Muckelroy and Baker 1979; 1980a), which culminated in his quite seminal paper in *Antiquity* (Muckelroy 1980c). Another paper was worked up by others posthumously from his incomplete doctoral thesis and appeared in *The Proceedings of the Prehistoric Society* (Muckelroy 1981). This paper inevitably overlaps the content of the previous one and, overall, it less obviously reflects his matured views in a coherent fashion; we cannot know whether he would have subscribed wholeheartedly to its contents as drafted. After an interval of 30 years it is perhaps timely to reappraise Keith Muckelroy's deductions and the model at which he arrived.

As had Coombs (1976) and O'Connor (1980, 355–6) previously, Muckelroy realised that the Langdon Bay assemblage (then comprising 189 objects) was unique, that it had no parallels among hoard finds in Britain (Muckelroy 1981, 285), and that many of the individual objects had their best parallels on the Continent. He discovered that both western French types and more easterly types were present. Some of the core distributions concerned can actually be viewed in a different light now (see Chapter 3 and below), but he correctly identified that there were potentially varied regional production backgrounds to the assemblage. Nevertheless, he did not jump to the conclusion that this implied a complex, wide-ranging itinerary for the boat presumed to have carried the cargo. He had recognised that a limited series of hoards also contained a mixture of 'western' and 'eastern' types (although sometimes one or other direction is represented by only a single object); apart from two outliers, these hoards were distributed along a north–south axis running from Picardy to Cher in northern France (Muckelroy 1980c, 103, fig 1).

Another key component of his analysis lay in the recognition that the fragmentary nature of much of the material in the assemblage was not generally the result of post-depositional damage in the marine environment. The nature of the breaks instead showed that they must have derived from fragmentation prior to deposition during the Bronze Age; he suggested that deliberate scrapping was intended to 'make them more manageable shapes for packing … It is thus clear that this is a cargo of scrap …' (*ibid*, 101). He deduced that there was a considerable inter-regional trade in scrap normally hidden from archaeological view, a trade that frequently carried types well beyond their normal spheres of circulation. Thus, he was able to conclude that the mix available for transportation across the Channel could easily have been present in the systemic sphere in areas of northern France, even though this mix was only attested to a limited degree among the metalwork deposited in that region. The most economic interpretation was to see the assemblage as having come in its entirety from northern France, possibly from areas not far from the coast (Muckelroy 1981, 287).

On the question of context, although no boat remains survived on the Langdon Bay site Muckelroy's careful evaluation of the assemblage and its relationship to terrestrial material led him to conclude that it represented a cargo in transit – a classic case of 'exchange frozen in time' (Muckelroy 1980c, 108). On the other hand, the small number of objects recovered from Salcombe at that stage (seven) severely limited interpretation of that site, especially since only three objects were in good enough condition to identify their specific types. Nevertheless, these too were seen to be split between western and eastern French origins (*ibid*, 106); and, having eliminated other explanations, he believed that this find too could be treated as a cargo (Muckelroy and Baker 1979, 205).

One of the strengths of Muckelroy's approach to the interpretation of Bronze Age metalwork and metalworking was that he took stock of the relevant ethnographic evidence drawn from small-scale societies. Mike Rowlands' recent publications had been influential. Muckelroy realised that many of the objects in the seabed assemblages were at or beyond the limits of their 'home territories' (1980c, 106), and this raised for him the possibility that those objects were no longer vested with the symbolic values attached by the society that created and used them; instead, they had come to be devalued or revalued to serve merely as a source of metal, as 'scrap', regardless of whether they were fragmentary or complete. He found support from the ethnographic evidence (citing in particular the work of Weber, in addition to that of Rowlands) for the notion that metalwork could have just such alternative values depending on the context of circulation – either within the boundaries of groups for whom the types were meaningful, or outside those boundaries.

It was this background that led Muckelroy to propose a two-tier model for the circulation of bronze (*ibid*, 107). Not only did it involve dichotomy in the way that specific types, local or alien, were regarded, but he also envisaged quite different 'levels' of activity: a low level of regional production and circulation and a high level of scrap bronze moving between regions, balancing inequalities in supply and demand. This secondary deduction was presumably influenced by the fact that the unique circumstance of the Langdon assemblage showed that large quantities could be involved in inter-regional metal exchange. By contrast, most land-based hoards were of quite modest size, and the few British Middle Bronze Age examples that were larger (though these are not exactly contemporary, being of the Taunton stage) could be shown consistently to have 'strong overseas links' and usually also fragmentary pieces: that is, scrap (*ibid*); hence, their compositions had some similarity to the Langdon assemblage. He realised that a different pattern obtained among the contemporary French hoards, more of which were of larger size and contained a higher frequency of fragmentary material; this pattern has since been elucidated more fully for the Rosnoën type hoards (Nallier and Le Goffic 2008, 155, tab 1).

For Muckelroy, then, the process of inter-regional commodity exchange could best be recognised through the exceptional circumstance of shipwrecked cargoes. In contrast, terrestrial deposits, or the great majority of them, related instead to internal processes of production and circulation. Shortly after Muckelroy was writing, Richard Bradley (eg 1985) made a quite different set of connections, inspired by Gregory's (1982) reappraisal of gifts and commodities within small-scale economies. Bradley's model held many land-based hoards to represent commodity exchange (eg Bradley 1985), although the validity of the relationship between circulation in the

systemic sphere and deposition was later challenged (Needham 1990a, 130–32).

Although in principle Muckelroy acknowledged the occurrence of ritual deposition of metalwork (Muckelroy and Baker 1979, 205; Muckelroy 1980c, 107), he saw the hoards as unproblematically reflecting material in circulation in the given region (as did most specialists working in Britain at the time). His clear recognition that maritime sites pointed to the existence of elements of circulation that might be hidden from archaeological view was seemingly only relevant to foreign types that were melted down quickly as they entered new territory; all locally acceptable types were presumably expected to be represented proportionally in the archaeological record.

However, much evidence, ranging from casting equipment to metalwork assemblages on settlement sites, demonstrates the falsity of such an assumption and, meanwhile, the growing appreciation that most hoards might also be ritually deposited has put their composition in a different perspective (see, for example, Needham 2007c for a summary of these issues). On any interpretation, they are unlikely often to be complete sets of material in use: as ritual deposits they are likely to be specially chosen compositions to serve particular purposes, but even as more economically governed deposits they are most likely to represent a small fraction of the metalwork in contemporary circulation locally, omitting an unknown fraction of the material which was successfully recycled into new castings. So, the typical size of hoards constitutes a dangerous basis from which to deduce scales of production or circulation; moreover, the specific contents of hoards may not fully or proportionally represent the range of types in circulation. While this observation may undermine the characterisation of Muckelroy's two-tier model, it does not invalidate his emphasis on the contextual-cum-compositional dichotomy between the maritime and terrestrial metalwork assemblages and the specific implications drawn from their differences. We have reconsidered those contrasts ourselves in this volume in order to define the distinctions and explain as best as possible what gave rise to them.

Another facet of Muckelroy's model is also unsatisfactory. He sometimes characterised the inter-regional exchange in scrap metal as being 'long-distance' trade (Muckelroy 1980c, 107; 1981, 291), a term which implies the 'directed' trade (ie single transaction) of material across intervening territories; yet, elsewhere, he accepts that even the far-displaced objects were probably shifting 'step-by-step … between industrial regions' in a down-the-line mode (Muckelroy 1981, 292). It is possible that the contradiction arose as a result of trying to accommodate the cross-Channel element necessary in any exchanges involving Britain and mainland Europe. If so, it was an unfortunate muddying of the water. Once societies on either side of the Channel (or any other stretch of water) decided they needed to engage in exchange, of whatever kind, then, in effect, they would be interacting as neighbours, for there are no intervening social groups (unless mariners themselves were a separate social entity). The fact that the intervening sea may present unusual difficulties compared with those involved in equivalent land-based interactions is, of course, relevant to the effort that must be expended and the risks that must be faced, but the short crossings of the Channel are not, in continental terms, long distances and Muckelroy himself favoured the Langdon Bay cargo having been picked up from 'somewhere in the lower Seine/Somme region' (*ibid*, 287).

Muckelroy asked yet other pertinent questions, such as who instigated the cross-Channel exchanges and were specialist mariners involved. He argued that exchange was likely to have been instigated by the demand side of the equation – that is, by the need of groups in southern Britain to obtain metal (Muckelroy 1980c, 108). This position seems logical until we consider two other factors. The first is the point that he himself acknowledged: we do not know what goods or services went in return (*ibid*), and so cannot possibly evaluate the importance of those to the reciprocating groups. The second is the possibility that these were part of a sustainable relationship, rather than opportunistic exchanges. The flow of metal, vital though it was, may have taken place within a broader skein of interactions that were valued for more than just economic reasons.

On the question of specialism, Muckelroy reasoned that specialist seamen were probably responsible. This interpretation stemmed from a combination of the obvious investment required to make the boats, a perceived clash between the best seasons for harvesting crops and sea crossings, and the fact that the Langdon Bay find lacked ingot material or foundry waste (Muckelroy 1980c, 108; 1981, 291, 294–5). Three later finds of raw metal barely change the picture in this last respect, especially when one considers, for example, the Uluburun and Rochelongues sites in the Mediterranean, both with considerable quantities of ingots, and now the large 2010 haul from Salcombe.[2] Muckelroy argued that, if considerable skill and labour were necessary to make seaworthy boats (see more recently Clark 2004a; Van der Noort 2006; Helms 2009), then it did not make sense to leave them idle; if exchange was not the sole occupation of the boat's crew, then they must have otherwise specialised in fishing. His specific argument against seamen-cum-farmers, based on timetable clashes, is rather dubious: crops need relatively little tending during the growing months up until harvesting, other than the warding off of browsing animals. Moreover, early societies were not prone to making modern rational decisions on labour specialisation; the season(s) in which to conduct seaborne trade would typically be fitted around the essential activities of those involved, unless specialists did exist for some entirely different reasons. These caveats do not mean that there could not be specialist mariners, but simply that Muckelroy conscripted poor evidence in their support.

Likewise, the dearth of raw metal may be a red herring. He argued that this absence showed that the assemblage in transit had been divorced from the realm of metalworkers; this interpretation in itself may not be an unreasonable proposition, but it hardly bears on whether the transit was conducted by specialists or part-timers. The absence of raw metal could, alternatively, simply mean that the regional system of origin, presumed in this case to be northern France, did not typically have much ingot material circulating (the ingot hoard subsequently found at Saint-Valery-sur-Somme (Blanchet and Mille 2009) is Early Bronze Age). Indeed, Muckelroy himself implicitly recognised that the distribution of 'raw metal' in regions distant from the copper sources may actually have been in the form of scrapped bronze objects.

If specialist mariners may still be a matter for debate, Muckelroy's arguments for overt specialisation in the building of boats are more persuasive. While being cautious not to be too precise on the status held, he recognised that the boat-builder was likely to have been accorded some kind of distinctive status, likening this role to the position often discussed for metalworkers of the period (Muckelroy 1981, 294). The status of the boat-builder in the Bronze Age world is a theme taken up more recently by Mary Helms (2009).

A final point of critique may be directed at Muckelroy's dismissal of socio-political connections across the Channel (Muckelroy 1980c, 108; 1981, 293–4), connections advocated in preceding years by scholars on both sides of the water (especially Jacques Briard and Colin Burgess). He based his rejection of these connections on select differences in the acceptance of bronze metalwork types, notably the near absence of median-winged axes and Rosnoën spearheads in Britain. Presumably also, following ethnographic precedence, he was willing to see the exchanges across the Channel as constituting 'subsistence oriented external trade' that could operate without social bonds. This assumption may be questionable as there was clearly a steady flow of metal into southern Britain from the Continent during much of the Bronze Age (its character, percentage contribution, and ultimate sources changing over time; eg Rohl and Needham 1998). Even though the evidence does not allow us to quantify the rate at which it took place it seems inconceivable that there was not a perception on the part of contemporary communities of this being a regular need and thus potentially benefiting from sustained relationships. Such relationships need not necessarily cause cultural convergence, but they can promote alliances secured by other kinds of exchange and social interaction. In fact, in the decades following Muckelroy's publications much more evidence has come to light for elements of strong parallelism between the material culture and settlement structures of southern Britain and northern France going well beyond the metalwork repertoire (eg papers in Bourgeois and Talon 2005; Clark 2009). These studies add weight to those bronze types that patently are closely connected stylistically and suggest, collectively, that there were many values and ways of doing things shared by communities on both sides of the Channel, even if individual regional groups chose to distinguish themselves in certain ways.

Exposing the weaknesses of some of Muckelroy's interpretations from three decades ago is, of course, a necessary step to steering ourselves towards a better understanding of these important sites and the interactions they represent. Muckelroy's contribution was, nevertheless, profound, for he was asking new questions of the evidence as result of his unique viewpoint, that of a maritime archaeologist.

Present perspectives

On account of its size and diversity, it is the Langdon assemblage which gives us the best opportunity to examine the 'catchment' of one of the seabed finds. Analytically we can take two different approaches (Fig 5.4):

- A 'tentacled' view, collating all the 'core' areas for types present: that is, those areas where finds of the relevant parallels are at their densest
- A 'restrictive' view, reducing to a minimum the potential source areas, taking account of less-dense distributions and even the possibility of zones of hidden circulation

In both these approaches the concern is with the range of places in which the bronzes were first created. This location is *not* the same as the place or places in which the assembled bronzes came together shortly before their deposition at Langdon Bay, a question which also needs to be addressed.

However, one implicit assumption in earlier work seems to be that the whole assemblage should be explained in a unitary fashion, that all the material was on board for the same reason – the sheer quantity suggesting a cargo. Any assumed homogeneity in raison d'être needs to be reappraised; following the outline given above for the potential components of a shipwreck site, there may be ship's equipment and the personal possessions of the crew and passengers as well as the cargo being carried on the specific voyage. There may even be a further category, especially if the conduct of seaborne exchange was in the hands of full-time specialists; it may be a mistake to assume that all of the cargo was a single consignment going from zone A to zone B. What ended up being wrecked may have been a palimpsest of two or more overlapping consignments, or may have included small amounts of material which just happened to get left behind in the boat from earlier voyages for one reason or another. In either of these scenarios there could easily be objects that had orig-

inally been moving in a totally different direction to that of the final voyage.

A simple tentacled view gives us a wide geographical catchment, within which the potential continental connections form a 180° fan from Brittany in the west to northern Germany in the east, with Langdon Bay occupying the pivot (Fig 5.5). However, there is also the strong possibility of a British contribution to the assemblage, which, moreover, might actually erode the case for some of the continental source zones, particularly that of north-eastern Germany for the Hademarschen socketed axes and the Middle Elbe region for conical ferrules.

Socketed axes/chisels had become an established local type in the south of Britain during the Taunton phase; so, even if it is accepted that they were initially inspired from the east, their successors of closely related styles in the Penard phase need no external stimulus to account for them. At present, the closer shores of the Continent do not look likely to be the source, partly because of the rarity of socketed axes/chisels in northern France and the Low Countries, but more definitively because the few recovered finds there are virtually all unlooped examples (Chapter 3). This difference would seem a rather unlikely bias to arise in the process of selective deposition given the otherwise similar properties of the looped and unlooped versions of this implement type. So, provisionally, it is deduced that there was a difference in the population of socketed axes/chisels on the two sides of the Channel and that the southern side is unlikely to have been the source of the looped examples from Langdon.

Given the marine context and the obvious use of the seaways, one could return to the idea that, even though not of the initial stimulus phase, these socketed axes/chisels had come to Langdon from north-east Germany. This scenario is not impossible: Muckelroy saw such separated clusters of similar types as a potential consequence of his higher level of 'long-distance' exchanges in metal (Muckelroy 1980c, 107). A particular type might regularly enter this exchange system and be conveyed through various regions as scrap, but stimulate imitation by local metalworkers, finally, only at some remove. However, we can draw in a final piece of evidence: the trend towards lower tin in the socketed axes (all but one have under 10.5% – Northover, Chapter 3). This observation is not significant at the object level, as many other individual objects in the assemblage have such low tin, but, as a group, it may be significant that it can be matched in a good number of Penard compositions in Britain, especially among the unassociated swords (Rohl and Needham 1998, 224–6, appendix 3; see also the discussion in Northover 1988, 133–6). Overall, then, given reasonable parallels onshore in Britain, there is no need to invoke a north-east German origin for the socketed axes/chisels. Instead, it is most likely that they were manufactured by Penard metalworkers in Britain.

The case of the conical ferrule gives another potential leap-frog connection eastwards. In this

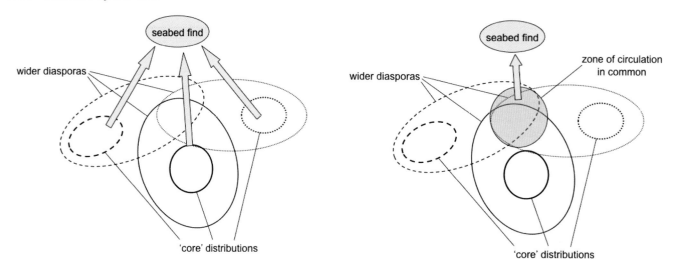

Fig 5.4   Models for viewing the geographical catchment of key object types in the Langdon Bay assemblage: a) a tentacled view; b) a restrictive view

case, Penard *was* the critical phase of connection. Although geographically well removed from the Channel coasts, it is not difficult to envisage the occasional long-distance displacement of the supposed central European prototypes, especially given the easy route via the rivers Main and Rhine (see Fig 5.5). However, an alternative, indigenous origin for the British ferrules is feasible, for there is a series of short conical ferrules or fittings dating to the Taunton phase (O'Connor 1980, 90–1 – there are additional finds since). It is by no means implausible that British metalworkers could have realised the scope for elongating this small fitting to adapt it for other purposes, notably to furnish spear butts. With this hypothesis, the direction of stimulus might be reversed, always supposing that the two regional groups did not spring up independently of one another. The Langdon find favours the former interpretation over the latter only *if* we accept that it is an assemblage entirely of continental material; but it is this interpretation that we are trying to assess from the empirical evidence and the socketed axes, at the very least, suggest the presence of British-made pieces.

In fact, some other object types need to be considered as potentially of British origin. These are types that may be found on both sides of the Channel, though not all with equal frequency. Notched-butt Group IV rapiers/dirks and palstaves of Langdon types 1–3 are both much more common finds on the insular side, the former category widely spread through Britain and Ireland (Burgess and Gerloff 1981, pls 123B and 124), the latter more confined to southern Britain. Yet both occur in northern France, and to suggest that they were not indigenous types there simply because recovered finds are fewer would be over-simplistic and potentially fallacious. One must conclude, then, that the actual examples of these two types encountered at Langdon Bay *could* just as easily have originated on the south side of the Channel, despite the variable densities

in the map of recovery. Tanged-and-collared chisels may come into the same category, even though most of the specific parallels identified so far are from Britain.

For two types, finds are so rare anywhere that known occurrences give no clues whatsoever. The hooked knife has been closely paralleled in only two other finds, one in Manche, close to the southern shore of the Channel, the other from near Grimsby in eastern England (Chapter 3). Class 2 flesh-hooks are known in only slightly greater numbers (assuming Langdon Bay No 149 is correctly identified), but their distribution is intriguing (Needham and Bowman 2005, 112, fig 6a, 110, table 7). Three finds are known from East Anglia, but these have strongly triangular prong sections, whereas No 149 appears to have been more square or diamond-shaped prior to erosion – a form typical, instead, of the handful of examples outside Britain. This fine point of detail may suggest that it is intrusive in terms of the British scene even though the type was clearly adopted in at least one British region. However, the swelling at the presumed socket/prong junction is currently only known on the British examples and two in the slightly later Hío hoard (Pontevedra, Spain). The other European finds are from Bois-du-Roc, Charente, and, at considerable remove, three from the island of Sicily (Needham and Bowman 2005). Taking account of the rarity of flesh-hook deposition in the Bronze Age, it must be assumed that this type was more widely used than is currently apparent, and future finds may suddenly alter the distribution. Nevertheless, it can be ventured that the Langdon example is most likely to have had an origin in lands somewhere to the south.

The remaining continental connections for Langdon types, including some of the major types present, are again across the Channel. Candidate source areas, seen from the tentacled view, range from Brittany across to the Low Countries and

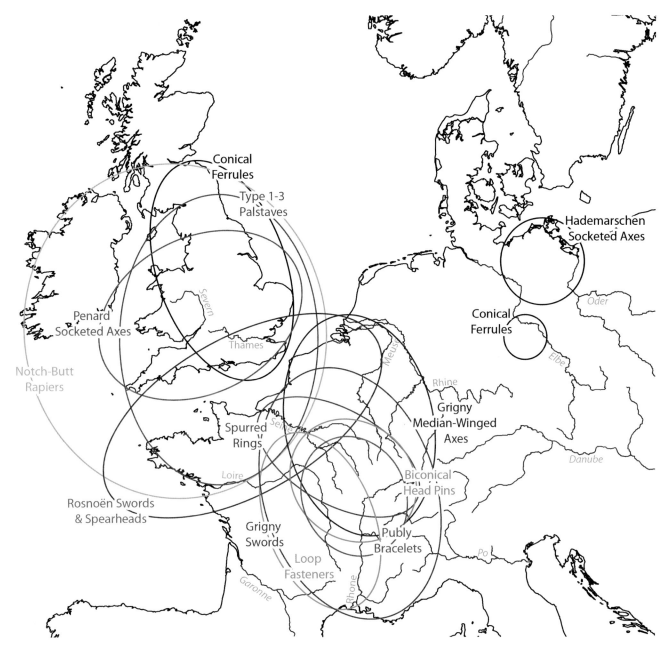

*Fig 5.5   Zones of most frequent occurrence of close parallels for the main types from Langdon Bay. The full
geographical spreads of these types are not shown for clarity; refer to text for full discussion*

down towards the Mediterranean. In fact, the prevailing axis of connection is in a zone southwards
between the Seine and the Rhine, by way of eastern
France to the Rhône corridor (see Fig 5.5). The
median-winged axes are dominant in terms of their
gross mass and significant in terms of their regionally diagnostic typology, but they are only the most
obvious category. A wide range of other types can be
best paralleled in this direction, some of them almost
certainly emanating from the same culture zone as
the winged axes. They include certain individual
swords: the Grigny type example (No 169) and the
Rixheim-related hilt (No 167). More generally, the
lozenge-section blades (Nos 165, 177, 179), even
when combined with a Rosnoën hilt-plate, are also

most likely to be from northern or eastern France;
if furnished with other hilt-plates, they could have
originated in regions still further south or east. The
source area of the leaf-blade knife (No 207 and,
perhaps, No 205) is more or less coincident with the
core area for the Grigny type median-winged axes;
and a further knife/dirk (No 197) is also tentatively
seen to originate thereabouts. The best parallels
have been found in this region for a range of fittings
and ornaments – the ribbed bracelet (No 153), pin
head (No 152), spurred ring pendant fragment (No
146), and strigil-like implement (No 144), while
the loop fastener (No 157) has parallels in an overlapping zone stretching further to the south and
centred on the Rhône corridor. Finally, the principle

of a knobbed ferrule (No 355) might also be traced to eastern France.

Three types remain to be discussed, all familiar in the Rosnoën tradition: classic Rosnoën swords, Rosnoën palstaves, and long-socket spearheads. One view would be to see these types as coming from a distinct source zone centred on Brittany, which is often assumed to be the heart of Rosnoën production. However, since they are all likely to have been in production in at least part of the territory between the Seine and the Meuse (as discussed above – 'origins, foreign-ness, and the problem of hidden circulation'), a more restrictive view would be that these Rosnoën-tradition elements could have been picked up from closer shores – indeed, within the south-pointing zone just outlined.

With regard to the continental component of the Langdon Bay assemblage, there is thus no compelling need to invoke its assembly from a wide range of geographical sources. Even so, we cannot rule out minor components which had a different background from the great majority, not least the likelihood of some southern British material. It may be significant that the common continental axis seen from the restrictive viewpoint leads to a culture zone around eastern France which was on the doorstep of the western Alps, where copper production was prodigious in the later Bronze Age. This model therefore identifies an exchange axis that was tapping into the network distributing metal away from those mined sources.

Nevertheless, the fact that the bulk of the material at Langdon was of types (the palstaves, most swords, and rapiers/dirks) appropriate to the Channel-flanking lands is clear evidence that this was not a case of the long-distance export of metal direct from the mining area. Indeed, it cannot be assumed either that there was a significant contribution directly from the first strong cultural heartland *en route*, that of the middle Rhine/Alsace-Lorraine, since the median-winged axes found at Langdon Bay could have emanated from production zones further north. It is much more likely that we are witnessing the more 'osmotic' flow of metal through networks that interlinked complex pools of metal in circulation, not individual points far-flung across the landscape. This model ties in with the evidence that the metal in the Langdon artefacts has probably been well recycled, and that there were at least two contributory impurity suites, one of which had echoes of the material in circulation in the Channel zone in the previous phase, that of Taunton/Baux-Sainte-Croix (Northover, Chapter 3).

So, having drawn tentative conclusions about the *ultimate* source of much of the metal, it is possible to suggest that the *immediate* source of the great majority of the actual objects was rather closer to the Strait of Dover. Nevertheless, some subtle variations in both impurity composition and lead isotope ratios make it clear that the various categories of object cannot all come from a single well-homogenised pool of metal in circulation. At least some

object categories were of metal that had a different recent history of mixing and/or recycling. Subtle variation in tin values can also potentially relate to almost imperceptible changes from one regional circulation stock to another, as suggested for the socketed axes/chisels.

It is helpful to consider compositions against the yardstick presented by the palstaves and most of the blade weapons, for these are types explicitly indigenous to the Channel regions and referable to Rosnoën and Penard traditions. The first difference drawn out by Peter Northover (Chapter 3) lies in the median-winged axes, for which the distributions of both lead and nickel are shifted relative to those for these Rosnoën/Penard types. Moreover, principal components analysis brought out further divergent trends in their respective antimony and silver levels. This evidence suggests the production of most or all of the median-winged axes within a distinct metal-working tradition which had a different balance of metal inputs ('inputs' include both metal brought into the region from outside during the given phase and metal which was retained in circulation from earlier use). One interpretation would be to suggest that median-winged axes found in northern France were all manufactured further to the south, but the alternative is a degree of spatial overlap between this manufacturing tradition and that of Rosnoën.

Even among the median-winged axes there may be significant variation. Two of eight analysed for lead isotopes yielded ratios which were drifted downwards from the main cluster on the traditional plots. This difference appears to be associated with higher trends in antimony, silver, and lead and is likely to reflect metal that had either a shorter history of recycling since extraction or less adulteration from a more general pool of metal in circulation in the region in question. These two factors may be tied together in a given metal-flow system and could suggest these two objects were 'closer' to the main source metal(s). At any rate, these compositional trends hint at a more complex spectrum in which a minority of the type had a variant background.

Two more of the lead isotope-analysed objects (a rapier and a socketed axe) are distinguished, in contrast, by a drift upwards from the main cluster of isotopic ratios; they suggest an ultimate metal source very distinct from that of the two median-winged axes just discussed. In fact, these may be moving towards the more extreme ratios seen in four of the six lead isotope-analysed objects from Salcombe; all four are blade weapons, one being the distinctive Saint-Ouen (or Pépinville A) type sword with its explicit connection to the Seine Basin. At present, it is impossible to be definitive about the metal contribution that was causing these higher lead isotope ratios. Their deviance from the lower-ratio group, although suggesting a distinct ore body, does not necessarily point to a different geographical zone because there is frequently multi-stage ore formation in limited metalliferous zones. Nevertheless, these two minor groups are at opposite poles of the main cluster and may actually represent two main contributory inputs to the metal stock in circulation, a stock that was otherwise becoming more homogenised through repeated mixing. This pattern has been referred to as a 'mixing spectrum' elsewhere and its position on the lead isotope plots seems to replicate closely that for Taunton-phase metalwork in south-east Britain (Rohl and Needham 1998, plots 30A and 30C – IMPLI 13). It would appear that there were similar metal inputs into the stock in circulation in the Channel zone across the two phases, a conclusion supported by similarity in the impurity patterns. One clear change that may be identified, however, is a decline in nickel from Taunton to Penard; this decline can potentially be explained by growth in the input of the metal represented by the median-winged axes at Langdon.

On the basis of the above discussion there is no need to suppose the collection of the Langdon material from a wide range of geographical or cultural regions. A majority of the assemblage could easily have been drawn from metalwork in circulation in a relatively restricted part of the opposite Channel shore. It is possible that one significant component, in particular the majority of median-winged axes, had been produced further inland, but its source need not have been as far away as the Alpine foreland. Overall, it may be that the Langdon assemblage fits a distance-decay profile in which the quantity of material present declines rapidly with distance from the Strait of Dover.

If the source-region of the winged axes was, in fact, further inland than that of the 'Rosnoën' metalwork this would introduce another crucial question: would this material have been specifically sought in the course of a mission which ventured inland to that region, or would it instead have constituted material already held in the circulation stock of the coastal communities? The latter scenario is eminently possible, as we know from the finds of median-winged axes scattered through the coastal territories that they played a part in the coastal metal-use system even if not produced locally. Objects more certain to have been produced further afield are too few to sustain any argument for longer-distance voyaging in pursuit of metal acquisition. Even the possibility of British-produced objects in the assemblage does not really weaken the case for a 'single-point' collection on the continental shore, once allowance has been made for both on-board equipment and potential left-overs from former voyages, as outlined above.

Nothing said here firmly excludes the possibility that a more complex itinerary was involved in the amassing of the continental part of the Langdon assemblage; but, on the other hand, there is no compelling evidence for anything beyond a fairly straightforward one-trip collection from a location in the coastal territories of northern France or the Low Countries, whether on the coast itself or inland from it. To draw this conclusion does not mean that there was no specialisation involved, either in the maritime venture or in the connecting land-based processes of accumulation and organising exchange. Conducting both inter-group exchange and maritime transportation were high-profile matters for Bronze Age communities, as in almost any period, and were too vital for the replenishment of bronze stocks to be left to opportunism or in inexpert hands.

Although it is not, as yet, an especially large assemblage, a case might be made for the Penard assemblage found at Salcombe having a similar distance-decay profile to that suggested for Langdon Bay. The bulk of the material is unproblematically typical of the nearest part of the Continent, Armorica; indeed, some could even be from the adjacent British shore. The palstave-adze (S6) seems to be especially characteristic of parts of Britain and Ireland at this time. From further afield comes the Saint-Ouen sword (S15), probably a product of the Seine Basin; and it is possible that two eroded blades were of related type (S16 and S17). Meanwhile, the *strumento* comes from a very remote region indeed. Again, a distance-decay profile is indicated with the implication that the most distant representatives could merely be the small minority of material that has passed successfully through a chain of interactions without having been destroyed or melted down. These 'tail-ends' of the distribution are not sufficient evidence in themselves for any form of direct contact over large distances. Looking at the Salcombe Penard assemblage in this way allows the provisional hypothesis that it may have been drawn in entirety from items in circulation in the lands flanking the western Channel, even though the ultimate origin of a minority of objects lay further afield.

Conclusion on the nature of the seabed assemblages

Given the taphonomic and logistical difficulties posed by the marine environment, it is almost impossible to be sure that any set of material recovered from the sea represents a complete or near complete assemblage as deposited. In some cases, the recovered material may be only the tip of the iceberg. Therefore, making any meaningful comparison between seabed and land assemblages is fraught with difficulty. This is a major obstacle when interpretation is heavily dependent on like-for-like comparisons and is most acute for the many seabed sites for which no survey has been undertaken. Not only is there a high chance that a greater number of objects was originally present at many of the sites, but there is also little doubt that the recovered objects are not a faithful representation of the actual seabed assemblage in terms of object completeness, size, and, indeed, type.

For the two key assemblages covered in this volume, however, more can be ventured partly because underwater survey work has begun to redress the recovery biases that are endemic for casually retrieved material. While the Salcombe Penard assemblage is of only moderate size (but still growing), the Langdon Bay assemblage is already known to have been of exceptional size by comparison with contemporary terrestrial finds. This factor in itself begins to draw these two assemblages apart from currently recognised practices of metalwork deposition. Their distinction is further reinforced by both diversity in object category and the high incidence of 'foreign' types when compared with contemporary assemblages in the closest terrestrial zone (Britain). Indeed, even the potential source areas for the foreign types lack closely comparable deposits.

In addition to the lack of comparanda among contemporary terrestrial hoards, it has also been shown that the two key assemblages do not mirror the accumulated assemblages from reaches of rivers, for these typically span more than one metalworking phase. Langdon Bay and the other multiple-object seabed finds seem to be characterised by each belonging to a single metalwork phase, while Salcombe appears on current evidence to be a fortuitous palimpsest of two separated phase groups. It is not possible to regard the seabed finds as extensions of the practices of deposition that account for the riverine metalwork. Similarly, although there are a handful of phase-specific metalwork assemblages potentially from comparable topographic situations in river mouths or estuaries across western Europe, these too differ in certain key respects. It is clear then that, whatever the explanation for the two large seabed assemblages, they represent a deposition phenomenon that has not hitherto been recognised.

A second interpretative difficulty stems from the fact that contextual evidence from the marine environment is rarely adequate to establish whether assemblages constituted 'closed groups', even when they are clearly of a single metalworking phase. Phase-specific deposits such as these need not necessarily be single events and the above discussion has explored the possibility of multiple-stage deposition which, for some reason, was tied to the workings of a phase-specific exchange network. In our view, however, the collective evidence is not in favour of a steady accumulation of ritual deposits at the same location.

Above all, what distinguishes the aggregate seabed assemblage, and *par excellence* those from Langdon Bay and Salcombe, is the high incidence of 'foreign' object types. This feature, in combination with the high diversity of types and categories, very much gives the impression that they are more faithful to a life-assemblage than the great mass of terrestrial and riverine deposits which were governed by selective deposition. These points all suggest that Langdon Bay, Salcombe, and perhaps some of the other multi-object assemblages are better representations of material circulating in the systemic sphere, particularly in the maritime interaction sphere, than we normally encounter. Rather than some highly dramatic and flamboyant form of conspicuous consumption, one must err instead towards these two assemblages being the residues of former wrecked ships – a conclusion that Keith Muckelroy's considered analysis brought him to many years ago.

Of one thing we can be sure: regular adventuring on the high seas, a major occupation of the Channel Bronze Age, must have brought its casualties. Bronze Age shipwrecks are almost certainly going to continue to be a feature of the maritime archaeological record.

Notes to Chapter 5

1. http://www.britishmuseum.org/research/search_the_collection_database.aspx
2. http://www.britishmuseum.org/research/search_the_collection_database.aspx

Appendix 1   Dimensions, condition and lead isotope data of artefacts from the Langdon Bay and Salcombe assemblages

Completeness

1. Complete
2. Small loss (eg loop, blade corner)
3. Large fragment (estimated greater than half present)
4. Approximately half
5. Small fragment (rather less than half)

Cutting edge profile(s)

A. Sharp
B. Rounded off
C. Very rounded (allowing for a wide variety of thicknesses at the edge)

Surface feature retention – fine morphology and decoration

a. Distinct features survive
b. Poor definition, but discernible features which are almost certainly original
c. Hint of features, but origin uncertain
d. Generally amorphous with no fine morphology

* Significant irregularities or anomalies in outline believed to be of post-depositional formation; may include surface hollows and perforations.

Condition of breaks

1. Crisp fracture
2. Slightly rounded
3. Well rounded and smooth
L   Loop only lacking
() Uncertain breaks – applies to completeness categories 1 and 1–2 only

Bending, twisting and other features

o   Unbent
b1. Slight bend
b2. Marked bend
b3. Doubled over
c. Concretion attached (significant amount)
s. Stones trapped in orifices (loops, wings)
t1. Slight twist down length, judged to be due to damage rather than initial manufacture

Catalogue No	East (OSGBE)	North (OSGBN)	British Museum Accession No	Site Code	Site ID	Object Type	Breadth (mm)	Width (mm)	Length (mm)	Weight (g)
1			1977 0402 01	LB	X	median-winged axe	25.0	38.3	200.0	497.0
2			1977 0402 02	LB	X	median-winged axe	41.0	46.0	222.0	881.0
3			1977 0402 03	LB	X	median-winged axe	31.0	40.0	211.0	543.0
4			1977 0402 04	LB	X	median-winged axe	34.0	40.0	198.0	749.0
5			1977 0402 05	LB	X	median-winged axe	28.0	37.0	179.5	546.0
6			1977 0402 06	LB	X	median-winged axe	38.0	47.0	215.0	809.0
7			1977 0402 07	LB	X	median-winged axe	35.0	43.0	204.0	693.5
8			1977 0402 08	LB	X	median-winged axe	39.0	42.0	216.0	778.5
9			1977 0402 09	LB	X	median-winged axe	44.0	45.0	221.0	831.0
10			1977 0402 10	LB	X	median-winged axe	39.0	41.0	189.5	701.0
11			1977 0402 11	LB	X	median-winged axe	24.0	38.0	192.5	499.5
12			1977 0402 12	LB	X	median-winged axe	24.0	39.0	189.5	632.5
13			1977 0402 13	LB	X	median-winged axe	22.0	38.0	184.0	464.5
14			1977 0402 14	LB	X	median-winged axe	29.0	40.0	197.5	573.0
15			1977 0402 15	LB	X	median-winged axe	26.0	43.0	210.0	635.0
16			1977 0402 16	LB	X	median-winged axe	34.5	42.5	203.0	629.0
17			1977 0402 17	LB	X	median-winged axe	42.0	45.0	211.0	737.0
18			1977 0402 18	LB	X	median-winged axe	22.0	38.5	199.0	440.0
19			1977 0402 19	LB	X	median-winged axe	38.5	42.5	215.0	709.0
20			1977 0402 20	LB	X	median-winged axe	36.0	39.0	194.5	703.0
21			1977 0402 21	LB	X	median-winged axe	44.0	44.0	221.0	865.0
22			1977 0402 22	LB	X	median-winged axe	36.0	48.0	225.0	740.5
23			1977 0402 23	LB	X	median-winged axe	45.0	46.0	226.0	763.0
24			1977 0402 24	LB	X	median-winged axe	30.0	45.5	204.0	635.0
25			1977 0402 25	LB	X	median-winged axe	32.0	39.0	202.5	527.0
26			1977 0402 26	LB	X	median-winged axe	34.0	42.5	207.0	571.0
27			1977 0402 27	LB	X	median-winged axe	20.5	38.5	174.0	451.0
28			1980 0201 01	LB	LB77.03	median-winged axe	18.5	36.5	193.0	409.5
29			1980 0201 02	LB	LB77.07	median-winged axe	26.5	35.0	174.0	528.7
30			1980 0201 03	LB	LB77.09	median-winged axe	19.0	43.5	186.0	694.7
31	634020	141725	1980 0201 11	LB	LB78.03	median-winged axe	28.0	40.5	211.5	620.4
32	634089	141755	1980 0201 12	LB	LB78.05	median-winged axe	30.5	44.0	216.0	808.2
33	634136	141775	1980 0201 13	LB	LB78.11	median-winged axe	27.5	42.0	206.0	691.2
34	634135	141776	1980 0201 14	LB	LB78.12	median-winged axe	31.0	42.0	202.5	656.6
35	634134	141780	1981 0702 05	LB	LB79.02	median-winged axe	26.0	39.0	190.0	729.8
36	634135	141781	1981 0702 03	LB	LB79.11	median-winged axe	44.0	47.5	211.0	846.5
37	634133	141787	1981 0702 01	LB	LB79.22	median-winged axe	42.0	44.5	225.0	758.7
38	634136	141784	1981 0702 02	LB	LB79.30	median-winged axe	43.5	41.5	221.0	807.1
39	634133	141791	1981 0702 06	LB	LB79.34	median-winged axe	32.5	35.5	189.5	413.6
40	634140	141776	1981 0702 04	LB	LB79.38	median-winged axe	29.0	39.5	208.0	582.8
41	634138	141787	1982 0603 01	LB	LB80.09	median-winged axe	43.0	40.5	235.0	724.0
42	634167	141798	1983 0501 02	LB	LB81.36	median-winged axe	41.0	42.5	215.0	658.2
43	634171	141805	1984 0701 01	LB	LB82.40	median-winged axe	32.5	40.3	226.0	572.5

Bending & Twisting	Break Condition	Feature Retention	Cutting Edge Profile	Completeness	Analysis No	206/204 ratio (Mean)	207/206 ratio (Mean)	208/206 ratio (Mean)	Previous publication of analysis and other notes
o	X	d	C	1	Do.118				
o,s,c	X	b	B	1	Do.119				
o	(3)	d	C	1	Do.120				
o,c	X	d*	C	1	Do.121				
o	X	c/d	C	1	Do.122				
o,c	(2)	b	C	1	Do.123	18.2527	0.85817	2.10560	
o,s,c,	(3)	d	C	1	Do.124				
o,s,c	(3)	c	C	1	Do.125				
o,c	X	b	B/C	1	Do.126				
o,c	2/3	c*	C	1-2	Do.127				
?b1,c	X	d*	C	1	Do.128				
o,c	X	d	C	1	Do.129				
o,c	X	d	C	1	Do.130	18.3203	0.85497	2.09873	
o	(3)	c/d*	C	1	Do.131				
o,c	X	c/d*	C	1	Do.132				
o,c	X	d	C	1	Do.133				
o,c	X	a/b	A/B	1	Do.134				
t1	(3)	d*	C	1	Do.135				
o,c,s	X	c	B/C	1	Do.136				
o	X	c	C	1	Do.137				
o	X	b	B	1	Do.138				
o,c	X	c	B/C	1	Do.139				
o	X	a	A	1	Do.177				
b1	(3)	d	B/C	1	Do.140				
o	X	d	B	1	Do.141				
o,c	X	c	B	1	Do.142				
o	(3)	d*	C	1	Do.143				
b1	X	d	C	1	Do.170				
o	X	d	C	1	Do.167	18.2121	0.85970	2.10890	
o	X	d	C	1	Do.169				
o	X	c	B/C	1	Do.161	18.2020	0.86100	2.11216	Rohl & Needham 1998
o,s	X	c	C	1	Do.157	18.3460	0.85473	2.10076	Rohl & Needham 1998
o	X	b	C	1	Do.158	18.1920	0.86170	2.11393	Rohl & Needham 1998
o	X	c	B	1	Do.159?	18.1980	0.86023	2.10990	Rohl & Needham 1998
o	X	d	C	1	Do.050				
o,s	X	b	A/B	1	Do.047				
o,s,c	X	a/b	A/B	1	Do.046				
o,s	X	a/b	C	1	Do.045				
o,s	X	d*	B/C	1	Do.052				
o	X	c/d*	B/C	1	Do.048				
o,c	X	a	A/B	1	X				
o	X	a	A/B	1	X				
o,c	X	a	A	1	X				

Catalogue No	East (OSGBE)	North (OSGBN)	British Museum Accession No	Site Code	Site ID	Object Type	Breadth (mm)	Width (mm)	Length (mm)	Weight (g)
44	634168	141815	1985 0801 01	LB	LB83.15	median-winged axe	18.5	34.0	187.0	269.3
45	634139	141788	Replica	LB	LB80.18	median-winged axe	X	X	X	X
46			1977 0402 29	LB	X	median-winged axe	34.0	38.5	109.5	361.0
47	634139	141780	1981 0702 07	LB	LB79.42	median-winged axe	37.5	37.5	112.0	399.0
48	634167	141805	1984 0701 02	LB	LB82.19	median-winged axe	31.0	39.5	130.0	435.3
49			1984 0701 03	LB	LB82.44	median-winged axe	23.5	36.0	96.5	187.0
50			1984 0701 46	LB	LB82.52	median-winged axe	21.0	27.0	82.0	93.9
51			1977 0402 28	LB	X	median-winged axe	38.0	46.5	112.0	513.0
52	634135	141781	1981 0702 08	LB	LB79.16	median-winged axe	43.0	49.0	115.0	476.0
53	634135	141792	1981 0702 09	LB	LB79.63	median-winged axe	11.5	38.0	71.0	139.6
54	634144	141788	1982 0603 02	LB	LB80.32	median-winged axe	5.5	37.5	37.5	41.0
55	634166	141795	1983 0501 04	LB	LB81.32	median-winged axe	11.5	37.0	69.5	152.6
56			1984 0701 47	LB	LB82.53	median-winged axe	8.0	33.0	46.5	58.2
57			1977 0402 30	LB	X	median-winged axe	27.5	33.5	67.5	254.6
58	634139	141783	1981 0702 10	LB	LB79.58	median-winged axe	49.5	35.5	76.5	403.6
59	634153	141791	1983 0501 03	LB	LB81.18	median-winged axe	34.5	37.5	35.5	151.2
60	634169	141797	1984 0701 05	LB	LB82.04	median-winged axe	14.5	36.3	31.0	64.8
61	634171	141805	1984 0701 04	LB	LB82.39	median-winged axe	35.5	33.5	67.0	234.4
62	634132	141790	1981 0702 11	LB	LB79.26	axe blade fragment	13.5	41.5	58.0	185.4
63	634167	141798	1983 0501 05	LB	LB81.53	axe blade fragment	11.5	46.0	42.0	108.9
64	634170	141797	1984 0701 11	LB	LB82.05	axe blade fragment	9.0	33.7	58.0	68.8
65			1977 0402 32	LB	X	?axe blade fragment	13.0	32.5	58.0	103.0
66	634166	141792	1983 0501 38	LB	LB81.26	?axe fragment	12.0	25.0	25.5	37.3
67			1977 0402 31	LB	X	axe blade fragment	17.0	50.0	68.0	205.5
68	634111	141767	1980 0201 17	LB	LB78.10	palstave blade fragment	16.0	48.5	65.5	188.6
69			1977 0402 42	LB	X	palstave, type 1	26.0	40.5	158.5	427.2
70			1977 0402 43	LB	X	palstave, type 1	24.0	38.5	161.5	377.2
71			1991 0302 01	LB	LB89.05	palstave, type 1	25.5	36.0	129.0	241.6
72			1984 0701 07	LB	LB82.23	palstave, type 1	20.5	41.5	164.0	330.4
73			1977 0402 40	LB	X	palstave, type 1	27.0	44.5	187.0	545.4
74			1984 0701 09	LB	LB82.08	palstave, type 1	22.0	44.0	163.5	404.0
75			1977 0402 38	LB	X	palstave, ?type 1	24.0	45.0	192.0	549.7
76	634135	141781	1981 0702 17	LB	LB79.12	palstave, ?type 1	22.5	34.5	153.0	298.8
77	634133	141790	1981 0702 15	LB	LB79.27	palstave, ?type 1	21.0	30.5	129.5	237.8
78	634138	141788	1982 0603 03	LB	LB80.08	palstave, ?type 1	25.0	36.0	81.5	200.6
79	634169	141799	1977 0402 39	LB	X	palstave, ?type 1	20.5	35.0	146.5	370.7
80	634172	141795	1977 0402 55	LB	X	palstave, type 2	24.0	38.5	181.0	456.9
81			1984 0701 10	LB	LB82.09	palstave, type 2	27.0	38.0	180.0	507.2
82			1984 0701 06	LB	LB82.27	palstave, type 2	34.0	43.0	163.5	443.9
83			1983 0501 06	LB	LB81.07	palstave, type 2	33.5	37.0	148.0	465.8
84			1977 0402 49	LB	X	palstave, ?type 2	21.5	30.0	143.5	271.4
85	634151	141789	1977 0402 59	LB	X	palstave, ?type 2	27.0	32.0	160.5	378.7
86	634171	141805	1981 0702 13	LB	LB79.37	palstave, ?type 2	32.5	46.0	122.0	393.0

Bending & Twisting	Break Condition	Feature Retention	Cutting Edge Profile	Completeness	Analysis No	206/204 ratio (Mean)	207/206 ratio (Mean)	208/206 ratio (Mean)	Previous publication of analysis and other notes
o	X	c	A/B	1	X				
X	X	X	X	X	X				
o	3	b	X	4	Do.145				
o,c	3	d	X	4	Do.055				
o,s,c	3	c	X	4	X				
o	3	c	X	4	X				
o	3	b	X	4	X				
o,c,s	2/3	c	B/C	4	Do.146	18.1840	0.86093	2.11076	
o,s,c	2&3	b	A/B	4	Do.053				
o	3	d*	X	5	Do.070				
o	3	c	X	5	X				
o	3	b	X	5	X				
o	3	c	X	5	X				
o	3	d	X	5	Do.144				
o	1/2	a/b	X	4-5	Do.059				
o	3	b	X	5	X				
X	3	d	X	5	X				
o	3	b	X	5	X				
o	3	d	X	5	Do.078				
o	2	c	B	5	X				
o	3	d	A/B	5	X				
o	3	d	B/C	(5)	Do.091				
o	3	c	X	5	X				
o,?b1	3	c	B	5	Do.090				
o	2/3	b	B	5	Do.155				
o,s	X	c	B/C	1	Do.184?				
o,c	3 L	b	B	2	Do.081				
b1	L	a/b	A/B	1	Do.231				
o,s	3 L	c	B	2	X				
o,c	2/3L	b/c	C	2	Do.082				
o	X	b	B/C	1	X				
o,c	3 L	d	C	2	Do.084				
o	2&3	d*	A/B	2	Do.051				
t1	3 L	c/d*	C	2	Do.057				
o,s	3	b	C	3	X				
o,c	3 L	c/d	C	2	Do.083				
o,s	3 L	b/c	C	2	Do.093	18.1800	0.86105	2.11116	Rohl & Needham 1998
o	3 L	c	A/B	2	X				
o,c	X	a	B/C	1	Do.233				
o,c	3	a/b	C	2	Do.210				
o	3 L	d*	C	2	Do.099	18.2300	0.85967	2.11049	Rohl & Needham 1998
o,c	(3)	d	B	1-2	Do.115				
o,c	3	b	X	3	Do.054				

Catalogue No	East (OSGBE)	North (OSGBN)	British Museum Accession No	Site Code	Site ID	Object Type	Breadth (mm)	Width (mm)	Length (mm)	Weight (g)
87	634132	141785	1977 0402 41	LB	X	palstave, type 3	33.0	43.5	174.0	654.6
88			1980 0201 04	LB	LB77.08	palstave, type 3	33.0	43.5	188.0	639.5
89	634169	141799	1980 0201 16	LB	LB78.06	palstave, type 3	30.0	43.0	188.5	693.7
90			1980 0201 15	LB	LB78.04	palstave, ? type 3	29.0	48.0	154.0	507.2
91			1981 0702 16	LB	LB79.46	palstave, ? type 3	33.0	45.0	190.5	757.5
92	634138	141787	1984 0701 08	LB	LB82.42	palstave, type 4	25.5	32.0	111.0	244.4
93	634150	141786	1977 0402 35	LB	X	palstave	28.0	37.0	92.0	201.0
94	634170	141799	1977 0402 56	LB	X	palstave	27.0	38.5	153.0	473.5
95			1977 0402 37	LB	X	palstave	28.0	36.0	156.0	474.4
96			1982 0603 04	LB	LB80.14	palstave	15.0	24.0	119.0	96.2
97			1977 0402 44	LB	X	palstave	18.5	39.0	172.0	323.1
98	634086	141752	1977 0402 45	LB	X	palstave	20.0	38.0	155.0	323.0
99	634138	141780	1977 0402 46	LB	X	palstave	16.5	35.0	148.5	282.4
100			1977 0402 57	LB	X	palstave	26.0	35.0	171.0	340.1
101	634140	141778	1983 0501 07	LB	LB81.09	palstave	22.5	32.5	151.5	312.4
102			1981 0702 14	LB	LB79.05	palstave	19.0	34.5	142.0	247.5
103			1977 0402 36	LB	X	palstave	22.0	34.5	151.5	315.4
104			1977 0402 47	LB	X	palstave	21.5	30.5	146.5	284.3
105			1977 0402 53	LB	X	palstave	22.0	34.0	168.0	348.6
106			1977 0402 54	LB	X	palstave	26.5	36.5	160.5	428.3
107			1977 0402 58	LB	X	palstave	18.5	33.5	148.5	265.7
108	634133	141789	1981 0702 12	LB	LB79.28	palstave	16.5	29.5	143.5	181.6
109			1984 0701 48	LB	LB82.47	palstave	22.5	29.0	135.0	228.0
110			1984 0701 49	LB	LB82.48	palstave	19.5	33.0	152.0	227.0
111			1977 0402 48	LB	X	palstave	18.0	31.5	125.0	183.8
112			1977 0402 50	LB	X	palstave	17.5	31.0	115.5	176.4
113			1977 0402 52	LB	X	palstave	15.5	30.0	118.5	172.9
114	634133	141791	1981 0702 18	LB	LB79.33	palstave	18.0	35.5	130.0	241.7
115			1984 0701 50	LB	LB82.46	palstave	19.0	31.0	128.0	236.6
116			1977 0402 33	LB	X	?palstave	11.5	16.5	105.5	60.3
117			1977 0402 34	LB	X	?palstave	13.5	20.5	123.5	116.0
118	634136	141775	1980 0201 19	LB	LB78.15	socketed axe/chisel	18.0	25.5	92.0	896.0
119			1977 0402 92a	LB	X	socketed axe/chisel	23.5	31.0	71.5	113.8
120			1980 0201 18	LB	LB78.07	socketed axe/chisel	25.5	34.0	120.0	196.3
121	634088	141756	1977 0402 51	LB	X	socketed axe/chisel	13.5	38.0	115.5	139.5
122			1981 0702 19	LB	LB79.41	socketed axe/chisel	18.0	34.0	83.0	96.5
123	634165	141818	1984 0701 53	LB	LB82.49	socketed axe/chisel	11.0	30.7	92.0	93.1
124			1984 0701 52	LB	LB82.50	socketed axe/chisel	13.5	30.0	104.0	90.5
125			1981 0702 20	LB	LB79.44	socketed axe/chisel	13.0	22.0	90.0	42.4
126			1984 0701 51	LB	LB82.51	socketed axe/chisel	13.0	19.5	81.0	54.0
127	634142	141773	1977 0402 89	LB	X	socketed axe/chisel	16.0	21.5	101.0	68.7
128	634141	141775	1985 0801 02	LB	LB83.01	socketed axe/chisel	10.0	25.0	53.0	39.9
129			1985 0801 03	LB	LB83.03	socketed axe/chisel	12.0	23.0	57.0	53.4

Bending & Twisting	Break Condition	Feature Retention	Cutting Edge Profile	Completeness	Analysis No	206/204 ratio (Mean)	207/206 ratio (Mean)	208/206 ratio (Mean)	Previous publication of analysis and other notes
t1,s,c	X	c	C	1	Do.178				
o	X	a/b	C	2	Do.168				
t1,c	X	b/c	C	1	Do.156	18.2190	0.85882	2.10631	Rohl & Needham 1998
o	3	c	C	3	Do.160	18.1850	0.86107	2.11165	Rohl & Needham 1998
o	3 L	d	C	2	Do.049				
o,s,c	2/3	b	X	3	X				
o	2/3	c	X	4	Do.087				
o	3 L	d	C	2	Do.092				
o	3 L	c/d	B	2	Do.085				
t1	X	d	C	2-3	Do.202				
o,s	(3)	d*	C	1-2	Do.104				
b1,c	(3)	d	C	1-2	Do.103				
o	(3)	d*	C	1-2	Do.102				
b1	3 L	d*	B/C	2	Do.117				
o,s	3 L	c	C	2	X				
b1	3 L	d	C	2	Do.056	18.2007	0.86060	2.11100	
o	3 L	d*	C	2	Do.086				
o	3	d	C	2	Do.101				
o,c	3 L	d	C	2	Do.095	18.2320	0.86142	2.11455	Rohl & Needham 1998
c,b1	3 L	d	C	2	Do.094	18.2060	0.85962	2.10868	Rohl & Needham 1998
o	X	d	C	1-2	Do.116				
o	X	d*	B/C	1-2	Do.186				
b1	X	d	C	2	X				
o	X	d	B	2	X				
b1	3	d*	C	2-3	Do.100				
b1	3	d*	B/C	3	Do.098				
o	3 L	d*	C	2-3	Do.096	18.2310	0.85998	2.10800	Rohl & Needham 1998
o	3	d*	B/C	3	Do.058				
o	X	d	C	1-3	X				
o	X	d*	X	(1-3)	Do.089				
o	X	d	X	(1-3)	Do.088				
o,s,c	3&2	b/c	C	3	Do.152				
o	2/3	c	X	3-4	Do.181				
o	3	c	A/B	2	Do.162	18.1240	0.86370	2.11475	Rohl & Needham 1998
o	2&3	d*	C	4	Do.097				
o	1	c/d	C	3-4	Do.062				
o,s,c	3	d	C	4	Do.226				
o	2	b	A/B	3	Do.225				
?b1	3	d	B/C	4	Do.068				
o	3	c	B/C	3	Do.224				
o	3&1	d	C	3-4	Do.029	18.2090	0.86030	2.11045	
o,c	3	c	B	4	X				
o,c	3	d	C	4-5	X				

Catalogue No	East (OSGBE)	North (OSGBN)	British Museum Accession No	Site Code	Site ID	Object Type	Breadth (mm)	Width (mm)	Length (mm)	Weight (g)
130	634171	141795	1984 0701 12	LB	LB82.22	socketed hammer	21.0	22.0	59.0	95.8
131	634138	141785	1982 0603 05	LB	LB80.15	socketed hammer	19.5	27.0	65.5	91.2
132	634133	141785	1981 0702 21	LB	LB79.19	?socketed hammer	11.0	16.5	49.5	35.3
133			1980 0201 20	LB	LB78.20	?socketed hammer	15.0	23.0	51.5	67.3
134	634019	141722	1980 0201 21	LB	LB78.01	hooked knife	21.5	21.0	151.0	105.9
135	634133	141789	1981 0702 22	LB	LB79.29	tanged chisel	7.5	13.0	124.0	21.7
136	634135	141787	1981 0702 23	LB	LB79.31	tanged chisel	7.0	16.5	66.5	13.8
137			1980 0201 22	LB	LB78.16	tanged chisel	8.5	16.0	114.5	30.6
138	634138	141787	1982 0603 06	LB	LB80.13	tanged chisel	10.5	19.0	134.0	33.7
139	634148	141784	1982 0603 07	LB	LB80.69	tanged chisel	4.5	16.5	83.0	9.6
140	634139	141788	1982 0603 08	LB	LB80.16	tanged chisel	5.5	13.0	75.0	8.3
141	634138	141787	1982 0603 09	LB	LB80.10	awl	5.0	5.5	129.0	17.5
142	634152	141791	1983 0501 08	LB	LB81.15	shank (?awl)	X	3.3	65.0	2.3
143	634140	141788	1982 0603 10	LB	LB80.22	shank	2.0	2.5	44.0	0.7
144	634155	141791	1983 0501 09	LB	LB81.19	shank	X	3.5	81.5	4.6
145	634168	141797	1983 0501 10	LB	LB81.40	shank	X	3.5	47.0	3.1
146	634140	141788	1982 0603 41	LB	LB80.21	spurred ring	2.5	4.5	41.0	1.4
147			1984 0701 59	LB	LB82.59	?tang/anvil spike	7.0	11.5	61.5	24.3
148			1980 0201 23	LB	LB78.14	?flesh-hook prong	X	15.5	118.5	56.2
149	634162	141791	1983 0501 15	LB	LB81.25	?tang/anvil spike	6.5	8.0	43.5	6.2
150			1977 0402 91	LB	X	pin	X	4.5	125.0	6.7
151	634172	141795	1984 0701 41	LB	LB82.24	pin	X	8.0	48.0	2.7
152	634168	141804	1984 0701 42	LB	LB82.18	pin-head	X	9.7	15.5	7.4
153	634167	141794	1983 0501 12	LB	LB81.29	bracelet	6.0	12.0	40.0	15.7
154	634167	141798	1983 0501 13	LB	LB81.34	bracelet	6.0	15.5	34.5	19.2
155	634160	141831	1985 0801 04	LB	LB83.02	bracelet	5.5	6.5	64.0	17.3
156	634170	141795	1984 0701 43	LB	LB82.01	?bracelet/ring-handle	8.0	8.5	37.5	11.7
157	634151	141792	1983 0501 14	LB	LB81.10	loop fastener	4.0	15.5	58.5	12.5
158	634156	141792	1983 0501 11	LB	LB81.21	?fitting	5.0	5.5	48.0	8.2
159			1980 0201 10	LB	LB77.10	rivet	X	8.0	16.5	4.4
160	634138	141787	1982 0603 40	LB	LB80.07	rivet	X	8.5	16.0	4.5
161			1983 0501 16	LB	LB81.31	rivet	X	4.5	16.0	1.1
162	634169	141804	1984 0701 14	LB	LB82.32	sword	5.0	29.5	182.5	83.5
163	634171	141805	1984 0701 13	LB	LB82.41	sword	7.5	32.0	212.5	136.9
164	634172	141804	1983 0501 18	LB	LB81.14	sword	6.5	23.5	111.5	65.8
165	634152	141788	1983 0501 19	LB	LB81.13	sword	7.0	27.5	79.5	50.7
166	634151	141793	1977 0402 68	LB	X	sword	6.0	27.0	165.5	98.9
167			1980 0201 24	LB	LB78.08	sword	3.5	31.5	54.0	13.5
168	634088	141756	1981 0702 34	LB	LB79.36	sword	5.0	29.5	24.5	7.1
169			1977 0402 65	LB	X	sword	6.5	25.0	195.0	135.5
170			1985 0801 07	LB	LB83.13	?sword	5.0	27.0	196.0	76.1
171			1977 0402 71	LB	X	?sword	6.0	30.5	158.0	96.8
172			1977 0402 72	LB	X	?sword	6.5	24.5	124.5	53.8

Bending & Twisting	Break Condition	Feature Retention	Cutting Edge Profile	Completeness	Analysis No	206/204 ratio (Mean)	207/206 ratio (Mean)	208/206 ratio (Mean)	Previous publication of analysis and other notes
o,c	X	b	X	1	Do.218				
o,c	3	d	C	4	Do.203				
o	2	d	?	3-5	Do.079				
o	3&1	d	X	5(?)	Do.147				
o,s,c	2	c	B	2-3	Do.201				
o	X	d	B/C	1	Do.072				
o	3?	c/d	A/B	1-3	Do.063				
o	X	c	B	1	Do.151				
o	X	c*	A	1	Do.204				
o	X	d	B	1	Do.205				
o	X	d*	A	3	Do.206				
b1(?)	(3)	a	A	1-2	Do.207				
b1	X	?	A	?	X				
o	3	c	A	X	X				
b1	3	b	X	?	Do.211				
b2	3	c	X	?	X				
o	2	a	(A)	?	Do.209				
o	3	b	X	?	Do.227				
b2	X	b	X	1	Do.153				
o	2	?	B	3-5	X				
b1,t1	X	d	C	?1-2	X				
o	X	b	A	1	X				
o	3	b	X	5	Do.221				
o	2	b	X	5	Do.213				
o	2	c	X	5	X				
o	X	c	X	1(2)	Do.228				
b1	2	a	X	5	X				
o,c	X	b	X	1	Do.214				
X	3	?	X	?	Do.212				
o	X	b	X	1	Do.175				
o	X	a	X	1	X				
o	X	b	X	1	X				
b1	3	c	A	4-5H	X				
o,s,c	3	b	A/B	4-5H	Do.219				
o	3	b/c	B	5H	X				
o	2	b	B	5H	X				
o	3	a/b	A/B	5H	X				
b1	1	b	X	5H	Do.163				
o	3	a/b	X	5H	Do.003	18.1808	0.86095	2.11055	
b1	3	c	B	4-5H	Do.110				
o	3	c	B	4-5II	X				
b2,t1	3	c/d	C	5H	Do.182?				
o,c	3	c/d	C	5H	Do.105				

Catalogue No	East (OSGBE)	North (OSGBN)	British Museum Accession No	Site Code	Site ID	Object Type	Breadth (mm)	Width (mm)	Length (mm)	Weight (g)
173			1977 0402 73	LB	X	?sword	8.5	27.5	140.0	97.2
174			1980 0201 06	LB	LB77.01	?sword	7.0	24.5	458.0	222.9
175	634139	141783	1981 0702 28	LB	LB79.60	?sword	7.0	25.5	95.5	58.0
176			1991 0302 03	LB	LB89.02	?sword	6.0	27.0	205.0	99.4
177	634139	141783	1981 0702 49	LB	LB79.55	sword blade fragment	7.5	27.0	80.0	60.2
178	634148	141784	1982 0603 34	LB	LB80.67	sword blade fragment	5.5	23.0	82.0	51.8
179	634172	141793	1984 0701 38	LB	LB82.21	sword blade fragment	5.5	21.0	59.0	30.9
180			1977 0402 61	LB	X	sword blade fragment	5.5	23.0	87.0	51.8
181	634132	141790	1981 0702 43	LB	LB79.23	sword blade fragment	5.5	21.5	161.0	95.6
182	634139	141788	1981 0702 52	LB	LB79.06	sword blade fragment	5.0	24.0	61.0	32.7
183	634148	141785	1981 0702 50	LB	LB79.59	sword blade fragment	5.0	23.0	74.0	39.9
184	634167	141817	1985 0801 05	LB	LB83.09	rapier	6.0	25.0	459.0	184.9
185			1982 0603 15	LB	LB80.19	rapier/dirk	5.0	28.5	122.5	50.5
186			1982 0603 19	LB	LB80.65	rapier/dirk	4.0	29.5	52.0	15.8
187	634135	141778	1981 0702 24	LB	LB79.47	rapier	7.0	24.0	408.0	167.1
188			1977 0402 60	LB	X	rapier/dirk	6.0	22.0	123.5	132.7
189	634131	141800	1977 0402 70	LB	X	rapier/dirk	4.5	24.0	134.5	54.0
190	634136	141790	1980 0201 25	LB	LB78.13	rapier/dirk	6.0	30.5	130.5	66.9
191	634148	141777	1980 0201 27	LB	LB78.17	dirk	5.0	28.5	114.5	34.3
192	634171	141793	1981 0702 33	LB	LB79.62	dirk	3.0	18.0	83.5	12.3
193	634169	141799	1982 0603 11	LB	LB80.26	rapier/dirk	4.0	20.5	126.0	30.2
194	634169	141799	1983 0501 20	LB	LB81.44	rapier/dirk	4.0	21.5	81.0	23.6
195	634170	141797	1984 0701 19	LB	LB82.12	dirk	5.5	20.5	174.5	58.9
196	634169	141799	1984 0701 16	LB	LB82.17	rapier	6.0	25.0	291.0	142.4
197	634170	141805	1984 0701 15	LB	LB82.06	dirk(?ex-sword)	7.0	25.0	177.0	68.6
198	634146	141790	1984 0701 18	LB	LB82.10	rapier/dirk (?reworked)	4.0	24.5	66.5	24.6
199	634137	141787	1984 0701 33	LB	LB82.38	knife	3.5	12.5	141.0	24.7
200			1982 0603 14	LB	LB80.37	knife	3.5	15.0	127.0	20.7
201	634136	141784	1982 0603 13	LB	LB80.02	knife	4.0	18.5	144.5	36.8
202	634139	141783	1977 0402 66	LB	X	knife	6.0	21.0	155.5	51.6
203	634169	141804	1981 0702 26	LB	LB79.35	knife	5.5	23.0	150.5	54.7
204			1981 0702 29	LB	LB79.53	knife	3.5	17.5	101.5	20.6
205	634146	141782	1984 0701 20	LB	LB82.33	knife	5.0	26.5	136.5	54.2
206	634170	141805	1977 0402 64	LB	X	knife	3.5	21.5	76.0	19.0
207			1982 0603 16	LB	LB80.28	knife	3.5	21.5	102.5	22.0
208			1984 0701 21	LB	LB82.34	knife (?ex-sword)	4.0	23.0	103.0	39.2
209			1992 0301 01	LB	LB90.03	knife (?ex-sword)	5.5	26.0	106.5	44.1
210	634021	141723	1983 0501 17	LB	LB81.45	?sword	5.0	20.0	424.0	100.8
211	634133	141784	1991 0302 02	LB	LB89.01	?sword	5.0	16.5	365.0	104.3
212	634135	141787	1981 0702 25	LB	LB79.48	?sword	5.5	22.0	281.0	91.3
213	634141	141775	1980 0201 26	LB	LB78.02	hilt fragment, ?sword	5.0	20.0	152.0	44.5
214	634138	141785	1982 0603 12	LB	LB80.17	hilt fragment, ?sword	5.5	18.5	177.0	51.3
215	634139	141788	1977 0402 69	LB	X	hilt fragment	5.5	23.0	139.0	38.0

Bending & Twisting	Break Condition	Feature Retention	Cutting Edge Profile	Completeness	Analysis No	206/204 ratio (Mean)	207/206 ratio (Mean)	208/206 ratio (Mean)	Previous publication of analysis and other notes
b1	3	c/d	C	5	Do.106				
b1	X	c	C	1	Do.166				
o	3	c*	C	5H	Do.008				
o	2?	d*	C	4-5H	X				
o	2	b	A	5	Do.022				
b1	3	c	C	5	X				
b1	2	b	B	5	X				
o	3	c	B	5	Do.113				
o	2	c	A/B	4-5	Do.026				
o	3	c*	A	5	Do.071				
o	3	d*	B	5	Do.064				
o	X	b	B	1	X				
o	3	c	C	4-5H	X				
b1	2	b	A/B	5	X				
b1	X	c/d*	C	1	Do.060				
b3,t1	3	c/d	C	3-4H	Do.114				
t1	3	d	B	3-5H	Do.183	18.1499	0.86250	2.11360	
o	3	d	C	3-5H	Do.154				
o	1	d	C	3-5H	Do.150				
b1	X	c	A/B	1	Do.004	18.1924	0.86060	2.10980	
b1	3	d	C	3-5H	X				
o	3	d	B/C	4-5H	X				
o	X	c	B/C	1	X				
o	X	c	B	1	X				
o	X	b*	B/C	?1	Do.220				
o	1	b	A	5H	X				
o	X	c	A/B	1	X				
o	1	a	A	2	X				
o	(3)	c	A/B	1/2	X				
o	X	b	A/B	1	Do.109				
o	X	b?c	A/B	1	Do.024				
o	X	b/c	A	1	Do.009				
o	X	b	A	1	X				
b1	X	b	A/B	1	Do.185				
o	X	b	A/B	1	Do.208				
o,c	X	c	A/B	1/2	X				
o	X	b/c	A/B	?1	X				
b1	X	d	C	1	X				
o	X	d	C	1	X				
b1,t1	2	c/d*	C	3-4H	Do.061				
b1	3	d	B/C	3-5H	Do.164				
b1	3	c	B/C	3-5H	X				
b1	1	c	B	3-5H	Do.107				

Catalogue No	East (OSGBE)	North (OSGBN)	British Museum Accession No	Site Code	Site ID	Object Type	Breadth (mm)	Width (mm)	Length (mm)	Weight (g)
216	634141	141789	1980 0201 05	LB	LB77.04	hilt fragment	2.5	11.0	197.0	21.6
217	634148	141784	1981 0702 31	LB	LB79.09	hilt fragment, ?sword	5.5	24.5	75.0	40.3
218	634146	141790	1981 0702 30	LB	LB79.32	hilt fragment, ?sword	6.5	27.5	91.5	59.9
219	634169	141795	1981 0702 27	LB	LB79.39	hilt fragment	5.0	18.0	148.0	35.9
220	634169	141795	1982 0603 18	LB	LB80.23	hilt fragment	4.0	18.0	92.0	24.3
221	634154	141833	1982 0603 17	LB	LB80.38	hilt fragment	4.5	20.0	108.5	36.4
222	634170	141798	1983 0501 21	LB	LB81.01	hilt fragment	4.5	20.0	100.0	32.8
223	634169	141799	1983 0501 23	LB	LB81.42	hilt fragment	7.0	28.5	29.0	26.0
224	634169	141799	1983 0501 22	LB	LB81.43	hilt fragment	6.5	22.5	29.0	13.3
225	634170	141798	1984 0701 28	LB	LB82.07	hilt fragment	5.0	21.0	102.0	41.1
226	634169	141799	1984 0701 17	LB	LB82.11	hilt fragment, ?sword	6.0	26.0	85.0	46.2
227	634168	141804	1984 0701 27	LB	LB82.13	hilt fragment	5.0	18.0	160.0	45.7
228	634169	141804	1984 0701 22	LB	LB82.29	hilt fragment	4.0	23.0	129.5	41.0
229	634170	141805	1984 0701 25	LB	LB82.20	hilt fragment	4.0	13.0	135.0	17.2
230			1984 0701 24	LB	LB82.30	hilt fragment	3.0	13.0	148.0	25.3
231			1984 0701 23	LB	LB82.31	hilt fragment	4.5	26.7	168.5	57.9
232	634182	141781	1984 0701 54	LB	LB82.54	hilt fragment	3.0	17.5	134.0	22.5
233	634182	141781	1984 0701 56	LB	LB82.56	hilt fragment	5.0	24.0	83.0	37.7
234			1985 0801 06	LB	LB83.07	hilt fragment	4.0	18.5	132.0	28.0
235			1985 0801 08	LB	LB83.08	hilt fragment	4.0	22.0	89.0	18.5
236			1984 0701 30	LB	LB82.35	blade fragment	5.5	22.0	137.5	59.0
237			1977 0402 62	LB	X	blade fragment	6.0	21.5	164.5	89.7
238			1977 0402 63	LB	X	blade fragment	5.0	16.5	160.0	63.8
239			1977 0402 67	LB	X	blade fragment	4.0	16.5	115.5	35.0
240			1977 0402 74	LB	X	blade fragment	3.0	12.0	142.5	17.6
241			1977 0402 75	LB	X	blade fragment	3.0	10.5	100.0	12.5
242			1977 0402 76	LB	X	blade fragment	4.5	17.0	135.0	39.2
243			1977 0402 77	LB	X	blade fragment	2.5	13.0	60.5	6.5
244			1977 0402 78	LB	X	blade fragment	3.0	15.5	120.5	19.6
245			1977 0402 79	LB	X	blade fragment	3.5	15.0	141.0	30.4
246			1977 0402 80	LB	X	blade fragment	5.0	16.5	178.0	54.6
247			1977 0402 81	LB	X	blade fragment	3.5	13.5	120.5	24.2
248			1977 0402 82	LB	X	blade fragment	4.0	13.0	151.0	34.9
249			1977 0402 83	LB	X	blade fragment	4.0	13.5	135.0	32.1
250			1977 0402 84	LB	X	blade fragment	5.0	18.5	133.5	54.3
251			1977 0402 85	LB	X	blade fragment	6.0	16.5	98.5	49.6
252			1977 0402 86	LB	X	blade fragment	4.0	16.5	96.0	36.1
253			1977 0402 87	LB	X	blade fragment	4.0	14.5	95.0	26.2
254			1977 0402 88	LB	X	blade fragment	4.0	12.5	152.0	28.7
255			1977 0402 92b	LB	X	blade frag (in axe)	X	X	74.0	X
256			1980 0201 07	LB	LB77.02	blade fragment	4.0	13.5	202.0	40.1
257	634107	141764	1980 0201 09	LB	LB77.05	blade fragment	4.0	13.5	111.0	31.0
258			1980 0201 08	LB	LB77.06	blade fragment	4.0	14.5	78.0	20.4

Bending & Twisting	Break Condition	Feature Retention	Cutting Edge Profile	Completeness	Analysis No	206/204 ratio (Mean)	207/206 ratio (Mean)	208/206 ratio (Mean)	Previous publication of analysis and other notes
b1,t1	3	d*	B	3-5H	Do.172				
o	3	c	C	5H	Do.005				
b1	3	c/d*	C	5H	Do.017				
o	3	c	B	3-5H	Do.025				
o	3	d	B/C	3-5H	X				
b1	3	d	C	3-5H	X				
o	3	d	C	3-5H	X				
o	3	c	X	5H	X				
o	3	c	X	5H	X				
o,c	1	d	C	4-5?H	X				
o	2	c	B	5H	X				
o	3	d*	C	3-5?H	X				
b1,t1	3	d*	C	3-5H	X				
b1	?	d*	C	?1H	X				
b1	3	d	B/C	3-5?H	X				
o	3	d	B/C	3-5H	X				
b1	3	d	B/C	2-5H	X				
o	3	c*	B	4-5H	X				
b1	3	d	B	3-5?H	X				
o	2	d	B/C	4-5H	X				
o	3	b	A/B	3-5T	X				
b1	3	c/d	B	3-5	Do.112				
b1	3	d	C	3-5	Do.111				
o,s	3	d	C	4-5	Do.108				
b1	3	d	C	3-5T	Do.044				
o	3	d	B/C	4-5T	Do.043				
b2	3	d*	C	4-5T	Do.042				
b1	3	d*	B/C	5T	Do.041				
o	3	c	B	2-5T	Do.040				
b1	3	c	A/B	3-5T	Do.039				
b1	3	d	C	3-5T	Do.038				
b1	3	d	B/C	3-5T	Do.037				
b1,t1	3	d	C	3-5	Do.036				
b1	3&1	d	B/C	3-5	Do.035				
b1	3	c	A/B	4-5	Do.034				
b1	3	c	B/C	4-5	Do.033				
b1	3	d	C	4-5	Do.032				
b1	3	d	B/C	4-5	Do.031	18.1780	0.86150	2.11270	
o	3	d*	C	3-5T	Do.030				
b1	3	d*	B/C	?	Do.180				
b1	3	d*	C	3-5	Do.173				
o	3	d	C	5	Do.174				
t1	3	d	C	5	Do.171				

Catalogue No	East (OSGBE)	North (OSGBN)	British Museum Accession No	Site Code	Site ID	Object Type	Breadth (mm)	Width (mm)	Length (mm)	Weight (g)
259			1980 0201 29	LB	LB78.09	blade fragment	5.0	16.5	48.5	19.6
260	634134	141779	1980 0201 30	LB	LB78.18	blade fragment	5.5	13.0	218.0	49.1
261	634135	141780	1980 0201 28	LB	LB78.19	blade fragment	3.0	16.0	90.0	17.8
262	634133	141784	1981 0702 32	LB	LB79.01	blade fragment	4.5	20.0	82.0	30.4
263	634132	141785	1981 0702 39	LB	LB79.03	blade fragment	2.0	10.0	79.5	6.1
264	634133	141783	1981 0702 55	LB	LB79.04	blade fragment	2.5	11.0	56.0	4.7
265	634133	141785	1981 0702 54	LB	LB79.07	blade fragment	3.5	13.0	66.5	13.6
266	634133	141784	1981 0702 36	LB	LB79.08	blade fragment	3.0	11.0	109.0	15.1
267	634134	141782	1981 0702 40	LB	LB79.10	blade fragment	4.5	11.5	73.5	10.4
268	634134	141782	1981 0702 51	LB	LB79.13	blade fragment	5.5	20.5	75.0	39.7
269	634134	141782	1981 0702 35	LB	LB79.14	blade fragment	5.5	18.0	110.0	31.5
270	634133	141785	1981 0702 48	LB	LB79.15	blade fragment	4.0	11.0	81.0	11.7
271	634133	141785	1981 0702 42	LB	LB79.17	blade fragment	3.5	12.5	139.0	30.0
272	634132	141786	1981 0702 47	LB	LB79.18	blade fragment	4.0	15.0	84.5	22.5
273	634133	141787	1981 0702 59	LB	LB79.20	blade fragment	4.0	14.5	44.5	13.3
274	634132	141790	1981 0702 44	LB	LB79.21	blade fragment	6.5	20.0	119.0	80.0
275	634132	141790	1981 0702 60	LB	LB79.24	blade fragment	5.5	21.5	29.0	16.7
276	634137	141785	1981 0702 45	LB	LB79.25	blade fragment	6.0	16.0	95.0	41.6
277	634139	141780	1981 0702 37	LB	LB79.40	blade fragment	3.5	10.0	80.0	10.9
278	634137	141787	1981 0702 46	LB	LB79.43	blade fragment	4.5	17.0	92.5	34.1
279	634137	141787	1981 0702 53	LB	LB79.51	blade fragment	5.0	16.5	81.5	29.5
280	634138	141785	1981 0702 58	LB	LB79.52	blade fragment	6.0	18.0	50.0	25.4
281	634139	141783	1981 0702 38	LB	LB79.54	blade fragment	2.5	11.0	76.0	4.9
282	634139	141782	1981 0702 41	LB	LB79.56	blade fragment	5.0	15.5	59.5	12.1
283	634139	141783	1981 0702 57	LB	LB79.57	blade fragment	3.0	13.0	53.5	10.5
284	634139	141783	1981 0702 56	LB	LB79.61	blade fragment	4.5	16.0	53.5	16.6
285	634137	141787	1982 0603 25	LB	LB80.01	blade fragment	3.5	13.7	66.5	8.1
286	634138	141785	1982 0603 37	LB	LB80.03	blade fragment	3.0	14.0	59.0	7.7
287	634140	141781	1982 0603 26	LB	LB80.05	blade fragment	2.0	7.5	54.0	2.2
288	634140	141781	1982 0603 35	LB	LB80.06	blade figment	4.5	15.0	85.0	21.6
289	634138	141787	1982 0603 29	LB	LB80.11	blade fragment	4.0	17.0	167.0	54.8
290	634138	141787	1982 0603 20	LB	LB80.12	blade fragment	4.0	19.0	142.0	39.0
291	634139	141788	1982 0603 38	LB	LB80.04	blade fragment	2.0	7.0	59.0	3.2
292	634169	141720	1982 0603 21	LB	LB80.20	blade fragment	2.5	14.0	94.0	14.9
293	634141	141788	1982 0603 36	LB	LB80.24	blade fragment	5.0	20.5	64.0	25.6
294	634145	141781	1982 0603 39	LB	LB80.25	blade fragment	2.5	13.0	43.5	6.4
295	634146	141782	1982 0603 24	LB	LB80.29	blade fragment	4.0	11.5	75.5	11.0
296	634144	141790	1982 0603 28	LB	LB80.30	blade fragment	2.0	11.0	27.5	1.8
297	634144	141788	1982 0603 31	LB	LB80.31	blade fragment	4.0	15.5	122.0	32.8
298	634145	141790	1982 0603 30	LB	LB80.34	blade fragment	4.0	17.0	143.5	37.0
299	634145	141790	1982 0603 22	LB	LB80.35	blade fragment	3.5	13.0	83.0	11.4
300	634145	141789	1982 0603 32	LB	LB80.36	blade fragment	4.0	17.0	115.5	37.7
301	634148	141785	1982 0603 33	LB	LB80.66	blade fragment	3.5	16.0	88.5	18.0

Bending & Twisting	Break Condition	Feature Retention	Cutting Edge Profile	Completeness	Analysis No	206/204 ratio (Mean)	207/206 ratio (Mean)	208/206 ratio (Mean)	Previous publication of analysis and other notes
o	3	d	B	5	Do.165				
b1	3	d	C	3-4T	Do.149				
b1	3	d	B	4-5T	Do.148				
o	3	b*	A/B	5	Do.012				
b1,t1	3	d*	B	3-5	Do.066				
o	3	d*	B	5	Do.080				
t1	3	d	C	4-5	Do.016				
b1	3	d*	B/C	3-5T	Do.073				
b1	3	d*	C	4-5T	Do.011				
o	2	d	A/B	5	Do.006				
b1	3	b	B	4-5T	X				
b2	3	d*	C	3-5	Do.076				
b1	3	d*	B/C	3-5	Do.023				
b1	3	d*	B/C	4-5	Do.014				
b1	3	d	B/C	5	Do.013				
o	3	d	B/C	4-5	Do.007				
b1	3	b/c	A/B	5	Do.065				
b1	3	c	B/C	4-5	Do.010				
o	1	d	C	4-5T	Do.074				
b1	3	d	C	4-5	Do.018				
o	3	b/c	B	4-5?T	Do.015				
o	3	c*	B	5	Do.020				
b1	3	d*	B	3-5T	Do.021				
b1	3	d	C	4-5T	Do.069				
o	3	d	A/B	5	Do.067				
b1	3	d	B	5	Do.019				
o	3	d	B	3-5T	X				
o	3	c	B	4-5	X				
b1	3	d	B/C	4-5T	X				
o	3	d	C	3-5	X				
o	3	d*	B/C	3-5	X				
o	2	a	A	3-5T	X				
o	3	d*	C	3-5	X				
o	3	c	B/C	3-5T	X				
o	2&3	b	A	4-5	X				
o	3	d	B/C	4-5	X				
b1	3	c	B	3-5T	X				
o	2	c	A	5T	X				
o	3	c*	B/C	3-5	X				
b1	3&1	c	B	3-5	X				
o	2	b	A	3-5T	X				
b1	3	c	A/B	3-5	X				
t1	3	d*	C	3-5	X				

Catalogue No	East (OSGBE)	North (OSGBN)	British Museum Accession No	Site Code	Site ID	Object Type	Breadth (mm)	Width (mm)	Length (mm)	Weight (g)
302	634148	141784	1982 0603 23	LB	LB80.68	blade fragment	3.0	10.5	86.0	12.1
303	634145	141791	1982 0603 27	LB	LB80.70	blade fragment	4.0	15.5	53.0	11.2
304	634146	141790	1983 0501 24	LB	LB81.02	blade fragment	3.5	12.5	71.0	9.9
305	634147	141790	1983 0501 25	LB	LB81.03	blade fragment	2.0	8.5	58.5	3.8
306	634147	141790	1983 0501 34	LB	LB81.04	blade fragment	3.5	14.5	46.5	9.3
307	634147	141792	1983 0501 33	LB	LB81.05	blade fragment	3.0	15.5	35.5	9.2
308	634148	141790	1983 0501 32	LB	LB81.06	blade fragment	3.5	12.5	70.5	13.8
309	634149	141793	1983 0501 28	LB	LB81.08	blade fragment	4.0	14.0	143.5	42.4
310	634136	141825	1983 0501 26	LB	LB81.12	blade fragment	5.0	19.5	213.0	91.7
311	634154	141786	1983 0501 30	LB	LB81.16	blade fragment	4.5	17.5	61.5	22.3
312	634155	141791	1983 0501 31	LB	LB81.20	blade fragment	4.0	18.0	50.0	15.3
313	634157	141793	1983 0501 36	LB	LB81.22	blade fragment	5.5	20.0	60.0	29.8
314	634159	141793	1983 0501 27	LB	LB81.24	blade fragment	5.0	18.0	156.5	64.8
315	634166	141793	1983 0501 35	LB	LB81.27	blade fragment	4.0	22.0	37.5	16.1
316	634167	141802	1983 0501 29	LB	LB80.43	blade fragment	4.0	17.0	91.0	27.4
317	634171	141792	1983 0501 01	LB	LB79.50	blade fragment	4.5	13.5	146.0	31.9
318	634163	141811	1984 0701 37	LB	LB82.02	blade fragment	5.0	17.0	144.0	58.4
319	634163	141811	1984 0701 26	LB	LB82.03	blade fragment	5.0	17.0	160.0	46.7
320	634169	141799	1984 0701 34	LB	LB82.14	blade fragment	3.5	14.0	161.0	31.4
321	634169	141799	1984 0701 39	LB	LB82.15	blade fragment	3.0	14.5	90.0	25.5
322	634169	141801	1984 0701 36	LB	LB82.25	blade fragment	4.5	17.0	168.5	67.4
323	634170	141800	1984 0701 35	LB	LB82.26	blade fragment	3.0	19.0	91.0	15.6
324	634170	141799	1984 0701 29	LB	LB82.28	blade fragment	4.0	16.0	269.0	79.8
325	634170	141805	1984 0701 31	LB	LB82.36	blade fragment	4.5	21.0	84.0	35.4
326	634170	141805	1984 0701 32	LB	LB82.37	blade fragment	5.0	20.0	142.0	53.0
327			1984 0701 40	LB	LB82.45	blade fragment	2.0	9.0	73.0	5.2
328			1984 0701 55	LB	LB82.55	blade fragment	5.0	17.0	111.0	35.6
329			1984 0701 57	LB	LB82.57	blade fragment	4.5	20.0	68.0	26.9
330			1984 0701 58	LB	LB82.58	blade fragment	4.7	19.0	81.5	36.4
331	634166	141816	1985 0801 14	LB	LB83.04	blade fragment	2.5	10.5	49.0	6.3
332	634167	141817	1985 0801 16	LB	LB83.06	blade fragment	3.0	18.0	49.0	10.3
333	634167	141817	1985 0801 10	LB	LB83.10	blade fragment	4.5	13.0	104.0	27.7
334	634174	141800	1985 0801 12	LB	LB83.11	blade fragment	4.0	12.5	124.0	63.9
335	634172	141804	1985 0801 09	LB	LB83.12	blade fragment	6.0	17.5	196.0	84.8
336	634171	141808	1985 0801 11	LB	LB83.14	blade fragment	5.0	14.0	102.0	24.2
337	634173	141803	1985 0801 13	LB	LB83.16	blade fragment	4.0	13.5	66.0	19.2
338	634170	141813	1985 0801 17	LB	LB83.18	blade fragment	4.0	20.0	69.0	27.3
339	634169	141814	1985 0801 18	LB	LB83.19	blade fragment	3.0	8.0	84.0	7.9
340	634154	141852	1985 0801 19	LB	LB83.20	blade fragment	6.5	18.0	165.0	53.8
341	634182	141840	1985 0801 20	LB	LB83.21	blade fragment	2.5	13.5	84.0	11.5
342			1991 0302 04	LB	LB89.03	blade fragment	4.5	19.0	132.0	59.4
343			1991 0302 05	LB	LB89.04	blade fragment	2.0	9.5	88.0	7.1
344			1992 0301 02	LB	LB90.01	blade fragment	4.0	14.0	46.0	8.8

Bending & Twisting	Break Condition	Feature Retention	Cutting Edge Profile	Completeness	Analysis No	206/204 ratio (Mean)	207/206 ratio (Mean)	208/206 ratio (Mean)	Previous publication of analysis and other notes
o	3	d	C	3-5T	X				
b1	2	c	A/B	4-5T	X				
o	3	d	B	4-5T	X				
b1	3	d	B	4-5T	X				
o	3	c	B/C	5	X				
o	3	d	A/B	5	X				
b1	3	d*	C	4-5	X				
b1	3	d	C	4-5	X				
b1	3	d	C	3-5	X				
b1	3	c	A/B	4-5	X				
b1	2	b	A	5	X				
b1,t1	2	c	C	5	X				
o	3	d*	C	4-5	X				
o	3	d	B	5	X				
b1,c	3	d	B/C	5	X				
b1	3	d	C	3-5	X				
o	3	d	B/C	4-5	X				
b2	3	d*	C	3-5	X				
b1	3	d*	A/B	3-5	X				
b1	3	d	C	4-5	X				
b2,t1	3	c*	C	3-5	X				
o	3	d	B	4-5	X				
b1	2	d	C	3-4T	X				
o	3	b	A	3-5T	X				
o	3	b	A/B	3-5T	X				
o	3	d	B	4-5	X				
o	3	c	B	4-5	X				
b1	3	d*	C	4-5	X				
o	3	d	B	5	X				
b1	3	d	B/C	5	X				
o	3	c	B	5	X				
b2	3	c	A/B	4-5T	X				
b3,c	X	d	B/C	3-5T	X				
b2	3	c	B/C	3-5T	X				
b2	3	d	C	4-5T	X				
b2	3	a/b	B	5	X				
o	3	d	B	5	X				
o	3	c	B	4-5	X				
b1	2?	d*	C	3-5	X				
o	3	d	B	4-5	X				
b1	2/3	c	B	5	X				
o	3	d*	A/B	5	X				
b2	3	d*	C	5T	X				

Catalogue No	East (OSGBE)	North (OSGBN)	British Museum Accession No	Site Code	Site ID	Object Type	Breadth (mm)	Width (mm)	Length (mm)	Weight (g)
345			1992 0301 03	LB	LB90.02	blade fragment	3.0	15.5	59.0	16.2
346			1992 0301 04	LB	LB90.04	blade fragment	3.0	11.5	50.0	6.5
347	634186	141769	1985 0801 15	LB	LB83.05	?blade fragment	3.5	17.0	60.0	14.1
348			1977 0402 93	LB	X	?blade fragment	5.5	25.0	26.5	9.5
349	634144	141790	1982 0603 42	LB	LB80.33	spearhead	21.5	31.0	152.0	114.5
350			1977 0402 95	LB	X	spearhead	22.0	28.5	162.5	87.5
351			1977 0402 94	LB	X	spearhead	21.0	39.5	70.0	84.6
352	634141	141775	1981 0702 62	LB	LB79.45	spearhead	19.5	35.5	67.0	48.2
353	634216	141821	1985 0801 23	LB	LB83.22	spearhead	5.0	20.0	41.0	9.7
354			1977 0402 90	LB	X	ferrule	13.0	18.5	97.0	41.0
355	634170	141798	1984 0701 44	LB	LB82.16	ferrule	X	24.5	31.0	37.9
356	634153	141791	1983 0501 39	LB	LB81.17	casting jet	9.5	17.0	29.5	15.8
357	634174	141800	1985 0801 21	LB	LB83.17	casting jet/lump	13.5	20.5	24.0	19.1
358	634156	141794	1983 0501 40	LB	LB81.23	lump	16.0	X	46.5	106.7
359			1981 0702 61	LB	LB79.49	lump	6.5	19.0	33.0	18.7
360	634169	141795	1983 0501 37	LB	LB81.41	unidentified	8.0	24.5	49.0	47.5
361			1977 0402 92c	LB	X	unidentified frags in socket of No 119	X	X	X	X
362	634173	141800	1984 0701 45	LB	LB82.43	rod – modern	X	14.0	120.0	130.4
363	634210	141852	1985 0801 22	LB	LB83.23	lump – modern	15.0	18.0	18.0	27.5
S 01			2005 0503 04	SB	0409050001	palstave	33.5	40.5	177.0	467.2
S 02			2005 0503 07	SB	0409120005	palstave	27.0	40.0	102.0	251.2
S 03	275964	36144	1981 0305 01	MS	MS78.01	palstave	23.0	31.0	144.0	255.7
S 04	275897	36261	1981 0305 02	MS	MS78.03	palstave	21.5	30.0	126.5	218.9
S 05			2005 0503 05	SB	0409050002	palstave	27.5	36.5	180.0	356.0
S 06			2005 0503 06	SB	0409040001	palstave-adze	18.0	16.5	132.5	53.7
S 07			2005 0503 03	SB	0409050003	*strumento con immanicatura a cannone*	17.0	46.0	121.5	58.8
S 08			2005 0503 01	SB	0409120004	gold bracelet	6.0	56.5	66.5	87.3
S 09			2005 0503 02	SB	outlier	gold torc fragment	X	8.5	53.5 (diam.)	24.1
S 10			Whereabouts unknown	SB	site B?	cauldron handle?	X	X	X	X
S 11			2005 0503 17	SB	0409120003	sword	5.0	23.5	492.0	173.8
S 12			2005 0503 14	SB	0409120010	sword hilt fragment	6.0	26.5	119.0	50.0
S 13			2005 0503 13	SA	site A no 36	sword blade fragment	6.5	25.0	230.0	153.8
S 14			2005 0503 16	SB	0409120002	?sword blade fragment	3.5	19.5	290.0	60.9
S 15	276095	36245	1981 1103 01	MS	MS77.01	sword	7.0	40.5	643.0	476.9
S 16	276084	36180	1981 1103 02	MS	MS77.02	?sword blade fragment	4.0	19.4	358.0	109.6
S 17	276039	36059	1981 1103 03	MS	MS77.03	?sword blade fragment	8.0	21.5	289.0	123.1
S 18	276094	36245	1983 1004 01	MS	MS82.01	sword hilt fragment	5.0	42	208.0	138
S 19			2005 0503 08	SB	0409120007	?sword hilt fragment	6.5	27.5	63.0	35.1
S 20			2005 0503 15	SB	0409120001	?sword blade fragment	4.5	19.5	170.0	56.7
S 21			2005 0503 09	SB	0409040002	hilt fragment	5.5	26.0	73.0	28.3
S 22	276089	36134	1981 0305 04	MS	MS79.01	blade fragment	3.5	13.0	420.0	74.7

Bending & Twisting	Break Condition	Feature Retention	Cutting Edge Profile	Completeness	Analysis No	206/204 ratio (Mean)	207/206 ratio (Mean)	208/206 ratio (Mean)	Previous publication of analysis and other notes
b1	3	d	B	5	X				
b1	3	b	A/B	5	X				
b1	3	d*	C	5	X				
o	X	d	X	X	Do.027				
o,c	X	c*	A/B	1	X				
b1	1	b	A	2	Do.176	18.1800	0.86096	2.11056	
o,c	2/3	c	A/B	4-5	Do.028				
o	3	c/d	B/C	4-5	Do.077				
o	3	d	C	5	Do.230				
b1	3	c	X	?3-5	Do.179				
o,c	2	b	X	5	Do.222				
o,c	X	c	X	1	Do.216				
X	3	c	X	?1	Do.229				
o,s,c	X	?	X	1	Do.217				
o	?	d?	X	?	Do.075				
t1	X	X	X	?	Do.215				
X	X	X	X	X	X				
b1	1/2	X	X	?	Do.223				Analysis identified as modern brass
X	X	a	X	1	X				
o	X	b	B	1	MS11				
o	2/3	a/b	A	4	MS21				
o	3	b	B	2		18.2290	0.86089	2.11389	Rohl & Needham 1998, no 194
o	3	a/b	B	2		18.2270	0.86124	2.11403	Rohl & Needham 1998, no 195
o,c	2L	b*	C	2	MS13				
b1	X	d	A	2	MS12				
b1	2/3	b	X	3	MS36				
b1?	X	b	X	1					
b2	2	a	X	5					
X	X	X	X	X					Found on Salcombe Cannon site 2001; object missing, never deposited at BM
b1	X	b	A	1-2	MS16				
o	3	c*	B	5	MS14				
b1	3	a	A	4	MS20				
b1	2	b	A/B	3-4	MS23				
o	X	a	A	1		18.0150	0.86983	2.12582	Rohl & Needham 1998, no 191
b1	X	b	A/B	3-4		18.1200	0.86582	2.12125	Rohl & Needham 1998, no 192
b2	X	c	B	3-4		18.1020	0.86542	2.11931	Rohl & Needham 1998, no 193
b1	2/3	b	A	4		18.4470	0.84802	2.08390	Rohl & Needham 1998, no 197
o	3	c	B	5	MS18				
b1	2	b	B	3-5	MS19				
X	3	d	B/C	5	MS17				
b1	X	d	C	1-2		18.0400	0.86871	2.12409	Rohl & Needham 1998, no 196

Catalogue No	East (OSGBE)	North (OSGBN)	British Museum Accession No	Site Code	Site ID	Object Type	Breadth (mm)	Width (mm)	Length (mm)	Weight (g)
S 23	275957	36209	1981 0305 03	MS	MS78.02	blade fragment	4.5	17.5	223.0	55.1
S 24			2005 0503 10	SB	0409120011	blade fragment (?hilt)	4.0	18.0	141.5	29.3
S 25			2005 0503 12	SB	0409050004	blade fragment (?hilt)	3.5	15.5	185.0	23.5
S 26			2005 0503 11	SB	0409050005	blade fragment	2.5	9.0	158.0	13.5
S 27			2005 0503 18	SB	0409120006	rectangular block/weight	11.5	20.5	28.5	44.7
S 28			2005 0503 19	SB	0409120009	tin lump	X	14.0	15.5	5.8
S 29			2005 0503 21	SB	0409120012	iron awl with bone handle	4.5	5.5	49.5	X
S 30			2005 0503 20	SB	0409120008	ring - modern	3.5	1.5	20.5 (diam.)	2.3

Bending & Twisting	Break Condition	Feature Retention	Cutting Edge Profile	Completeness	Analysis No	206/204 ratio (Mean)	207/206 ratio (Mean)	208/206 ratio (Mean)	Previous publication of analysis and other notes
o	1	d	B	3-4					
o	3	d*	B	4-5	MS22				
b1	3	d	B	3-5	MS24				
b1	2	d	C	3-5	MS26				
o	X	c?	X	1	MS15				
X	X	X	X	X	MS25				
c	X	X	X	X					
X	X	X	X	X					

Appendix 2　Results of metal analyses carried out on the Langdon Bay material

No.	Do	Type	British Museum Accession No	Fe	Co	Ni	Cu	Zn	As	Sb	Sn	Ag	Bi	Pb	Au	S
1	118	Median-winged axe	P1977.04-02.1	0.04	0.04	0.17	88.90	0.01	0.19	0.05	10.25	0.10		0.26	0.00	
2	119	Median-winged axe	P1977.04-02.2	0.06	0.08	0.28	86.13	0.01	0.08	0.08	12.48	0.07		0.46	0.03	
3	120	Median-winged axe	P1977.04-02.3	0.04	0.04	0.07	87.09	0.03	0.09	0.01	11.94	0.09		0.19	0.00	
4	121	Median-winged axe	P1977.04-02.4	0.08	0.02	0.21	89.47	0.01	0.22	0.04	9.54	0.05		0.21	0.01	
5	122	Median-winged axe	P1977.04-02.5	0.05	0.03	0.16	88.96	0.00	0.29	0.01	9.86	0.07		0.27	0.00	
6	123	Median-winged axe	P1977.04-02.6	0.05	0.03	0.06	85.64	0.02	0.29	0.18	12.93	0.19	0.08	0.10	0.03	0.16
7	124	Median-winged axe	P1977.04-02.7	0.05	0.06	0.15	87.67	0.01	0.32	0.10	10.42	0.09	0.08	0.30	0.00	0.61
8	125	Median-winged axe	P1977.04-02.8	0.01	0.04	0.15	87.40	0.00	0.24	0.05	10.69	0.04	0.04	0.58	0.00	0.50
9	126	Median-winged axe	P1977.04-02.9	0.03	0.03	0.18	87.79	0.04	0.15	0.07	10.75	0.06	0.06	0.22	0.06	0.36
10	127	Median-winged axe	P1977.04-02.10	0.01	0.02	0.14	87.95	0.03	0.14	0.03	10.39	0.05	0.01	0.09	0.01	0.89
11	128	Median-winged axe	P1977.04-02.11	0.06	0.05	0.16	88.16	0.05	0.20	0.08	10.33	0.12	0.00	0.20	0.00	0.42
12	129	Median-winged axe	P1977.04-02.12	0.08	0.06	0.19	87.93	0.01	0.28	0.07	10.47	0.09	0.05	0.07	0.01	0.42
13	130	Median-winged axe	P1977.04-02.13	0.23	0.02	0.15	89.21	0.00	0.09	0.22	9.19	0.19	0.03	0.09	0.00	0.25
14	131	Median-winged axe	P1977.04-02.14	0.16	0.02	0.14	87.43	0.00	0.27	0.05	11.00	0.02	0.05	0.15	0.01	0.30
15	132	Median-winged axe	P1977.04-02.15	0.06	0.07	0.12	85.85	0.00	0.17	0.06	12.35	0.07	0.01	0.20	0.08	0.64
16	133	Median-winged axe	P1977.04-02.16	0.03	0.05	0.21	85.91	0.01	0.20	0.04	12.69	0.06	0.04	0.14	0.04	0.33
17	134	Median-winged axe	P1977.04-02.17	0.04	0.04	0.16	89.00	0.00	0.13	0.05	9.57	0.00	0.05	0.05	0.03	0.59
18	135	Median-winged axe	P1977.04-02.18	0.08	0.04	0.15	88.44	0.00	0.23	0.05	10.32	0.04	0.01	0.18	0.00	0.22
19	136	Median-winged axe	P1977.04-02.19	0.37	0.04	0.09	88.49	0.00	0.11	0.05	10.15	0.06	0.06	0.15	0.00	0.16
20	137	Median-winged axe	P1977.04-02.20	0.02	0.02	0.19	88.36	0.00	0.14	0.09	10.08	0.00	0.03	0.16	0.01	0.40
21	138	Median-winged axe	P1977.04-02.21	0.03	0.03	0.13	86.84	0.09	0.20	0.06	11.85	0.08	0.02	0.36	0.00	0.08
22	139	Median-winged axe	P1977.04-02.22	0.01	0.01	0.17	87.16	0.01	0.18	0.07	11.92	0.06	0.01	0.18	0.00	0.03
23	177	Median-winged axe	P1977.04-02.23	0.04	0.05	0.15	88.83	0.06	0.09	0.05	9.99	0.05	0.04	0.15	0.06	0.25
24	140	Median-winged axe	P1977.04-02.24	0.04	0.02	0.17	88.36	0.00	0.07	0.04	10.78	0.05	0.05	0.10	0.00	0.08
25	141	Median-winged axe	P1977.04-02.25	0.08	0.02	0.07	89.98	0.01	0.11	0.03	8.21	0.06	0.00	0.10	0.01	1.09
26	142	Median-winged axe	P1977.04-02.26	0.06	0.04	0.16	88.19	0.03	0.26	0.03	10.81	0.06	0.01	0.11	0.01	0.06
27	143	Median-winged axe	P1977.04-02.27	0.05	0.03	0.16	89.06	0.00	0.15	0.03	9.45	0.05	0.03	0.21	0.03	0.49
28	170	Median-winged axe	P1980.02-01.1	0.03	0.01	0.17	89.79	0.01	0.28	0.04	9.00	0.02	0.05	0.16	0.03	0.17
29	167	Median-winged axe	P1980.02-01.2	0.13	0.06	0.45	88.67	0.00	0.04	0.03	10.11	0.03	0.03	0.20	0.00	0.04
30	169	Median-winged axe	P1980.02-01.3	0.04	0.04	0.14	85.47	0.03	0.23	0.04	12.90	0.08	0.04	0.23	0.03	0.09
31	161	Median-winged axe	P1980.02-01.11	0.02	0.04	0.12	89.74	0.02	0.06	0.08	8.95	0.10	0.02	0.26	0.00	0.37
32	157	Median-winged axe	P1980.02-01.12	0.24	0.06	0.13	87.91	0.00	0.25	0.11	10.27	0.12	0.05	0.66	0.00	0.02
33	158	Median-winged axe	P1980.02-01.13	0.02	0.02	0.11	88.09	0.05	0.23	0.05	10.23	0.04	0.00	0.10	0.03	0.60
34	159	Median-winged axe	P1980.02-01.14	0.04	0.04	0.15	88.69	0.00	0.13	0.05	10.38	0.06	0.06	0.15	0.01	0.09
35	50	Median-winged axe	P1981.07-02.5	0.12	0.07	0.20	87.53	0.01	0.45	0.15	10.72	0.09	0.05	0.31	0.00	0.07
36	47	Median-winged axe	P1981.07-02.3	0.05	0.02	0.23	88.68	0.03	0.13	0.04	9.76	0.08	0.03	0.31	0.00	0.25
37	46	Median-winged axe	P1981.07-02.1	0.07	0.02	0.21	88.28	0.00	0.20	0.06	10.04	0.09	0.06	0.25	0.07	0.35
38	45	Median-winged axe	P1981.07-02.2	0.01	0.04	0.17	88.49	0.00	0.16	0.08	9.98	0.03	0.05	0.23	0.05	0.41
39	52	Median-winged axe	P1981.07-02.6	0.04	0.04	0.13	87.86	0.00	0.19	0.07	10.89	0.07	0.00	0.29	0.00	0.20

No.	Do	Type	British Museum Accession No	Fe	Co	Ni	Cu	Zn	As	Sb	Sn	Ag	Bi	Pb	Au	S
40	48	Median-winged axe	P1981.07-02.4	0.11	0.02	0.13	88.02	0.01	0.16	0.02	10.07	0.05	0.05	0.51	0.00	0.64
46	145	Median-winged axe frag.	P1977.04-02.29	0.06	0.04	0.16	87.43	0.00	0.19	0.07	10.76	0.08	0.04	0.25	0.00	0.66
47	55	Median-winged axe frag.	P1981.07-02.7	0.18	0.02	0.16	88.66	0.03	0.14	0.04	9.37	0.07	0.03	0.16	0.01	0.87
51	146	Median-winged axe frag.	P1977.04-02.28	0.03	0.02	0.27	87.39	0.05	0.32	0.04	11.02	0.05	0.02	0.19	0.00	0.24
52	53	Median-winged axe frag.	P1981.07-02.08	0.04	0.02	0.20	88.42	0.04	0.01	0.01	10.57	0.09	0.08	0.12	0.01	0.07
53	70	Median-winged axe frag.	P1981.07-02.09	0.22	0.01	0.32	86.42	0.01	0.14	0.00	12.46	0.04	0.00	0.03	0.00	0.09
57	144	Median-winged axe frag.	P1977.04-02.30	0.08	0.02	0.17	86.94	0.00	0.13	0.02	11.59	0.05	0.01	0.16	0.00	0.28
58	59	Median-winged axe frag.	P1981.07-02.10	0.05	0.04	0.18	86.68	0.00	0.16	0.03	12.37	0.07	0.03	0.10	0.00	0.02
62	78	Axe blade fragment	P1981.07-02.11	0.03	0.04	0.13	90.18	0.01	0.17	0.07	8.71	0.01	0.03	0.25	0.00	0.10
65	91	Axe blade fragment	P1977.04-02.32	0.01	0.02	0.24	88.23	0.00	0.17	0.07	10.69	0.03	0.04	0.10	0.05	0.15
67	90	Axe blade fragment	P1977.04-02.31	0.02	0.01	0.21	86.82	0.00	0.21	0.04	11.94	0.02	0.03	0.06	0.00	0.37
68	155	Palstave fragment	P1980.02-01.17	0.09	0.01	0.15	88.94	0.00	0.24	0.06	9.95	0.03	0.05	0.11	0.00	0.13
69	184	Palstave 1	P1977.04-02.42	0.02	0.03	0.26	86.09	0.01	0.26	0.02	12.52	0.03	0.05	0.12	0.00	0.34
70	81	Palstave 1	P1977.04-02.43	0.04	0.03	0.21	87.57	0.03	0.18	0.01	11.32	0.06	0.03	0.10	0.05	0.06
71	231	Palstave 1	P/LB89/5	0.03	0.03	0.14	88.84	0.00	0.22	0.04	9.85	0.08	0.01	0.15	0.01	0.32
73	82	Palstave 1	P1977.04-02.40	0.05	0.01	0.27	88.93	0.01	0.18	0.04	10.04	0.01	0.04	0.08	0.01	0.13
75	84	Palstave 1?	P1977.04-02.38	0.03	0.02	0.16	87.99	0.00	0.18	0.05	10.56	0.05	0.04	0.42	0.07	0.10
76	51	Palstave 1?	P1981.07-02.17	0.09	0.04	0.15	87.19	0.06	0.21	0.05	11.06	0.02	0.03	0.39	0.08	0.42
77	57	Palstave 1?	P1981.07-02.15	0.02	0.03	0.29	87.72	0.00	0.32	0.02	11.00	0.03	0.06	0.06	0.03	0.14
79	83	Palstave 1?	P1977.04-02.39	0.03	0.06	0.21	85.67	0.01	0.52	0.08	12.34	0.07	0.12	0.39	0.01	0.15
80	93	Palstave 2	P1977.04-02.55	0.02	0.03	0.21	87.83	0.00	0.11	0.01	10.80	0.04	0.04	0.11	0.04	0.46
82	233	Palstave 2	P1984-07-01.6	0.04	0.03	0.08	85.83	0.01	0.19	0.02	13.14	0.02	0.02	0.23	0.00	0.13
83	210	Palstave 2	P1983.05-01.6	0.20	0.02	0.17	84.06	0.01	0.22	0.03	14.50	0.08	0.04	0.38	0.08	0.06
84	99	Palstave 2?	P1977.04-02.49	0.05	0.02	0.64	87.21	0.02	0.32	0.14	10.57	0.04	0.02	0.09	0.03	0.46
85	115	Palstave 2?	P1977.04-02.59	0.02	0.01	0.19	88.31	0.05	0.02	0.01	10.55	0.01		0.12	0.00	
86	54	Palstave 2?	P1981.07-02.13	0.02	0.04	0.23	87.72	0.00	0.15	0.03	11.20	0.02	0.03	0.16	0.00	0.18
87	178	Palstave 3	P1977.04-02.41	0.01	0.02	0.16	88.38	0.00	0.14	0.04	9.75	0.05	0.04	0.09	0.03	1.00
88	168	Palstave 3	P1982.02-01.4	0.11	0.03	0.25	88.72	0.04	0.11	0.06	10.33	0.02	0.03	0.10	0.00	0.01
89	156	Palstave 3	P1980.02-01.16	0.02	0.03	0.17	87.09	0.00	0.12	0.05	11.87	0.05	0.01	0.09	0.08	0.03
90	160	Palstave 3	P1980.02-01.15	0.02	0.01	0.19	87.63	0.00	0.19	0.08	11.38	0.03	0.05	0.16	0.00	0.04
91	49	Palstave 3	P1981.07-02.16	0.03	0.02	0.18	88.70	0.03	0.11	0.04	9.83	0.06	0.06	0.39	0.05	0.28
93	87	Palstave fragment	P1977.04-02.35	0.03	0.01	0.16	88.33	0.01	0.10	0.00	10.93	0.03	0.03	0.10	0.02	0.02
94	92	Palstave	P1977.04-02.56	0.05	0.03	0.29	87.31	0.00	0.22	0.02	11.41	0.03	0.10	0.06	0.00	0.14
95	85	Palstave	P1977.04-02.37	0.01	0.01	0.10	78.27	0.00	0.12	0.00	10.86	0.01	0.01	0.00	0.00	10.12
96	202	Palstave	P1982.06-03.4	0.07	0.05	0.26	88.66	0.02	0.31	0.07	10.07	0.04	0.02	0.13	0.00	0.09
97	104	Palstave	P1977.04-02.44	0.01	0.03	0.16	86.74	0.00	0.19	0.09	11.14	0.06	0.00	0.24	0.00	0.48
98	103	Palstave	P1977.04-02.45	0.04	0.03	0.16	89.78	0.00	0.21	0.03	8.94	0.09	0.00	0.14	0.00	0.19
99	102	Palstave	P1977.04-02.46	0.06	0.04	0.20	88.35	0.00	0.08	0.06	10.45	0.18	0.01	0.06	0.00	0.14
100	117	Palstave	P1977.04-02.57	0.01	0.04	0.21	89.68	0.04	0.09	0.09	9.22	0.06		0.26		
102	56	Palstave	P1977.07-02.14	0.05	0.13	0.10	88.84	0.00	0.24	0.03	10.02	0.07	0.03	0.13	0.05	0.05
103	86	Palstave	P1977.04-02.36	0.02	0.01	0.20	88.76	0.00	0.09	0.07	10.19	0.04	0.01	0.13	0.07	0.13
104	101	Palstave	P1977.04-02.47	0.01	0.02	0.16	89.13	0.00	0.32	0.04	9.91	0.04	0.01	0.04	0.00	0.09
105	95	Palstave	P1977.04-02.53	0.06	0.03	0.21	89.25	0.03	0.22	0.05	8.94	0.07	0.09	0.48	0.03	0.35
106	94	Palstave	P1977.04-02.54	0.01	0.05	0.21	86.64	0.00	0.18	0.04	12.09	0.07	0.03	0.23	0.01	0.14

No.	Do	Type	British Museum Accession No	Fe	Co	Ni	Cu	Zn	As	Sb	Sn	Ag	Bi	Pb	Au	S
107	116	Palstave	P1977.04-02.58	0.04	0.01	0.16	89.58	0.01	0.59	0.01	8.95	0.10		0.25	0.03	
108	186	Palstave	P1981.07-02.12	0.02	0.03	0.15	89.61	0.01	0.22	0.02	9.40	0.06	0.03	0.11	0.03	0.10
111	100	Palstave	P1977.04-02.48	0.01	0.01	0.14	90.79	0.03	0.14	0.03	8.48	0.07	0.03	0.04	0.01	0.02
112	98	Palstave	P1977.04-02.50	0.02	0.03	0.20	89.83	0.00	0.10	0.03	9.41	0.06	0.00	0.14	0.00	0.02
113	96	Palstave	P1977.04-02.52	0.04	0.03	0.18	90.14	0.03	0.19	0.03	8.61	0.06	0.03	0.22	0.00	0.19
114	58	Palstave	P1981.07-02.18	0.01	0.02	0.16	87.69	0.00	0.23	0.00	11.15	0.03	0.03	0.13	0.05	0.25
116	89	Palstave?	P1977.04-02.33	0.03	0.04	0.18	89.64	0.00	0.10	0.02	9.26	0.04	0.03	0.27	0.00	0.20
117	88	Palstave?	P1977.04-02.34	0.01	0.00	0.18	86.99	0.00	0.06	0.03	12.28	0.01	0.01	0.10	0.00	0.08
118	152	Socketed axe/chisel	P1980.02-01.19	0.01	0.02	0.17	88.35	0.00	0.10	0.09	10.40	0.06	0.01	0.03	0.00	0.57
119	181	Socketed axe/chisel	P1977.04-02.92	0.01	0.03	0.17	91.98	0.00	0.14	0.00	7.34	0.01	0.02	0.07	0.01	0.02
120	162	Socketed axe/chisel	P1980.02-01.18	0.10	0.02	0.12	88.94	0.00	0.07	0.01	10.08	0.03	0.04	0.08	0.01	0.29
121	97	Socketed axe/chisel	P1977.04-02.51	0.00	0.04	0.19	89.83	0.00	0.20	0.05	9.16	0.09	0.07	0.07	0.01	0.05
122	62	Socketed axe/chisel	P1981.07-02.19	0.02	0.02	0.15	88.05	0.00	0.23	0.04	10.98	0.05	0.02	0.16	0.00	0.05
123	226	Socketed axe/chisel	P1984.07-01.53	0.02	0.03	0.26	88.98	0.01	0.05	0.03	9.96	0.05	0.01	0.13	0.05	0.23
124	225	Socketed axe/chisel	P1984.07-01.52	0.04	0.03	0.17	89.96	0.00	0.32	0.05	8.87	0.05	0.00	0.17	0.00	0.03
125	68	Socketed axe/chisel	P1981.07-02.20	0.03	0.03	0.23	89.73	0.00	0.20	0.06	9.29	0.06	0.01	0.08	0.01	0.03
126	224	Socketed axe/chisel	P1984.07-01.51	0.04	0.02	0.20	89.34	0.00	0.05	0.06	9.66	0.05	0.09	0.17	0.00	0.03
127	29	Socketed axe/chisel	P1977.04-02.89	0.04	0.06	0.50	90.27	0.01	0.25	0.06	8.24	0.02		0.23	0.06	
130	218	Socketed hammer	P1984.07-01.12	0.02	0.01	0.12	85.91	0.03	0.65	0.00	12.27	0.04	0.01	0.21	0.06	0.07
131	203	Socketed hammer	P1982.06-03.5	0.06	0.03	0.23	92.41	0.02	0.11	0.03	6.80	0.03	0.02	0.04	0.06	0.01
132	79	Socketed hammer?	P1981.07-02.21	0.03	0.03	0.28	82.64	0.00	0.24	0.09	16.20	0.03	0.04	0.10	0.00	0.00
133	147	Socketed hammer?	P1980.02-01.20	0.00	0.02	0.25	85.80	0.05	0.22	0.05	13.12	0.03	0.00	0.08	0.00	0.04
134	201	Hooked knife	P1980.02-01.21	0.14	0.02	0.19	89.77	0.02	0.52	0.03	8.86	0.03	0.00	0.10	0.03	0.02
135	72	Tanged chisel	P1981.07-02.22	0.07	0.04	0.24	85.68	0.01	0.14	0.08	12.79	0.03	0.02	0.25	0.01	0.29
137	151	Tanged chisel	P1980.02-01.22	0.02	0.05	0.21	85.31	0.02	0.30	0.05	13.35	0.05	0.02	0.16	0.01	0.10
138	204	Tanged chisel	P1982.06-03.6	0.10	0.03	0.13	90.96	0.02	0.11	0.04	8.07	0.06	0.07	0.11	0.01	0.01
139	205	Tanged chisel	P1982.06-03.7	0.09	0.01	0.14	87.65	0.00	0.26	0.01	10.77	0.07	0.03	0.65	0.01	0.05
140	206	Tanged chisel	P1982.06-03.8	0.01	0.02	0.20	92.57	0.00	0.17	0.01	6.47	0.02	0.02	0.05	0.00	0.22
141	207	Awl	P1982.06-03.9	0.05	0.04	0.14	90.48	0.08	0.27	0.02	7.77	0.06	0.01	0.24	0.05	0.56
144	211	Shank	P1983.05-01.9	0.05	0.03	0.19	90.12	0.00	0.16	0.02	8.61	0.08	0.03	0.15	0.00	0.33
146	209	Spur	P1982.06-03.41	0.08	0.01	0.07	84.17	0.01	0.22	0.03	14.50	0.08	0.04	0.38	0.08	0.06
147	227	Tang/anvil spike?	P1984.07-01.59	0.07	0.02	0.14	89.05	0.01	0.05	0.04	9.97	0.04	0.02	0.19	0.00	0.24
148	153	Flesh-hook prong?	P1980.02-01.23	0.02	0.03	0.28	88.43	0.00	0.03	0.04	10.47	0.00	0.00	0.18	0.04	0.25
152	221	Pin-head	P1984.07-01.42	0.03	0.03	0.15	88.87	0.00	0.05	0.01	9.90	0.12	0.05	0.36	0.00	0.10
153	213	Bracelet	P1983.05-01.12	0.25	0.02	0.16	87.27	0.00	0.11	0.05	11.65	0.06	0.04	0.14	0.00	0.04
155	228	Bracelet	P1985.08-01.4	0.11	0.01	0.12	88.85	0.03	0.10	0.08	9.82	0.08	0.00	0.29	0.00	0.08
157	214	Loop fastener	P1983.05-01.14	0.10	0.02	0.17	86.89	0.01	0.43	0.05	11.32	0.08	0.06	0.41	0.00	0.11
158	212	Fitting (loop)	P1983.05-01.11	0.08	0.03	0.23	89.69	0.00	0.05	0.03	9.00	0.05	0.00	0.07	0.01	0.47
159	175	Rivet	P1980.02-01.10	0.15	0.03	0.20	90.05	0.00	0.02	0.01	9.12	0.00	0.05	0.00	0.01	0.02
163	219	Rosnoën sword	P1984.07-01.13	0.06	0.01	0.24	88.66	0.00	0.08	0.01	10.09	0.06	0.01	0.03	0.03	0.34
167	163	Sword	P1980.02-01.24	0.02	0.04	0.24	88.72	0.05	0.03	0.01	10.36	0.06	0.00	0.16	0.00	0.00
168	3	Sword	P1981.07-02.34	0.04	0.04	0.39	84.96	0.01	0.13	0.05	13.32	0.04	0.06	0.16	0.00	0.50
169	110	Sword	P1977.04-02.65	0.05	0.05	0.15	97.77	0.00	0.24	0.05	0.12	0.05	0.01	0.33	0.00	0.71
171	182	?Sword	P1977.04-02.71	0.01	0.03	0.17	90.16	0.00	0.15	0.04	9.08	0.01	0.01	0.07	0.01	0.01
172	105	?Sword	P1977.04-02.72	0.01	0.08	0.05	89.19	0.00	0.11	0.01	10.23	0.01	0.01	0.04	0.04	0.01
173	106	?Sword	P1977.04-02.72	0.04	0.03	0.25	86.35	0.05	0.26	0.07	12.38	0.02	0.02	0.11	0.00	0.28
174	166	?Sword	P1980.02-01.6	0.05	0.02	0.16	87.54	0.01	0.12	0.02	11.15	0.09	0.07	0.11	0.00	0.34
175	8	?Sword	P1981.07-02.28	0.04	0.02	0.15	88.92	0.03	0.10	0.05	9.51	0.04	0.05	0.29	0.05	0.52

No.	Do	Type	British Museum Accession No	Fe	Co	Ni	Cu	Zn	As	Sb	Sn	Ag	Bi	Pb	Au	S
177	22	Sword blade fragment	P1981.07-02.49	0.00	0.02	0.21	88.90	0.00	0.03	0.04	9.95	0.03	0.01	0.12	0.04	0.44
180	113	Sword blade fragment	P1977.04-02.61	0.08	0.01	0.18	85.71	0.01	0.17	0.01	13.38	0.01	0.03	0.05	0.04	0.09
181	26	Sword blade fragment	P1981.07-02.43	0.05	0.01	0.09	88.23	0.01	0.20	0.02	10.81	0.04	0.01	0.00	0.00	0.26
182	71	Sword blade fragment	P1981.07-02.52	0.04	0.02	0.17	87.64	0.00	0.26	0.05	11.46	0.01	0.03	0.06	0.01	0.10
183	64	Sword blade fragment	P1981.07-02.50	0.03	0.03	0.18	88.28	0.03	0.20	0.07	10.09	0.08	0.01	0.42	0.00	0.35
187	60	Rapier	P1981.07-02.24	0.07	0.03	0.21	85.60	0.04	0.23	0.04	13.29	0.06	0.00	0.11	0.04	0.04
188	114	Rapier/dirk	P1977.04-02.60	0.01	0.02	0.19	88.03	0.00	0.15	0.03	10.82	0.05	0.01	0.08	0.00	0.30
189	183	Rapier/dirk	P1977.04-02.70	0.09	0.03	0.22	89.03	0.00	0.26	0.16	9.65	0.04	0.03	0.16	0.03	0.08
190	154	Rapier/dirk	P1980.02-01.25	0.01	0.02	0.22	88.13	0.00	0.16	0.02	10.09	0.02	0.03	0.19	0.00	0.77
191	150	Dirk	P1980.02-01.27	0.02	0.05	0.11	87.62	0.00	0.10	0.02	11.61	0.03	0.00	0.10	0.03	0.06
192	4	Dirk	P1981.07-02.33	0.06	0.02	0.68	83.37	0.01	0.49	0.15	14.78	0.02	0.05	0.11	0.00	0.08
197	220	Dirk, ex-sword?	P1984.07-01.15	0.37	0.03	0.03	88.07	0.11	0.05	0.05	9.90	0.12	0.05	0.36	0.00	0.10
202	109	Knife	P1977.04-02.66	0.01	0.03	0.20	88.99	0.00	0.15	0.09	9.14	0.00	0.02	0.15	0.05	0.74
203	24	Knife	P1981.07-02.26	0.08	0.02	0.18	85.72	0.00	0.08	0.03	12.97	0.05	0.00	0.21	0.05	0.37
204	9	Knife	P1981.07-02.29	0.05	0.03	0.16	89.39	0.01	0.20	0.07	9.33	0.10	0.05	0.13	0.03	0.17
206	185	Knife	P1977.04-02.64	0.04	0.02	0.17	87.91	0.03	0.20	0.03	10.83	0.02	0.01	0.18	0.00	0.32
207	208	Knife	P1982.06-03.16	0.03	0.01	0.04	85.36	0.00	0.21	0.00	13.98	0.00	0.03	0.05	0.03	0.03
212	61	?Sword	P1981.07-02.05	0.02	0.04	0.17	89.81	0.01	0.00	0.01	9.63	0.03	0.01	0.17	0.00	0.02
213	164	Hilt fragment	P1980.02-01.26	0.25	0.02	0.16	89.87	0.04	0.25	0.03	8.39	0.07	0.01	0.09	0.00	0.59
215	107	Hilt fragment	P1977.04-02.69	0.02	0.10	0.07	87.45	0.01	0.31	0.01	10.80	0.12	0.08	0.17	0.00	0.43
216	172	Hilt fragment	P1980.02-01.5	0.16	0.05	0.15	91.22	0.03	0.17	0.01	7.64	0.04	0.06	0.03	0.00	0.25
217	5	Hilt fragment	P1981.07-02.31	0.10	0.01	0.13	89.18	0.00	0.16	0.02	9.43	0.06	0.03	0.05	0.00	0.47
218	17	Hilt fragment	P1981.07-02.30	0.02	0.04	0.41	89.09	0.01	0.26	0.03	9.71	0.00	0.00	0.13	0.04	0.02
219	25	Hilt fragment	P1981.07-02.27	0.01	0.03	0.36	87.29	0.01	0.10	0.06	10.94	0.00	0.01	0.06	0.00	0.66
238	111	Blade fragment	P1977.04-02.63	0.10	0.03	0.21	87.32	0.00	0.23	0.00	11.12	0.04	0.01	0.33	0.00	0.21
239	108	Blade fragment	P1977.04-02.67	0.02	0.02	0.11	88.49	0.01	0.31	0.03	10.38	0.04	0.01	0.10	0.03	0.11
240	44	Blade fragment	P1977.04-02.74	0.03	0.02	0.19	88.25	0.03	0.31	0.06	10.79	0.04	0.01	0.08	0.03	0.01
241	43	Blade fragment	P1977.04-02.75	0.04	0.05	0.21	86.25	0.07	0.15	0.04	12.13	0.05	0.04	0.13	0.04	0.56
242	42	Blade fragment	P1977.04-02.76	0.05	0.03	0.17	89.40	0.00	0.12	0.10	9.59	0.06		0.18	0.00	
243	41	Blade fragment	P1977.04-02.77	0.01	0.03	0.17	91.59	0.00	0.12	0.04	7.66	0.07		0.06	0.00	
244	40	Blade fragment	P1977.04-02.78	0.02	0.05	0.17	86.86	0.00	0.19	0.05	12.20	0.07		0.18	0.00	
245	39	Blade fragment	P1977.04-02.79	0.02	0.02	0.13	89.53	0.01	0.06	0.06	9.83	0.01		0.09	0.00	
246	38	Blade fragment	P1977.04-02.80	0.02	0.02	0.20	92.24	0.01	0.13	0.01	6.81	0.07		0.27	0.05	
247	37	Blade fragment	P1977.04-02.81	0.02	0.02	0.16	88.81	0.06	0.08	0.01	10.42	0.06		0.12	0.00	
248	36	Blade fragment	P1977.04-02.82	0.01	0.02	0.19	89.20	0.04	0.01	0.04	10.05	0.04		0.20	0.00	
249	35	Blade fragment	P1977.04-02.83	0.09	0.02	0.39	91.52	0.00	0.07	0.05	7.48	0.03		0.10	0.03	
250	34	Blade fragment	P1977.04-02.84	0.02	0.05	0.36	85.68	0.01	0.16	0.04	12.99	0.09		0.10	0.00	
251	33	Blade fragment	P1977.04-02.85	0.08	0.06	0.11	94.04	0.00	0.17	0.00	5.01	0.03		0.06	0.01	
252	32	Blade fragment	P1977.04-02.86	0.08	0.02	0.21	90.97	0.03	0.01	0.04	8.18	0.09		0.12	0.00	
253	31	Blade fragment	P1977.04-02.87	0.01	0.02	0.32	88.11	0.17	0.07	0.02	10.42	0.07		0.40	0.08	
254	30	Blade fragment	P1977.04-02.88	0.05	0.02	0.18	92.66	0.00	0.14	0.01	6.51	0.02		0.06	0.00	
255	180	Blade fragment in axe	P1977.04-02.92	0.02	0.04	0.19	88.24	0.00	0.18	0.04	10.03	0.03	0.02	0.14	0.00	0.82
256	173	Blade fragment	P1980.02-01.7	0.06	0.03	0.04	88.53	0.00	0.13	0.10	10.36	0.07	0.01	0.33	0.00	0.09
257	174	Blade fragment	P1980.02-01.9	0.03	0.00	0.16	91.80	0.00	0.04	0.04	7.25	0.00	0.03	0.09	0.01	0.42

No.	Do	Type	British Museum Accession No	Fe	Co	Ni	Cu	Zn	As	Sb	Sn	Ag	Bi	Pb	Au	S
258	171	Blade fragment	P1980.02-01.8	0.04	0.02	0.14	90.43	0.03	0.03	0.05	8.17	0.07	0.01	0.13	0.04	0.65
259	165	Blade fragment	P1980.02-01.29	0.00	0.01	0.14	89.19	0.01	0.03	0.02	10.25	0.05	0.06	0.03	0.00	0.01
260	149	Blade fragment	P1980.02-01.30	0.01	0.05	0.42	86.48	0.04	0.24	0.09	12.11	0.03	0.03	0.31	0.00	0.04
261	148	Blade fragmcnt	P1980.02-01.28	0.01	0.02	0.21	86.51	0.00	0.24	0.04	11.44	0.01	0.02	0.60	0.03	0.39
262	12	Blade fragment	P1981.07-02.32	0.06	0.03	0.19	88.96	0.00	0.17	0.04	9.93	0.02	0.02	0.07	0.00	0.27
263	66	Blade fragment	P1981.07-02.39	0.18	0.03	0.12	85.60	0.00	0.17	0.01	13.41	0.05	0.05	0.03	0.00	0.07
264	80	Blade fragment	P1981.07-02.55	0.06	0.04	0.16	89.99	0.03	0.14	0.03	8.62	0.06	0.04	0.20	0.00	0.30
265	16	Blade fragment	P1981.07-02.54	0.08	0.01	0.18	89.10	0.00	0.12	0.07	9.91	0.03	0.05	0.12	0.00	0.07
266	73	Blade fragment	P1981.07-02.36	0.12	0.04	0.15	87.91	0.03	0.17	0.02	10.82	0.03	0.05	0.38	0.00	0.01
267	11	Blade fragment	P1981.07-02.40	0.10	0.04	0.23	87.91	0.01	0.08	0.04	10.59	0.05	0.00	0.06	0.00	0.58
268	6	Blade fragment	P1981.07-02.51	0.02	0.01	0.09	89.47	0.00	0.13	0.02	9.58	0.03	0.03	0.06	0.00	0.19
270	76	Blade fragment	P1981.-7-02.48	0.08	0.01	0.13	90.12	0.00	0.28	0.04	8.82	0.05	0.04	0.08	0.06	0.17
271	23	Blade fragment	P1981.07-02.42	0.05	0.03	0.27	88.92	0.02	0.05	0.01	10.16	0.05	0.02	0.10	0.08	0.02
272	14	Blade fragment	P1981.07-02.47	0.01	0.03	0.23	90.95	0.00	0.10	0.04	7.92	0.08	0.02	0.06	0.00	0.21
273	13	Blade fragment	P1981.07-02.59	0.01	0.01	0.15	90.47	0.03	0.06	0.03	8.72	0.01	0.04	0.15	0.01	0.04
274	7	Blade fragment	P1981.07-02.44	0.01	0.05	0.15	86.73	0.02	0.06	0.01	12.27	0.06	0.04	0.29	0.01	0.13
275	65	Blade fragment	P1981.07-02.60	0.09	0.06	0.18	87.65	0.03	0.21	0.07	11.11	0.04	0.04	0.28	0.00	0.03
276	10	Blade fragment	P1981.07-02.45	0.08	0.03	0.09	90.58	0.00	0.03	0.01	8.40	0.09	0.03	0.05	0.00	0.28
277	74	Blade fragment	P1981.07-02.37	0.04	0.03	0.14	88.91	0.00	0.22	0.06	10.28	0.07	0.04	0.00	0.00	0.01
278	18	Blade fragment	P1981.07-02.46	0.06	0.02	0.20	91.80	0.00	0.03	0.02	7.23	0.04	0.02	0.28	0.07	0.02
279	15	Blade fragment	P1981.07-02.53	0.03	0.01	0.11	87.06	0.00	0.09	0.06	11.75	0.06	0.00	0.29	0.05	0.21
280	20	Blade fragment	P1981.07-02.58	0.07	0.02	0.36	86.11	0.00	0.23	0.08	12.75	0.02	0.00	0.18	0.00	0.03
281	21	Blade fragment	P1981.07-02.38	0.08	0.01	0.16	91.07	0.02	0.18	0.03	7.41	0.09	0.03	0.17	0.01	0.29
282	69	Blade fragment	P1981.07-02.41	0.01	0.04	0.11	88.78	0.01	0.06	0.11	10.31	0.04	0.01	0.18	0.03	0.06
283	67	Blade fragment	P1981.07-02.57	0.05	0.03	0.15	89.86	0.00	0.15	0.11	8.97	0.04	0.03	0.11	0.01	0.33
284	19	Blade fragment	P1981.07-02.56	0.03	0.02	0.09	89.08	0.01	0.12	0.03	9.43	0.06	0.00	0.00	0.04	0.86
348	27	Blade fragment	P1977.04-02.93	0.03	0.01	0.17	88.37	0.00	0.02	0.02	11.01	0.02		0.15	0.06	
350	176	Spearhead	P1977.04-02.95	0.10	0.03	0.44	91.79	0.05	0.00	0.02	6.86	0.08	0.07	0.10	0.05	0.20
351	28	Spearhead	P1977.04-02.94	0.05	0.01	0.18	89.19	0.02	0.22	0.04	8.22	0.04		1.46	0.00	
352	77	Spearhead	P1981.07-02.62	0.04	0.03	0.19	91.49	0.04	0.17	0.00	7.44	0.00	0.01	0.17	0.00	0.18
353	230	Spearhead	P1985.08-01.23	0.07	0.02	0.17	86.54	0.01	0.05	0.11	12.44	0.04	0.02	0.15	0.01	0.11
354	179	Ferrule	P1977.04-02.90	0.06	0.02	0.23	87.38	0.05	0.22	0.09	11.50	0.07	0.06	0.04	0.00	0.02
355	222	Ferrule, knobbed	P1984.07-01.44	0.14	0.02	0.19	85.92	0.01	0.40	0.05	12.31	0.07	0.01	0.20	0.00	0.37
356	216	Jet	P1983.05-01.29	0.17	0.03	0.04	89.77	0.04	0.12	0.00	9.00	0.05	0.03	0.02	0.08	0.30
357	229	Jet/lump	P1985.08-01.21	0.01	0.03	0.13	88.36	0.00	0.05	0.05	10.58	0.09	0.00	0.31	0.00	0.15
358	217	Lump	P1983.05-01.40	0.01	0.02	0.16	91.60	0.00	0.48	0.04	7.18	0.05	0.00	0.05	0.01	0.23
359	75	Lump	P1981.07-02.61	0.02	0.06	0.12	88.77	0.04	0.28	0.00	10.24	0.09	0.03	0.13	0.00	0.03
360	215	Unclassified	P1983.05-01.37	0.12	0.02	0.13	87.16	0.01	0.30	0.06	11.65	0.05	0.01	0.11	0.00	0.07
362	223	Modern rod	P1984.07-01.45	0.37	0.01	0.12	68.84	27.43	0.13	0.00	1.65	0.04	0.03	1.36	0.01	0.01

Appendix 3 Results of metal analyses carried out on the Salcombe material

Analysis No.	Ref No.	Object	Fe	Co	Ni	Cu	Zn	As	Sb	Sn	Ag	Bi	Pb	Au	Cd	S	Al	Si	Mn
MS 11/Mean	S1	Palstave	0.05	0.04	0.15	88.06	0.01	0.21	0.02	11.27	0.04	0.03	0.10	0.01	0.00	0.01	0.00	0.00	0.00
MS 12/Mean	S6	Palstave-adze	0.02	0.02	0.25	92.83	0.01	0.10	0.01	6.62	0.02	0.02	0.02	0.02	0.00	0.01	0.00	0.04	0.01
MS 13/Mean	S5	Palstave	0.05	0.04	0.19	88.42	0.01	0.14	0.02	10.73	0.07	0.01	0.19	0.02	0.00	0.08	0.00	0.02	0.01
MS 14/Mean	S12	Sword hilt fragment	0.15	0.03	0.18	88.36	0.02	0.12	0.05	10.50	0.06	0.01	0.25	0.01	0.00	0.25	0.00	0.01	0.01
MS 15/Mean	S27	Block/weight	0.01	0.03	0.21	88.95	0.01	0.10	0.04	10.23	0.07	0.00	0.09	0.04	0.00	0.14	0.01	0.05	0.01
MS 16/Mean	S11	Sword?	0.05	0.02	0.22	88.37	0.00	0.15	0.06	10.77	0.04	0.01	0.03	0.05	0.00	0.13	0.00	0.10	0.00
MS 17/Mean	S21	Hilt fragment	0.02	0.00	0.07	91.39	0.01	0.03	0.00	8.25	0.02	0.02	0.03	0.02	0.00	0.07	0.00	0.06	0.01
MS 18/Mean	S19	Sword hilt fragment?	0.37	0.01	0.11	90.12	0.03	0.06	0.02	8.80	0.04	0.05	0.08	0.01	0.00	0.27	0.00	0.02	0.01
MS 19/Mean	S20	Sword blade fragment?	0.04	0.01	0.14	88.80	0.01	0.09	0.01	10.56	0.06	0.03	0.04	0.01	0.00	0.18	0.01	0.00	0.01
MS 20/Mean	S13	Sword blade fragment	0.12	0.04	0.21	91.35	0.00	0.10	0.01	7.72	0.07	0.03	0.07	0.04	0.00	0.16	0.00	0.07	0.01
MS 21/Mean	S2	Palstave	0.05	0.02	0.17	88.34	0.00	0.09	0.01	11.01	0.04	0.03	0.02	0.03	0.00	0.15	0.00	0.03	0.01
MS 22/Mean	S24	Blade fragment	0.13	0.04	0.12	89.15	0.03	0.12	0.09	9.81	0.04	0.01	0.09	0.02	0.00	0.28	0.00	0.05	0.01
MS 23/Mean	S14	Sword blade fragment?	0.02	0.01	0.11	91.66	0.00	0.01	0.01	7.75	0.02	0.00	0.03	0.02	0.00	0.31	0.00	0.03	0.00
MS 24/Mean	S25	Blade fragment	0.25	0.02	0.20	89.57	0.01	0.07	0.01	9.42	0.01	0.01	0.04	0.02	0.00	0.33	0.00	0.02	0.01
MS 25/Mean	S28	Tin lump	0.01	0.01	0.02	0.03	0.01	0.00	0.00	99.32	0.00	0.01	0.03	0.04	0.00	0.01	0.05	0.46	0.00
MS 26/Mean	S26	Blade fragment	0.23	0.03	0.17	90.03	0.02	0.10	0.01	9.08	0.04	0.03	0.05	0.02	0.00	0.19	0.00	0.02	0.01
MS 27/Mean	050625 0002	Narrow blade (rapier?)	0.12	0.03	0.15	91.65	0.01	0.06	0.01	7.59	0.04	0.01	0.07	0.03	0.00	0.15	0.00	0.07	0.00
MS 28/Mean	050918 0002	Palstave	0.05	0.02	0.20	88.62	0.00	0.14	0.04	10.55	0.07	0.03	0.08	0.02	0.00	0.11	0.01	0.06	0.01
MS 29/Mean	050918 0001	Wire-drawing die?	0.11	0.02	0.11	77.44	0.03	0.08	0.00	21.89	0.01	0.01	0.07	0.01	0.00	0.14	0.00	0.08	0.00
MS 30/Mean	050918 0003	Block/weight	0.06	0.03	0.16	90.84	0.07	0.10	0.05	8.27	0.08	0.04	0.20	0.00	0.00	0.06	0.01	0.01	0.01
MS 31/Mean	050716 0001	Hilt/blade fragment	0.06	0.03	0.14	91.25	0.00	0.07	0.01	8.26	0.06	0.00	0.04	0.03	0.00	0.02	0.00	0.03	0.00
MS 32/Mean	050711 0002	Hammer	0.02	0.03	0.14	86.74	0.00	0.16	0.05	12.49	0.04	0.00	0.17	0.02	0.00	0.11	0.00	0.03	0.01
MS 33/Mean	051008 0001	Rapier hilt fragment	0.11	0.01	0.15	89.96	0.01	0.10	0.03	9.18	0.03	0.00	0.06	0.00	0.00	0.13	0.01	0.23	0.00
MS 34/Mean	050917 0001	Rapier hilt fragment	0.12	0.03	0.24	89.87	0.02	0.20	0.13	9.08	0.05	0.02	0.05	0.01	0.00	0.13	0.01	0.05	0.00
MS 35/Mean	050917 0003	Rapier fragment	0.08	0.03	0.22	90.21	0.02	0.11	0.03	9.05	0.02	0.04	0.05	0.04	0.00	0.03	0.01	0.06	0.01
MS 36/Mean	S7	*Strumento*	0.04	0.02	0.23	88.19	0.02	0.16	0.02	11.05	0.08	0.02	0.10	0.03	0.00	0.01	0.00	0.02	0.00
R3111/Mean	BM 1888.09-01.05	*Strumento*	0.11	0.04	0.03	90.62	0.04	0.27	0.02	8.37	0.04	0.00	0.24	0.04	0.00	0.06	0.03	0.08	0.02

Notes: S nos refer to the catalogue (Appendix 1); other reference nos are site find numbers for finds made in 2005.
Analyses for S3, S4, S15, S16 and S22 are published in Rohl & Needham 1998, 225.

Appendix 4 Metal sampling and analysis

by J P Northover

Cut samples were removed with a jeweller's piercing saw with a blade with 32 teeth/cm either from cutting edges, butts or fractures. Drilled samples were taken with a handheld model-maker's electric drill with a 0.9mm diameter bit. All samples were hot mounted, either in a copper-filled acrylic resin (for the first 182 samples) or a carbon-filled thermo-setting resin (for the final 32). All were ground and polished to a 1μm diamond finish.

The initial samples, labelled between Do 3 and Do 186, were analysed using the CAMEBAX then in the Department of Materials, University of Oxford. Operating conditions were an accelerating voltage of 25kV, a beam current of 30nA and an X-ray take-off angle of 40E; pure element and mineral standards were used with count times of 10s per element. Ten elements (iron, cobalt, nickel, copper, zinc, arsenic, antimony, tin, silver, and gold) were acquired using point analysis so that the arsenic Kα line could be used without interference from lead. Lead was estimated separately by an area analysis method with the area percentage then converted to a weight percentage. Detection limits were generally 100ppm with the exception of approximately 300ppm for gold.

The re-analysis added bismuth and sulphur, with copper, tin, bismuth, sulphur, and lead being analysed over a 50μm square raster to give corrected, quantitative data for elements that are dispersed in small inclusions rather than in solid solution. The final 32 samples were analysed using the JEOL 8800 electron microprobe currently in the Department of Materials, University of Oxford. Operating conditions were similar but with an accelerating voltage of 20kV, and the analyses made over a raster of 30 × 50μm Aluminium, silicon, and manganese have been added to the standard elements set for bronze, but here only silicon was detected, almost certainly associated with corrosion products. In all cases a minimum of three analyses was made per sample: Appendix 3 gives the mean composition for each sample. For the sake of uniformity, Al, Si, and Mn are not listed in the table.

After analysis, the cut samples were examined metallographically in both the as-polished and etched states. The etch used was an acidified aqueous solution of ferric chloride further diluted with ethanol.

Bibliography

Abaz, B, Beyneix, A & Mateu, A, 1992 Une hache de type de Rosnoën à Gontaud-de-Nogaret (Lot-et-Garonne), *Bulletin de la Société Préhistorique Française*, **89**, 277–8

Aitkins, B M, 1978 [Letter to K Muckelroy, Jesus College, Cambridge] (personal communication June 1978). Langdon Bay Archive: 1A/2

Albanese Procelli, R M, 1993 *Ripostigli di Bronzi della Sicilia nel Museo Archeologico di Siracusa*. Palermo: Accademia Nazionale di Scienze, Lettere e Arti di Palermo

Albanese Procelli, R M, 2003 Produzione metallurgica di età protostorica nella Sicilia centro-occidentale, in *Quarte giornate internazionali di studi sull'area elima: Erice, 1–4 dicembre 2000. Atti / il presente volume è stato curato da Alessandro Corretti*, volume 1. Pisa: Scuola Normale Superiore, 11–28

Allen, J R L, 2002 Retreat rates on soft-sediment cliffs: the contribution from dated fishweirs and traps on Holocene coastal outcrops, *Proc Geol Ass*, **113**, 1–8

Allen, M J & Gardiner, J, 2000 *Our changing coast: a survey of the intertidal archaeology of Langstone Harbour, Hampshire*, CBA Res Rep **124**. York: Council for British Archaeology

Anderson, T, 1994 A Bronze Age Burial from St Margaret's-at-Cliffe. *Archaeol Cantiana*, **114**, 357–61

Anon, 1927 The Huelva Hoard (Spain), *Antiquity*, **1**(1), 106–7

Anon, 1978a [Letter to K Muckelroy, Jesus College, Cambridge, with geological information] (personal communication 7 March 1978). Moor Sands Archive: 2/15

Anon, 1978b Committee for aerial photography, Cambridge [Letter to K Muckelroy, Jesus College, Cambridge] (Personal communication 17 April 1978). Moor Sands Archive: 2/15

Anon, 1982 National Maritime Museum communication with general information relating to 10–25 July 1982 session at Langdon Bay Bronze Age site, 2 July 1982. Langdon Bay Archive: 1A/3

ApSimon, A M & Greenfield, E, 1972 The excavation of Bronze Age and Iron Age settlements at Trevisker, St. Eval, Cornwall, *Proc Prehist Soc*, **38**, 302–81

Armbruster, B R & Louboutin, C, 2004 Parures en or de l'Âge du Bronze de Balinghem et Guînes (Pas-de-Calais): les aspects technologiques, *Antiquités Nationales*, **36**, 133–46

Armbruster, B R & Pernot, M, 2006 La technique du tournage utilisée à l'Âge du Bronze final pour la fabrication d'épingles de bronze trouvées en Bourgogne, *Bulletin de la Société Préhistorique Française*, **103**, 305–11

Baines, J M, 1973 A Late Bronze Age spearhead from Pett, *Sussex Archaeol Collect*, **111**, 110

Baker, P, 1977a [Letter to K Muckelroy, Jesus College, Cambridge] (personal communication 4 August 1977). Moor Sands Archive: 2/3

Baker, P, 1977b [Letter to J Munday, National Maritime Museum] (personal communication 16 July 1977). Moors Sands Archive: 2/2

Baker, P, 1977c [Letter to K Muckelroy, Jesus College, Cambridge] (personal communication 13 September 1977). Moors Sands Archive: 2/3

Baker, P, 1977d [Letter to W Gibbons, Sec, Advisory Committee on Historic Wrecks. Dept of Trade (Marine Division)] (personal communication 19 October 1977). Moor Sands Archive: 2/4

Baker, P, 1977e *Techniques of archaeological excavation*. London: Batsford

Baker, P, 1980 Salcombe Bronze Age Wreck Project: Report to Advisory Committee on Historic Wreck Sites, 14 October 1980. Moor Sands Archive: 1/2

Baker, P, 1982 [Letter to Dr N Flemming] (personal communication 9 March 1982). Langdon Bay Archive: 1A/3

Baker, P, 2004 [Letter to D Parham, Bournemouth University] (personal communication 1 August 2004). Moor Sands Archive: 2/15

Baker, P & Branigan, K, 1978 Two Bronze Age swords from Salcombe, Devon, Notes and News, *Int J Naut Archaeol*, **7**(2), 149–51

Balaam, N D, Smith, K & Wainwright, G J, 1982 The Shaugh Moor project: fourth report – environment, context and conclusion, *Proc Prehist Soc*, **48**, 203–78

Ballantyne, C K & Harris, C, 1994 *The periglaciation of Great Britain*. Cambridge: University of Cambridge Press

Barham, A J & Bates, M R, 1990 *The Holocene prehistory and palaeoenvironment of the Dour Valley catchment. A geoarchaeological assessment report for Dover District Council*, Geoarchaeological Service Facility Technical Report 90/04. London: Geoarchaeological Service Facility University College London

Bass, G F, 1966 *Archaeology underwater*. New York: Praeger

Bass, G F, 1967 *Cape Gelidonya: a Bronze Age shipwreck*. Philadelphia: American Philosophical Society

Bass, G F, 1972 *A history of seafaring based on underwater archaeology*. New York: Walker

Bastien, G & Yvard, J-C, 1980 Objets en bronze de la Seine Parisienne, *Bulletin de la Société Préhistorique Française*, **77**, 245–50

Batchellor, W, 1828 *A new history of Dover and Dover Castle*. Dover

Bates, M R, 1998 Locating and evaluating archaeology below the alluvium: the role of sub-surface stratigraphical modelling, *Lithics*, **19**, 4–8

Bates, M R & Barham, A J, 1993a Recent observations of tufa in the Dour Valley, Kent, *Quat Newslett*, **71**, 11–25

Bates, M R & Barham, A J, 1993b *Dover A20 road and sewer scheme environmental archaeological and palaeoenvironmental field and laboratory assessment report*, Geoarchaeological Service Facility Technical Report 93/03. London: Geoarchaeological Service Facility University College London

Bates, M R & Whittaker, K, 2004 Landscape evolution in the Lower Thames Valley: implications of the archaeology of the earlier Holocene period, in J Cotton &

D Field (eds) *Towards a New Stone Age: aspects of the Neolithic in south-east England*, CBA Research Report **137**. York: Council for British Archaeology, 50–70

Bates, M R, Barham, A J, Jones, S, Parfitt, K, Parfitt, S A, Pedley, M, Preece, R C, Walker, M J C & Whittaker, J E, 2008 Holocene sequences and archaeology from the Crabble Paper Mill site, Dover, UK and their regional significance, *Proc Geol Ass*, **119**(3–4), 299–327

Bates, M R, Corke, B, Parfitt, K & Whittaker, J E, 2011 A geoarchaeological approach to the evolution of the town and port of Dover: prehistoric to Saxon periods, *Proc Geol Ass*, **122**, 157–76

Beck, C & Shennan, S, 1991 *Amber in prehistoric Britain*, Oxbow Monograph **8**. Oxford: Oxbow Books

Bellam, J, 1996 A Middle Bronze Age pin from Broomhill Sands, Camber, East Sussex, and its context, *Sussex Archaeol Collect*, **134**, 217–19

Bennett, P, 1988 Archaeology and the Channel Tunnel, *Archaeol Cantiana*, **106**, 1–24

Betzler, P, 1974 *Die Fibeln in Süddeutschland, Österreich und der Schweiz I*, Prähistorische Bronzefunde **XIV**/3. Munich: Beck

Billard, C, 1993 Éléments sur le peuplement de la Basse Vallée de la Seine à partir de l'étude de matériaux de dragage, *Revue Archéologique de l'Ouest*, **10**, 55–87

Billard, C, Eluère, C & Jezegou, M-P, 2005 Découverte de torques en or de l'Âge du Bronze en Mer de Manche, in J Bourgeois & M Talon (eds) *L'Âge du Bronze du Nord de la France dans son Contexte Européen*. Paris: Comité des Travaux Historiques et Scientifiques, 287–301

Blanchet, J-C, 1984 *Les premiers métallurgistes en Picardie et dans le nord de la France*, Mémoires de la Société Préhistorique Française **17**. Paris: Société Préhistorique Française

Blanchet, J-C & Mille, B, 2009 Découverte exceptionelle d'un dépôt de lingots de l'age du Bronze ancien a Saint-Valery-sur-Somme, in A Richard, P Barral, A Daubigny, G Kaenel, C Mordant & J-F Piningre (eds) *L'Isthme Européen Rhin-Saône-Rhône dans la Protohistoire. Approches Nouvelles en Hommage à Jacques-Pierre Millotte*, Annales Literaires de l'Université de Franche-Comté **860**. Besançon: Presses Universitaires de Franche-Comté, 177–82

Blanchet, J-C and Mohen, J-P, 1977 Le dépôt du Bronze Final de Saint-Just-en-Chaussée (Oise), *Bulletin de la Société Préhistorique Française* **74**, 472–81

Blanchet, J-C & Mordant, C, 1987 Les premières haches à rebords et à butée dans le basin Parisien et le Nord de la France, in J-C Blanchet (ed) *Les Relations entre le Continent et les Iles Britanniques à l'Âge du Bronze: Actes du Colloques de Lille dans le cadre du 22ème Congrès préhistorique de France, 2–7 septembre 1984*, Supplément à la Revue Archéologique de Picardie. Amiens, Revue Archéologique de Picardie, 89–118

Blanchet, J-C, Bréart, B, Collart, J-L, Pommepuy, C, Bayard, D & Berredjeb, T, 1989 Picardie. *Gallia Informations* **1989**(1), 185–276

Bocquet, A, 1969 Isère préhistorique et protohistorique, *Gallia Préhistoire*, **12**, 121–400

Boon, G, 1978 National Museum of Wales [Letter to K Muckelroy, Jesus College, Cambridge] (personal communication 11 April 1978). Moor Sands Archive: 2/15

Bourgeois, J & Talon, M (eds), 2005 *L'Âge du Bronze du Nord de la France dans son Contexte Européen*. Paris: Comité des Travaux Historiques et Scientifiques

Bowman, S & Needham, S, 2007 The Dunaverney and Little Thetford flesh-hooks: history, technology and their position within the later Bronze Age Atlantic zone feasting complex, *Antiq J*, **87**, 53–108

Bradley, R, 1985 *Consumption, change and the archaeological record*, University of Edinburgh Department of Archaeology Occasional Paper **13**. Edinburgh: University of Edinburgh

Bradley, S L, Milne, G A, Teferle, F N, Bingley, R M & Orliac, E J, 2009 Glacial isostatic adjustment of the British Isles: new constraints from GPS measurements of crustal motion, *Geophysical Journal International*, **178**, 14–22

Brailsford, J, 1953 *Later prehistoric antiquities of the British Isles*. London: British Museum

Brandherm, D, 2007 *Las espadas del Bronce Final en la Péninsula Iberica y Baleares*, Prähistorische Bronzefunde **IV**/16. Stuttgart: Franz Steiner Verlag

Brandherm, D & Burgess, C, 2008 Carp's-tongue problems, in F Verse, B Knoche, J Graefe, M Hohlbein, K Schierhold, C Siemann, M Uckelmann & G Woltermann (eds) *Durch die Zeiten... Festschrift für Albrecht Jockenhövel zum 65. Geburtstag*, Internationale Archäologic, Studia Honoraria **28**. Rahden: Marie Leidorf, 133–68

Brandherm, D & Moskal-del Hoyo, M, 2010 Las espadas en lengua de carpa – aspectos morfológicos, metalúrgicos y culturales, *Trabajos de Prehistoria*, **67**, 431–56

Branigan, K, 1977 [Letter to K Muckelroy, Jesus College, Cambridge] (personal communication October 1977). Moor Sands Archive: 2/12

Briard, J, 1958a Le dépôt de Penavern en Rosnoën (Finistère), *Travaux du Laboratoire Anthropologie et de Préhistoire de la Faculté des Sciences de Rennes*. Rennes: Laboratoire d'anthropologie et de préhistoire, Faculté des Sciences, 24–34

Briard, J, 1958b Le dépôt de fondeur de Menez-Tosta en Gouesnach (Finistère), *Travaux du Laboratoire Anthropologie et de Préhistoire de la Faculté des Sciences de Rennes*. Rennes: Laboratoire d'anthropologie et de préhistoire, Faculté des Sciences, 2–23

Briard, J, 1965 *Les dépôts bretons et l'Age du Bronze atlantique*. Rennes: Université de Rennes

Briard, J (ed), 1984 *Paléométallurgie de la France Atlantique: Age du Bronze (1)*. Rennes: Travaux du Laboratoire 'Anthropologie-Préhistoire-Protohistoire-Quaternaire armoricains'

Briard, J (ed), 1985 *Paléométallurgie de la France Atlantique: Age du Bronze (2)*. Rennes: Travaux du Laboratoire 'Anthropologie-Préhistoire-Protohistoire-Quaternaire armoricains'

Briard, J & Bigot, B, 1989 Le Bronze Atlantique: de Tréboul aux haches à talon en Armorique, in *Dynamique du Bronze Moyen en Europe occidentale, Actes du 113ᵉ Congrès des Sociétés Savantes, Strasbourg 1988*. Paris: Editions du CTHS, 523–36

Briard, J, Cordier, G & Gaucher, G, 1969 Un dépôt de la fin du Bronze Moyen à Malassis, commune de Chéry (Cher), *Gallia Préhistoire*, **12**, 37–73

Briard, J, Éluère, C, Mohen, J-P & Verron, G, 1982–3 Mission au British Museum: objets de l'Âge du Bronze trouvés en France – les ensembles, *Antiquités Nationales*, **14/15**, 34–58

Briard, J & Onnée, Y, 1972 *Le Dépôt du Bronze Final de Saint-Brieuc-des-Iffs (Île-et-Vilaine)*, Travaux du Laboratoire Anthropologie Préhistoire-Protohistoire et Quarternaire Armoricains. Rennes: Université de Rennes

Briard, J & Onnée, Y, 1980 L'Âge du Bronze, du Poudouvre au Clos-Poulet, in *Éléments pour une Préhistoire du Nord-est de l'Armorique Bretonne*, Dossiers de Centre Régional Archéologique d'Alet. Saint Malo: Centre Régional Archéologique d'Alet, 45–98

Briard, J, Onnee, Y & Peuziat, J, 1980 Les bronziers de Rosnoën (1000 av. J-C): les dépôts de Logonna-Quimerc'h, Plougoulm et Coray, *Bulletin de la Société Archéologique du Finistère*, **108**, 51–67

Briard, J & Verron, G, 1976a *Typologie des objets de l'Age du Bronze en France, Fascicule III: Haches (1)*. Paris: Société Préhistoriques Francaise, Commission du Bronze

Briard, J & Verron, G, 1976b *Typologie des objets de l'Age du Bronze en France, Fascicule IV: Haches (2), Herminettes*. Paris: Société Préhistoriques Francaise, Commission du Bronze

Brindley, A L, 2007 *The dating of food vessel and urns in Ireland*. Bronze Age Studies **7**. Galway: Department of Archaeology, National University of Ireland

Bristow, C R, Mortimore, R & Wood, C, 1997 Lithostratigraphy for mapping the chalk of southern England, *Proc Geol Ass*, **108**, 293–316

British Geological Survey, 2000 *Kingsbridge, Salcombe and Start Point, England and Wales Sheet 355 & 356, Solid and Drift Geology. Scale 1:50,000. Provisional Series*. Nottingham: British Geological Survey

British Museum, 1979a Minutes of the Committee on Excavation and Fieldwork, 22 March 1979. Moor Sands/Langdon Bay Archive: British Museum files

British Museum, 1979b Report of the Dept of Prehistoric and Romano-British Antiquities to the Trustees' Committee on Excavation and Fieldwork, October 1979. Moor Sands/Langdon Bay Archive: British Museum files

Britton, D, 1963 Traditions of metal-working in the later Neolithic and Early Bronze Age of Britain: part 1, *Proc Prehist Soc*, **29**, 258–325

Britton, D, 1968 The bronzes, in M A Cotton and S S Frere (eds) Ivinghoe Beacon excavations, 1963–5, *Rec Buckinghamshire*, **18**, 187–260

Brown, M A & Blin-Stoyle, A E, 1959 A sample analysis of British Middle and Late Bronze Age material using optical spectrometry, *Archaeometry*, Supplement **2**, 188–208

Browne, D, 1975 *Principles and practice in modern archaeology*. London: Hodder & Stoughton

Brun, P & Mordant, C (eds), 1988 *Le groupe Rhin-Suisse-France orientale et la notion de civilisation des Champs d'Urnes*, Mémoires du Musée de Préhistoire d'Ile-de-France **1**. Nemours: Musée de Préhistoire d'Ile-de-France

Burgess, C B, 1968a The later Bronze Age in the British Isles and north-western France, *Archaeol J*, **125**, 1–45

Burgess, C B, 1968b *Bronze Age metalwork in Northern England*. Newcastle upon Tyne: Oriel Press

Burgess, C B, 1976 Burials with metalwork of the later Bronze Age in Wales and beyond, in G C Boon & J M Lewis (eds) *Welsh antiquity: essays mainly on prehistoric topics presented to H N Savory upon his retirement as Keeper of Archaeology*. Cardiff: National Museum of Wales, 81–104

Burgess, C B, 1980 *The Age of Stonehenge*. London: Dent

Burgess, C B, 1995 A Bronze Age rapier from Catterick Bridge, *Yorkshire Archaeol J*, **67**, 1–5

Burgess, C B, 2012 South Welsh socketed axes and other carp's tongue conundrums, in W J Britnell & R J Sylvester (eds) *Reflections on the Past: Essays in Honour of Frances Lynch*. Welshpool: Cambrian Archaeological Association, 237–53

Burgess, C B, Coombs, D & Davies, D G, 1972 The Broadward complex and barbed spearheads, in F Lynch & C Burgess (eds) *Prehistoric man in Wales and the west: essays in honour of Lily F Chitty*. Bath: Adams & Dart, 211–83

Burgess, C B & Gerloff, S, 1981 *The dirks and rapiers of Great Britain and Ireland*, Prähistorische Bronzefunde IV/7. Munich: Beck

Burgess, C B & O'Connor, B, 2008 *Iberia, the Atlantic Bronze Age and the Mediterranean, in* S Celestino, N Rafel & X-L Armada (eds) *Contacto cultural entre el Mediterráneo y el Atlántico (siglos XII–VIII ane): La precolonización a debate*. Madrid: Consejo Superior de Investigaciones Científicas, Escuela Española de Historia y Arqueología en Roma, 41–58

Butler, J J, 1963 Bronze Age Connections across the North Sea: a study in prehistoric trade and industrial relations between the British Isles, the Netherlands, North Germany and Scandinavia c1700–700 BC. *Palaeohistoria*, **9**, 1–286

Butler, J J, 1987 Bronze Age connections: France and the Netherlands, *Palaeohistoria*, **29**, 9–34

Butler, J J, 1995/6 Bronze Age metalwork and amber in the Netherlands (part II:1): catalogue of flat axes, flanged axes and stopridge axes, *Palaeohistoria*, **37/38**, 159–243

Butler, J J & Steegstra, H, 1997–8 Bronze Age metal and amber in the Netherlands (II: 2): catalogue of the palstaves, *Palaeohistoria*, **39/40**, 163–275

Butler, J J & Steegstra, H, 1999–2000 Bronze Age metal and amber in the Netherlands (III: I): catalogue of the winged axes, *Palaeohistoria*, **41**(2), 127–48

Cantet, J-P, 1991 Les influences de Bronze atlantique en Gascogne gersoise, in C Chevillot & A Coffyn (eds) *L'Age du Bronze atlantique: ses faciès, de L'Écosse a L'Andalousie, et leurs relations avec le bronze continental et la Méditerranée*, Actes du 1er Colloque du Parc Archéologique de Beynac. Beynac-et-Cazenac: Association des Musées du Sarladais, 193–202

Carpenter, C, 1978 Property Services Agency, Ancient Monuments Branch [Letter to K Muckelroy, Jesus College, Cambridge] (personal communication 4 April 1978). Moor Sands Archive: 2/15

Carter, R W G, 1988 *Coastal Environments*. London: Academic Press

Casparie, W A, 1984 The three Bronze Age footpaths XVI (Bou), XVII (Bou) and XVIII (Bou) in the raised bog of southeast Drenthe (the Netherlands), *Palaeohistoria*, **26**, 41–94

Champion, T, 1980 Settlement and environment in later Bronze Age Kent, in J Barrett and R Bradley (eds) *Settlement and society in the British later Bronze Age*, BAR Brit Ser **83**, 2 vols. Oxford: British Archaeological Reports, 223–46

Charles, J A, 1978 [Letter to K Muckelroy, Jesus College, Cambridge] (personal communication October 1978). Moor Sands Archive: 2/12

Cherry, J, 1977 [Letter to I H Longworth, Keeper, Dept of Prehistoric and Romano-British Antiquities, British Museum with minutes of general meeting of Council of Nautical Archaeology] (personal communication 8

July 2003). Langdon Bay/Moor Sands Archive: British Museum files

Clark, J, 2011 [email to D Parham, Bournemouth University] (personal communication 4 March 2011)

Clark, P (ed), 2004a *The Dover Bronze Age boat*. Swindon: English Heritage

Clark, P (ed), 2004b *The Dover Bronze Age boat in context: society and water transport in prehistoric Europe.* Oxford: Oxbow Books

Clark, P (ed), 2009 *Bronze Age Connections: Cultural Contact in Prehistoric Europe.* Oxford: Oxbow Books

Clarke, D L, 1970 *Beaker Pottery of Great Britain and Ireland*. Cambridge: Cambridge University Press

Coffyn, A, 1985 *Le Bronze Final atlantique dans la Péninsule Iberique*, Publications du Centre Pierre Paris **11**. Paris: Diffusion de Boccard

Coles, J M, 1963–4 Scottish Middle Bronze Age metalwork, *Proc Soc Antiq Scotl*, **97**, 82–156

Coles, J M, 1972 *Field archaeology in Britain*. London: Methuen and Co Ltd

Collard, M, Darvill, T & Watts, M, 2006 Ironworking in the Bronze Age? Evidence from a 10th century BC settlement at Hartshill Copse, Upper Bucklebury, West Berkshire, *Proc Prehist Soc*, **72**, 367–421

Colquhoun, I & Burgess, C B, 1988 *The swords of Britain*, Prähistorische Bronzefunde **IV**/5. Munich: Beck

Coombs, D, 1976 The Dover harbour bronze finds – a Bronze Age wreck?, *Archaeol Atlantica*, **1**, 193–5

Coombs, D, 2001 Metalwork, in F Pryor (ed) *The Flag Fen Basin: archaeology and environment of a fenland landscape.* London: English Heritage, 255–98

Cordier, G & Gruet, M, 1975 L'Âge du Bronze et le premier Âge du Fer en Anjou, *Gallia Préhistoire*, **18**, 157–287

Costa, S, Delahaye, D, Freiré-Diaz, S, Davidson, R, Di Nocera, L and Plessis, E, 2004 Quantification of the Normandy and Picardy chalk cliff retreat by photogrammetric analysis, in R N Mortimore and A Duperret (eds), *Coastal chalk cliff instability*, Geological Society Engineering Geology Special Publication **20**. London: Geological Society, 139–48

Coudrin, [no initial], 1905 Trouvaille de l'époque du bronze faite à Kergoff en Noyal-Pontivy (Morbihan), *Bulletin de la Société Polymathique de Morbihan*, 144–53

Cowen, J, 1952 A bronze sword from Folkestone, *Archaeol Cantiana*, **65**, 90–92

Cowie, T, 1994 A Bronze Age gold torc from the Minch, *Hebridean Naturalist*, **12**, 19–21

Cowie, T & Hall, M, 2001 Late Bronze Age metalwork from Scottish rivers: a rediscovered sword from the River Firth near Cambus, Clackmannanshire, in its wider context, *Tayside and Fife Archaeol J*, **7**, 1–15

Cowie, T & Hall, M, 2010 A new look at the Late Bronze Age metalwork from the Tay, in D Strachan *Carpow in Context: a late Bronze Age logboat from the Tay.* Edinburgh: Society of Antiquaries of Scotland, 151–62

Craddock, T & Craddock, B R, 1997 The inception of metallurgy in south-west Britain: hypotheses and evidence, in P Budd and D Gale (eds) *Prehistoric extractive metallurgy in Cornwall.* Truro: Cornwall Archaeological Unit, 1–14

Cunliffe, B, 1978 *Hengistbury Head*. London: Paul Elek

Cunliffe, B, 1991 *Iron Age communities in Britain*, 3rd edn. London: Routledge

Cunliffe, B, 2001 *Facing the ocean: the Atlantic and its peoples*. Oxford: Oxford University Press

Daniel, G, 1980 Obituary: Keith Muckelroy, *The Times*, 13 September, 14

Darvill, T, 2006 Beyond Hartshill Copse: early ironworking in Britain and its wider context, in M Collard *et al* 2006, 406–16

Davey, P J, 1973 Bronze Age metalwork in Lincolnshire, *Archaeologia*, **104**, 51–127

Davey, P J & Forster, E, 1975 *Bronze Age Metalwork from Lancashire and Cheshire.* Liverpool: University of Liverpool Department of Archaeology work notes 1

Davey, P J & Knowles, G C, 1972 The Appleby hoard, *Archaeol J*, **128**, 154–61

David-Elbiali, M, 2000 *La Suisse occidentale au IIe millénaire av J-C*, Cahiers d'archéologie romande de la bibliothèque historique vaudoise **80**. Lausanne: Cahiers d'archéologie romande

De Mulder, G, 1993 Bronzen baggervondsten uit de Schelde te Moerzeke (O-Vl), *Lunula*, **1**, 37–40

Dean, M, 1981 Langdon Bay Archaeological Project Annual Report. Langdon Bay Archive: 2A/2

Dean, M, 1982a Proposal for underwater work 1982 (submitted to Dr S McGrail, Archaeological Research Centre, National Maritime Museum, 28 February 1982). Langdon Bay Archive: 1A/2

Dean, M, 1982b [Letter to Dr I H Longworth, Keeper, Dept of Prehistoric and Romano-British Antiquities, British Museum] (personal communication 24 March 1982). Moor Sands/Langdon Bay Archive: British Museum files

Dean, M, 1982c Underwater Archaeologist, National Maritime Museum. Moor Sands, Salcombe, 1982 report. 19 October 1982. Moor Sands Archive: 1/2

Dean, M, 1982d Langdon Bay Archaeological Project Annual Report. Langdon Bay Archive: 2A/2

Dean, M, 1983a Aims for fieldwork in 1983 on the Bronze Age site at Langdon Bay (submitted to Dr S McGrail, Archaeological Research Centre, National Maritime Museum, 16 November 1982). Langdon Bay Archive: 1A/2

Dean, M, 1983b Langdon Bay Archaeological Project Annual Reports. Langdon Bay Archive: 2A/2

Dean, M, 1983c [Note to Dr S McGrail, Archaeological Research Centre, National Maritme Museum] (personal communication 23 August 1983). Langdon Bay Archive: 1A/6

Dean, M, 1984a [Letter to I Milligan, Dept of Transport] (personal communication 7 February 1984). Langdon Bay Archive: 1A/3

Dean, M, 1984b Langdon Bay Archaeological Project Annual Reports. Langdon Bay Archive: 2A/2

Dean, M, 1984c Evidence for possible prehistoric and Roman wrecks in British waters, *Int J Naut Archaeol*, **13**, 78–80

Dean, M, 1985 Langdon Bay Archaeological Project Annual Reports. Langdon Bay Archive: 2A/2

Dean, M, 1987a Archaeological Diving Unit Reports. Langdon Bay Archive: 2A/2

Dean, M, 1987b Langdon Bay Archaeological Project Annual Reports. Langdon Bay Archive: 2A/2

Dean, M, 1988 Archaeological Diving Unit, Report No. ADU 034, 22 November 1988. Moor Sands Archive: 1/2

Dean, M, 1990a [Letter to A Moat] (personal communication 26 January 1990). Langdon Bay Archive: 1A/2

Dean, M, 1990b Archaeological Diving Unit Report. Langdon Bay Archive: 2A/2

DCMS, 1973 *Protection of Wrecks Act 1973 (Revised*

Statute), Chap. 33, Section 1:1(a). Available: www. opsi.gov.uk/RevisedStatutes/Acts/ukpga/1973/ cukpga_19730033 Accessed: 31 March 2011

DoE (Heritage Division), 1989 Minutes of the Advisory Committee on Historic Wreck Sites, December 1989. Langdon Bay Archive: 1A/2

Donnelly, J P, Cleary, P, Newby, P and Ettinger, R 2004 Coupling instrumental and geological records of sea-level change: Evidence from southern New England of an increase in the rate of sea-level rise in the late 19th century, *Geophysical Research Letters*, **31**, doi:10.1029/2003GL018933

DoT (Marine Division), 1978 *Statutory Instruments* (1978 No. 764). London: HMSO

DoT (Marine Division), 1979 *Statutory Instruments* (1979 No. 56). London: HMSO

DoTr (Marine Directorate), 1986 [Letter to M Dean, ref MNA 58/26/064] (personal communication 27 November 1986). Langdon Bay Archive: 1A/2

DoTr (Marine Directorate), 1989 [Letter to M Dean, ref MNA 58/26/054] (personal communication 19 December 1989). Langdon Bay Archive: 1A/2

Desittere, M & Weissenborn A M, 1977 *Catalogus voorwerpen uit de metaaltijden*. Gent: Oudheidkundige Musea, Bijloke-museum

Dixon, F, 1849 On bronze or brass relics, celts &c, found in Sussex, *Sussex Archaeol Collect*, **2**, 260–69

Dornbusch, U, 2005a *Controls on chalk cliff erosion in the eastern Channel*, English Scientific Geomorphology Reports. Beaches at Risk Phase 1. Available: http:// www.geog.susx.ac.uk/BAR/publish.html Accessed: 25 March 2011

Dornbusch, U, 2005b *Retreat of chalk cliffs and downwearing of shore platforms in the eastern Channel during the last century*, English Scientific Geomorphology Reports. Beaches at Risk Phase 1. Available: http:// www.geog.susx.ac.uk/BAR/publish.html Accessed: 25 March 2011

Duncombe, J, 1772 [Untitled letter], *The Gentleman's Magazine*, **42**, 266

Duperret, A, Genter, A, Martinex, A & Mortimore, R N, 2004 Coastal chalk cliff instability in NW France: role of lithology, fracture pattern and rainfall, in R N Mortimore & A Duperret (eds) *Coastal chalk cliff instability*, Geological Society Engineering Geology Special Publication **20**. London: Geological Society, 33–56

Durrance, E M & Laming, D J C, 1982 *The geology of Devon*. Exeter: University of Exeter

Earll, R, 1978 Projects Coordinator, Underwater Conservation Programme [Letter to K Muckelroy, Jesus College, Cambridge] (personal communication 19 February 1978)

Earll, R, 1979 Appendix I: A biological assessment of the site, in K Muckelroy and P Baker The Bronze Age site off Moor Sand, near Salcombe, Devon: An interim report on the 1978 season, *Int J Naut Archaeol Underwater Explor*, **8**(3), 189–210

Ehrenberg, M R 1977 *Bronze Age spearheads from Berkshire, Buckinghamshire and Oxfordshire*, BAR Brit Ser **34**. Oxford: British Archaeological Reports

Ehrenberg, M, 1982 The contents of the Acton Park, Rhosnesney, Denbighshire hoard, *Bull Board Celtic Stud*, **30**, 165–7

Elsted, W P, 1856 Proceedings at meetings of the Archaeological Institute, January 4th, 1856, *Archaeol J*, **13**, 98–104

Eluère, C, 1982 *Les ors préhistoriques*, L'Âge du Bronze en France **2**. Paris: Picard

Eogan, G, 1965 *Catalogue of Irish bronze swords*. Dublin: Stationery Office

Eogan, G, 1967 The associated finds of gold bar torcs, *J Roy Soc Antiq Ir*, **97**, 129–75

Eogan, G, 1983 *Hoards of the Irish later Bronze Age*. Dublin: University College

Eogan, G, 1994 *The accomplished art: gold and goldworking in Britain and Ireland during the Bronze Age*. Oxford: Oxbow Books

Eogan, G, 2001 A composite late Bronze Age chain object from Roscommon, Ireland, in W H Metz, B L van Beek & H Steegstra (eds) *Patina: essays presented to Jay Jordan Butler on the occasion of his 80th birthday*. Groningen: privately published, 231–40

Escalon de Fonton, M, 1970 Informations archéologiques. Circonscription Languedoc-Rousillon, *Gallia Préhistorie*, **13**, 513–49

Evans, J, 1881 *The ancient bronze implements, weapons, and ornaments of Great Britain and Ireland*. London: Longmans

Farley, M, 1978 A middle Bronze Age 'chisel' from Ivinghoe, *Rec Buckinghamshire*, **20**, 675–6

Flinder, A, 1977 Advisory Committee on Historic Wreck Sites [Letter to K Muckelroy, Jesus College, Cambridge] (personal communication 8 October 1977)

Floyd, P A, Holdsworth, R E and Steele, S A, 1993 Geochemistry of the Start Complex greenschists: Rhenohercynian MORB? *Geological Magazine*, **130**, 345–52

Fontijn, D R, 2002 *Sacrificial landscapes: cultural biographies of persons, objects and 'natural' places in the Bronze Age of the southern Netherlands, c. 2300–600 BC*, Analecta Praehistorica Leidensia **33/34**. Leiden: University of Leiden

Fontijn, D, 2009 Land at the other end of the sea? Metalwork circulation, geographical knowledge and the significance of British/Irish imports in the Bronze Age of the Low Countries, in P Clark (ed) *Bronze Age connections: cultural contact in prehistoric Europe*. Oxford: Oxbow Books, 129–48

Fordham, S & Mould, Q, 1982 The South Hams survey, in N D Balaam, K Smith & G J Wainwright (eds) The Shaugh Moor project: fourth report – environment, context and conclusion, *Proc Prehist Soc*, **48**, 261–6

Fox, A, 1957 Excavations on Dean Moor in the Avon valley 1954–1956. The late Bronze Age settlement, *Trans Devon Ass*, **89**, 18–77

Fox, A, 1995 Tin ingots from Bigbury Bay, *Proc Devon Archaeol Exploration Soc*, **53**, 11–23

Fox, A & Britton, D, 1969 A continental palstave from the ancient field system on Horridge Common, Dartmoor, *Proc Prehist Soc*, **35**, 220–28

Fox, C, 1923 *The archaeology of the Cambridge region*. Cambridge: Cambridge University Press

Gabillot, M, 2003 *Dépôts et Production Métallique du Bronze Moyen en France Nord-Occidentale*, BAR Int Ser **1174**. Oxford: British Archaeological Reports

Gallay, G, 1988 *Die mittel- und spätbronze- sowie älterisenzeitlichen Bronzedolche in Frankreich und auf den britischen Kanalinseln*, Prähistorische Bronzefunde **VI**/7. Munich: Beck

Gardes, P, 1991 Le Bronze Final dans les Landes: état de la question, in C Chevillot & A Coffyn (eds) *L'Age du*

Bronze Atlantique. Beynac-et-Cazenac: Association des Musées du Sarladais, 183–92

Gaucher, G, 1981 *Sites et Cultures de l'Âge du Bronze dans le Bassin Parisien*, Gallia Préhistoire Supplément **XV**. Paris: Centre National de la Recherche Scientifique

Gaucher, G & Robert, Y, 1967 Les dépôts de bronze de Cannes-Écluse (Seine-et-Marne), *Gallia Préhistoire*, **10**, 169–223

Gehrels, R 2006 The sea-level history and coastal geomorphology of Moor Sands, South Devon. Unpublished report.

Gehrels, W R, 2010 Late Holocene relative sea-level changes and crustal motion around the British Isles: lessons for the 21st century, *Quat Sci Rev*, **29**, 1648–60

Gehrels, W R, Kirby, J R, Prokoph, A, Newnham, R M, Achterberg, E P, Evans, H, Black, S and Scott, D B, 2005 Onset of recent rapid sea-level rise in the western Atlantic Ocean, *Quaternary Science Reviews*, **24**, 2083–100

Gehrels, W R, Marshall, W A, Gehrels, M J, Larsen, G, Kirby, J R, Eiriksson, J, Heinemeier, J and Shimmield, T, 2006 Rapid sea-level rise in the North Atlantic Ocean since the first half of the 19th century, *The Holocene*, **16 (7)**

Gerloff, S, 1986 Bronze Age class A cauldrons: typology, origins and chronology, *J Roy Soc Antiq Ir*, **116**, 84–115

Gerloff, S, 2004 Hallstatt fascination: 'Hallstatt' buckets, swords and chapes from Britain and Ireland, in H Roche, E Grogan, J Bradley, J Coles & B Raftery (eds) *From megaliths to metal: essays in honour of George Eogan*. Oxford: Oxbow Books, 124–54

Gerloff, S, 2007 Reinecke's ABC and the chronology of the British Bronze Age, in C Burgess, P Topping & F Lynch (eds) *Beyond Stonehenge: essays in honour of Colin Burgess*. Oxford: Oxbow Books, 117–61

Gerloff, S, 2010 *Atlantic cauldrons and buckets of the late Bronze and early Iron Ages in Western Europe*, Prähistorische Bronzefunde, **II**/18. Stuttgart: Franz Steiner Verlag

Giardino, C, 1995 *Il Mediterraneo occidentale fra XIV ed VIII secolo a.c. cerchi minerarie e metallurgiche* [*The west Mediterranean between the 14th and 8th centuries BC Mining and metallurgical spheres*], BAR Int Ser **612**. Oxford: British Archaeological Reports

Giardino, C, 2004 I Ripostigli, in D C Genick (ed) *L'Età del Bronzo Recente in Italia: Atti del Congresso Nazionale di Lido di Camaiore, 26–29 Ottobre 2000*. Lucca: M. Baroni

Gibbard, P L, 1995 The formation of the Strait of Dover, in R C Preece (ed) *Island Britain: a Quaternary perspective*, Geological Society Special Publication **96**. London: Geological Society, 15–26

Gibbons, W, 1977 Advisory Committee on Historic Wreck Sites, Dept of Trade (Marine Division) [Letter to P Baker] (personal communication 6 December 1977). Moor Sands Archive: 2/4

Gibbons, W, 1978a Dept of Trade (Marine Division) Ref MNA 58/26/054 [Letter to K Muckelroy] (personal communication 25 May 1978). Langdon Bay Archive: 1A/2

Gibbons, W, 1978b Dept of Trade (Marine Division) Ref MNA 58/26/054 [Letter to K Muckelroy] (personal communication 12 July 1978). Langdon Bay Archive: 1A/2

Gomez de Soto, J, 1985 Haches à talon massives de l'Age

du Bronze final dans le Centre-Ouest, *Bulletin de la Société d'Émulation de la Vendée*, 227–36

Gomez de Soto, J, 1995 *Le Bronze Moyen en Occident: la Culture des Duffaits et la Civilisation des Tumulus*, L'Âge du Bronze en France **5**. Paris: Picard

Gouge, P & Peake, R, 2005 Aux marges du Bronze atlantique: sites et chronologies de la région du confluent Seine-Yonne, in J Bourgeois & M Talon (eds) *L'Âge du Bronze du Nord de la France dans son Contexte Européen*. Paris: Comité des Travaux Historiques et Scientifiques, 333–60

Greatorex, C, 2003 Living on the margins? The late Bronze Age landscape of the Willingdon levels, in D Rudling (ed) *The archaeology of Sussex to AD 2000*. Great Dunham: Heritage, 89–100

Green, H S, 1973 Archaeology and the M5 motorway, *Proc Somerset Archaeol Natur Hist Soc*, **117**, 33–46

Green, H S, 1985 Four Bronze Age sword-finds from Wales, *Bull Board Celtic Stud*, **32**, 283–7

Green, J, 1977 *The Loss of the Verenigde Oostindische Compagnie Jacht Verguide Draeck, Western Australia in 1656*, BAR Int Ser **36**. Oxford: British Archaeological Reports

Gregory, C A, 1982 *Gifts and commodities*. London: Academic Press

Griffith, F M & Quinnell, H, 1999a Barrows and ceremonial sites in the Neolithic and earlier Bronze Age, in R Kain & W Ravenhill (eds) *Historical atlas of south-west England*. Exeter: Exeter University Press, 55–61

Griffith, F M & Quinnell, H, 1999b Settlement, c. 2500 BC to c. AD 600, in R Kain & W Ravenhill (eds) *Historical atlas of south-west England*. Exeter: Exeter University Press, 62–8

Griffith, F M & Wilkes, E M, 2006 The land seen from the sea? Coastal archaeology and place-names of Bigbury Bay, Devon, *Archaeol J*, **163**, 67–91

Grinsell, L V, 1992 The Bronze Age round barrows of Kent, *Proc Prehist Soc*, **58**, 355–84

Grove, J M, 2002 *The Little Ice Age*, 2nd edn. London: Routledge

Grove, L R A, 1954 Two bronze socketed axes from West Peckham, *Archaeol Cantiana*, **68**, 10

Gupta, S, Collier, J, Potter, G & Palmer-Felgate, A, 2005 Catastrophic flood geomorphology in the English Channel compared with Martian outflow channels, *Geophysical Research Abstracts*, **7**, 10803

Hall, E T, 1978a Littlemore Scientific Engineering Co [Letter to K Muckelroy, Jesus College, Cambridge] (personal communication 21 March 1978). Moor Sands Archive: 2/15

Hall, E T, 1978b [Letter to K Muckelroy, Jesus College, Cambridge] (personal communication 23 May 1978). Moor Sands Archive: 2/15

Halliwell, G & Parfitt, K, 1985 The prehistoric land surface in the Lydden Valley: an initial report, *Kent Archaeol Rev*, **82**, 39–43

Harbison, P, 1969 *The axes of the early Bronze Age in Ireland*, Prähistorische Bronzefunde **IX**/1. Munich: Beck

Harding, A F, 1993 Europe and the Mediterranean in the Bronze Age: cores and peripheries, in C Scarre and F Healy (eds) *Trade and exchange in prehistoric Europe*, Oxbow Monograph **33**. Oxford: Oxbow Books, 153–60

Harding, A F, 2000 *European societies in the Bronze Age*. Cambridge: Cambridge University Press

Harding, A, Šumberová, R, Knüsel, C & Outram, A, 2007

Velim: violence and death in Bronze Age Bohemia. Prague: Archeologický ústav AV ČR

Harris, C S, Hart, M B, Varley, P M & Warren, C D, 1996 *Engineering geology of the Channel Tunnel.* London: Thomas Telford

Hasenson, A, 1980 *The history of Dover harbour.* London: Aurum Special Editions

Hawkes, C F C, 1942 The Deverel Urn and the Picardy pin: a phase of Bronze Age settlement in Kent, *Proc Prehist Soc*, **8**, 26–47

Hawkes, C F C, 1955 *Grave-groups and hoards of the British Bronze Age*, Inventaria Archaeologica, GB. 1–8. London: International Congress of Prehistoric and Protohistoric Sciences

Helms, M W, 2009 The master(y) of hard materials: thoughts on technology, materiality and ideology occasioned by the Dover boat, in P Clark (ed) *Bronze Age connections: cultural contact in prehistoric Europe.* Oxford: Oxbow Books, 149–58

Holdsworth, R E, 1989 The Start–Perranporth line: a Devonian terrane boundary in the Variscan orogen of SW England?, *Journal of the Geological Society*, **146**, 419–21

Holme, N A, 1978 Marine Biological Association of the UK [Letter to K Muckelroy, Jesus College, Cambridge] (personal communication 20 March 1978). Moor Sands Archive: 2/15

Inventory of bronze objects recovered as of 5 August, 1979 Langdon Bay Archive: 1A/2

Jeannet, A, 1968 Catalogue des objets de l'Age du Bronze du Musée de Tournus (Saône-et-Loire), *Revue Archéologique de l'Est et du Centre-Est*, **19**, 69–97

Keeley, H, Allison, E, Branch, N, Cameron, N, Dobinson, S, Ellis, I, Ellison, P, Fairbairn, A, Green, C, Hunter, R, Lee, J, Locker, A, Lowe, J, Palmer, A, Robinson, E, Stewart, J & Wilkinson, K, 2004 The environmental evidence in P Clark (ed) *The Dover Bronze Age boat.* Swindon: English Heritage, 229–50

Kibbert, K, 1980 *Die Äxte und Beile im mittleren Westdeutschland I*, Prähistorische Bronzefunde **IX**/10. Munich: Beck

Kibbert, K, 1984 *Die Äxte und Beile im mittleren Westdeutschland II*, Prähistorische Bronzefunde **IX**/13. Munich: Beck

Kubach, W, 1973 Westeuropäische formen in einem frühurnenfelderzeitlichen Depotfund aus dem Rhein bei Mainz, *Archäologisches Korrespondenzblatt*, **3**, 299–307

Kytlicová, O, 2007 *Jungbronzezeitliche Hortfunde in Böhmen*, Prähistorische Bronzefunde **XX**/12. Stuttgart: Franz Steiner

Lanting, J N & van der Plicht, J, 2001/2 De ^{14}C-chronologie van de nederlandse pre- en protohistorie, IV: bronstijd en vroege ijzertijd, *Palaeohistoria*, **43/44**, 117–262

Lawrence, M & Dean, M, 1996 Archaeological Diving Unit Report. Langdon Bay Archive: 2A/2

Lawson, A, 1979a A late Middle Bronze Age hoard from Hunstanton, Norfolk, in C Burgess & D Coombs (eds) *Bronze Age hoards: some finds old and new*, BAR Brit Ser **67**. Oxford: British Archaeological Reports, 42–92

Lawson, A, 1979b A late Bronze Age hoard from West Caister, Norfolk, in C Burgess & D Coombs (eds) *Bronze Age hoards: some finds old and new*, BAR Brit Ser **67**. Oxford: British Archaeological Reports, 173–9

Lawson, A, 1984 An unusual Bronze Age sword from Highclere, Hampshire, *Proc Hampshire Fld Club*, **41**, 281–4

Lawson, A, 1999 The Bronze Age hoards of Hampshire, in A F Harding (ed) *Experiment and design: archaeological studies in honour of John Coles.* Oxford: Oxbow Books, 94–107

Lawson, A J & Farwell, D E, 1991 Archaeological investigation following the discovery of a hoard of palstaves near New Inn Farmhouse, Marnhull, Dorset, *Proc Dorset Natur Hist Archaeol Soc*, **112**, 131–8

Le Roux, C T & Thollard, P, 1990 Gallia Informations – Bretagne, *Gallia Préhistoire*, **33**, 1–80

Leman, P, 1978 Informations archéologiques – Circonscription du Nord-Pas-de-Calais, *Gallia Préhistorie*, **21**, 447–68

Lindendauf, A, 2003 The sea as a place of no return in ancient Greece, *World Archaeol*, **35**, 416–33

Liversage, D, 2000 *Interpreting impurity patterns in ancient bronze: Denmark*, Nordiske Fortidsminer Serie C, **1**. Copenhagen: Det Koneglige Nordiske Oldskriftselskab

Liversage, D and Northover, J P, 1998 Prehistoric trade monopolies and bronze supply in northern Europe, in C Mordant, M Pernot & V Rychner (eds) *L'Atelier du bronzier en Europe du XXe au VIIIe siècle avant Notre Ère, I (Session de Neuchâtel).* Paris: Èditions du CTHS, 137–52

Long, A J, Scaife, R G & Edwards, R J, 2000 Stratigraphic architecture, relative sea-level and models of estuary development in southern England: new data from Southampton Water, in K Pye & J Allen (eds) *Coastal and estuary environments, sedimentology, geomorphology and geoarchaeology*, Geological Society Special Publication **175**. London: Geological Society, 253–80

Long, A J, Waller, M P & Plater, A J, 2007 *Dungeness and Romney Marsh: barrier dynamics and marshland evolution.* Oxford: Oxbow Books

Longworth, I H, 1977a Unpublished report (11 February 1977) from British Museum, Keeper of Prehistoric and Romano-British Antiquities, No A3/47/51/012. Moor Sands/Langdon Bay Archive: British Museum files

Longworth, I H, 1977b [Letter to D Wilson] (personal communication 10 February 1977). Moor Sands/Langdon Bay Archive: British Museum files

Longworth, I H, 1979a Unpublished report (21 February 1979) from British Museum, Keeper of Prehistoric and Romano-British Antiquities, No A3/81/47/2. Moor Sands/Langdon Bay Archive: British Museum files

Longworth, I H, 1979b [Letter to K Muckelroy, Jesus College, Cambridge] (personal communication 31 May 1979). Moor Sands Archive: 2/5

Longworth, I H, 1980 Unpublished submission for funds from Keeper, Dept of Prehistoric and Romano-British Antiquities to British Museum Board of Trustees (11 February 1980). Moor Sands/Langdon Bay Archive: British Museum files

Longworth, I H, 1981 [Letter to Dr T Hall. Research Laboratory for Archaeology and History of Art, Oxford] (personal communication 18 December 1981). Moor Sands/Langdon Bay Archive: British Museum files

Longworth, I H, 1983 [Letter to the Director, British Museum] (personal communication 21 March 1983). Moor Sands/Langdon Bay Archive: British Museum files

Longworth, I H, 1984 *Collared urns of the Bronze Age in*

Great Britain and Ireland. Cambridge: Cambridge University Press

Lynch, F, 1991 *Prehistoric Anglesey: the archaeology of the island to the Roman conquest,* 2nd edn. Llangefni: Anglesey Antiquarian Society

McDakin, C, 1900 Coast erosion. Dover Cliffs. Read before the British Association 18 September 1899, Dover, Standard Office

McDonald, K, 1978 *The treasure divers.* London: Pelham

McDonald, K, 1994 *Shipwrecks of the South Hams: the wreckwalker's guide to the coast path from Erme to Dart.* Kingsbridge: Wreckwalker Books

McGrail, S, 1978a Archaeological Research Centre, National Maritime Museum [Letter to K Muckelroy, Jesus College, Cambridge] (personal communication 25 April 1978). Moor Sands Archive: 2/3

McGrail, S, 1978b [Letter to K Muckelroy, Jesus College, Cambridge] (personal communication 27 April 1978). Moor Sands Archive: 2/2

McGrail, S, 1979 [Letter to K Muckelroy, Jesus College, Cambridge] (personal communication 11 January 1979). Moor Sands Archive: 2/2

McGrail, S., 1980 [Letter to A Moat] (personal communication, 15 October 1980). Langdon Bay Archive: 1A/3

McGrail, S, 1983a [Letter to Dr I H Longworth, Keeper, Dept of Prehistoric and Romano-British Antiquities, British Museum] (personal communication 5 May 1983). Moor Sands/Langdon Bay Archive: British Museum Files

McGrail, S, 1983b [Letter to Dr I H Longworth, Keeper, Dept of Prehistoric and Romano-British Antiquities, British Museum] (personal communication 2 September 1983). Langdon Bay Archive: 1A/6

McGrail, S, 1993 Prehistoric seafaring in the Channel, in C Scarre and F Healy (eds) *Trade and exchange in prehistoric Europe.* Oxford: Oxbow Books, 199–210

Mäder, A, 2002 *Die spätbronzezeitlichen und spätlatènezeitlichen Brandstellen und Brandbestattugen in Elgg (Kanton Zürich). Untersuchungen zu Kremation und Bestattungsbrauchtum,* Zürcher Archäologie 8–9. Zürich/Egg: Fotorotar AG

Mäder, A & Sormaz, T, 2000 Die Dendrodaten der beginnenden Spätbronzezeit (Bz D) von Elgg ZH-Breiti, *Jahrbuch der Schweizerischen Gesellschaft für Ur- und Frühgeschichte,* **83,** 65–78

Malcolm, J O, 1977 Institute of Oceanographic Sciences [Letter to K Muckelroy, Jesus College, Cambridge] (personal communication December 1977). Moor Sands Archive: 2/7

Manby, T, 1980 Bronze Age settlement in east Yorkshire, in J Barrett & R Bradley (eds) *Settlement and society in the British later Bronze Age,* BAR Brit Ser **83.** Oxford: British Archaeological Reports, 307–70

Marcigny, C, Colonna, C, Ghesquière, E & Verron, G, 2005a *La Normandie à l'Aube de l'Histoire: les Décourvertes Archéologiques de l'Âge du Bronze 2300–800 avJ-C* Paris: Somogy Éditions d'Art

Marcigny, C, Ghesquière, E, Clément-Sauleau, S & Verney, A, 2005b L'Âge du Bronze en Basse-Normandie: definition par le mobilier céramique, une première tentative, in J Bourgeois and M Talon (eds) *L'Âge du Bronze du Nord de la France.* Paris: Comité des Travaux Historiques et Scientifiques, 303–32

Marolles, C, 1991 Découverte de fragments d'épées en bronze sur le site des 'Hautes-Chanvières', à Mairy (Ardennes), *Préhistoire et Protohistoire en Champagne-Ardennes,* **15,** 75–80

Marsden, P, 1986 The origin of the Council for Nautical Archaeology. *International Journal of Nautical Archaeology,* **15,** 179–183 doi: 10.1111/j.1095-9270.1986.tb00574.x

Marsden, P R V, 2005 *Sealed by time: the loss and recovery of the Mary Rose,* Archaeology of the Mary Rose **1.** Portsmouth: Mary Rose Trust

Marsille, L, 1913 Les dépôts de l'Âge du Bronze dans le Morbihan, *Bulletin de la Société Polymathique de Morbihan,* 49–109

Martin, C, 1975 *Full fathom five.* London: Chatto & Windus

Martin, E, Plouviez, J & Row, H, 1981 Archaeology in Suffolk: archaeological finds, 1980, *Proc Suffolk Inst Archaeol Hist,* **35,** 73–6

Massey, A C, 2004 Holocene sea-level changes along the Channel coast of south-west England. Unpubl PhD thesis, University of Plymouth, Plymouth

Massey, A C, Gehrels, W R, Charman, D J, Milne, G A, Peltier, W R, Lambeck, K & Selby, K A, 2008 Relative sea-level change and postglacial isostatic adjustment along the coast of south Devon, United Kingdom, *J Quat Sci,* **23,** 415–33

May, V, 1971 The retreat of Chalk Cliffs, *Geogr J,* **137,** 203–6

May, V & Heeps, C, 1985 The nature and rates of change on chalk coastlines, *Zeitschrift für Geomorphologie NF Supplementband,* **57,** 81–94

Mayer, E F, 1977 *Die Äxte und Beile in Österreich,* Prähistorische Bronzefunde **IX**/9. Munich: Beck

Megaw, B R S & Hardy, E M, 1938 British decorated axes and their diffusion during the earlier part of the Bronze Age, *Proc Prehist Soc,* **4,** 272–307

Milligan, I, 1978 Dept of Trade (Marine Division) [Letter to K Muckelroy, Jesus College, Cambridge] (personal communication 1 December 1978). Langdon Bay Archive: 1A/2

Millotte, J-P, Cordier, G & Abauzit, P, 1968 Essai de typologie protohistorique: les haches à ailerons medians, *Revue Archéologique de l'Est et du Centre-Est,* **19,** 7–67

Moat, A, 1978a [Letter to K Muckelroy, Jesus College, Cambridge] (personal communication 19 October 1978). Langdon Bay Archive: 1A/2

Moat, A, 1978b Lecture to Diving Officers' Conference, 26 November 1978. Langdon Bay Archive: 1A/4

Moat, A, 1979 [Letter to K Muckelroy, Jesus College, Cambridge] (Personal communication, 9 April 1979). Langdon Bay Archive: 1A/2

Moat, A, 1980 [letter to S McGrail] (personal communication, 25 October 1980). Langdon Bay Archive: 1A/3

Moat, A, 1981 [Notes from lecture to Council for Kentish Archaeology, spring meeting] (personal communication March 1981). Langdon Bay Archive: 1A/4

Moat, A, 1986 [Letter to M Dean] (personal communication 13 October 1986). Langdon Bay Archive: 1A/2

Moat, A, 1987 Summary of diving operations during the 1987 season, 13 October 1987. Langdon Bay Archive: 1A/2

Moat, A, 1988 [Letter to M Dean] (personal communication 17 October 1988). Langdon Bay Archive: 1A/2

Moat, A, 1989a [Letter to Dept of Transport (Marine Directorate)] (personal communication 25 March 1989). Langdon Bay Archive: 1A/2

Moat, A, 1989b Working report for 1 June to 15 October 1989, 16 October 1989. Langdon Bay Archive: 1A/2

Moat, A, 1990 [Letter to M Dean] (personal communication 19 October 1990). Langdon Bay Archive: 1A/2

Moat, A, 1993 Langdon Bay Archaeological Project Annual Reports. Langdon Bay Archive: 2A/2

Moat, A & Baker, P, 1980 Langdon Bay Archaeological Project: Preliminary report, 1980. Moor Sands/Langdon Bay Archive: British Museum Files

Mohen, J-P, 1977 *L'Age du bronze dans la région de Paris*. Paris: Editions des Musées Nationaux

Mohen, J-P & Bailloud, G, 1987 *La Vie Quotidienne: les Fouilles du Fort Harrouard*, L'Âge du Bronze en France **4**. Paris: Picard

Monteagudo, L, 1977 *Die Beile auf der Iberischen Halbinsel*, Prähistorische Bronzefunde **IX**/6. Munich: Beck

Moody, G, 2008 *The Isle of Thanet: from prehistory to the Norman Conquest*. Stroud: The History Press

Mordant, C, Mordant, D & Prampart, J-Y, 1976 Le dépôt de bronze de Villethierry (Yonne), *Gallia Préhistoire*, IXe supplement

Morey, C R, 1976 The natural history of Slapton Ley Nature Reserve IX: the morphology and history of the lake basins, *Field Studies* **4**, 353–68.

Morey, C R, 1983 The evolution of a barrier-lagoon system – a case study from Start Bay, *Proceedings of the Ussher Society*, **5**, 454–9.

Morris, R, 1972 *HMS Colossus: the story of the salvage of the Hamilton Treasures*. London: Hutchinson

Mortimore, R N, Lawrence, J, Pope, D, Duperret, A & Genter, A, 2004 Coastal cliff geohazards in weak rock: the UK Chalk cliffs of Sussex, in R N Mortimore & A Duperret (eds) *Coastal chalk cliff instability*, Geological Society Engineering Geology Special Publication **20**. London: Geological Society, 3–32

Moskal, M, 2007 Późnobrązowe miecze z językiem karpia na terenie Europy, in J Chochorowski (ed) *Studia nad epoką brązu i wczesną epoką żelaza w Europie. Księga poświęcona Profesoriwi Markowi Gedlowi na pięćdziesięciolecie pracy w Uniwersytecie Jagiellońskim*. Kraków: Wydawnictwo Uniwersytetu Jagiellońskiego, 465–531

Mottershead, D N, 1971 Coastal head deposits between Start Point and Hope Cove, Devon, *Field Studies*, **3**, 433–53

Mottershead, D N, 1982 Coastal spray weathering of bedrock in the supratidal zone at East Prawle, south Devon, *Field Studies*, **5**, 663–84

Mottershead, D N, 1989 Rates and patterns of bedrock denudation by coastal salt spray weathering: a seven-year record, *Earth Surface Processes and Landforms*, **14**, 383–98

Mottershead, D N, 1994 Tafoni on coastal slopes, south Devon, UK, *Earth Surface Processes and Landforms*, **19**, 543–63

Mottershead, D N, 1997 *Classic landforms of the south Devon coast*. Sheffield: The Geographical Association and The British Geomorphological Research Group

Muckelroy, K, 1975 Ten years of underwater archaeology, *Triton*, **20**(4), 17–18

Muckelroy, K, 1976 The integration of historical and archaeological data concerning an historic wreck site; the 'Kennemerland', *World Archaeol*, **7**(3), 280–89

Muckelroy, K, 1977a Outline for Salcombe swords expedition, No 1, 15–18 October 1977. Moor Sands Archive: 1/2

Muckelroy, K, 1977b The Salcombe Swords, unpublished report. Moor Sands Archive: 1/2

Muckelroy, K, 1977c [Letter to Prof K Branigan] (personal communication 19 October 1977). Moor Sands Archive: 2/12

Muckelroy, K, 1977d [Letter to M Rule, Mary Rose Trust] (personal communication 20 October 1977). Moor Sands Archive: 2/15

Muckelroy, K, 1977e Dive log for 15 October 1977. Moor Sands Archive: 4/2

Muckelroy, K, 1977f [Letter to P Baker] (personal communication 2 November 1977). Moor Sands Archive: 2/3

Muckelroy, K, 1977g [Letter to P Baker] (personal communication 4 November 1977). Moor Sands Archive: 2/3

Muckelroy, K, 1977h [Letter to I H Longworth, Keeper, Dept of Prehistoric and Romano-British Antiquities, British Museum] (personal communication 23 December 1977). Moor Sands Archive: 2/5

Muckelroy, K, 1978a The Salcombe Bronze Age Wreck: Prospectus for the 1978 season. Moor Sands Archive: 1/2

Muckelroy, K, 1978b [Letter to Mrs M Stevens, 8 The Ridgeway River, Dover] (personal communication 11 February 1978). Langdon Bay Archive: 1A/2

Muckelroy, K, 1978c [Verbal report to I Kinnes, British Museum, Dept of Prehistoric and Romano-British Antiquities as noted in letter to The Keeper, Conservation, BM] (personal communication 25 May 1978). Moor Sands/Langdon Bay Archive: British Museum Files

Muckelroy, K, 1978d Working sequence for each area of site, May 1978. Langdon Bay Archive: 1A/10

Muckelroy, K, 1978e Report written in support of application for designation to protect wreck site at Langdon Bay to Dept of Trade (Marine Division), June 1978. Langdon Bay Archive: 1A/3

Muckelroy, K, 1978f [Letter to P Baker] (personal communication 4 June 1978). Moor Sands Archive: 2/3

Muckelroy, K, 1978g [Letter to R Valentine, Director General, BSAC] (personal communication 9 June 1978) Langdon Bay Archive: 1A/2

Muckelroy, K, 1978h [Letter to S McGrail, Archaeological Research Centre, National Maritime Museum] (personal communication 3 September 1978). Moor Sands Archive: 2/2

Muckelroy, K, 1978i Salcombe Bronze Age Wreck Project: a preliminary report, September 1978. Moor Sands Archive: 1/2

Muckelroy, K, 1978j [Letter to Dr D Coombs, Dept of Archaeology, University of Manchester] (personal communication 1 October 1978). Langdon Bay Archive: 1A/2

Muckelroy, K, 1978l Salcombe Bronze Age Wreck Project, *NATNEWS*, 1978(3), 1

Muckelroy, K, 1978m [Letter to Dr D Coombs, Dept of Archaeology, University of Manchester] (personal communication 12 October 1978). Langdon Bay Archive: 1A/2

Muckelroy, K, 1978n [Letter to D C Langmead, Deputy Curator, Hydrographic Dept, MOD, Taunton] (personal communication 22 October 1978). Langdon Bay Archive: 1A/2

Muckelroy, K, 1978o [Letter to M Oram, Dover Branch, BSAC] (personal communication 28 November 1978). Langdon Bay Archive: 1A/2

Muckelroy, K, 1978p [Application for licence to excavate, to Dept of Trade (Marine Division)] (personal communication exact date unknown). Langdon Bay Archive: 1A/2

Muckelroy, K, 1979a The Bronze Age site at Langdon Bay,

near Dover, Kent: a prospectus for the 1979 season (1 January 1979). Langdon Bay Archive: 1A/2

Muckelroy, K, 1979b Salcombe Bronze Age Wreck Project: proposed programme of work. Moor Sands Archive: 1/2

Muckelroy, K, 1979c Notes for site working, 18 March 1979. Langdon Bay Archive: 1A/11

Muckelroy, K, 1979d [Letter to J Hazard, Director of Coaching, BSAC] (personal communication 4 April 1979). Moor Sands Archive: 2/15

Muckelroy, K, 1979e [Letter to P Baker] (personal communication 2 May 1979). Moor Sands Archive: 2/3

Muckelroy, K, 1979f [Letter to S McGrail, Archaeological Research Centre, National Maritime Museum] (personal communication 3 May 1979), Langdon Bay Archive: 1A/2

Muckelroy, K, 1979g [Letter to A Bax, Plymouth Ocean Projects] (personal communication 2 June 1979). Moor Sands Archive: 2/15

Muckelroy, K, 1979h The Bronze Age site off Moor Sand, Salcombe, Devon: an interim report on the 1979 season. Moor Sands Archive: 1/2

Muckelroy, K, 1979i [Letter to I Milligan, Dept of Trade (Marine Division)] (personal communication 26 June 1979). Langdon Bay Archive: 1A/2

Muckelroy, K, 1979j [Letter to I W Milligan, Dept of Trade (Marine Division)] (personal communication 17 October 1979). Moor Sands Archive: 2/4

Muckelroy, K, 1980a [Letter to A Moat] (personal communication 30 January 1980). Langdon Bay Archive: 1A/2

Muckelroy, K, 1980b [Letter to I H Longworth, Keeper, Dept of Prehistoric and Romano-British Antiquities, British Museum] (personal communication 23 July 1980). Langdon Bay Archive: 1A/2

Muckelroy, K, 1980c Two Bronze Age cargoes in British waters, *Antiquity*, **54**(211), 100–109

Muckelroy, K, 1981 Middle Bronze Age trade between Britain and Europe: a maritime perspective, *Proc Prehist Soc*, **47**, 275–97

Muckelroy, K & Baker, P, 1978 Salcombe Bronze Age Wreck Project: notes for participants. Moor Sands Archive: 3/7

Muckelroy, K & Baker, P, 1979 The Bronze Age site off Moor Sand, near Salcombe, Devon: an interim report on the 1978 season, *Int J Naut Archaeol*, **8**, 189–210

Muckelroy, K & Baker, P, 1980a The Bronze Age site off Moor Sand, near Salcombe, Devon: an interim report on the 1979 season. *Int J Naut Archaeol*, **9**, 155–8

Muckelroy, K & Baker, P, 1980b In pursuit of a Bronze Age hoard, *Diver*, November 1980, 16–19

Müller-Karpe, H, 1959 *Beiträge zur Chronologie der Urnenfelderzeit nördlich und südlich der Alpen*, Römisch-Germanische Forschungen **23**. Berlin: De Gruyter

Musson, R M W, Neilson, G and Burton, P W, 1984 *Macroseismic reports on historical British Earthquakes*, Global seismology unit **208**. Edinburgh: Natural environment research council

Nallier, R & Le Goffic, M, 2008 Rosnoën 60 ans après. Compléments et révision concernant le dépôt de l'Âge du Bronze final de Penavern (Finistère), *Bulletin de la Société Préhistorique Française*, **105**, 131–57

Needham, S P, 1979 The extent of foreign influence on Early Bronze Age axe development in southern Britain, in M Ryan (ed) *The origins of metallurgy in Atlantic Europe*. Dublin: Stationery Office, 265–93

Needham, S P, 1980 A bronze from Winterfold Heath, Wonersh, and its place in the British narrow-bladed palstave sequence, *Surrey Archaeol Collect*, **72**, 37–47

Needham, S P, 1981 Valuation of 1980 finds from Langdon Bay [Letter to Dr I H Longworth, Keeper, Dept of Prehistoric and Romano-British Antiquities, British Museum] (personal communication 29 December 1981). Moor Sands/Langdon Bay Archive: British Museum files

Needham, S P, 1982a Archaeological assessment of the Langdon Bay project, 1974–1981 (unpublished report). Langdon Bay Archive: 1A/2

Needham, S P, 1982b *The Ambleside hoard*, British Museum Occasional Paper **39**. London: British Museum Press

Needham, S P, 1983 The early Bronze Age axeheads of central and southern England. Unpubl PhD thesis, University College, Cardiff

Needham, S P, 1987 The Bronze Age, in J Bird & D G Bird (eds) *The archaeology of Surrey to 1540*. Guildford: Surrey Archaeological Society, 97–137

Needham, S P, 1988 A group of early Bronze Age axes from Lydd, in J Eddison & C Green (eds) *Romney Marsh: evolution, occupation, reclamation*. Oxford University Committee for Archaeology Monograph **24**. Oxford: Oxford University Committee for Archaeology, 77–82

Needham, S P, 1990a *The Petters late Bronze Age metalwork: an analytical study of Thames Valley metalworking in a settlement context*, British Museum Occasional Paper **70**. London: British Museum

Needham, S P, 1990b The Penard-Wilburton succession: new metalwork finds from Croxton (Norfolk) and Thirsk (Yorkshire), *Antiq J*, **70**, 253–70

Needham, S P, 1991 [Letter to Dr I H Longworth, Keeper, Dept of Prehistoric and Romano-British Antiquities, British Museum] (personal communication 5 July 1991). Moor Sands/Langdon Bay Archive: British Museum files

Needham, S P, 1992 The structure of settlement and ritual in the Late Bronze Age of south-eastern Britain, in C Mordant and A Richard (eds) *L'Habitat et l'Occupation du Sol à l'Age du Bronze en Europe*, Documents Préhistoriques **4**. Paris: Comité des Travaux Historiques et Scientifiques, 49–69

Needham, S P, 1993 A Bronze Age goldworking anvil from Lichfield, Staffordshire, *Antiq J*, **73**, 125–32

Needham, S P, 2005 Yarmouth, Isle of Wight: Middle Bronze Age base-metal scatter (2003 T392), in *Treasure Annual Report 2003*. London: DCMS, 20–21

Needham, S P, 2007a Cirencester area, Gloucestershire: Bronze Age gold and base-metal scatter, in *Treasure Annual Report 2004*. London: DCMS, 26–33

Needham, S P, 2007b The great divide, in C Haselgrove and R Pope (eds) *The earlier Iron Age in Britain and the near continent*. Oxford: Oxbow Books, 39–63

Needham, S P, 2007c Bronze makes a Bronze Age? Considering the systemics of Bronze Age metal use and the implications of selective deposition, in C Burgess, P Topping & F Lynch (eds) *Beyond Stonehenge: essays in honour of Colin Burgess*. Oxford: Oxbow Books, 278–87

Needham, S P, 2008 Bronze palstave-adze, in A Mudd & B Pears *Bronze Age Field System at Tower's Fen, Thorney, Peterborough: Excavations at 'Thorney*

Borrow Pit' 2004–2005, BAR Brit Ser **471**. Oxford: British Archaeological Reports, 71–3

Needham, S P, 2009 Encompassing the sea: 'maritories' and Bronze Age maritime interactions, in P Clark (ed) *Bronze Age connections: cultural contact in prehistoric Europe*. Oxford: Oxbow Books, 12–37

Needham, S P & Bowman, S, 2005 Flesh-hooks, technological complexity and the Atlantic Bronze Age feasting complex, *European J Archaeol*, **8**, 93–136

Needham, S P & Burgess, C B, 1980 The later Bronze Age in the lower Thames valley: the metalwork evidence, in J Barrett & R Bradley (eds) *Settlement and society in the British later Bronze Age*. BAR Brit Ser **83**. Oxford: British Archaeological Reports, 437–69

Needham, S P & Dean, M, 1987 La cargaison de Langdon Bay à Douvres (Grandes Bretagne): la signification pour les échanges à travers la Manche, in J-C Blanchet (ed) *Les Relations Entre le Continent et les Îles Britanniques à l'Âge du Bronze*. Amiens: Supplément à la Revue Archéologique de Picardie, 119–24

Needham, S P & Giardino, C, 2008 From Sicily to Salcombe: a Mediterranean Bronze Age object from British coastal waters, *Antiquity*, **82**, 60–72

Needham, S P & Hook, D R, 1988 Lead and lead alloys in the Bronze Age: recent finds from Runnymede Bridge, in E A Slater & J Tate (eds) *Science and Archaeology, Glasgow 1987*, BAR Brit Ser **196**. Oxford: British Archaeological Reports, 259–74

Needham, S P & Rigby, V, 2003 The roll-headed copper alloy pins, in P Hutchings, Ritual and riverside settlement: a multi-period site at Princes Road, Dartford, *Archaeol Cantiana*, **123**, 41–79

Needham, S P, Ramsey, C B, Coombs, D, Cartwright, C & Pettitt, P, 1997 An independent chronology for British Bronze Age metalwork: the results of the Oxford Radiocarbon Accelerator, *Archaeol J*, **154**, 55–107

Needham, S P, Parfitt, K & Varndell, G (eds), 2006 *The Ringlemere Cup: precious cups and the beginning of the Channel Bronze Age*, British Museum Research Publication **163**. London: British Museum Press

Needham, S P, Varndell, G & Worrell, S, 2007 A Late Bronze Age hoard of gold and bronze from near Berwick-upon-Tweed, Northumberland, in C Burgess, P Topping & F Lynch (eds) *Beyond Stonehenge: essays in honour of Colin Burgess*. Oxford: Oxbow Books, 397–402

Needham, S P, Northover, J P, Uckelmann, M & Tabor, R, 2012 South Cadbury: the last of the bronze shields? *Archäologisches Korrespondenzblatt* **42**, 473–92

Newman, P, 2003 *Deckler's Cliff field system, East Portlemouth, Devon*, Archaeological Investigation Report Series A1/16/2003. Swindon: English Heritage

Nicholson, S M, 1980 *Catalogue of the prehistoric metalwork in Merseyside County Museums*, University of Liverpool Department of Archaeology work notes **2**. Liverpool: University of Liverpool

Norfolk Museums Service, 1977 *Bronze Age metalwork in Norwich Castle Museum*, 2nd edn. Norwich: Norfolk Museums Service

Northover, J P, 1980 The analysis of Welsh Bronze Age metalwork [appendix] in H N Savory (ed) *Guide catalogue to the Bronze Age collections*. Cardiff: National Museum of Wales, 229–43

Northover, J P, 1983 The exploration of the long-distance movement of bronze in Bronze and early Iron Age Europe, *Bull Inst Archaeol Univ London*, **19**, 1982/3, 45–72

Northover, J P, 1988 Appendix 2: The analysis and metallurgy of British Bronze Age swords, in I Colquhoun and C Burgess *The swords of Britain*. Prähistorische Bronzefunde **IV**/5. Munich: Beck, 130–46

Northover, J P, 1989 The gold torc from Saint Helier, Jersey, *Annual Bulletin of the Société Jersiaise*, **25**, 112–37

Northover, J P, 1995 Late Bronze Age drawplates in the Isleham hoard, in B Schmid-Sikimić & P della Casa (eds) *Trans Europam: Beiträge zur Bronze- und Eisenzeit zwischen Atlantik und Altai – Festschrift für Margarita Primas*. Bonn: Dr Rudolf Habelt, 15–22

Northover, J P, 1997 Metalworking waste from Erlenbach-Obstgartenstrasse, in C Fischer (ed) *Innovation und Tradition in der Mittel- und Spätbronzezeit: Gräber und Siedlungen in Neftenbach, Fällanden, Dietikon, Pfäffikon und Erlenbach*, Monographien der Kantonsarchäologie Zürich **28**. Zürich: Direktion der öffentlichen Bauten des Kantons Zürich, Hochbauamt, Abteilung Kantonsarchäologie, 99–101

Northover, J P, 2001 Bronze Age metalwork of the Isle of Wight, in W H Metz, B L van Beek & H Steegstra (eds) *Patina: essays presented to Jay Jordan Butler on the occasion of his 80th birthday*. Groningen: privately published, 431–48

Novák, P, 1975 *Die Schwerter in der Tschechoslowakei I*, Prähistorische Bronzefunde **IV**/4. Munich: Beck

O'Connor, B, 1980 *Cross-Channel relations in the later Bronze Age*, BAR Int Ser **91**. Oxford: British Archaeological Reports

O'Connor, B, 2009 The bronze metalwork, in L Ladle & A Woodward *Excavations at Bestwall Quarry, Wareham 1992–2005, Volume 1: the prehistoric landscape*, Dorset Natural History & Archaeological Society Monograph **19**. Dorchester: Dorset County Museum, 272–5

O'Connor, B & Woodward, P J, 2003 A group of Middle Bronze Age socketed axes from east Dorset, *Proc Dorset Natur Hist Archaeol Soc*, **125**, 144–6

Oram, M, 1979 Scientific bursary report on Langdon Bay Project from Chairman, Dover branch, BSAC, April 1979. Langdon Bay Archive: 1A/2

Pare, C F E, 1999 Weights and weighing in Bronze Age central Europe, in *Eliten in der Bronzezeit: Ergebnisse zweier Kolloquien in Mainz und Athen*, Römisch-Germanischen Zentralmuseums Monographien **43**/2. Mainz: RGZM, 421–514

Parfitt, K, 1983 Dover Archaeological Group; Hacklinge Holes, Worth, *Archaeol Cantiana*, **99**, 290

Parfitt, K, 1993 The Dover Boat, *Curr Archaeol*, **133**, 4–8

Parfitt, K, 1994 A possible Bronze Age grave at Walmer 1910, *Kent Archaeol Rev*, **116**, 133–5

Parfitt, K, 1995 Ripple Farm gold ring. Archive note, Dover Archaeological Group

Parfitt, K, 1997 Waldershare bronze hoard. Archive notes held at Dover Museum

Parfitt, K, 2004 A search for the prehistoric harbours of Kent, in P Clark (ed) *The Dover Bronze Age boat in context: society and water transport in prehistoric Europe*. Oxford: Oxbow Books, 99–105

Parfitt, K, 2006 Ringlemere and ritual and burial landscapes of Kent, in S P Needham, K Parfitt and G Varndell (eds) *The Ringlemere Cup: precious cups and the beginning of the Channel Bronze Age*, British Museum Research Publication **163**. London: British Museum Press, 47–52

Parfitt, K & Champion, T, 2004 The boat in its cultural setting, in P Clark (ed) *Dover Bronze Age boat*. Swindon: English Heritage, 264–75

Parfitt, K & Corke, B, 2003 The Dover–Deal bulk supply water-main, in *Canterbury's archaeology 2001–2002*. Canterbury: 26th Annual Report of Canterbury Archaeological Trust, 35–6

Parham, D & Palmer, M, 2006 Questioning the wrecks of time, *Brit Archaeol*, **91**(Nov/Dec 2006), 42–4

Pászthory, K & Mayer, F F, 1998 *Die Äxte und Beile in Bayern*, Prähistorische Bronzefunde **IX**/20. Stuttgart: Franz Steiner

Peake, R & Delattre, V, 2005 L'apport des analyses C¹⁴ à l'étude de la nécropole de l'Âge du Bronze de Marolles-sur-Seine, *Revue Archéologique du Centre*, **44**, 5–25

Pearce, S M, 1973 Three prehistoric implements from Devon, *Proc Devon Archaeol Soc*, **31**, 58

Pearce, S M, 1977 Curator of Antiquities, Royal Albert Memorial Museum [Letter to K Muckelroy, Jesus College, Cambridge] (personal communication 7 November 1977). Moor Sands Archive: 2/12

Pearce, S M, 1983 *The Bronze Age metalwork of south western Britain*, BAR Brit Ser **120**. Oxford: British Archaeological Reports

Pearce, W J, 1978 Asst Sec, British Academy [Letter to K Muckelroy, Jesus College, Cambridge] (personal communication 2 June 1978). Moor Sands Archive: 2/6

Pedley, H M, 1990 Classification and environmental models of cool freshwater tufas, *Sedimentary Geology*, **68**, 143–54

Philp, B J, 1976 Brief discussion of the significance of the finds, in S Stevens (ed) Major discovery of Bronze Age implements at Dover, *Kent Archaeol Rev*, **43**, 67–73

Philp, B J, 1981 *The excavation of the Roman forts of the Classis Britannica at Dover. 1970–1977*, Kent Archaeological Rescue Unit Monograph Series **3**. Dover: Kent Archaeological Rescue Unit

Philp, E G J, 1989 *The Roman house with Bacchic murals at Dover*, Kent Archaeological Rescue Unit Monograph Series **5**. Dover: Kent Archaeological Rescue Unit

Pryor, F, 2001 *The Flag Fen Basin: archaeology and environment of a fenland landscape*. London: English Heritage

Przybyła, M S, 2009 *Intercultural contacts in the western Carpathian area at the turn of the 2nd and 1st millennia BC*. Warsaw: National Centre for Culture

Radley, A, 1934 A bronze palstave from Arncliffe in Litton Dale, W Yorkshire, *Yorkshire Archaeol J*, **31**, 95–6

Rahtz, P A, 1958 Dover: Stembrook and St. Martin-le-Grand, *Archaeol Cantiana*, **72**, 111–37

Ramsey, G, 1993 Damaged butts and torn rivet holes: the hafting and function of Middle Bronze Age 'dirks' and 'rapiers', *Archeomaterials*, **7**, 127–38

Reid, C, 1913 *Submerged forests*. Cambridge: Cambridge University Press

Reim, H, 1974a *Die spätbronzezeitlichen Griffplatten-, Griffdorn- und Griffangelschwerter in Ostfrankreich I*. Prähistorische Bronzefunde **IV**/3, Munich: Beck

Reim, H, 1974b Bronze- und Urnenfelderzeitliche Griffangelschwerter im nordwestlichen Voralpenraum und in Oberitalien, *Archäologisches Korrespondenzblatt*, **4**, 17–26

Renfrew, C, 1974 *British prehistory, a new outline*. London: Duckworth

Richter, I, 1970 *Der Arm- und Beinschmuck der Bronze- und Urnenfelderzeit in Hessen und Rheinhessen*. Prähistorische Bronzefunde **X**/1, Munich: Beck

Rigold, S E, 1969 The Roman haven of Dover, *Archaeol J*, **126**, 78–100

Roberts, S, 1992 Dept of Environment (Heritage Division) [Letter to A Moat] (personal communication 3 April 1992). Langdon Bay Archive: 1A/2

Robinson, N D, 1986 Lithostratigraphy of the Chalk Group of the North Downs, southeast England, *Proc Geol Ass*, **97**, 141–70

Robinson, W, 1979 Dept of Archaeology, National Museum of Wales, Cardiff [Letter to K Muckelroy] (personal communication 28 February 1979). Langdon Bay Archive: 1A/2

Rohl, B M & Needham, S P, 1998 *The circulation of metal in the British Bronze Age: the application of lead isotope analysis*, British Museum Occasional Paper **102**. London: British Museum

Rohl, B M & Northover, J P, 2001 Analysis of the metalwork, in F Pryor (ed) *The Flag Fen Basin: archaeology and environment of a Fenland landscape*. Swindon: English Heritage, 298–308

Roth, H, 1974 Ein Ledermesser der Atlantischen Bronzezeit aus Mittelfranken, *Archäologisches Korrespondenzblatt*, **4**, 37–47

Roudil, J L, 1972 *L'Âge du Bronze en Languedoc Oriental*, Mémoires de la Société Préhistorique Française **10**. Paris: Klincksieck

Rowlands, M J, 1976 *The production and distribution of metalwork in the middle Bronze Age of southern Britain*, BAR Brit Ser **31**. Oxford: British Archaeological Reports

Ruiz-Gálvez, M (ed), 1995 *Ritos de Pasos y Puntos de Paso: La Ría de Huelva en el Mundo del Bronce Final Europeo*. Madrid: Universidad Complutense

Rychner, V & Klänstchi, N, 1995 *Arsenic, nickel et antimoine*, Cahiers d'archéologie romande de la Bibliothèque historique vaudoise **63–64**. Lausanne: Cahiers d'archéologie romande

Samson, A V M, 2006 Offshore finds from the Bronze Age in north-western Europe: the shipwreck scenario revisited, *Oxford J Archaeol*, **25**, 371–88

Samson, B L, 1999 Langdon Bay Archaeological Project Annual Report. Langdon Bay Archive: 2A/2

Savory, H N, 1980 *Guide catalogue of the Bronze Age collections*. Cardiff: National Museum of Wales

Schauer, P, 1971 *Die Schwerter in Süddeutschland, Österreich und der Schweiz I*, Prähistorische Bronzefunde **IV**/2. Munich: Beck

Schmidt, P K & Burgess, C B, 1981 *The axes of Scotland and northern England*, Prähistorische Bronzefunde **IX**/7. Munich: Beck

Scott Robertson, W A, 1878 Gold torques from Dover. *Archaeol Cantiana*, **12**, 317–20

Shennan, I & Horton, B, 2002 Holocene land- and sea-level changes in Great Britain, *J Quat Sci*, **17**, 511–26

Shephard-Thorn, E R, 1988 *Geology of the country around Ramsgate and Dover. Memoir for 1:50,000 sheets 274 and 290 (England and Wales)*. London: HMSO

Sherwin, G A, 1942 A second bronze hoard of Arreton type found in the Isle of Wight, *Antiq J*, **22**, 198–201

Silvester, R J, 1980 The prehistoric open settlement at Dainton, south Devon, *Proc Devon Archaeol Soc*, **38**, 17–48

Smith, M A, 1958 *Late Bronze Age hoards in the British Museum*. Inventaria Archaeologica, GB. 35–41; International Congress of Prehistoric and Protohistoric Sciences. London: British Museum

Smith, M A, 1959a *Middle Bronze Hoards from southern*

England, Inventaria Archaeologica GB. 42–47; International Union of Prehistoric and Protohistoric Sciences. London: Garraway

Smith, M A, 1959b Some Somerset hoards and their place in the Bronze Age of southern Britain, *Proc Prehist Soc*, **25**, 144–87

Society of Antiquaries, 1982 Research fund notes for applicants for grants. Langdon Bay Archive: 1A/3

Sparks, B W, 1978 [Letter to K Muckelroy, Jesus College, Cambridge] (personal communication 6 June 1978). Langdon Bay Archive: 1A/2

Stebbing, W P D, 1934 An early Iron Age site at Deal, *Archaeol Cantiana*, **46**, 207–9

Stebbing, W P D, 1936 Discoveries in the neighbourhood of Deal during 1936, *Archaeol Cantiana*, 48, 235–7

Stebbing, W P D, 1956 Researches and discoveries in Kent – research and record east Kent, 1955–56, *Archaeol Cantiana*, **70**, 267

Stevens, S, 1976 Major discovery of Bronze Age implements at Dover. *Kent Archaeol Rev*, **40**, 67–73

Stratham, S P H, 1899 *History of the castle, town and port of Dover*. London

Taylor, J J, 1980 *Bronze Age goldwork of the British Isles*. Cambridge: Cambridge University Press

Taylor, R, 1980 An Armorican socketed axe from the sea off Chesil Beach, Dorset, *Archaeol Atlantica*, **3**, 133–7

Thévenot, J-P, 1985 Informations archéologiques: circonscription de Bourgogne, *Gallia Préhistoire*, **28**, 171–210

Thomas, C, 1963 A flat axe from Praa Sands, *Cornish Archaeol*, **2**, 77

Threipland, L M & Steer, K A, 1951 Excavation at Dover, 1945–1947, *Archaeol Cantiana*, **64**, 130–49

UKHO, 1998 *Salcombe Harbour. Admiralty Standard Chart 0028, 1:12,500*. Taunton: UKHO

Ussher, W A E, 1904 *The geology of the country around Kingsbridge and Salcombe (explanation of sheets 355 and 356)*. London: Memoirs of the Geological Survey of England and Wales

Valentine, R, 1979 [Letter to A Moat, Secretary, Dover BSAC] (personal communication 14 March 1979). Langdon Bay Archive: 1A/2

Valentine, R, 2003 *BSAC: The Club 1953–2003*. London: Circle Books

Van der Noort, R, 2006 Argonauts of the North Sea – a social maritime archaeology for the 2nd millennium BC, *Proc Prehist Soc*, **72**, 267–87

van Geel, B & Renssen, H, 1998 Abrupt climatic change around 2,650 BP in north-west Europe: evidence for climatic teleconnections and a tentative explanation, in A S Issar & N Brown (eds) *Water, environment and society in times of climatic change*. Dordrecht: Kluwer, 21–41

Van Gijssel, K & van der Valk, B, 2006 Shaped by water, ice and wind: the genesis of the Netherlands, in L P Kooijmans, P W van den Broeke, H Fokkens & A L van Gijn (eds) *The prehistory of the Netherlands*. Amsterdam: Amsterdam University Press, 45–74

Verlaeckt, K, 1992 Metalen voorwerpen uit de Bronstijd, gevonden op het grondgebied van de Provincie Oost-Vlaanderen, *Archeologisch Jaarboek Gent 1992*, 49–130

Verlaeckt, K, 1996 Opgevist verleden: een bronzen zwaard van de Sandettié-bank (Nauw van Calais), *Lunula*, **4**, 52–3

Verney, A, 1988 *L'Industrie des Haches à Talon de Type*

Normand en France, unpublished thesis (Mémoire de Maîtrise). Paris: University of Paris I

Verney, A, 1989 La place des haches à talon de type Normand dans l'étude du Bronze Moyen en France, in *La Culture des Tumulus et la Dynamique du Bronze Moyen en Europe Occidentale*, Actes du 113e Congrès des Sociétés Savantes. Strasbourg: Comité des Travaux Historiques et Scientifiques, 479–89

Verney, A & Verron, G, 1998 Les dépôts de Condé-sur-Noireau (Calvados) et Chailloué (Orne): leur apport à la caractérisation de l'horizon de Rosnoën, *Journée Préhistorique et Protohistorique de Bretagne*, 47–9

Verron, G, 1973 Informations archéologiques. Circonscription de Haute et Basse Normandie, *Gallia Préhistoire*, **16**, 361–99

Waller, M P & Long, A J, 2003 Holocene coastal evolution and sea-level change on the southern coast of England: a review, *J Quat Sci*, **18**, 351–9

Waller, M P & Long, A J, 2011 The Holocene coastal deposits of Sussex: a re-evaluation, in M Waller, E Edwards & L Barber (eds) *Romney Marsh: persistence and changes in a coastal lowland*. Sevenoaks: Romney Marsh Research Trust, 1–21

Warmenbol, E, 1989 Le dépôt de haches à ailerons de Maaseik (Limburg), *Jahrbuch des Römisch-Germanischen Zentralmuseums Mainz*, **36**, 277–99

Warmenbol, E, 1990a Un petit dépôt du Bronze Final découvert à Yvoir (Namur), *Helinium 30*, 79–92

Warmenbol, E, 1990b De Bronstijd en -Nijverheid in West-Vlaanderen: een status quaestionis, *Westvlaamse Archaeologica*, **6**, 33–48

Warmenbol, E, 1991 Le Bronze Final atlantique entre côte et Escaut, in C Chevillot & A Coffyn (eds) *L'Âge du Bronze atlantique: ses faciès, de L'Écosse a L'Andalousie, et leurs relations avec le bronze continental et la Méditerranée*, Actes du 1er Colloque du Parc Archéologique de Beynac. Beynac-et-Cazenac: Association des Musées du Sarladais, 89–110

Warmenbol, E, 1992 Le matériel de l'Âge du Bronze: le seau de la drague et le casque du héros, in E Warmenbol *et al* 1992, 67–122

Warmenbol, E, Cabuy, Y, Hurt, V & Cauwe, N, 1992 *La collection Edouard Bernays: Néolithique et Age du Bronze, époques gallo-romaine et médiévale*. Bruxelles: Musées Royaux d'Art et d'Histoire

Weatherup, D R M, 1982 Armagh County Museum archaeological acquisitions: the collection of Armagh Natural History and Philosophical Society, *J Roy Soc Antiq Ir*, **112**, 51–71

Wegner, G, 1976 *Die vorgeschichtlichen Flussfunde aus dem Main und aus dem Rhein bei Mainz*, Materialhefte zur Bayerischen Vorgeschichte **30**. Kallmünz/Opf: M Lassleben

Wheeler, M, 1954 *Archaeology from the earth*. Oxford: Clarendon

Williams, A, 1937 Bronze implements from Swansea, Glamorgan, *Archaeol Cambrensis*, **92**, 333

Winder, T, 1923 Submerged forest in Bigbury Bay at Thurlestone Sands, South Devon, *Trans Devon Ass*, **55**, 120–23

Woodruff, C H, 1874 On Celtic tumuli in east Kent, *Archaeol Cantiana*, **9**, 16–30

Woodruff, C H, 1880 An account of discoveries made in Celtic tumuli near Dover, Kent, *Archaeologia*, **45**, 53–6

Woodworth, P L & Player, R 2003 The permanent service

for mean sea level: an update to the 21st century, *Journal of Coastal Research*, **19**, 287–295.

Worden, W H, 1978 Chief Fisheries Officer, Devon Sea Fisheries District [Letter to K Muckelroy, Jesus College, Cambridge] (personal communication 21 February 1978). Moor Sands Archive: 2/10

Worsfold, F H, 1943 A report on the Late Bronze Age site excavated at Minnis Bay, Birchington, Kent, 1938–40, *Proc Prehist Soc*, **9**, 28–47

Wright, E V, 1990 *The Ferriby Boats: seacraft of the Bronze Age*. London: Routledge

Yalçin, Ü, Paulak, C & Slotta, R (eds), 2005 *Das Schiff von Uluburun: Welthandel vor 3000 Jahren*. Bochum: Deutsches Bergbau-Museum

Yates, D, 2007 *Land, power and prestige: Bronze Age field systems in southern England*. Oxford: Oxbow Books

Yates, D & Bradley, R, 2010 Still water, hidden depths: the deposition of Bronze Age metalwork in the English Fenland, *Antiquity*, **84**, 405–15

Index

Entries in bold refer to the Figures